A-Level
Economics

Revising for Economics exams can be a real labour of love... But don't fret — this spectacular all-in-one CGP book has everything you need to score top Marx.

Like a Swiss-Army revision book, it covers AQA, Edexcel Economics A *and* OCR. Inside you'll find everything you need to learn for both years of the course, plus exam-style questions for every topic, and a section of advice from CGP's exam experts!

We've also thrown in a free Online Edition, so you can revise digitally (the future is now).

A-Level revision? It has to be CGP!

Contents

Section Nine — Aggregate Demand and Aggregate Supply

Section Ten — Government Economic Policy Objectives

Section Eleven — Macroeconomic Policy Instruments

Section Twelve — The Financial Sector

Section Thirteen — The Global Economy

Section Fourteen — Economic Development

Do Well in Your Exam

This book is suitable for:

AQA, Edexcel Economics A, OCR

There are notes on the pages that tell you which bits you need for your specification:

- Notes at the top of pages in **bold** tell you which exam boards the **page** is for (or **pages** if the topic covers more than one page).

- Notes in the margins point out if **part** of a page is only for some boards.

Published by CGP

Editors:
Sarah George, Chris Lindle, Tom Miles, Sarah Oxley, Andy Park, Michael Weynberg

Contributors:
John Grant, Alison Hazell, Samantha Uppal

With thanks to Michael Bushell for the proofreading.
With thanks to Jan Greenway for the copyright research.

ISBN: 978 1 78294 347 1

Printed by Elanders Ltd, Newcastle upon Tyne.
Clipart from Corel®

Based on the classic CGP style created by Richard Parsons.

An Introduction to Economics

So, here it is — your shiny new Economics book. Ready to get down to business... or economics? Good. Let's get cracking. **This page is for AQA, Edexcel and OCR.**

Economics is a Social Science

1) Economics is considered to be a **social science** because it looks at the **behaviour** of **humans**, either as individuals or as part of organisations (such as firms and governments), and their use of **scarce resources** (see p.6 for more).

2) The **methodology** that economists use to tackle Economics is **similar** to the methodology used by scientists in **natural** and **other sciences** (e.g. Biology). Economists will:

- Develop **theories** and create economic **models** to explain phenomena (e.g. how exchange rates are determined).
- Use **simplifying assumptions** to limit the number of variables in an investigation.
- **Test** theories and models against relevant known facts, making use of observation, deduction, graphs, statistics and other tools.
- Use **empirical data** to improve and revise their economic models.
- Use economic models to make **predictions**.

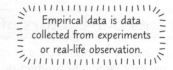

Empirical data is data collected from experiments or real-life observation.

3) However, **unlike** in natural sciences, economists **can't** conduct **controlled laboratory experiments** where only one variable is changed at a time. For example, if an economist examines the impact of price on the demand for cheese, they can't keep consumers' income constant — in the **real world**, income won't remain constant.

4) To get around the problem of the existence of multiple variables in an economy, economists use the **assumption** known as *ceteris paribus*, which is Latin for '**all other things remaining equal**'.

5) Economists use *ceteris paribus* when they're looking at the **relationship** between **two factors** (e.g. price and demand). They'll **assume** that **only** these two factors change and **all other factors** (e.g. income, changes in taste) that would have an effect on any other variable being considered **remain the same**.

6) Using *ceteris paribus* enables economists to **develop theories** and **models**, and **make predictions**.

Economic Decisions might not always make the most Economic Sense

Because Economics deals with real people, you have to keep in mind that the **decisions** made by **individuals**, **firms** or **governments** will often be based on **opinions** and **judgements**. For example, decisions might be based on:

- **Normative statements** (see below), which are people's **opinions**.
- **Moral views** and **value judgements** (e.g. the view that people shouldn't live in poverty, so wealth should be shared).
- **Political judgements** (e.g. lowering taxes may win votes for a government).
- **Short-term positive consequences** of a decision, regardless of long-term consequences (e.g. reducing taxes may win an election, but it will reduce the government's income and may lead to public spending cuts).

There are Two Kinds of economic statement

Before moving on to more specific things, you need to know about the **two** kinds of **statements** you can make in economics.

POSITIVE statements

Positive statements are **objective** statements that can be **tested** by referring to the available **evidence**.

- For example:
  "A reduction in income will increase the amount of people shopping in pound shops."
- With suitable data collected over a period of time, you should be able to tell if the above claim is true or false.

Positive statements are important because they can be **tested** to see whether **economic ideas** are **correct**.

NORMATIVE statements

Normative statements are **subjective** statements which contain a **value judgement** — they're **opinions**.

- For example:
  "The use of fossil fuels should be taxed more highly than the use of renewable fuels."
- It's not possible to say whether the above statement is true or not — only whether you agree or disagree with it.

Normative statements are also important because **value judgements** influence **decision-making** and **government policy**, e.g. a political party in government may wish to increase taxes for the rich to redistribute income to the poor.

The Economic Problem

If you condensed Economics down to one statement it'd be something like: Economics is all about satisfying infinite wants and needs with limited resources. "What does that mean?", I hear you ask. Well, read on and find out... **For all boards.**

Economics — how best to satisfy Infinite Desires using Limited Resources

1) Everyone has certain basic **needs** in life — e.g. food, water, a place to live, and so on.
   Everyone also has an infinite list of things they **want** — e.g. designer clothes, smartphones, holidays, houses.

2) However, there's a **limited** amount of **resources** available to satisfy these needs and wants (i.e. resources are **scarce**).

3) These facts lead to the **basic economic problem**:

   How can the available scarce resources be used to satisfy **people's infinite needs and wants** as effectively as possible?

There are Four Factors of Production

The scarce resources (inputs) used to make the things people want and need (outputs) can be divided into four **factors of production**. These factors are: **Land**, **Labour**, **Capital** and **Enterprise**.

Individuals and firms are rewarded for providing these factors, e.g. with wages or rent.

Land: including all the Natural Resources in and on it

As well as actual 'territory', **land** includes all the Earth's **natural resources**:

- **non-renewable** resources, such as natural gas, oil and coal
- **renewable** resources like wind or tidal power, or wood from trees
- **materials** extracted by mining (e.g. diamonds and gold)
- **water**
- **animals** found in an area

Non-renewable resources will eventually run out if we carry on using them.

Renewable resources can regrow or regenerate. But some renewable resources have to be used carefully if they're not to run out — e.g. to be sustainable, enough trees need to be planted to replace those that are used.

1) Nearly all things that fall under the category of 'land' are **scarce** — there **aren't enough** natural resources to satisfy the demands of everyone.

2) One exception is **air**, but even this isn't as simple as it first looks...

   - Air is **not** usually considered a scarce resource — there's enough for **everyone** to have as much as they want.
   - But this **doesn't** mean all air is equally good — air can be **polluted**, as can be seen in a lot of big cities.
   - In fact, the **environment** is considered by some people to be a **scarce resource**.

Because there's enough air for everyone to have as much as they want, in theory it's **impossible** to **sell** it. (*Why would you **buy** it when you can get it **for free**?*) Economists call things like this **free goods**.

Things that are **scarce** and which can therefore be traded are known as **economic goods**.

Labour: the Work done by People

In the UK, the number of people of working age with a job is around 30 million.

1) Labour is the **work done** by those **people** who contribute to the production process. The population who are available to do work is called the **labour force**.

2) There's usually also a number of people who are **capable** of working and who are **old enough** to work, but who **don't** have a job. Economists refer to these people as **unemployed**.

3) There are also people who **aren't** in **paid employment** but still provide things people need or want, e.g. homemakers.

4) Different people have different levels of education, experience or training. These factors can make some people more 'valuable' or productive in the workplace than others — they have a greater amount of **human capital**.

Capital: Equipment used in producing goods and services

1) **Capital** is the equipment, factories and schools that help to produce goods or services.

2) **Capital** is different from **land** because capital has to be **made** first.

3) Much of an economy's capital is **paid for** by the **government** — e.g. a country's road network is a form of capital.

Enterprise: willingness to take a Risk to make a Profit

Enterprise refers to the people (**entrepreneurs**) who take **risks** and create things from the other three factors of production.

1) They set up and run **businesses** using any of the factors of production available to them.

2) If the business **fails**, they can **lose** a lot of money. But if the business **succeeds**, the **reward** for their risk-taking is **profit**.

The Economic Problem

Scarcity requires the Careful Allocation of Resources

1) **Economic activity** involves **combining** the factors of production to create **outputs** that people can **consume**. The **purpose** of any economic activity is to **increase** people's **economic welfare** by creating outputs that **satisfy** their various **needs** and **wants**.

2) In Economics a wide range of things count as **economic activity**.

3) One form of economic activity is the making of **goods** and the provision of **services** (i.e. creating outputs).

   - **GOODS:** 'Physical' products you can **touch** — such as washing machines, books or a new factory.
   - **SERVICES:** 'Intangible' things — such as medical check-ups, teaching, or train journeys.

4) **Consumption** (i.e. buying or using) is also a form of **economic activity**. When you consume something, you're trying to satisfy a **need** or a **want**. You can consume both goods and services.

   Lots of other things are also classified as economic activity, such as doing housework, DIY and bringing up children (even though you might not get paid for doing it).

5) Since there's an **endless** array of things that could be produced and consumed, but only **limited resources**, this leads to three fundamental questions:
   - **What** to produce?
   - **How** to produce it?
   - **Who** to produce it **for**?

Economic Agents react to Incentives

1) The **agents** ('participants') in an economy can usually be thought of as:

   Producers — firms or people that make goods or provide services.

   Consumers — people or firms who buy the goods and services.

   Governments — a government sets the rules that other participants in the economy have to follow, but also produces and consumes goods and services.

2) Each of these **economic agents** has to make **decisions** that affect how resources are allocated. For example:
   - **Producers** decide what to make, and how much they're willing to sell it for.
   - **Consumers** have to decide what they want to buy, and how much they're willing to pay for it.
   - **Governments** have to decide how much to intervene in the way producers and consumers act.

3) In a **market economy** (see page 10), all economic agents are assumed to be **rational** (see page 14), which means they'll make the decisions that are best for **themselves**. These decisions will be based on economic **incentives**, such as making profit or paying as little as possible for a product.

4) Considering people's incentives helps to answer those fundamental questions above.
   - **What to produce?** This will be those goods that firms can make a profit from.
   - **How to produce it?** Firms will want to produce the good in the most efficient way they can, in order to maximise their profits.
   - **Who to produce it for?** Firms will produce goods for consumers who are willing to pay for those goods.

   So in effect consumers decide what is to be produced. Producers won't want to produce things that nobody wants to buy.

Warm-Up Questions

Q1 What is the basic economic problem?

Q2 What are the four factors of production? Give an example of each.

Q3 Give three different types of economic agent.

PRACTICE QUESTIONS

Exam Question

Q1 State and explain three factors of production which would be necessary for opening a new restaurant. [6 marks]

Learn the facts about factors of production...

Economics is a funny one... you might think it's going to be all about banks and money and stuff. But there's a bit of groundwork to do before you get to all of that. It's interesting though, and getting your head around all of this will definitely help you later on. Those four factors of production are at the heart of everything in economics, by the way... so learn them well.

Production Possibility Frontiers

Production possibility frontiers (PPFs) — also known as production possibility curves (PPCs) or production possibility boundaries (PPBs) — show the maximum amount of two goods or services an economy can produce. **For all boards.**

Production Possibility Frontiers show the **Maximum** possible output

The basic problem in Economics is how best to allocate scarce resources. A **production possibility frontier** (PPF) shows the options that are available when you consider the production of just **two types** of goods or services.

1) The PPF below shows the **maximum** number of **houses** (on the horizontal axis) and **vehicles** (on the vertical axis) that can be made, using the **existing** level of resources in an economy.

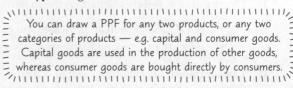

You can draw a PPF for any two products, or any two categories of products — e.g. capital and consumer goods. Capital goods are used in the production of other goods, whereas consumer goods are bought directly by consumers.

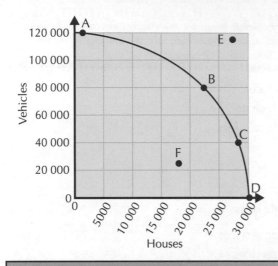

2) Points A, B, C and D (and every other point on the PPF) are all achievable **without** using any **extra** resources. However, they are **only** achievable when **all** the available resources are used as **efficiently** as is actually possible.

- Notice how, as you move along the curve from A to B, you're building **more houses** (about 22 500 instead of 1000) but **fewer vehicles** (80 000 instead of 120 000).

- Moving along the curve from A to B like this corresponds to allocating **more resources** to the production of houses, and **fewer resources** to the production of vehicles.

- In other words, there's a **trade-off** between 'building more houses' and 'making more vehicles' — to do **more** of one, you have to do **less** of the other.

> A **trade-off** is when you have to choose between conflicting objectives because you **can't** achieve all your objectives at the **same time**. It involves **compromising**, and aiming to achieve **each** of your objectives **a bit**.

3) All points **on** the PPF are **productively efficient** (see p.58) because all resources are used as efficiently as possible to produce the **maximum possible output**. However, **not** all points on the PPF are **allocatively efficient** (see p.56) because not all points will reflect the production of goods that people **want** or **need** — e.g. if all resources are used to produce vehicles, this might not match society's need for houses.

All the different points on the PPF represent a different choice about how to use the available scarce resources.

4) Point E lies **outside** the PPF, so it **isn't achievable** using the **current level** of resources in the economy. To build that many houses and vehicles at the same time, **extra** (or **better**) **resources** would need to be found.

5) Point F lies **inside** the PPF (rather than **on** it) — this means making this mix of goods is **productively inefficient**. With the current level of resources, you could build more houses **without** making fewer vehicles (or more vehicles **without** making fewer houses).

Opportunity Cost is the next best thing that you're forced to give up

1) The trade-off described above involves an **opportunity cost**.

2) An opportunity cost is what you **give up** in order to do something else — i.e. it's the cost of any choice that's made.

3) So moving from A to B on the PPF above means you have the opportunity to build 21 500 extra houses as long as you **give up** the opportunity to make 40 000 vehicles. In other words, the **opportunity cost** of building 21 500 extra houses is the lost production of 40 000 vehicles.

> The opportunity cost of a decision is the next best alternative that you give up in making that decision.

4) Opportunity cost is a key concept in Economics which is used to ensure a more **efficient allocation** of **resources**. For example, **consumers** use the concept to **choose** what to **spend** their **income** on; **producers** use it to look at the **profit forgone** by not making an **alternative product**; and **governments** use it to look at the **lost value** to **society** from the policies they choose **not** to implement.

5) However, there are some **problems** with using the concept of opportunity cost:

- Often, not all alternatives are known.
- Some factors don't have alternative uses.
- There may be a lack of information on alternatives and their costs.
- Some factors (e.g. land) can be hard to switch to an alternative use.

Production Possibility Frontiers

Economic Growth shifts the PPF

1) A PPF shows what's possible using a **particular level** of resources (e.g. a particular number of people, a particular amount of capital and raw materials, and so on).

2) If this level of resources is **fixed**, then movements **along** the PPF just show a **reallocation** of those resources.

3) However, if the total amount of resources **changes**, then the PPF itself **moves**.

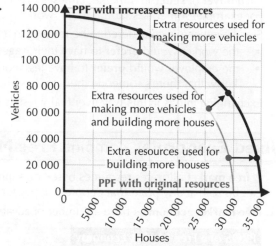

- For example, **increased resources** (e.g. an increase in the total number of workers) would mean that the total possible **output** of that economy would also **increase** — so the PPF **shifts outward**.

- For the economy shown by this PPF, the extra output could be **either** more houses **or** more vehicles **or** a combination of both.

4) **Improved technology** or **improvements** to **labour** (e.g. through training) can also shift the PPF outwards, because it allows **more output** to be produced using the **same resources**.

5) An **outward shift** of the PPF shows **economic growth**.

6) When **fewer** total resources are available (e.g. after some kind of **natural disaster**), the opposite happens — the PPF **shifts inwards**, showing that the total possible output has **shrunk**. This shows **negative economic growth**.

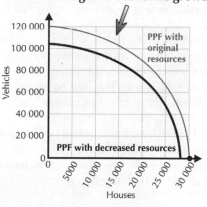

7) In this example, the possible output has **grown** because of improved technology. However, this particular technology can only help with **house-building** — this means the PPF has been stretched in only the **horizontal direction**.

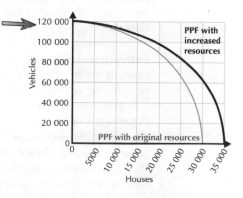

Warm-Up Questions

Q1 Explain what a production possibility frontier (PPF) shows.

Q2 What is meant by a trade-off?

Q3 Describe why a PPF might move outwards. What does it mean if it moves inwards?

Exam Questions

Q1 Look at the diagram on the right. Which of the following combinations of cars and butter cannot currently be produced in this economy using the existing resources?
A) Only W
B) Only X
C) Only W, Y and Z
D) Only Y and Z
[1 mark]

Q2 Use the diagram on the right to explain the term opportunity cost. [5 marks]

Decisions, decisions, decisions...

It's important to get your head round these PPFs. Think of different points on a PPF as representing different decisions you could make about how you want to allocate your all-too-scarce resources. Then they don't seem (quite) as bad.

Markets and Economies

*Markets are a way to allocate resources to different economic activities. But sometimes governments decide that things would work out better if things weren't left entirely up to the market. **These pages are for all boards.***

Markets are a method for Allocating Scarce Resources

1) **Markets** are a way of **allocating resources**. They **don't** have to be a place, or involve the exchange of physical objects.

2) Each **buyer** or **seller** in a market **chooses** to exchange something they have for something they'd prefer to have instead. For example, someone's labour (their 'work') is a resource. If they have a job, they exchange their labour for a salary.

3) Since everyone is considered to be **rational** in a free market (see p.14), an economist would assume that:
   - the worker would **prefer** to have their wages, but less free time,
   - the employer would **prefer** to have less money, and to know that there's someone there to do some work.

   Any exchange can only happen because different people or organisations value things differently.

4) Exchanging things in this way eventually results in a particular **allocation of resources**.

Mixed Economies combine Free Markets and Government Intervention

1) A **free market** allocates resources based on **supply and demand** and the **price mechanism**. In other words, **anything** can be sold at **any price** that people will pay for it. (See Section 2 for more about the free market.)

2) **Free market economies** have a number of advantages... but there are also some downsides.

PROS of a Free Market Economy

- **Efficiency** — As **any** product can be bought and sold, only those of the **best value** will be in **demand**. So firms have an **incentive** to try to make goods in as efficient a way as possible.
- **Entrepreneurship** — In a market economy, the **rewards** for good ideas (e.g. new, better products, or better ways to make existing products) can make entrepreneurs a lot of money. This encourages risk-taking and innovation.
- **Choice** — The **incentives** for innovation can lead to an increase in **choice** for consumers. (And in a free market, consumers aren't restricted to buying only what the government recommends.)

CONS of a Free Market Economy

- **Inequalities** — Market economies can lead to huge **differences in income** — this can be controversial, since many people think particularly large differences are **unfair**. And in a completely free market, anyone who is unable to work (even if it's not their fault) would receive no income.
- **Non-profitable goods may not be made** — For example, drugs to treat **rare** medical conditions may never sell enough for a firm to make any profit, so these would not be made.
- **Monopolies** — Successful businesses can become the only supplier of a product — this **market dominance** can be abused (see p.85).

3) In a **command** (or **planned**) economy, it's the **government** (not markets) that decides how resources should be allocated. **Communist countries** (e.g. the former USSR) have command economies, but they're **much rarer** since the **collapse** of **communism** in the **late 20th century**. However, some countries **still** have command economies, such as **North Korea**.

PROS of a Command Economy

- **Maximise welfare** — Governments have more control over the economy, so they can **prevent** **inequality** and **redistribute income fairly**. They can also ensure the production of goods that people **need** and are **beneficial** to **society**.
- **Low unemployment** — The government can try to provide everyone with a **job** and a **salary**.
- **Prevent monopolies** — The market dominance of monopolies can be **prevented** by the government.

CONS of a Command Economy

- **Poor decision-making** — A **lack of information** means that governments may make **poor** (and **slow**) decisions about what needs to be produced.
- **Restricted choice** — Consumers have a **limited choice** in what they can **consume**, and firms will make what they're **told** to make.
- **Lack of risk-taking and efficiency** — Government-owned firms have **no incentive** to **increase efficiency**, **take risks** or **innovate**, because they **don't** need to make profit.

4) **Market failure** happens when free markets result in **undesirable outcomes** — for example, traffic congestion is seen as a market failure.

   See Section 5 for more about market failure.

5) **Governments** often intervene when there's a market failure.
   - They might **change the law**, or **offer tax breaks** (e.g. reduce taxes for anyone carrying out particular activities), or create some other kind of **incentive** to try to influence people's behaviour.
   - Governments can also intervene in the economy by **buying** or **providing** goods or services.

6) When both the **government** and **markets** play a part in allocating resources, this is called a **mixed economy**.

Markets and Economies

A **Mixed Economy** has a **Public Sector** and a **Private Sector**

1) In a mixed economy, the government is known as the **public sector**.
2) Businesses that are privately owned make up the **private sector**.
3) Private-sector organisations usually have to **break even** or make a **profit** to survive.
4) **Most** countries have a mixed economy, including the UK — there are **no** purely free market economies where the government doesn't intervene in some way.
5) In a **pure free market economy** there would be **no public sector** and in a **pure command economy** there would be **no private sector**.

> There's also a third sector, known as the voluntary sector. This sector includes charities and other non-profit-making organisations.

EDEXCEL ONLY

Smith, Marx and Hayek were Influential Economic Thinkers

Adam Smith (1723-1790)

- Smith's ideas have shaped **traditional economic theory**. He was a big believer in the **free market** and described how its **'invisible hand'** (see p.28) would **allocate resources** in **society's best interests**.
- He said that this came about because **consumers** and **producers** are motivated by **self-interest** — consumers are motivated to **maximise** their **own benefits** and producers are **motivated to maximise profit** (see p.13). In the free market, consumers' **demand** and producers' **supply** will lead to price levels being set at a point which benefits them **both** (for more on the price mechanism, see p.28).
- Smith pointed out that in order for the free market to **work properly** there **couldn't** be any **monopolies** (see p.62) and there would have to be **low barriers to entry** (see p.60) to **maximise competition** (see p.56).
- Smith also wrote about **specialisation** and the **division of labour** — there's more on that on p.37.

Karl Marx (1818-1883)

- Marx was **critical** of the **free market** and argued that it created a situation where a **small ruling class** of **producers** (the **bourgeoisie**) **dominated** and **exploited** the **larger** working class of **wage earners** (the **proletariat**).
- Marx argued that **profit-maximising** bourgeois producers would **exploit** workers (e.g. paying them low wages and giving them few rights) until the proletariat eventually rose up in a **revolution** and took over. This would then lead to the workers **controlling production** and **everyone** having a **share** in the **ownership** of **resources**.
- Marx's ideas led to the rise of **communism** in the **20th century**, but his ideas contained little about **how command economies** would work. Many communist countries **collapsed** in the late 20th century, which led to the **discrediting** of communism and command economies, but Marx's ideas are becoming more popular now.

Friedrich Hayek (1899-1992)

- Hayek was a **keen supporter** of the **free market system** and a **critic** of **command economies**. He argued that governments **shouldn't intervene** to **allocate resources** because governments **lack** the **information** required to allocate them in the way that's most beneficial to society.
- Hayek believed that **individual** consumers and producers have the **best knowledge** of what they **want** or **need**, and so the allocation of resources should be left to them and the **price mechanism**.
- Hayek saw the price mechanism as a way for producers and consumers to **communicate** (this is the idea of price acting as a **signalling device** between consumers and producers, see p.28). The price level set by the forces of supply and demand would show what both consumers and producers **want** and will naturally allocate resources in a much more **efficient** way than governments can.

Warm-Up Questions

Q1 Give two advantages and two disadvantages of a free market economy.

Q2 Explain what is meant by the terms: 'mixed economy', 'public sector' and 'private sector'.

Exam Question

Q1 Explain why a command economy tends to lead to a lack of efficiency. [5 marks]

Do some economics exam practice — but don't forget to market...

Free markets are one of those things that sound really good in theory, but in practice one or two problems tend to crop up. This is why mixed economies are currently all the rage in world economics (apart from in a couple of places).

Economic Objectives

Before we get stuck into the objectives of different economic agents, you need to learn a little bit of background theory on the margin and maximising utility. Once you've got that clear you'll be all set to look at those economic agents. **All boards.**

Economists use the concept of the **Margin**

1) The margin is the **change** in a variable caused by an **increase of one unit** of another variable.

2) For example, the **marginal cost** of an ice cream is the **additional cost** of making **one additional** ice cream, i.e. it's the cost of the **final** ice cream produced.

3) Marginal cost can be calculated by finding the **difference** between the **total cost** at the new output level and the **total cost at one unit less than that**. For example:

> The **total cost** of producing **100** ice creams is **£100** and the **total cost** of producing **101** ice creams is **£102**. So, the **marginal cost** of producing the **101st** ice cream is £102 – £100 = **£2**.

4) A lot of economic theory is based on the **assumption** that people make **decisions** based on **marginal changes** — e.g. a person will make a decision on whether to work for one more hour or not, rather than decide whether to work at all.

5) The concept of the **margin** is important in understanding **how consumers act rationally** (see below), and you'll come across it again several more times in the A Level course. Examples include:

- **Marginal product** (**MP**) (see p.40)
- **Marginal revenue** (**MR**) (see p.46)
- **Marginal tax rate** (see p.172)

The concept of the margin is also used for many other things, for example, to explain **price** (see p.16) and **wage differentials** (see p.106); to help in the understanding of **externalities** (see p.75); to determine **profit maximising output** in **perfect competition** (see p.56); and to assess the **efficiency** of different **market structures**, such as **monopolies** (see p.62). It's also used to explain **marginal utility** and **rationality** (see below).

Economic Agents are assumed to be **Utility Maximisers**

1) **Traditional economic theory assumes** that economic agents (e.g. producers, consumers and workers) want to **maximise** their **utility**.

> *Utility roughly means 'well-being', 'happiness' or 'satisfaction'.*

2) **Different** economic agents will have **different ways** of maximising their utility, e.g. a consumer may want to maximise their happiness, and a producer may wish to maximise their profit (see next page).

3) Traditional economists argue that in order to maximise utility, economic agents must act **rationally**. This means that they'll make decisions based **solely** on trying to gain the maximum utility possible and **nothing else** will influence their decision making.

> *You can read about profit-maximising on p.49.*

You need to understand **How Consumers** act **Rationally**

1) To fully understand how **consumers** act rationally you need to know about **marginal utility**, **total utility** and the **law of diminishing marginal utility**:

- **Marginal utility** is the **benefit** gained from consuming **one additional** unit of a good.
- **Total utility** is the **overall benefit** gained from consuming a good.
- The **law of diminishing marginal utility** states that for **each additional unit** of a good that's consumed, the **marginal utility** gained **decreases**. For example, each additional biscuit eaten gives a consumer **less satisfaction** than the previous one.

2) A **rational consumer** will choose to consume a good at the point where **marginal utility = price**. For example, if the utility a person gains from eating a chocolate biscuit is worth 10p, then a rational consumer will pay 10p for it. If the utility gained from consuming a second biscuit is worth 8p, then that consumer will only want to pay 8p for the second biscuit.

"Biscuits... diminish in utility? Not likely!"

3) If marginal utility **decreases** with each extra good consumed then the **price** a consumer is willing to pay for each extra good will **decrease**. It's this law of diminishing marginal utility that explains why the **demand curve slopes downwards** (see p.16).

Economic Objectives

Different Economic Agents will have different Economic Objectives

Economic agents will usually have different objectives, but quite often these objectives are to maximise a particular quantity (e.g. profit). This page describes some of the traditional assumptions made about the objectives of economic agents, but includes a few other objectives too.

PRODUCERS

1) A firm's profit is their total revenue (money received by the firm, e.g. from sales) minus their total costs.

2) Firms are traditionally assumed to want to maximise profit — this could be for various reasons:
   - Profit means the firm can survive — loss-making firms might eventually have to close.
   - Greater profits allow firms to offer better rewards to the owner (or shareholders) and staff...
   - ...or profit can be reinvested in the business in the hope of making even more profits later. For example, a firm might want to invest in order to expand.

3) But firms may want to maximise other quantities instead, such as total sales or the firm's market share.
   - A large market share could lead to some monopoly power (see p.62) — this would mean that the firm could charge higher prices due to a lack of competition.
   - Bigger firms are often considered more prestigious and stable, so they can attract the best employees.

4) Some firms may also have ethical objectives — i.e. 'doing some good', even if it doesn't increase profits. For example, a firm may decide to buy all its raw materials from nearby suppliers in order to support the local economy, even if cheaper alternatives are available elsewhere.

CONSUMERS

1) Consumers are traditionally assumed to want to maximise their utility, while not spending more than their income (i.e. while living within their means).
   - Utility will involve different things for different people — e.g. some people might value the security of making large pension contributions, while others might want to spend their money on things like fast cars and holidays.
   - But whatever someone spends their money on, it's assumed they'll act rationally to increase their utility in the way that makes most sense to them.

2) Consumers can also act as workers — workers are assumed to want to maximise their income, while having as much free time as they need or want.

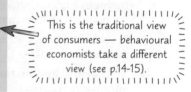 This is the traditional view of consumers — behavioural economists take a different view (see p.14-15).

GOVERNMENTS

1) Governments try to balance the resources of a country with the needs and wants of the population — i.e. economists assume that governments try to maximise the 'public interest'.

2) This is likely to include some or all of the following:
   - Economic growth — usually measured by growth in a country's GDP. Gross domestic product (see p.122).
   - Full employment — everybody of a working age, who is capable of working, having a job.
   - Equilibrium in the balance of payments — a balance between the payments into the country over a period of time and the payments out.
   - Low inflation — keeping prices under control, as high inflation can cause serious problems.

3) In practice, these are competing objectives — policies that help achieve one objective may make it more difficult to achieve another (e.g. extra government spending may help create jobs, but it could lead to higher inflation). See p.160-161 for more information.

Warm-Up Questions

Q1 Describe two economic objectives a firm might have.

Q2 What are governments assumed to be trying to maximise?

Exam Question

Q1 The table shows the total revenue earned by a shop selling chairs. What is the marginal revenue of the fourth chair?
A) £24   C) £50
B) £37   D) £195   [1 mark]

Quantity	Total Revenue (£)
1	60
2	110
3	158
4	195
5	219

Economic agents — they like to maximise stuff and wear dark sunglasses...

The objectives of economic agents discussed here are based on traditional views of what these agents wish to maximise. It's good to keep in mind that these traditional views are challenged by some economists — see the next page for more.

Behavioural Economics

Behavioural economics is a growing area of study in Economics. Governments, including the UK government, are beginning to use behavioural economics to create more effective economic policies. ***These pages are for AQA and Edexcel only.***

Behavioural Economics Challenges traditional economic theory

1) The **key assumptions** used in **traditional economic theory** are:
   - Economic agents are **utility maximisers**.
   - Economic agents are **rational**.

2) Behavioural economists **challenge** these assumptions because they're **not realistic**. They look at the impact of **social**, **psychological** and **emotional** factors on decision making to try to make more realistic predictions about the decisions that individuals make.

3) Behavioural economists **don't ignore** traditional economic theory — they try to **improve** upon it and make it more **relevant** to the real world.

Donald gained maximum utility from his bagpipes. No one else did.

Rationality is used to explain the actions of Economic Agents

1) Using the concept of utility maximisation, it's **assumed** that a **rational individual** (sometimes referred to as '*homo economicus*') will attempt to **maximise** their **utility** (or economic profit). They do this by **comparing** the **costs** and **benefits** of **alternatives**, and then choosing the option that maximises their net utility (or net profit).

2) However, acting rationally requires all economic agents to have the **information** they need to be able to **correctly** choose between alternatives. Traditional economic theories assume that everyone has **perfect** (or **symmetric**) **information** and the **ability** to **use** this information to make a **rational decision**.

3) In **real life**, economic agents will likely have **imperfect information** — they **won't** have all the information they need to make a rational decision and this will lead to **market failure** (for more see p.82).

4) **Asymmetric information** is another problem that **prevents rationality**. Asymmetric information occurs when **one party** has **more information** than the other in a transaction. For example, sellers often have more information than buyers as a seller will know how much a product actually cost to make and what its true value is (see p.82).

5) As a result, behavioural economists believe that **rationality alone** can't be used to **predict** consumer behaviour.

There are Many Reasons why consumers Don't act Rationally

1) Behavioural economists argue that there are a lot of **restrictions** on people's ability to make rational decisions:
   - The **time** available to make a decision is **limited**.
   - **Not all information** is **available**, and the information that's available may be **incorrect**.
   - People **might not** be able to **process** and **evaluate** the **vast amounts** of **data** involved in making a decision, and they **might not** be very good at **calculating** the **costs** of alternatives (this is known as **computation weakness**).

2) These **limits** on decision making are known as '**bounded rationality**'. Behavioural economists argue that bounded rationality means that people tend to **satisfice** (make a satisfactory decision) rather than **spend ages** trying to make a **rational decision** which maximises utility.

Behavioural Economists argue that individuals have Bounded Self-control

1) A **rational individual** (*homo economicus*) is **assumed** to have **total self-control** and will only act to maximise their utility.

2) However, behavioural economists argue that individuals have **limits** on their self-control, i.e. they have '**bounded self-control**'. For example, a consumer may have a **limited ability** to stop smoking, even though the act of smoking **doesn't** maximise their utility.

Behavioural Economics

Biases Stop individuals acting in an Economically Rational way

Behavioural economists believe that individuals are **influenced** by **biases** which affect their decision making. For example:

- **Rules of thumb** — simple, useful tools that **help** an individual make a decision, e.g. choosing the **middle-priced option** when faced with a range of different prices for similar products.
- **Anchoring** — this means placing **too much emphasis** on **one piece** of **information**, e.g. the **first price quoted** for a job can influence an individual's view of what's a **fair price**.
- **Availability bias** — this is where judgements are made about the **probability** of events occurring based on how **easy** it is to **remember** such events occurring, e.g. following a drought, people will **overestimate** the probability of a drought occurring the next year and make decisions based on this **assumption**.
- **Social norms** — an individual's behaviour can be **influenced** by the behaviour of their **social group** (this could be anything from a friendship group to the population of the whole world). For example, an individual may stop buying cigarettes if none of their friends smoke.
- **Habitual behaviour** — doing the **same thing over and over again**, e.g. individuals often choose to shop at the **same place** regardless of any rational reason for going **somewhere else**.

Fairness can affect decision making

1) In traditional economic theory, a **rational individual** may **give money** to **charity** because they **gain utility** from doing it (e.g. it makes them **feel good**). However, behavioural economists recognise that individuals and firms **don't** just act out of **self-interest** — they may have a sense of **fairness** and choose to act **altruistically**.

2) For example, a firm may pay their employees **above** the **minimum** or **market wage** (for more on wages see p.106-107 and p.116-117) because they think it's **fair** — they **aren't** guaranteed to receive any benefit from it.

Governments can use behavioural economic theory for their Policies

A government's **social** and **economic policies** need to work in the **real world** and using traditional economic theories based on **unrealistic assumptions** might not be very useful. As a result, governments may use behavioural economics to help them **create** their **policies**. There are a number of **observations** provided by behavioural economists that can be used by governments (and by producers) to **influence** the **decisions** of **individuals** or **firms**.

Choice architecture is where an **individual's choice** is **influenced** by **adapting** the way the choice is **presented**. This can be done in a number of ways:

- **Default options** — people are **more likely** to choose the 'default' option, so this can be used to encourage individuals to act in a certain way — e.g. employees might be **automatically enrolled** onto a pension scheme.
- **Framing** — the **context** in which information is **presented** can **influence** a decision, e.g. changing the wording of a choice could make an option more desirable, so charging a fee of £1 a day seems more appealing than £7 a week.
- **Nudges** — this is where some alternatives are made **easier** to **choose** than others **without removing** the **freedom** of choice, e.g. by **only** allowing smoking in certain areas, a government can 'nudge' people into quitting.
- **Restricted choice** — this occurs when people's choices are **restricted**, e.g. people are restricted to only being able to choose from a **limited number** of **schools** in their **local area**.
- **Mandated choices** — this is where people **have** to make a **decision**, e.g. a government may implement a policy where people **have** to **choose** whether or not they're willing to be organ donors.

Warm-Up Questions

Q1 What is bounded rationality?
Q2 List three biases that can occur in decision making.

Exam Question

Q1 How could behavioural economics contribute to the design of government policies to encourage individuals to save more?

[8 marks]

Here's a nudge — you better learn this stuff, it's important...

Behavioural economics is pretty interesting and provides a more realistic take on economic activity than the traditional theories. It does have its critics though, people don't like the idea that an individual's decisions might be influenced by things like framing and nudges — they think that consumers should have free will. However, behavioural economists would argue that rational individuals don't exist and people need help to make decisions that bring the most benefit to themselves and society.

Demand

Section 2 is all about markets, and to understand markets you'll need to know everything there is to know about demand and supply. Working out what demand is seems like a good place to start — so go on, get reading... ***These pages are for all boards.***

Markets are where Goods and Services are Bought and Sold

1) A **market** is anywhere **buyers** and **sellers** can exchange **goods** or **services**.

2) The **price charged** for and **quantity sold** of each good or service are **determined** by the levels of **demand** and **supply** in a market.

3) The levels of demand and supply in a market are shown using **diagrams**. These diagrams demonstrate the price level and quantity demanded/supplied of goods or services.

For information on supply, turn to p.22.

Demand for Goods or Services is Different at Different Prices

1) **Demand** is the **quantity** of a good/service that consumers are **willing and able** to buy at a **given price**, at a **particular time**.

2) A **demand curve** shows the relationship between **price** and **quantity demanded**. At any given point along the curve it shows the **quantity** of the good or service that would be bought at a particular **price**.

3) Here's an example of a demand curve:

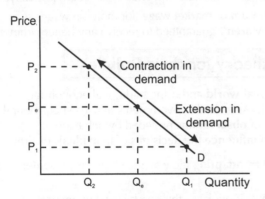

- At price P_e the quantity Q_e is demanded.
- A **decrease** in price from P_e to P_1 causes an **extension** in demand — it rises from Q_e to Q_1.
- An **increase** in price from P_e to P_2 causes a **contraction** in demand — it falls from Q_e to Q_2.
- So, **movement along** the **demand curve** is caused by **changes in price**.

Demand curves can be curved but are more often drawn as straight lines. They're usually labelled with a 'D'.

4) Demand curves usually **slope downwards**. This means that the **higher** the **price** charged for a good, the **lower** the **quantity demanded** — as shown by the diagram above.

5) In general, consumers aim to pay the **lowest price possible** for goods and services. As prices decrease **more consumers** are **willing and able** to purchase a good or service — so **lower prices** means **higher demand**.

6) The **relationship** between **price** and **quantity demanded** can also be explained using the **law of diminishing marginal utility** (see p.12).

Jamil could probably do with diminishing his own utilities.

Changes in Demand cause a Shift in the Demand Curve

1) A demand curve moves to the **left** (e.g. D_1) when there is a **decrease** in the **amount demanded** at **every price**.

2) A demand curve shifts to the **right** (e.g. D_2) when there is an **increase** in the **amount demanded** at **every price**.

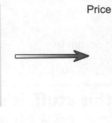

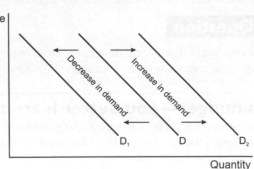

Demand

There are lots of **Factors** that can **Cause** a **Shift** in the **Demand Curve**

1) Changes in tastes and fashion can cause demand curves to shift to the **right** if something is **popular** and to the **left** when it is **out of fashion**.

2) Changes to people's **real income**, the amount of goods/services that a consumer can afford to purchase with their income, can affect the **demand** for **different types** of goods differently.

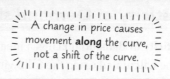
*A change in price causes movement **along** the curve, not a shift of the curve.*

- **Normal goods** (e.g. DVDs) are those which people will demand **more** of if their **real income increases**. This means that a **rise** in real income causes the **demand curve** to **shift** to the **right** — people want to buy more of the good at each price level.

- **Inferior goods** (e.g. cheap clothing) are those which people demand **less** of if their real income increases. This means that a **rise** in real income causes the **demand curve** to **shift** to the **left** — people demand less at each price level since they'll often switch to more expensive goods instead.

- A more **equal distribution** of income (i.e. a reduction in the difference between the incomes of rich and poor people) may cause the demand curve for **luxury goods** (e.g. sports cars) to shift to the **left** — and the demand curve for other items to shift to the **right**. This is because there'll be **fewer** really **rich** people who can afford **luxury** items, and **more** people who can afford **everyday** items.

Changes in demand in **One Market** can affect demand in **Other Markets**

Some markets are **interrelated**, which means that changes in **one** market **affect** a **related** market.

- **Substitute goods** are those which are alternatives to each other — e.g. beef and lamb. An **increase** in the **price** of one good will **decrease** the **demand** for it and **increase** the **demand** for its **substitutes** (this is also known as '**competitive demand**').

- **Complementary goods** are goods that are **often used together**, so they're in **joint demand** — e.g. strawberries and cream. If the **price** of strawberries **increases**, demand for them will **decrease** along with **demand** for cream.

- The introduction of a **new product** may cause the demand curve to shift to the **left** for goods that are **substitutes** for the new product and to the **right** for goods that are **complementary** to it.

- **Derived demand** is the demand for a good or a factor of production used in making another good or service. For example, an **increase** in the demand for **fencing** will lead to an **increased** derived demand for **wood**.

- Some goods have more than one use, e.g. oil can be used to make plastics or for fuel — this is **composite demand**. This means changes in the **demand curve** for **fuel** could lead to changes in the **supply curve** for **plastics**.

Warm-Up Questions

Q1 What causes a movement along a demand curve?

Q2 What causes a shift in a demand curve?

Q3 What are normal goods?

Q4 Give four examples of complementary goods.

Exam Questions

Q1 The decline in the housing market experienced in the UK during the period 2008-2012 led to building firms reducing their workload and to many tile retailers cutting down or delaying expansion plans. Explain the likely impacts of the decline of the UK housing market on tile manufacturers. [8 marks]

Q2 Cheese and crackers are complementary goods. Explain the likely impacts on the demand for crackers if the price of cheese dramatically increases. [4 marks]

I love complementary goods — always make me feel good about myself...

A market determines the price of a certain good (or service), and price will often affect demand. Demand links to the quantity sold — greater demand tends to lead to a greater quantity sold. There are loads of different factors that can influence demand, so make sure you learn how these affect the demand curve — those that change the level of demand cause the curve to shift.

Price, Income and Cross Elasticities of Demand

Elasticity of demand is a measure of how much the demand for a good changes with a change in one of the key influences on demand — the price of the good, the level of real income and the price of another good. **These pages are for all boards.**

Price Elasticity of Demand shows how Demand Changes with Price

1) **Price elasticity of demand** (**PED**) is a measure of how the quantity **demanded** of a good **responds** to a **change** in its **price**.

2) PED can be **calculated** using the following formula:

$$PED = \frac{\text{percentage change in quantity demanded}}{\text{percentage change in price}}$$

You can think of PED as the way that consumers react (how much of a good they demand) as the price changes.

3) Have a look at this example:

- When the **price** of a type of toy car **increased** from **50p** to **70p** the **demand** for them **fell** from **15** cars to **10** cars.

- The **percentage change** in **quantity demanded** would be: $\frac{\text{change in demand}}{\text{original demand}} \times 100 = \frac{-5}{15} \times 100 = -33.33\%$

- The **percentage change** in **price** would be: $\frac{\text{change in price}}{\text{original price}} \times 100 = \frac{20}{50} \times 100 = 40\%$

  A common exam mistake is to write PED as a percentage — it's not.

- So **PED** $= \frac{-33.33\%}{40\%} = -0.83$

4) Price elasticity of demand is **usually negative** because **demand falls** as **price increases** for most goods.

< means 'less than'
> means 'greater than'

PED can be Elastic, Inelastic or Unit Elastic

Elastic (Relatively Elastic) Demand: PED > 1

1) If the value of PED (ignoring any minus signs) is **greater than 1 (> 1)**, demand for the good is **elastic**. This means a **percentage change** in **price** will cause a **larger percentage change** in **quantity demanded**.

2) The **higher** the value of PED, the **more elastic** demand is for the good.

3) In diagram 1, price falls from **£50** to **£40** and an extra **45** units are demanded, which gives an **elastic** PED of **−7.5**.

$$PED = \frac{45/30 \times 100}{-10/50 \times 100} = -7.5$$

So a 1% change in price leads to a 7.5% change in demand.

4) **Perfectly elastic demand** has a PED of **± infinity** and any **increase** in **price** means that **demand** will **fall to zero** — see diagram 2. Consumers are willing to buy all they can obtain at P, but **none** at a **higher price** (above P).

Inelastic (Relatively Inelastic) Demand: 0 < PED < 1

1) The value of PED for goods with inelastic demand (ignoring any minus signs) is **between 0 and 1 (0 < PED < 1)**. This means a **percentage change** in **price** will cause a **smaller percentage change** in **quantity demanded**. The **smaller** the value of PED, the **more inelastic** demand is for the good.

2) In diagram 3, price falls from **£50** to **£40** (**20% decrease**) and only an extra **4** units (**8% increase**) are demanded. This gives an **inelastic** PED of **−0.4** which means for every 1% change in price there's a 0.4% change in demand.

3) **Perfectly inelastic demand** has a PED of **0** and any **change** in **price** will have **no effect** on the **quantity demanded** — see diagram 4. At any price (e.g. P_1 or P_2), the **quantity demanded** will be the **same**.

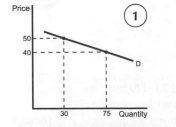

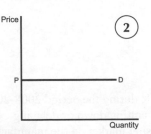

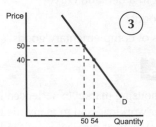

Unit Elasticity of Demand: PED = ±1

1) A good has **unit elasticity** (PED = ±1) if the size of the **percentage change** in **price** is **equal** to the size of the **percentage change** in **quantity demanded** — see diagram 5.

2) For example, here a **20% decrease** in price will lead to a **20% increase** in quantity demanded.

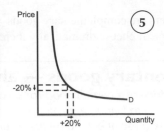

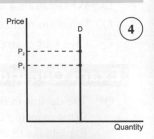

Jim's demand for bungee cord elasticity was at an all-time high.

Price, Income and Cross Elasticities of Demand

Income Elasticity of Demand shows how Demand Changes with Income

1) **Income elasticity of demand (YED)** measures how much the **demand** for a good changes with a **change in real income**.

2) YED can be **calculated** using the following formula: ⟹

$$YED = \frac{\text{percentage change in quantity demanded of a good}}{\text{percentage change in real income}}$$

3) Here's an example:

> If **real incomes increased** by **10%** and because of this the **demand** for **cameras** increased by **15%**, the income elasticity of demand for cameras would be: $YED = \frac{15\%}{10\%} = 1.5$

4) Here are examples of the meanings of different values of YED (ignoring any minus signs):

Income elastic: YED > 1

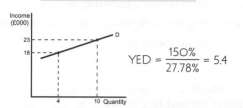

$$YED = \frac{150\%}{27.78\%} = 5.4$$

An increase in income of **£5000** leads to an increase in demand for the good of **6 units**. This gives an **elastic** (or **relatively elastic**) YED of **5.4**. So for every 1% increase in incomes, demand increases by 5.4%.

Income inelastic: YED < 1

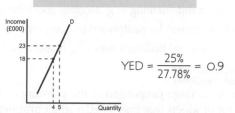

$$YED = \frac{25\%}{27.78\%} = 0.9$$

An increase in income of **£5000** leads to an increase in demand for the good of only **1 unit**. This gives an **inelastic** (or **relatively inelastic**) YED of **0.9**.

Perfectly inelastic: YED = 0

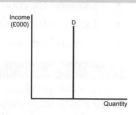

No matter how high incomes rise, **demand remains constant**.

You need to know about Cross Elasticity of Demand too

1) **Cross elasticity of demand (XED)** is a measure of how the **quantity demanded** of one good **responds** to a **change** in the **price** of another good.

2) XED can be **calculated** using the following formula: ⤺

$$XED = \frac{\text{percentage change in quantity demanded of good A}}{\text{percentage change in price of good B}}$$

3) If two goods are **substitutes** their XED will be **positive** and if they're **complements** their XED will be **negative**. For example:

> **Toy cars** and **teddy bears** are **substitutes**. If the **price** of toy cars **rose** by **40%**, the **demand** for teddy bears may **increase** by **20%**. $XED = \frac{20\%}{40\%} = 0.5$

> **Tennis rackets** and **tennis balls** are **complementary** goods. If the **price** of tennis rackets **rose** by **50%**, the **demand** for tennis balls may **fall** by **30%**. $XED = \frac{-30\%}{50\%} = -0.6$

Warm-Up Questions

Q1 Give the formula for PED.

Q2 What is income elasticity of demand?

Exam Question

Q1 The price of chococakes was reduced from £3 to £1.50, causing an increase in demand from 200 to 400. What is the price elasticity of demand for chococakes?

A) –1.0   B) –2.0   C) –0.5   D) +2.0

[1 mark]

Cross elasticity of demand — it's elasticity of demand on a bad day...

I'm sorry, I know that's terrible. Anyway, the key things to pick up here are that there are three elasticities of demand that you need to understand. Their names should give you a clue about what affects them. Well, except XED, which is a bit less obvious — it's like PED, but it's about two different goods (or services) rather than just the one. Read it over until it's clear in your head.

Uses of Elasticities of Demand

*Different factors influence the different elasticities of demand. Some factors influence more than one type of elasticity,
so make sure you study them well. PED also has implications for a firm's revenue.* **These pages are for all boards.**

Many Factors Influence the Price Elasticity of Demand

1) **Substitutes**

   The **more substitutes** a good has, the **more price elastic** demand is — if there are many
   substitutes available then consumers can easily **switch** to something else if the price rises.
   The **number of substitutes** a good has depends on how closely it's **defined**, e.g. peas have
   a number of substitutes (like carrots and sweetcorn), but vegetables as a group have fewer.

   > The most important
   > influence on elasticity is
   > the number of **substitutes**
   > a good has, but in the
   > exam you'll be expected to
   > know lots of influences.

2) **Type of good (or service)**

   - Demand for **essential items** (e.g. toilet paper) is price **inelastic**, but demand for **non-essential** items
     (e.g. tablet computers) tends to be price **elastic**.
   - Demand for goods that are **habit-forming** (e.g. alcohol and tobacco) tends to be price **inelastic**.
   - Demand for purchases that **cannot be postponed** (e.g. emergency plumbing services) tends to be price **inelastic**.
   - Demand for products with **several different uses** (e.g. water) tends to be price **inelastic**.

3) **Percentage of income spent on good**

   Demand for products that need a **large proportion** of the **consumer's income** (e.g. a fridge) is **more
   price elastic** than demand for products that only need a **small proportion** of **income** (e.g. toothpaste).
   Consumers are more likely to shop around for the **best price** for an expensive good.

4) **Time**

   In the **long run** demand becomes more **price elastic** as it becomes **easier** to change to **alternatives** because
   consumers have had the time to shop around. Also, in the long run, habits and loyalties can change.

Total Revenue and Price Elasticity of Demand

> Remember, PED will usually
> be negative, but we're
> ignoring minus signs here.

1) It's important for firms to understand the relationship between **total revenue**
   (price per unit × quantity sold) and a product's **price elasticity of demand**.

2) Elasticity **changes** along a **straight-line demand curve**:

   - PED changes along the demand curve from minus
     infinity at **high price/zero demand**, through an
     elasticity of minus **one** at the **midpoint**, to an elasticity
     of **zero** at **zero price/high quantity** demanded.

   - The n-shaped graph underneath shows how the **total
     revenue changes** as the point **moves along** the **demand
     curve** — i.e. as the price and quantity demanded change.

   - **Total revenue** is **maximised** when **PED = ±1** — the
     nearer a firm sets a product's price to the **mid-point** of
     the demand curve, the **higher** its **total revenue** will be.

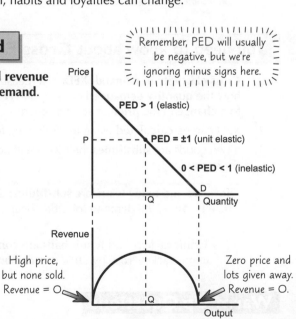

3) If a good has **elastic** demand, then:

   - A **reduction** in **price** will **increase** the firm's **total revenue**.
   - An **increase** in **price** will **reduce** the firm's **total revenue**.

   For example, a good has an **elastic** PED of −2.5. When the good's price is £5, 20 units are sold, giving a total
   revenue of **£100**. When **price falls** to £4, **demand rises** to 30 units and **total revenue increases** to **£120**.

4) However, if a good has **inelastic** demand, then:

   - A **reduction** in **price** will **reduce** the firm's **total revenue**.
   - An **increase** in **price** will **increase** the firm's **total revenue**.

   For example, a good has an **inelastic** PED of −0.5. When the good's price is £5, 20 units are sold, giving a
   total revenue of **£100**. When **price falls** to £4, **demand rises** to 22 units and **total revenue falls** to **£88**.

Uses of Elasticities of Demand

Income Elasticity of Demand is different for Normal and Inferior goods

Normal Goods

These goods have a **positive YED (0 < YED < 1)**. As **incomes rise, demand increases**. The size of the demand increase is dependent on the product's **elasticity**. If the YED of a product is **elastic (YED > 1)** then it's a **luxury (or superior) good**.

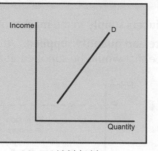

Inferior Goods

These goods have a **negative YED (YED < 0)** As **incomes rise, demand falls**. A rise in income will lead to the **inferior good** being **replaced** with one considered to be of **higher quality**.

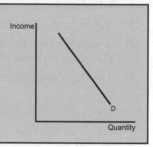

Normal goods are the most common type of good.

Cross Elasticity of Demand shows if goods are Substitutes or Complements

1) **Substitutes** have **positive** cross elasticities of demand (XEDs). A **fall** in the **price** of **one substitute** (e.g. rice) will **reduce** the **demand** for **another** (e.g. pasta). The **closer** the substitutes, the **higher** the **positive XED**. For example, ballpoint pens and fountain pens will have a **higher XED** compared to ballpoint pens and pencils.

2) Goods that are **complements** have **negative** XEDs. An **increase** in the **price** of a good (e.g. cheese) will lead to a **reduction** in **demand** for its **complements** (e.g. chutney).

3) Goods which have a **XED of zero** are **independent** (or **unrelated**) **goods** and **don't** directly affect the demand of each other — for example, bananas and slippers.

Knowledge of Elasticities of Demand is Useful for Firms and Governments

EDEXCEL & OCR

1) Information about **YED** can be used in **sales forecasting** — if the YED of a product and likely **changes** in **income** are known, then **sales levels** can be **predicted**. YED can also be used in **pricing policy** — a **reduction** in price for a normal good, when there's an **expected fall** in incomes, may **limit** the **expected reduction** in **demand** for the good.

2) A firm may choose to supply a **range** of goods with **various YEDs**. During a boom **demand** for a product with a **high YED** will **increase**, but demand for that product will **decrease** when the economy is in a recession. So a firm may also supply products with a **low YED** so that they can still **earn revenue** during a **recession**.

3) It's also useful for firms to know the **XEDs** of their goods because that will tell them how to **react** to **changes** in the **price** of **related products** to ensure they **maximise demand** for their products. For example, if a firm sells a product that has a close substitute and the substitute's price **drops**, they may choose to **lower** the price of their product to **reduce** the possible **fall** in demand for it.

4) It'd be very useful for governments to know how **demand** for goods might change during **booms** and **recessions** when they're setting their **policies**. For example, **demand** for **bus services** may **increase** with **falling incomes** in a recession, so a government would have to make sure that sufficient bus services were provided.

Warm-Up Questions

Q1 List four influences on PED.
Q2 What is the PED when a firm's revenue is maximised?
Q3 Do complements have positive or negative XED?

Exam Question

Q1 Explain how a firm can use knowledge of price elasticity of demand to maximise revenue. [6 marks]

Inferior? How dare you call my bespoke carrier bag raincoats inferior...

Well, who'd have thought it? If you charge too much for an elastic good you can actually reduce revenue. If firms and governments had perfect knowledge of all the different elasticities of demand then they'd be laughing. Unfortunately, though, they don't, which means there's a bit of guesswork involved and getting it wrong can lead to some pretty costly mistakes.

Supply

Like demand, supply is a key part of the market mechanism. But whereas demand is all about what consumers are willing and able to pay for, supply is all about firms' willingness to supply goods/services at different prices. **These pages are for all boards.**

Supply of Goods or Services is Different at Different Prices

1) **Supply** is the **quantity** of a **good or service** that **producers supply** to the **market** at a **given price**, at a **particular time**.

2) A **supply curve** shows the **relationship** between **price** and **quantity supplied**. At any given point along the curve it shows the **quantity** of the good or service that would be supplied at a particular **price**.

3) Here's an example of a supply curve:

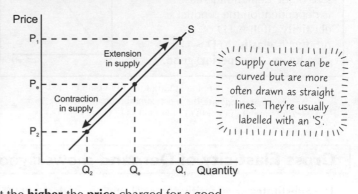

- At price P_e the quantity Q_e is supplied.
- An **increase** in price from P_e to P_1 causes an **extension** in supply — it **rises** from Q_e to Q_1.
- A **decrease** in price from P_e to P_2 causes a **contraction** in supply — it **falls** from Q_e to Q_2.
- So, **movement along** the supply curve is caused by **changes in price**.

Supply curves can be curved but are more often drawn as straight lines. They're usually labelled with an 'S'.

4) Supply curves usually **slope upwards**. This means that the **higher** the **price** charged for a good, the **higher** the **quantity supplied** — as shown by the diagram above.

5) **Producers** and **sellers** aim to **maximise** their **profits**. Other things being equal, the **higher** the **price** for a good or service the **higher** the **profit**. **Higher profit** provides an **incentive** to **expand production** and **increase supply**, which explains why the **quantity supplied** of a good/service **increases** as **price increases**.

6) However, increasing **supply** increases **costs**. Firms will only **produce more** if the **price increases** by **more** than the costs.

7) **Increased prices** mean that it will become **profitable** for **marginal firms** (these are firms that are just breaking even) to **supply** the **market** — increasing **market supply** levels.

In perfect competition, the supply curve is the marginal cost curve, see p.56.

Changes in Supply cause a Shift in the Supply Curve

1) A supply curve moves to the **left** (e.g. S_1) when there's a **decrease** in the **amount supplied** at **every price**.

2) A supply curve shifts to the **right** (e.g. S_2) when there's an **increase** in the **amount supplied** at **every price**.

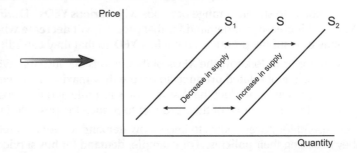

There are lots of Factors that can Cause a shift in the Supply Curve

Changes to the costs of production

An **increase** in one or more of the **costs of production** (e.g. raw materials, wages etc.) will **decrease producers' profits** and cause the supply curve to **shift to the left**. If a cost of production **decreased**, the supply curve would shift to the **right**. For example, an **increase** in the cost of **cocoa** will lead to a **reduction** in the **supply** of **chocolate**, but a **decrease** in the cost of **packaging** will lead to an **increase** in **supply**.

Improvements in technology

Technological improvements can **increase supply** as they **reduce the costs of production**. For example, improvements in the **energy efficiency** of commercial freezers could **reduce the energy costs** of a food company.

Supply

Changes to the productivity of factors of production

Increased productivity of a factor of production means that a company will get **more output** from a unit of the factor. For example, **more productive staff** will lead to an **increase** in **output** and shift the supply curve to the **right**.

Indirect taxes and subsidies

An **indirect tax** on a good effectively **increases costs** for a **producer** — this means that the **supply is reduced** and the supply curve is shifted to the **left**. A **subsidy** on a good encourages its production as it acts to **reduce costs** for **producers** — this leads to an **increased** level of supply and the supply curve **shifts right**.

For more on indirect taxes and subsidies see p.30-31 and p.86-88.

Changes to the price of other goods

If the **price of one product** (A) made by a firm **increases**, then a firm may **switch production** from a **less profitable** one (B) to **increase production of A** and make the most of the higher price that they can get for it. This **decreases** the supply of **product B**.

Number of suppliers

An **increase** in the number of **suppliers** in a market (including new firms) will **increase** supply to the market, shifting the supply curve to the **right**. A **decrease** in the **number of suppliers** will shift the curve to the **left**.

Joint Supply is when Goods or Services are Supplied Together

← AQA & OCR

1) **Joint supply** is where the **production** of **one good** or **service** involves the **production** of **another** (or several others) — it's another example of when markets are **interrelated**. For example, if **crude oil** is **refined** to make **petrol** this will also increase the supply of **butane** (another product that's made as a result of this process).

2) If the **price** of a product **increases**, then **supply** of it and any **joint products** will **also increase**. For example, if the **price** of **petrol increases**, the level of drilling for oil will rise and the **supply** of **petrol** and its **joint products** will **increase**.

You also need to know about Competitive Supply

← OCR ONLY

Competitive supply is where two (or more) **alternative goods** can be produced from the **same factors of production** (land, labour and capital). For example, land used to grow potatoes might be used to grow wheat, so it's up to the producer to **choose** the best way to use their factors of production.

Warm-Up Questions

Q1 What does a supply curve show?

Q2 What causes a contraction of supply?

Q3 Describe two factors that can cause a supply curve to shift.

PRACTICE QUESTIONS

Exam Questions

Q1 Which of the following would cause a movement along a supply curve?
   A) A cut in the price of the product.
   B) A new entrant into the market.
   C) An improvement in the technology used to make the product.
   D) An increase in the costs of the raw materials used to make the product.   [1 mark]

Q2 Which of the following would most likely lead to an increase in the supply of dolls' houses?
   A) An increase in the cost of wood-cutting machinery.
   B) The exit from the market of a major toy maker.
   C) A new doll's house construction method is introduced which speeds up production by 25%.
   D) An increase in the cost of glue.   [1 mark]

Personally, I've always thought Supply was a bit shifty...

Ah supply, that's just like demand but the line goes a different way... No, no, no, wait, don't be fooled into thinking it's really similar to demand — it's still important that you learn all about supply. Although learning about it should be made easier if you're well acquainted with demand, as you've got to learn about what happens when prices change and the curve shifts.

Price Elasticity of Supply

*These pages cover price elasticity of supply and the factors that can affect it. Be careful not to confuse it with price elasticity of demand (p.18) — it might seem similar but there are some differences to look out for. **These pages are for all boards.***

Price Elasticity of Supply shows how Supply Changes with Price

1) **Price elasticity of supply (PES)** is a measure of how the **quantity supplied** of a good **responds** to a **change in its price**.

2) PES can be **calculated** using the **following formula**:

$$PES = \frac{\text{percentage change in quantity supplied}}{\text{percentage change in price}}$$

You can think of PES as the way that suppliers react (how much of a good they supply) as the price changes.

3) Here's an example calculation:

- When the **price** of a smartphone **increased** from **£449** to **£485** the **supply** of them **increased** from **15000** to **21500**.

- The **percentage change** in **quantity supplied** would be: $\frac{\text{change in supply}}{\text{original supply}} \times 100 = \frac{6500}{15000} \times 100 = \textbf{43.33\%}$

- The **percentage change** in **price** would be: $\frac{\text{change in price}}{\text{original price}} \times 100 = \frac{36}{449} \times 100 = \textbf{8\%}$

  Don't forget that PES has no units — it's not a percentage.

- So **PES** $= \frac{43.33\%}{8\%} = \textbf{5.42}$

4) PES is **generally positive** since the **higher** the **price** the **greater** the **supply**.

PES can be Elastic, Inelastic or Unit Elastic

Elastic (Relatively Elastic) Supply: PES > 1

1) If the value of PES is **greater than 1 (> 1)**, supply of the good is **elastic**. This means a **percentage change in price** will cause a **larger percentage change in quantity supplied**.

2) The **higher the value** of PES, the **more elastic** supply is for the good.

3) In diagram 1, price increases from £5 to £7 and an extra 7 units are supplied, which gives an **elastic PES** of **8.75**.

$$PES = \frac{7/2 \times 100}{2/5 \times 100} = 8.75$$

So a 1% change in price leads to an 8.75% change in supply.

4) **Perfectly elastic supply** has a PES of ± **infinity** and any **fall** in **price** means that the **quantity supplied** will be reduced to **zero** — see diagram 2.

Inelastic (Relatively Inelastic) Supply: 0 < PES < 1

1) The value of PES for an inelastic good is **between 0 and 1 (0 < PES < 1)**. This means a **percentage change** in **price** will cause a **smaller percentage change** in **quantity supplied**. The **smaller** the value of PES, the **more inelastic** supply is.

2) In diagram 3, price increases from £2000 to £6000 (**200%**) and only an extra **2000** units (**100% increase**) are supplied. This gives an inelastic PES of 0.5 which means for every 1% change in price there is a 0.5% change in supply.

3) **Perfectly inelastic supply** has a PES of **0** and any **change** in **price** will have **no effect** on the **quantity supplied** — see diagram 4. At any price (e.g. P_1 or P_2), the **quantity supplied** will be the **same**.

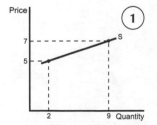

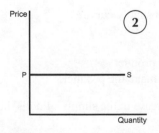

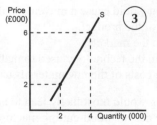

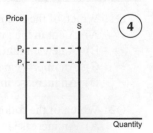

Unit Elasticity of Supply: PES = 1

1) A good has **unit elasticity** (PES = 1) if the percentage change in **quantity supplied** is **equal** to the percentage change in **price** — see diagram 5.

2) For example, a **50% increase** in price will lead to a **50% increase** in quantity supplied.

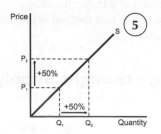

Supply of this floral outfit was low. Most people were glad about this.

Price Elasticity of Supply

A **High PES** is **Important** to **Firms**

1) Firms aim to **respond quickly** to **changes in price and demand**.
2) To do so they need to make their **supply** as **elastic** (i.e. responsive to price change) as possible.
3) Measures undertaken to **improve** the **elasticity** of **supply** include **flexible working patterns**, using the **latest technology** and having **spare production capacity**. For example, if a firm has spare production capacity it can quickly increase supply of a good without an increase in costs (e.g. the cost of building a new factory).

Supply is **Price Inelastic** in the **Short Run**

Over short periods of time firms can find it **difficult** to **switch production** from one good to another. This means that **supply** is likely to be **more price inelastic** in the **short run** compared to the **long run**.

SHORT RUN
- The **short run** is the **time period** when a firm's **capacity** is **fixed**, and at least one **factor of production** is **fixed**.
- **Capital** is often the factor of production that's **fixed** in the **short run** — a firm can recruit **more workers** and buy **more materials**, but it takes **time** to build additional production facilities. This means that it can be **difficult** to **increase production** in the **short run**, so supply in the short run is **inelastic**.

LONG RUN
- In the **long run** all the factors of production are **variable** — so in the **long run** a firm is able to **increase** its **capacity**.
- This means that supply is **more elastic** in the long run because firms have **longer** to react to **changes in price and demand**.

The distinction between **long run** and **short run** varies with **different industries** because **production times** and levels of **capital equipment** vary between industries. For example, the **long run** for a firm that makes sandwiches will be a **shorter time** than that of a firm that builds ships — to change production levels in ship building requires **more capital equipment**, **more planning** etc. Because ships take longer to produce than sandwiches, the **supply** of ships is more **inelastic**.

There are **Several Other Factors** that affect **PES**

The supply of agricultural products is more price inelastic in the short run than manufactured goods — plants take time to grow and livestock need nurturing over several years.

1) During periods of **unemployment** supply tends to be **more elastic** — it's **easy to attract new workers** if a firm wishes to expand.
2) **Perishable goods** (e.g. some fresh fruit and flowers) have an **inelastic supply** as they cannot be stored for very long.
3) Firms with **high stock levels** often have **elastic supply** — they're able to increase supply quickly if they want to.
4) Industries with more **mobile factors of production** (e.g. those that find it easy to expand their labour force and don't have production machinery/facilities that are difficult to relocate) tend to have **more elastic supply**. For example, industries that employ lots of unskilled workers may find it easy to increase their labour force.

Warm-Up Questions

Q1 What is the formula used to calculate PES?
Q2 What is perfectly elastic supply?
Q3 In the short run is supply price elastic or price inelastic?

Exam Questions

Q1 It has been calculated that bananas have a price elasticity of supply (PES) in the short run of 0.62. Suggest two reasons why bananas have an inelastic PES in the short run. [4 marks]

Q2 Explain why a company that specialises in making hand-made furniture with a small highly skilled workforce could find it difficult to increase supply in the short run. [4 marks]

My morning exercise is a jog around the block — I call it the short run...

The diagrams for PES are similar to those for PED (aside from the major difference of being supply curves rather than demand curves). However, remember that the one for unit elasticity is very different — it's a straight line rather than a curved one. It's important that you understand why firms are interested in PES and how time affects PES — it's all about the short and long run.

Market Equilibrium

*Here comes a key topic. On these pages you'll cover what it means when you have a pair of axes with both a demand and a supply curve on them and what they show about a market. **These pages are for all boards.***

A **Market** is in **Equilibrium** when **Supply Equals Demand**

1) At **equilibrium**, **price** and **output** are **stable** — there's a **balance** in the market and **supply** is **equal** to **demand**. **All products** that are presented for sale are **sold** and the market is **cleared**.

2) In a **free market**, **supply** and **demand** determine the **equilibrium price** and **quantity**.

3) This **free interaction** of supply and demand is known as **market forces**.

4) The **equilibrium point** can be found at the point where the **supply curve** and **demand curve meet**. This is shown in the example below:

> *When a market is cleared, the amount sellers wish to sell is equal to the amount that buyers demand.*

The table below shows the **supply** and **demand** for a teddy bear at various prices.

Price (£)	Quantity demanded per fortnight	Quantity supplied per fortnight
10	7000	1000
20	6000	2000
30	5000	3000
40	4000	4000
50	3000	5000
60	2000	6000
70	1000	7000

By looking at the data in this table you can see that the **equilibrium price** is **£40** — this is where the units **demanded** (4000) is **equal to** the units **supplied** (4000).

The equilibrium price and quantity are clear in the diagram above — it's at the point where the **supply** and **demand curves meet**.

5) When **supply** and **demand** aren't **equal** the market is in **disequilibrium**.

6) If there's **excess supply** or **excess demand** the market will be in **disequilibrium**.

> *In general, supply and demand curves are for the whole market, but they can also be used for individual firms or consumers.*

Excess Supply and Demand won't exist in a Free Market for long

Market forces act to remove **excess supply** or **demand**.

EXCESS SUPPLY

1) **Excess supply** is when the **quantity supplied** to a market is **greater** than the **quantity demanded**.

2) If the price for the teddy bear is set **above** the **equilibrium** (e.g. **£60**) there would be **excess supply** (a surplus) of **4000 units** (6000 supplied minus the 2000 demanded). This would cause the **price** to be **forced down**, **supply** to **contract** and **demand** to **extend** until the **equilibrium** was reached (£40 price and 4000 units supplied/demanded).

EXCESS DEMAND

1) **Excess demand** is when the **demand** for a good/service is **greater** than its **supply**.

2) If the price for the teddy bear is set **below** the **equilibrium** (e.g. **£20**) there would be **excess demand** of **4000 units** (6000 units demanded minus 2000 supplied). This would cause the **price** to be **forced up**, **demand** to **contract** and **supply** to **extend** until the **equilibrium** was reached (again, £40 price and 4000 units supplied/demanded).

Market Equilibrium

Shifts in Demand or Supply Curves will change the Market Equilibrium

1) If the **demand curve shifts**, assuming no change in the supply curve, then this will affect supply and price in the following ways:

- If **demand increases** from D to D_1 then the **price** will **increase** from P_e to P_1 and **supply** will **extend** from Q_e to Q_1, creating a new equilibrium.

- If **demand decreases** from D to D_2 then the **price** will **fall** to P_2 and **supply** will **contract** to Q_2, again creating a new equilibrium.

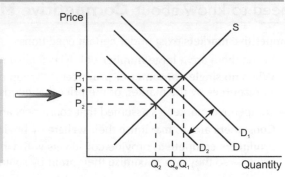

2) If the **supply curve shifts**, assuming no change in the demand curve, then this will affect demand and price in the following ways:

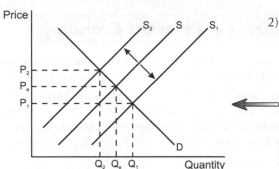

- If the **supply increases** from S to S_1 then the **price** will **fall** to P_1 and **demand** will **extend** to Q_1, creating a new equilibrium.

- If the **supply decreases** from S to S_2 then the **price** will **rise** to P_2 and **demand** will **contract** to Q_2, again creating a new equilibrium.

Elasticity will affect the Point of the New Equilibrium

1) **Price elasticity of supply** and **price elasticity of demand** influence the **size** of changes in the equilibrium price and quantity caused by supply and demand curve shifts.

2) For example, if the **demand curve** shifts to the **right** along an **elastic supply curve**, this will have a **larger effect** on **quantity** than price. The **opposite** is true for an **inelastic supply curve**.

Elasticity of PES/PED	Shifts in demand/supply curve has greater impact on:
Price **inelastic** supply or demand	Price
Price **elastic** supply or demand	Quantity

The Demand and Supply model involves several Assumptions

1) The demand and supply model involves several **assumptions**. For example, it's assumed that:
   - Supply and demand are **independent** of each other.
   - All markets are **perfectly competitive**.
   - *Ceteris paribus* (see p.5) applies.

2) These assumptions mean the model has **limited use** in the **real world**. However, the model can be useful as it gives a **broad picture** of how supply and demand works in a way that's **simple** and **easy** to **understand**.

AQA & OCR

Warm-Up Questions

Q1 When is a market in equilibrium?

Q2 What is excess supply?

Exam Question

Q1 Complete the following sentence. The equilibrium point in a free market
   A) is purely dependent on supply.
   B) will stay the same if there's a fall in supply.
   C) determines supply and demand.
   D) will move with a shift in the demand curve.

[1 mark]

In my experience there's never an excess supply of cake...

...there's always a shortage. How sad. Remember, disequilibrium can exist, but in free markets the price and quantity demanded (or supplied) will head back towards equilibrium levels (equilibrium is where the supply and demand curves cross).

Price and the Allocation of Resources

Prices are crucial for determining how resources are allocated within a market. **This page is for all boards.**

You need to know about **Competitive Markets**

1) **Competitive markets** exist under certain conditions:
   - When there are a **large number** of **buyers** (consumers) and **sellers** (producers).
   - When **no single consumer** or **producer** (or group of either) can **influence** the **allocation** of **resources** by the market, or the **price** that goods and services can be bought at.

2) In a competitive market it's assumed that consumers and producers act **rationally** (see p.12-14 for more):
   - **Consumers** aim to **maximise** their **welfare** by buying goods/services to **maintain** or **improve** their **quality of life**.
   - **Producers compete** to provide consumers with what they **want**, at the **lowest possible price** — so they can **maximise** their **profit** by selling to the **most customers**.

Price is the main way of **Allocating Resources** in a **Market Economy**

1) The **value** at which a good or service is **exchanged** is known as its **price**. Changes in the **demand** or **supply** of a good/service lead to changes in its **price** and to the **quantity bought/sold** — this is known as the **price mechanism**.

2) The price mechanism **allocates** goods/services in an **impersonal way** (known as the '**invisible hand**' of the market), as prices will change until equilibrium is achieved and supply equals demand. It's free from people's **biases** and **opinions**. The price mechanism also **coordinates** the decisions of **buyers** and **sellers**, e.g. how expensive something is will influence whether someone buys it and how much of it a producer supplies.

3) The price mechanism has the following **three functions**:
   - It acts as an **incentive** to firms — **higher prices** allow firms to produce more goods/services and **encourage increased production** and **sales** by providing **higher profits**.
   - It acts as a **signalling device** — **changes** in **price** show **changes** in **supply and/or demand** and act as a **signal** to producers and consumers. For example, a price increase is a **signal** to producers that demand is high, so this will encourage them to **increase production**.
   - It acts to **ration scarce resources** — if there's **high demand** for a good/service and its supply is **limited**, then the price will be **high**. Supply of the good will be **restricted** to those that can afford to pay a **high price**. The **opposite** applies for goods that are in **low demand** but in **high supply** — they'll have a **low price** and **many** will be sold.

4) The price mechanism is also used to **allocate** the **resources** used to **produce** goods/services. For example, if **demand** for **curtains increases**, the market will allocate (through the price mechanism) **more curtains** to **consumers**, **more labour** (e.g. seamstresses) for making curtains, and **more commodities** (e.g. cotton) to **curtain manufacturers**.

5) The price mechanism has **advantages** and **disadvantages**:

Advantages	Disadvantages
• Resources will be allocated efficiently to **satisfy** consumers' **wants** and **needs**. • The price mechanism can operate **without** the **cost** of **employing** people to **regulate** it. • **Consumers decide** what is and isn't produced by producers. • **Prices** are kept to their **minimum** as resources are used **as efficiently as possible**.	• **Inequality** in **wealth** and **income** is likely. • There will be an **under-provision** of **merit goods** and an **over-provision** of **demerit goods**, as the supply of and demand for these goods won't be at the socially optimal level (see p.78-79). • People with **limited skills** or **ability** to **work** will suffer **unemployment** or receive very **low wages**. • **Public goods** won't be produced (see p.80-81).

6) **Introducing** the price mechanism into an area of human activity can have **unintended consequences**. For example, offering **payment** for **blood donations** can **reduce** the **supply** of blood donors — donors often have **altruistic reasons** for giving blood and are **uncomfortable** about receiving payments. Another disadvantage of payments for blood donations is an **increase** in the **costs** of **screening** required to prevent '**unsuitable**' donors (e.g. drug users) donating.

Warm-Up Questions

Q1 Briefly explain what is meant by the term 'competitive market'.

Exam Question

Q1 Explain how prices can act as an incentive to firms. [4 marks]

So producers compete with low prices? Pretty sure some don't really try...

Prices are very important for allocating resources — they determine the levels of supply and demand for different goods/services.

Consumer and Producer Surplus

The consumer and producer surplus relate to the size of the benefit to consumers and producers from a given price level. When prices change, consumer and producer surpluses change. **This page is for all boards.**

Consumer and Producer Surpluses are above and below Equilibrium Price

Consumer Surplus

1) Everyone has **different** tastes, incomes and views on how much they're prepared to pay for a good/service.

2) When a consumer **pays less** for a good than the amount that they're **prepared to pay** for it, this **amount** of **money** is known as the **consumer surplus**. For example, if someone was prepared to pay **£10** for a good and bought it for **£8** then there would be a consumer surplus of **£2**.

3) So, the **consumer surplus** is the **difference** between the **price** that a consumer is **willing** to pay for a good or service and the **price** that they **actually pay** (the equilibrium price).

Producer Surplus

1) Different producers have **different** costs when making goods/services.

2) If a producer **receives more** for a product or service than the **price** they're **willing to accept**, the **extra earnings** are known as the **producer surplus**. For example, if the equilibrium price of a good is **£15** but a supplier would be happy to sell for **£10** then the producer surplus would be **£5**.

3) So, the **producer surplus** is the **difference** between the **price** that a producer is **willing** to supply a good or service at and the **price** that they **actually receive** for it (the equilibrium price).

The consumer and producer surplus can be shown on a diagram: ⟹

- **Consumer surplus** — the area **below** the demand curve and **above** the equilibrium price line.
- **Producer surplus** — the area **above** the supply curve and **below** the equilibrium price line.

> There's more on consumer and producer surpluses on p.64-65.

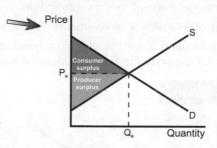

Changes in Supply and Demand affect Consumer and Producer Surplus

1) Anything that causes a **shift** in the **supply** or **demand curve** can lead to a **change** in the **price** of a good.

2) A change in price will bring a good **closer to** or **further away from** the amount the **buyer** was **willing** to **pay** or the **supplier** was **willing** to **sell** for and this will **change** the **consumer** and **producer surpluses**.

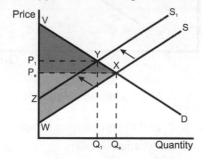

A shift in the **supply curve** from **S** to **S₁** means the **price** will **increase** from P_e to P_1 and **quantity** will **decrease** from Q_e to Q_1. The **consumer surplus changes** from **VP$_e$X** to **VP$_1$Y** and the **producer surplus changes** from **P$_e$WX** to **P$_1$ZY**.

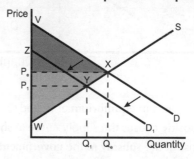

A shift in the **demand curve** from **D** to **D₁** means the **price** and **quantity** will **decrease** from P_e to P_1 and Q_e to Q_1 respectively. The **consumer surplus changes** from **VP$_e$X** to **ZP$_1$Y** and the **producer surplus changes** from **P$_e$WX** to **P$_1$WY**.

Warm-Up Questions

Q1 What is consumer surplus?

Q2 What is producer surplus?

Sir Plus — King Arthur's trusty accountant...

Consumer and producer surplus — it's all about you buying stuff for less than you're prepared to and producers selling stuff for more than they need to in order to cover their costs. When you find a bargain you have a consumer surplus, which is awesome.

Subsidies and Indirect Taxes

Subsidies and indirect taxes result in gains or losses for producers and consumers. **These pages are for Edexcel only.**

Subsidies and Indirect Taxes can affect Consumers and Producers

1) Governments sometimes provide **subsidies** to **encourage demand** for a good (e.g. energy-saving home insulation). A subsidy is money paid by the government to the **producer** of a good to make it **cheaper** than it would be otherwise.

2) Governments can also place a **tax** on a good (these are called **indirect taxes**) to **reduce** the **demand** for it (e.g. cigarettes and alcohol). The presence of a tax on a good aims to **discourage** people from buying it as the tax **raises** its **market price**.

3) **Taxes** and **subsidies** lead to **shifts** in the **supply curves** of **goods/services**, which cause **prices to change**.

4) The changes in price lead to an **extension** or **contraction** in **demand**.

Government subsidies for make-up increased Coco's demand.

The Benefit of Subsidies is divided between Consumers and Producers

1) Subsidies encourage **increased production** and a **fall** in **price**, which leads to an **increase in demand**. So, a subsidy **shifts** the **supply curve** to the **right**.

2) The **benefit** of a subsidy is received partly by the **producer** and partly by the **consumer**.

3) The relative amounts gained by producers (**producer gain**) and consumers (**consumer gain**) are dependent on the **price elasticities** of **demand** and **supply**. Here are a couple of examples:

For more on subsidies see p.88.

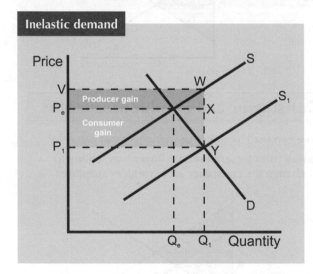

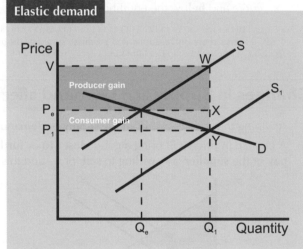

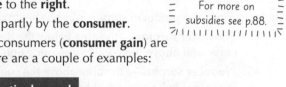

- The market is in **equilibrium** at P_e and Q_e **before** the subsidy is granted.
- The subsidy causes the supply curve to **shift** to S_1, the price to fall to P_1 and the quantity to increase to Q_1.
- The **cost** of the **subsidy** to the **government** is given by P_1VWY (the entire shaded-in box). This subsidy can be split into two parts: the **consumer gain** and the **producer gain**.

> The consumer gain is the fall in price from P_e to P_1 — they gain by paying less for the good than they would have if there was no subsidy (this would be P_e). The area of the consumer gain is P_1P_eXY (dark purple).

> The producer gain is equal to the difference between V and P_e — they gain by receiving extra revenue from the government that they can keep. The area of the producer gain is P_eVWX (light purple).

4) By comparing the two diagrams above it's clear that:
- The **more price inelastic** the **demand curve** is, the **greater** the **consumer's gain** is from the subsidy.
- The **more price elastic** the **demand curve**, the **greater** the **producer's gain** is from the subsidy.

Subsidies and Indirect Taxes

Indirect Taxes also affect both Consumers and Producers

1) Taxes **increase** the **price** of a good, which leads to a **reduction** in demand.
Taxation **shifts** the **supply curve** to the **left**.

2) As with subsidies, taxation has an impact on both the **producer** and the **consumer** of a good.
The **relative proportion** borne by producers and consumers is again **dependent** on
the **price elasticities** of **demand** and **supply**. Here are a couple of examples:

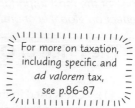
For more on taxation, including specific and *ad valorem* tax, see p.86-87

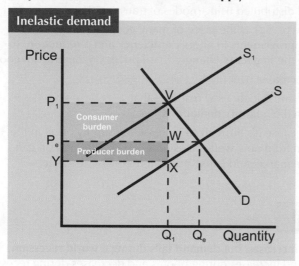
Inelastic demand

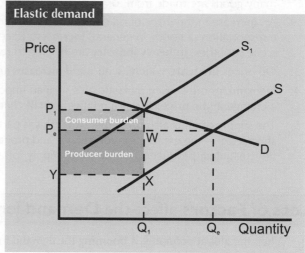
Elastic demand

- With **no taxation** the market is in **equilibrium** at P_e and Q_e.
- The tax causes the supply curve to shift to S_1, the price to increase to P_1 and the quantity to decrease to Q_1.
- The **revenue** for the **government** generated by the **tax** is given by P_1YXV (the entire shaded-in box).
This tax can be split into two parts: the **consumer burden** and the **producer burden**.

> The consumer burden is the rise in price from P_e to P_1 — they lose out by paying more for the good than if the tax wasn't in place (this would be P_e). The area of the consumer burden is P_1P_eWV (dark purple).

> The producer burden is equal to the difference between Y and P_e — they lose out by paying some of the revenue to the government. The area of the producer burden is P_eYXW (light purple).

3) By comparing the two diagrams above it's clear that:
- The more **price inelastic** the **demand curve**, the **greater** the **tax burden** for the **consumer**.
- The more **price elastic** the **demand curve**, the **greater** the **tax burden** for the **producer**.

Warm-Up Questions

PRACTICE QUESTIONS

Q1 A subsidy is introduced for a good with elastic demand.
Will the producer or consumer gain be larger?

Exam Questions

Q1 The diagram on the right shows the granting of a subsidy on a good.
Which of the following areas represents the producer gain?
A) EGIK
B) GOHL
C) FGIJ
D) EFJK

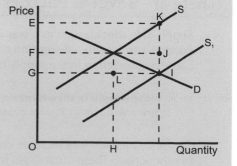

[1 mark]

Q2 If a government places a tax on a product, explain the effect it will have on its price and demand. [6 marks]

Indirect taxis — a burden on your holiday money...

Subsidies and indirect taxation both affect consumers and producers — but who's affected more depends on the price elasticity of demand. Make sure you understand how price elasticity affects the consumer and producer gains and burdens.

Demand and Supply — Oil

A lot of Section 2 is theoretical, but here are some pages that apply the theory to real-world markets. Oil is a commodity and is one of the most important resources in the world. Oil is key to most economic activity, so changes in its price can have a big effect on global economies. So, with that in mind, take a look at these lovely pages. **These examples are useful for all boards.**

The **Price** of **Oil** is **Very Important** for an **Economy**

1) Oil is used in the production of a huge variety of goods and it's used extensively for transportation. For example, many goods are made from, or packaged in, plastic and distributed using modes of transport that consume oil.

2) An increase in the price of oil can result in inflation (see p.152) as the price of many goods (and of the transportation of goods in general) increases. Recent improvements in energy efficiency and a reduction, in some countries, in heavy industry are helping to reduce the impact of changes in oil prices on the price of goods.

3) Oil prices fluctuate widely, with rapid increases and decreases over time.

4) Demand for oil is price inelastic. It's such an important and widely used resource that a change in the price causes a relatively small change in the quantity demanded.

5) The supply of oil is also price inelastic. This is partly because it's difficult to increase the supply of oil in the short term — the exploration for new oil and production from new wells takes time. Also, although oil can be stockpiled, producers don't want to supply lots to the market and cause prices to decrease too much.

Lots of **Factors** affect the **Demand** for **Oil**

1) When the global economy is booming the demand for oil increases, but demand falls during a world recession. This is because oil is used in most economic activity, so its demand increases during booms and decreases during recessions.

2) Speculators can affect the demand for oil because they buy and sell oil in the hope of making a profit from fluctuations in its price. For example, they could buy oil at $100 per barrel today with the hope of selling it next week when they predict the price will have risen to $120 per barrel — however, prices can fall and speculators can make large losses.

3) The value of the US dollar can affect the demand for oil. This is important because oil is priced in US dollars — if the value of the dollar is low then more oil can be purchased by speculators holding other currencies.

4) If the demand for products made from crude oil (e.g. plastics) increases then the derived demand for oil increases (see p.17 for more about derived demand).

5) The attractiveness of buying oil substitutes, e.g. biofuel, impacts demand for oil. As substitutes to oil become cheaper, more reliable and more readily available, this has a negative impact on demand for oil.

6) Weather conditions in major oil using countries can affect oil demand. For example, in cold conditions more oil is needed for heating.

The growth of emerging economies is increasing the demand for oil. For example, countries such as China and India are becoming increasingly large oil consumers.

7) As living standards improve then the demand for oil increases — this can be linked to an increased consumption of goods and services. Many of these goods/services will use oil in their manufacture and delivery. For example, people with a high income can afford to own a large house and several cars — this involves higher oil consumption than people with small houses who don't own a car.

There are **Several Factors** affecting the **Supply** of **Oil** in the **Short Run**

1) Supply-side shocks, such as a war in a major oil producing country, can lead to a disruption of oil supplies. This would cause a contraction in the supply of oil as shown on the diagram.

> If the supply of oil decreases from S to S_1 then the price will rise to P_1 and demand will contract to Q_1.

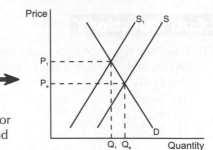

2) This price increase will increase costs to firms where oil is an important factor of production. These firms might increase prices to maintain their profits and this could have a knock-on effect on demand (it would decrease).

3) The Organisation of Petroleum Exporting Countries (OPEC) (an organisation whose members include several of the major oil exporting nations, such as Saudi Arabia and Venezuela) also has a major influence on the world supply of oil. This means that it can exert significant control over the price of oil.

4) OPEC members can agree to cut oil production levels (reduce supply), which causes oil prices to increase. Alternatively they can increase production levels (increase supply) to cause oil prices to decrease.

Demand and Supply — Oil

Different Factors affect the Supply of Oil in the Long Run

1) The **size** of remaining **oil reserves** — the **bigger** the remaining oil reserves, the **higher** the **supply** of oil will be in the **long run**. The estimates of the size of world oil reserves vary.

2) The **cost** of **extracting oil** from reserves — some reserves are **too expensive** to extract oil from at the moment, but if **demand** and **oil prices increase** then it might become **worth extracting** this harder to reach oil. Also an increase in price and demand could cause an **increase** in the **exploration** for new oil reserves.

3) The **efficiency** and **cost** of **technology** used in **exploiting** and **refining** the **oil** — the **cheaper** and **more efficient** the technology, the **lower** the cost of the oil due to the increased level of supply.

Michelle couldn't hide her excitement about the discovery of a new oil well.

Examples of changes to Demand and Supply of Oil

A large increase in the demand for oil

1) The **growth** of **emerging economies** is driving an **increased global demand** for **oil**.

2) This increase in demand can be shown on a diagram.
   - The **increase** in **demand** shifts the **demand curve** to the **right**.
   - The increase in demand can lead to an **increase** in **supply**.

3) Oil producers might **restrict** the use of **reserves** to keep the **price high**.

4) The **signalling effect** of the **price increase** can encourage an **increase** in **production**.

5) There will be a **delay** before this **additional supply** is **available** on the market.

6) **Demand** for oil in the **short run** is **price inelastic** — so this, with the inelastic supply curve, will lead to a large **increase** in **price**.

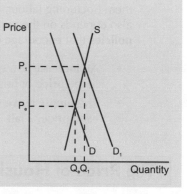

An expansion of fracking for oil

1) An **increase** in the scale of **fracking** activities (extraction of shale oil and gas) could lead to a **large increase** in the **supply** of **oil**.

2) This increase in supply can be shown on a diagram.
   - The **increase** in **supply** shifts the **supply curve** to the **right**. This increases output and causes the price to fall.
   - The **inelasticities** of supply and demand would lead to a **larger reduction** in **price** than the **increase** in **quantity**.

3) However, shale oil is **not a direct substitute** for **crude oil**, so the increase in its availability may not have a major effect on global oil prices.

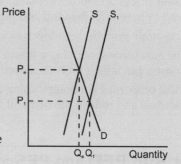

Warm-Up Questions

Q1 Is the price elasticity of demand for oil elastic or inelastic?

Q2 Give two factors that affect demand for oil.

Q3 What factors affect the supply of oil in the long run?

PRACTICE QUESTIONS

Exam Question

Q1 Biofuel is a substitute for crude-oil-derived fuels and it's marketed in many countries as an alternative to diesel. How would a large subsidy granted to UK biofuel suppliers affect the demand for crude oil? [12 marks]

Crude oil — it tells the most inappropriate jokes...

In the exam you'll get extracts about different markets and you'll need to use the theory you've learnt about demand and supply to explain what happens in them. If you learn the factors that affect the demand and supply of oil, then you'll have no trouble if you're asked about the oil market. Remember, factors affecting supply can be categorised into short run and long run factors.

Demand and Supply — Housing

The housing market is really important for an economy — there's always lots of demand for places to live and it's important to have a sufficient supply of housing in order for an economy to be successful.

Buying a House is an Investment

1) Houses can **rise** in value **over time** and they're seen as an **investment** — it's possible to invest in houses and make a **return** on the investment in the future.

2) However, a **fall** in house prices can result in **negative equity** — where the value of a property's **mortgage** is **greater** than the property's **market value**. This is **bad** for **home owners** — what they sell their house for won't pay off the amount they owe on it (the remainder of the mortgage). Unless they can pay off the remainder of their mortgage they can't move house.

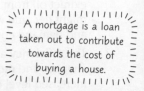

A mortgage is a loan taken out to contribute towards the cost of buying a house.

The Supply of Houses is the variety of houses available at a given time

1) The supply of houses is made up of **new build** and **pre-owned** houses that are available for a range of prices.

2) The supply of **new build houses** is partially dependent on the **costs** of building them (including labour, materials, land, and legal and planning costs). The supply also depends on the **number** and **size** of **building firms** and any **government policies** that encourage (or discourage) building new houses.

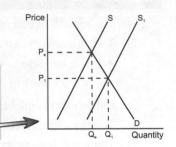

- An **increase** in the number of **new houses** built should lead to a **fall** in the **price** of houses. This is shown in the diagram on the right.
- The **supply curve** will shift to the **right**, leading to **more houses** being supplied at each price, a **fall** in the **equilibrium price** and a **rise** in the **equilibrium quantity**.

The Price of Housing is determined mainly by Demand Factors

1) The **state** of the **economy** has a big impact on the housing market — in areas of **high unemployment** houses have **lower prices** and **lower demand** (e.g. in some parts of north east England), but areas with **low unemployment** tend to have **high demand** and **high house prices** (e.g. parts of south east England).

2) **Economic growth**, high levels of **consumer confidence** and high **living standards** increase demand for housing.

3) The **substitute** for buying a house is **renting** one. A **fall** in the **cost** of renting may **decrease** the **demand** to **buy houses**, but falling rents could **reduce** the **supply** of properties for rent if landlords are **unwilling** to offer low rents.

4) Most properties are bought using a **mortgage**, so if, for example, **interest rates rise**, the cost of a **mortgage** will increase and **reduce** the **demand** for house purchases.

Short Run PED and PES for housing are Inelastic

1) There are **no close substitutes** for housing. This means the price elasticity of demand is **inelastic** — so a **rise** in **price** causes a **smaller reduction** in **demand**.

2) The price elasticity of supply is **inelastic** too. The **supply** of houses **can't** be quickly increased because it takes **time** to build new houses. Supply can also be **restricted** by the availability of **building materials**, **construction workers** and **suitable land**, and by **government regulations**.

3) Because supply can't increase much in the **short run**, an increase in demand can make **prices rise sharply**.

Dave was shocked to discover his builder's idea of 'minor refurbishment'.

House Prices have many Knock-on Effects

1) If house prices **rise** and lots of houses are bought and sold, then this might create more jobs in the **construction industry**.

2) **Higher** house prices **increase** the value of **people's assets** and can **increase consumer confidence** — this confidence can **encourage spending** and increase **investment**.

3) **Increased** house **sales encourage spending** on furniture, decorating and other household goods.

Demand and Supply — Transport

Finally, here's a bit of information on the transport market.

Transport is usually a Derived Demand

1) Transport is the **movement** of freight (goods) and passengers (people) from one place to another.

2) Transport is almost always a **derived demand** — it usually results from demand for other goods and services:
   - People want to **get to places** for work, leisure activities and holidays, and shopping and other chores.
   - Firms want to bring **factors of production together**, and bring **goods to customers**.

Demand for Transport is Income Elastic and Price Elastic

1) Transport as a **whole** has a **positive income elasticity of demand** (YED) — as real incomes increase the demand for transport increases (i.e. it's a normal good). However, each transport mode also has its **own** YED.

2) **Car** and **air travel** are generally considered to have a **positive YED**, but **bus travel** is thought to have a **negative YED** — bus travel is considered an **inferior good** (i.e. as incomes **rise**, demand for bus travel **falls**).

3) Demand for transport is also **price elastic** to some extent. People might cut back on **leisure travel** if prices rise, but **commuter travel** is less likely to be affected.

4) There's some **cross elasticity of demand** between transport modes that are suitable **substitutes** for one another.

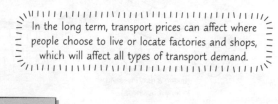
In the long term, transport prices can affect where people choose to live or locate factories and shops, which will affect all types of transport demand.

The Price Elasticity of Car Travel is Quite Low

1) **Demand** for **car travel** depends on several things, for example:
   - The **cost** of a **journey**, e.g. petrol — individuals will choose whether or not to drive depending on its **cost**. However, the **price elasticity** for travelling by car is **low** because people highly value the **convenience** and **comfort** of driving. This means that changes in the cost of driving **might not** have a large effect on its demand.
   - **Income** — car ownership and usage **rise** with real income, so **economic growth** causes an **increase** in car usage.
   - **Substitutes** — there are substitutes to car travel, such as travelling by **bus** or by **train**, and a reduction in their prices **might** reduce car usage. However, these modes of transport are often considered to be **poor substitutes** for cars, so **cross elasticity of demand** is **low**.
   - **Complements** — the **price** of **complementary goods**, such as **car insurance** or **parking**, can affect the demand for driving.

2) In the **short run** the **supply** of **roads** is **fixed** (until new ones can be built). This can lead to **excess demand** (shown on the diagram) for road space during busy periods, i.e. there will be **congestion** during rush hour.

3) Congestion can be **reduced** by introducing a **price** (**P** on the diagram, e.g. a **toll fare** or **congestion charge**) for using the road network. If the price is set at the **right level** this will **reduce demand** back to the level of **supply**.

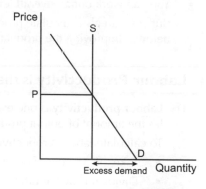

Warm-Up Questions

Q1 Give three factors which influence the demand for housing.

Q2 Is the supply of housing in the short run price elastic?

Q3 How will demand for transport be affected by a general increase in people's real income?

Q4 Give three factors which influence the demand for car travel.

Exam Questions

Q1 Discuss reasons why average house prices might vary between two areas of a country. [10 marks]

Q2 Explain the likely impact of higher fuel prices on the usage of cars. [4 marks]

My school football coach considered me to be a poor substitute...

So, here are two very different markets, but in the end it all comes down to how the market forces act. One very important thing you should learn is how important price elasticity of demand and supply are in determining price and output levels. Lovely stuff.

Production and Productivity

Before we get down to the more complicated Business Economics topics, here are a couple of pages to gently ease you in. Businesses produce things and they try to do it efficiently — you need to know how. **This page is for all boards.**

Production means Manufacturing something in order to Sell it

1) Production involves converting **inputs** (e.g. raw materials, labour) into **outputs** (things to sell).

2) The inputs can be any of the four **factors of production** — land, labour, capital and enterprise. **Inputs** can be:
   - **tangible** — things you can touch, like raw materials or machines.
   - **intangible** — 'abstract' things that can't be touched — like ideas, talent or knowledge.

3) The **outputs** produced should have an **exchangeable value** — they need to be something that can be sold.

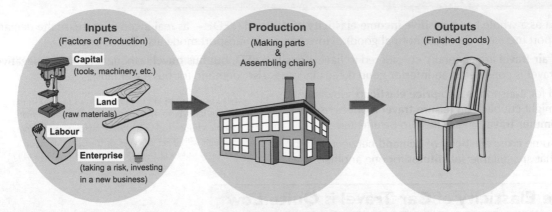

Inputs
(Factors of Production)

Capital
(tools, machinery, etc.)

Land
(raw materials)

Labour

Enterprise
(taking a risk, investing in a new business)

Production
(Making parts & Assembling chairs)

Outputs
(Finished goods)

Productivity is the output per Factor Employed

- **Productivity** is a way of measuring how efficiently a company or an economy is producing its output.
- It's defined as the **output per unit of input employed**. So if one company could take the same amount of inputs as another company, but produce more stuff, their productivity would be **greater**.
- You can work out an **overall** level of productivity (involving all four possible inputs).
- But you can also calculate productivity for **any one** of the four individual factors of production, e.g. labour (see below). Improving the productivity of any one of these **separate** factors should increase **overall productivity**.

Labour Productivity is the output per Worker or output per Hour Worked

1) **Labour productivity** is one example of measuring productivity for one factor. It's the amount of output produced **per worker** (or **per worker-hour**).

2) To calculate labour productivity:
   - Take the amount of output produced in a particular time.
   - Divide this by the **total** number of workers (or the total **hours worked** by all the workers).

3) Labour productivity allows workers to be **compared** against other workers. For example, labour productivity is calculated for **whole economies**, so that the productivity of the different labour forces can be compared.

4) Improvements in labour productivity can come about as a result of better **training**, more **experience**, improved **technology**, and so on. **Specialisation** can also improve labour productivity — if each worker performs tasks that they're **good at doing**, have **practised a lot** or have been **trained** to do, then they'll **produce more** than if they did lots of different tasks.

A fitter workforce is a more productive workforce.

Warm-Up Questions

Q1 What are the four types of input that go into producing something?

Q2 Give two examples of how the labour productivity of a firm could be improved.

PRACTICE QUESTIONS

Average CGP productivity — one joke per hour...

An hour well spent, eh? Right? Right...? There's no pleasing some people. Anyway, there's some pretty straightforward stuff here on production and productivity. Learning it won't get you the Nobel Prize for Economics, but it'll definitely be useful.

Specialisation

By specialising, we don't have to spend all our time making what we want or need. **This page is for all boards.**

Specialisation leads to a Division of Labour

1) People could **make** all the things they need and want **themselves**. They could grow their own **food**, make their own **clothes**, build their own **computers**, and so on. In **practice** though, this is very unlikely to work. What usually happens is that people and firms **specialise** — some people grow food, others make clothes, etc.

2) The **division of labour** is a **type** of **specialisation** where production is **split** into **different tasks** and **specific people** are **allocated** to each task, e.g. in making a stool — one person could make the legs and another could make the seats.

3) **Adam Smith** explained the **increase** in **productivity** that could be achieved through the division of labour. He said that **one untrained worker** wouldn't even make **20 pins per day**, but **10 workers**, **specialising** in different tasks, could make **48 000**.

4) There are **advantages** and **disadvantages** to specialisation, but overall an economy can produce **more stuff** if people and firms **specialise**. (It's not just individuals and firms that can specialise — whole **regions** and even **countries** can specialise to an extent. For example, there are loads of technology companies based in Silicon Valley in California.)

Advantages of Specialisation

- People can **specialise** in the thing they're **best** at. (Or by doing it, they learn to become better at it.)

- This can lead to **better quality** and a **higher quantity** of products for the same amount of effort overall — i.e. increased **labour productivity**.

- Specialisation is one way in which firms can achieve **economies of scale** (see p.42), e.g. a **production line** (where each person may perform just one or two tasks) is a form of specialisation.

- Specialisation leads to **more efficient** production — this helps to tackle the problem of **scarcity**, because if **resources** are used more efficiently, **more output** can be produced **per unit** of **input**.

- **Training costs** are **reduced** if workers are only trained to perform certain limited tasks.

Disadvantages of Specialisation

- Workers can end up doing **repetitive** tasks, which can lead to **boredom**.

- Countries can become **less self-sufficient** — this can be a problem if **trade** is **disrupted** for whatever reason (e.g. a war or dispute). For example, if a country specialises in **manufacturing**, and **imports** (rather than produces) all its **fuel**, then that country could be in trouble if it falls out with its fuel **supplier**.

- It can lead to a **lack** of **flexibility** — for example, if the companies eventually move elsewhere, the workforce left behind can struggle to **adapt**.

Coal mining in the UK is an example of this. When pits closed, many miners had non-transferable skills (this is structural unemployment — see p.150).

Trade means people can Buy the stuff they're no longer making Themselves

1) Specialisation means that **trade** becomes absolutely vital — economies (and individual people and firms) have to be able to **obtain** the things they're no longer making for themselves. This means it's **necessary** to have a **way** of **exchanging** goods and services between countries. (See p.198-201 for more on trade.)

2) **Swapping** goods with other countries is one way a country can get what it needs, e.g. a country which mines diamonds may want oil, while another country which produces oil may want diamonds. This way of trading goods is called a **barter system** — it's **very inefficient** because it takes a lot of **time** and **effort** to find traders to barter with.

3) The most **efficient** way of exchanging goods and services between countries is using **money** (with the use of **exchange rates** where necessary — see p.210). Money is a **medium of exchange** — it's something both buyers and sellers value and that means that countries can buy goods, even if sellers don't want the things that the buying country produces.

Money has **three** other functions too:

- **A measure of value** — e.g. the value given to a good (such as a barrel of oil) can be measured in US dollars.

- **A store of value** — e.g. an individual who receives a wage may wait before buying something if they know that the money they have will be of a similar value in future.

- **A standard (or method) of deferred payment** — money can be paid at a later date for something that's consumed now, e.g. people often borrow money to buy a car or pay university fees.

Warm-Up Questions

Q1 Give two advantages and two disadvantages of specialisation.

Q2 What are the four functions of money?

PRACTICE QUESTIONS

Money, eh? — Is there anything it can't do?

Money makes trade much easier, allowing specialisation — which has its own advantages and disadvantages for you to learn.

The Costs of a Firm

A firm could be anything from a dog-walking business to a giant multinational like an oil or technology company. What most firms have in common is that they sell goods or services to try to make profit. **These pages are for all boards.**

Firms generate **Revenue** and incur **Costs**

1) A firm is any sort of **business organisation**, like a family-run factory, a dental practice or a supermarket chain.
2) An **industry** is all the firms providing **similar** goods or services.
3) A **market** contains all the firms **supplying** a particular good or service **and** the firms or people **buying** it.
4) Firms generate **revenue** (money coming in) by **selling** their **output** (goods or services).
5) Producing this output uses **factors of production** (land, labour, capital and enterprise), and this has a **cost**.
6) The **profit** a firm makes is **its total revenue minus its total costs.** *Revenue and profit are explained properly later in the section.*
7) In the **long run** firms need to make profit to **survive**.

Economists include **Opportunity Cost** in the **Cost** of **Production**

- When economists talk about the **cost of production** they are referring to the **economic cost** of producing the output.
- The economic cost includes the **money cost** of factors of production that have to be paid for, but it also includes the **opportunity cost** of the factors that aren't paid for (e.g. a home office that a business is run from).
- The **opportunity cost** of a factor of production is the **money that you could have got** by putting it to its **next best use**. E.g. if you run your own business the money you **could earn** doing other work is the opportunity cost of your **labour**.
- So, in economics, cost isn't just a calculation of money spent — it takes into account **all** of the effort and resources that have gone into production.

In the **Short Run** some **Costs** are **Fixed**

1) The **short run** is the period of time when **at least one** of a firm's factors of production is **fixed**.
2) The short run isn't a specific length of time — it **varies from firm to firm**. For example, the short run of a **cycle courier** service could be **a week** because it can hire new staff with their own bikes quickly, but a **steel manufacturer** might have a short run of **several years** because it takes lots of time and money to build a new steel-manufacturing plant.
3) The **long run** is the period of time when **all factors of production** can be **varied**.
4) Costs can be **fixed** or **variable** in the short run:

FIXED COSTS	VARIABLE COSTS
- Fixed costs **don't vary with output** in the **short run** — they have to be paid whether or not anything is produced. - For example, the **rent on a shop** is a fixed cost — it's **the same** no matter what the sales are.	- Variable costs **do vary with output** — they increase as output increases. - The cost of the **plastic bags** that a shop gives to customers is a variable cost — the **higher sales** are, the **higher the overall cost** of the bags.

5) In the **long run all costs** are **variable**.

Total Cost and Average Cost include Fixed Costs and Variable Costs

Total cost (TC) is **all the costs** involved in producing a particular **level of output.**

The **total cost** (TC) for a particular output level is the **total fixed costs** (TFC) plus the **total variable costs** (TVC) for that **output level:** **TC = TFC + TVC**

Average cost (AC) is the **cost per unit produced.** *It's also called average total cost (ATC).*

Average cost (AC) is calculated by **dividing** total costs by the **quantity** produced (Q): **AC = TC ÷ Q**

Average fixed cost (AFC) = total fixed costs ÷ **quantity** produced: **AFC = TFC ÷ Q**

Average variable cost (AVC) = total variable costs ÷ **quantity** produced: **AVC = TVC ÷ Q**

The Costs of a Firm

Marginal Cost is the cost of Increasing Output by One Unit

Marginal cost (MC) is the **extra cost** incurred as a result of producing **the final** unit of output. ◄

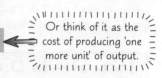
Or think of it as the cost of producing 'one more unit' of output.

Marginal cost is only affected by **variable costs** — fixed costs have to be paid even if **nothing** is produced. You can calculate it by finding the **difference** between total cost at the current output level (TC_n) and total cost at one unit **less** (TC_{n-1}): $MC = TC_n - TC_{n-1}$

Output	Total Fixed Costs (£)	Total Variable Costs (£)	Total Cost (£)	Average Cost (£)	Average Fixed Cost (£)	Average Variable Cost (£)	Marginal Cost (£)
0	60	—	60	—	—	—	—
1	60	70	130	130	60	70	70
2	60	120	180	90	30	60	50
3	60	180	240	80	20	60	60
4	60	260	320	80	15	65	80
5	60	360	420	84	12	72	100

60 + 360   420 ÷ 5   60 ÷ 5   360 ÷ 5   420 − 320

Marginal cost usually means the extra cost of producing 'the final unit' of output, but there's a more general formula that gives the extra cost of 'the last few units':

$$MC = \frac{\text{Change in TC } (\Delta TC)}{\text{Change in Quantity } (\Delta Q)}$$

These are the values substituted into the formulas.

Lowest Average Cost occurs when Marginal Cost equals Average Cost

1) Marginal cost (MC) **decreases initially** as output increases, then begins to **increase** in the short run because of the **law of diminishing returns**. (This is explained on page 40.)

2) So the **MC curve** is always **u-shaped**.

3) Changes in marginal cost affect average cost:

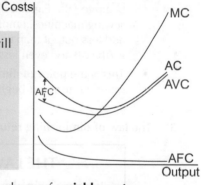

- When the marginal cost is **lower** than the average cost (AC), the average cost will be **falling**. This is because each extra unit produced will **decrease** the average cost (adding something smaller than the average will decrease the average).

- When the marginal cost is **higher** than the average cost (AC), the average cost will be **rising** because each extra unit produced will **increase** the average cost.

- So the marginal cost curve meets the average cost curve at the lowest average cost, i.e. **average cost** will be **lowest** when **MC = AC** — this is the point of **productive efficiency** (see p.58).

4) The MC curve also **meets** the AVC curve at the **minimum AVC**. (Marginal cost is made up of **variable costs**, so it increases and decreases AVC in the same way it does AC.)

5) This means AVC and AC curves also **always** form a **u-shape** in the **short run** — they both decrease until they reach a minimum, then begin to increase.

6) AFC (average fixed cost) **falls as output rises** because the total fixed cost is **spread** across the greater output.

Warm-Up Questions

Q1 What are fixed costs?

Q2 Where does the marginal cost curve meet the average cost curve?

Exam Questions

Q1 Firm X and Firm Y are producing the same product at the same output level and have the same variable costs. The fixed costs of Firm X are double the fixed costs of Firm Y. Firm X and Firm Y have the same:
   A) average fixed cost   B) marginal cost   C) fixed costs   D) total costs   [1 mark]

Q2 Explain why average fixed costs fall with increased output.   [2 marks]

Chat-up lines for economists #23 — "I'm a big fan of you-shaped curves"...

There are loads of terms and formulas here you need to know — get to grips with them before moving on. It's also really important to understand the relationship between marginal cost and average cost — the average cost curve falls when marginal cost is below it, and rises when marginal cost is above it. The marginal cost doesn't have to be falling for the average cost to fall.

The Law of Diminishing Returns

Firms can increase their output by adding more of their factors of production (e.g. getting more staff). In the long run they can add more of all of their factors of production. But in the short run only <u>some</u> factors can be increased, while others stay <u>fixed</u>. The short run effect of changing only some factors is explained by the law of diminishing returns. **For all boards.**

Increases in Output are Limited by Diminishing Returns in the Short Run

1) The **law of diminishing returns** explains what happens when a **variable factor** of production **increases** while other factors stay fixed. Because at least one factor stays **fixed**, the law of diminishing returns only applies in the **short run**.

2) When you increase **one factor** of production by **one unit**, but keep the others **fixed**, the **extra output** you get is called the **marginal product**. E.g. if you add one more unit of labour, the extra output is the **marginal product of labour**.

> **Marginal product** (MP) is the **additional output** produced by adding **one more unit** of a **factor input** (i.e. by adding one more unit of any of the **factors of production** being used).

Another term for marginal product is marginal returns.

- Initially, as you **add more** of a factor of production the **marginal product** will increase — each unit of input added will **add more** output than the one before.

- This might happen because more **specialisation** is possible with more of a particular factor. As more **people** are employed, for example, they can specialise in carrying out particular tasks.

- Eventually, if you **keep adding** units of **one factor** of production, the other **fixed factors** will begin to **limit** the additional output you get, and the marginal product will begin to **fall**. E.g. if a clothes manufacturer only has 5 sewing machines, employing a 6th machinist will probably add less output than employing the 5th did, and employing a 7th will add even less.

- This is the **point of diminishing returns** — the point where **marginal product** begins to **decrease** as input increases.

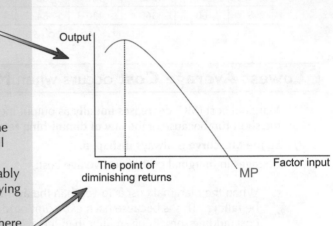

Output

The point of diminishing returns   MP   Factor input

3) The **law of diminishing returns** says that there is always a point where marginal product begins to decrease.

> ### THE LAW OF DIMINISHING RETURNS
> If **one variable factor** of production is **increased** while **other factors** stay **fixed**, eventually the **marginal returns** from the variable factor will begin to **decrease**.

This is also called the law of diminishing marginal returns, or the law of variable proportions.

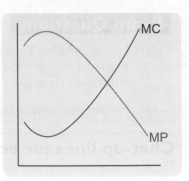

Andy's serves had really improved lately — he'd reached the point of diminishing returns.

Diminishing Marginal Returns increase Marginal Cost

1) **Marginal returns** (or marginal product, MP) are related to **marginal cost** (MC) — as shown in the diagram.
   - As marginal returns **rise**, marginal cost **falls**.
   - As marginal returns **fall**, marginal cost **rises**.
   The marginal cost curve is the mirror image of the marginal product curve.

2) Marginal cost will rise as marginal returns fall because, all other things being equal, if you're getting **less additional output** from each **unit of input** then the cost per unit of that output will be greater.

MC

MP

The Law of Diminishing Returns

Diminishing Marginal Returns eventually cause Productivity to Fall

1) The law of diminishing returns says that as the level of a variable factor input is increased, **marginal product** (or **marginal returns**) will eventually begin to diminish.

2) As the level of that factor input continues to be increased, the **average product** will eventually start to fall too, as shown on the right. The MP curve always meets the AP curve when the AP curve is at its **maximum**.

> Average product (AP) is the **output** produced **per unit** of **factor input**.

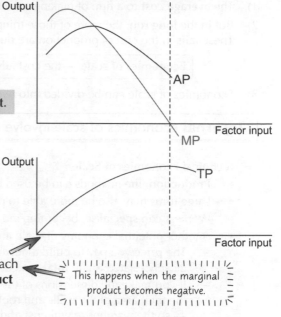

3) The average product is also known as **productivity**. For example, if the variable factor is labour, the **labour productivity** would be the average output **per worker** (or **per worker-hour**).

> ⌇ There's more on productivity on p.36. ⌇

So if a firm employs more and more people, it will eventually find that the **productivity** of those employees falls.

4) If you then keep adding more of the variable factor, you can even reach a stage where **adding further input** results in a **fall** in the **total product** — e.g. because workers start getting in each other's way.

> ⌇ This happens when the marginal product becomes negative. ⌇

> Total product (TP) is the **total output** produced using a particular combination of factor inputs.

> ⌇ See p.39 for more about marginal and average curves. ⌇

Productivity can be improved in various ways

1) There are various ways to increase **labour productivity** — for example, through **better training** or **better management**.

2) Improved **technology** can also help improve productivity — faster computers could allow employees to achieve more during their working day, for example.

3) Increasing productivity will allow a firm to **reduce** its **costs** of production.

> ⌇ Improved technology might also allow a firm to track its costs and productivity more accurately, meaning it can see when it's encountering the point of diminishing returns, for example. ⌇

Warm-Up Questions

Q1 What is the marginal product?

Q2 Does the law of diminishing returns apply in the long run or the short run?

Q3 If a firm is experiencing diminishing returns, will its total output always be falling?

PRACTICE QUESTIONS

Exam Question

Q1 The marginal cost curve of a firm is shown on the right.
   a) Explain the shape of the curve between A and B.   [3 marks]
   b) Explain the shape of the curve between B and C.   [3 marks]

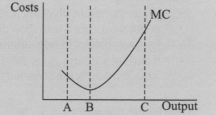

I fought the law of diminishing returns — and the law eventually won...

The key things to remember here are that diminishing returns only happen in the short run, and they don't have to mean decreasing output. It's pretty straightforward really — in the short run at least one factor of production stays fixed, so increasing the input of other factors will eventually lead to diminishing returns, which will mean an increase in marginal cost.

Economies and Diseconomies of Scale

In the long run firms can increase their scale of production by increasing <u>all</u> of their factors of production. ***For all boards.***

Economies of Scale can be Internal or External

1) The **average cost** to a firm of making something is usually quite high if they **don't** make very many of them.

2) But in the **long run**, the more of those things the firm makes, the more the average cost of making each one **falls**. These falls in the cost of production are due to **economies of scale**.

> Economies of scale — the cost advantages of production on a large scale.

See the long run average cost curve on p.44.

3) Economies of scale can be divided into two categories — **internal** and **external**.

Internal economies of scale involve changes Within a firm

Technical Economies of Scale

- **Production line** methods can be used by large firms to make a lot of things at a very low average cost.
- Large firms may also be more able to purchase other **specialised equipment** to help reduce average costs.
- Workers can **specialise**, becoming more efficient at the tasks they do, which might not be possible in a small firm.
- Another potential economy of scale arises from the **law of increased dimensions**. For example:
  - The **price** you pay to build a new warehouse might be closely related to the **total area of the walls and roof**, say.
  - If you make the dimensions of the walls and roof **twice as big**, the total **area** of the walls and roof will be **4 times greater** — so the warehouse will **cost about 4 times as much** to build.
  - But the **volume** of the warehouse will be **8 times greater**, meaning that you're getting more storage space for each pound you spend.
  - The same is true of things like **oil tankers** — e.g. bigger tankers reduce the cost of transporting each unit of oil.

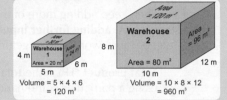

Purchasing Economies of Scale

- **Larger firms** making lots of goods will need **larger quantities** of raw materials, and so can often **negotiate discounts** with suppliers.
- Because large firms will be the **most important customers** of suppliers (as they'll put in the biggest orders), they'll be able to **drive a hard bargain**.

Managerial Economies of Scale

- **Large firms** will be able to employ **specialist** managers to take care of different areas of the business (e.g. finance, production, customer service). These specialist managers gain **expertise** and **experience** in a specific area of the business, which usually leads to better **decision-making** abilities in that area.
- And the number of managers a firm needs **doesn't** usually depend directly on the production scale — a firm probably won't need twice as many managers to produce twice as many goods. This **reduces** the management cost per unit.

Financial Economies of Scale

- Larger firms can often **borrow money** at a **lower** rate of **interest** — lending to them is seen by banks as less risky.

Risk-bearing Economies of Scale

- Larger firms can **diversify** into different **product areas** (e.g. make different things) and different **markets** (e.g. sell in different countries). This diversification leads to a **more predictable overall demand** — basically, if demand for one product in one country falls, there's likely to be a different product whose demand somewhere increases.
- It also means large firms are more able to take **risks** (e.g. by launching products that may or may not prove popular). If the product is unsuccessful, a large firm's other activities allow it to **absorb** the cost of **failure** more easily.

Marketing Economies of Scale

- **Advertising** is usually a **fixed cost** — this is spread over more units for large firms, so the cost **per unit** is lower.
- The **cost per product** of advertising several products may also be **lower** than the cost of advertising just one, e.g. a firm could advertise several products on a single flyer.
- Larger firms also benefit from **brand awareness** — products from a well-known brand will be **trusted** by consumers. This might mean a larger firm doesn't need to advertise as much to get sales.

Economies and Diseconomies of Scale

External economies of scale involve changes Outside a firm

- Local colleges may start to offer **qualifications** needed by **big local employers**, reducing the firms' training costs.
- Large companies locating in an area may lead to improvements in **road networks** or **local public transport**.
- If lots of firms doing **similar** or **related** things locate near each other, they may be able to **share resources** (e.g. research facilities). **Suppliers** may also decide to locate in the same area, reducing transport costs.

Extremely successful companies can gain Monopoly Power in a market

1) As a firm's **average cost** for making a product **falls**, it can sell that product at a **lower price**, undercutting its competition.

2) This can lead to a firm gaining a bigger and bigger **market share**, as it continually offers products at prices that are lower than the competition.

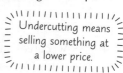
Undercutting means selling something at a lower price.

3) In this way, a firm can eventually force its competitors out of business and become the **only supplier** of the product — i.e. it will have a **monopoly**.

Diseconomies of Scale — Disadvantages of being big

1) Getting bigger isn't always good though — as a firm increases in size, it can encounter **diseconomies of scale**.

2) Diseconomies of scale cause average cost to **rise** as output rises. Diseconomies can be **internal** or **external**.

INTERNAL

- **Wastage** and **loss** can increase, as materials might seem in plentiful supply. Bigger warehouses might lead to more things getting **lost** or **mislaid**.
- **Communication** may become more difficult as a firm grows, affecting staff morale.
- Managers may be less able to **control** what goes on.
- It becomes more difficult to **coordinate** activities between different divisions and departments.
- A '**them and us**' attitude can develop between workers in different parts of a large firm — workers might put their department's interests before the company's, leading to less cooperation and lower efficiency.

EXTERNAL

- As a **whole industry** becomes bigger, the price of raw materials may **increase** (since demand will be greater).
- Buying large amounts of materials **may not** make them less expensive per unit. If local supplies aren't sufficient, more expensive goods from further afield may have to be bought.

High Fixed Costs create Large Economies of Scale

1) There are **huge economies of scale** in industries with **high fixed costs** but **low variable costs**. In some cases, the **structure** of whole industries can change to take advantage of this.

2) For example, **robot-based assembly lines** are very expensive to **set up**, but reduce the **labour** required to produce each unit. This means **fixed costs** will **increase** (as the loans used to buy the equipment need to be repaid), while **variable costs** (e.g. labour costs) **fall**.

This is an example of improved technology leading to changes in the structure of an industry.

3) As a firm grows by taking advantage of its large **economies of scale**, other firms in the industry may be **forced** to follow the same strategy, or shut down. The result is an industry **dominated** by a few large firms (or even just a single firm).

Warm-Up Questions

Q1 What's the difference between an internal economy of scale and an external one?

Q2 Give two examples of economies of scale.

PRACTICE QUESTIONS

Exam Question

Q1 Explain why companies do not always reduce their average cost of production as their output increases. [5 marks]

Risk-bearing economies of scale — when your business annoys grizzlies...

There are all sorts of economies of scale. But it's not all plain sailing for big firms — they can have difficulties too. This is why someone, somewhere invented the term 'diseconomy of scale'. I know, 'diseconomy' doesn't sound like a real word, but the effects are very real indeed. You know the drill... learn the stuff, cover the page, try to recall it all, and then try the questions.

Long Run Average Cost

The average cost curves on page 39 were short run average cost curves (SRAC curves), but to show economies and diseconomies of scale you need to use long run average cost curves (LRAC curves). **This page is for all boards.**

In the **Long Run** firms can **Move** onto **New Short Run Average Cost Curves**

1) In the **short run** a firm has at least one **fixed** factor of production. This means that it operates on a particular **short run average cost curve** (SRAC curve), e.g. $SRAC_1$ on the diagram below.

2) As a firm increases **output** in the short run by increasing **variable factors** of production, it moves **along** its short run average cost curve.

3) In the **long run** a firm can change **all factors** of production. When it does this it moves onto a **new SRAC curve**, e.g. $SRAC_2$.

> The **MINIMUM POSSIBLE AVERAGE COST** at each level of output is shown by a **LONG RUN AVERAGE COST CURVE** (LRAC curve).

4) SRAC curves can **touch** the LRAC curve, but they can't go **below** it.

5) For a firm to operate on its LRAC curve at a particular level of output, it has to be using the **most appropriate mix** of all factors of production.

6) This means that it may **not** be able to reduce costs to this minimum level in the **short run** (since in the short run, some factors are fixed).

7) But in the long run a firm can vary **all factors** of production and bring costs down to the level of the LRAC curve.

There's an SRAC curve that touches the LRAC curve at the minimum of both (e.g. $SRAC_3$).

> ### The shape of LRAC curves is determined by <u>internal</u> economies and diseconomies of scale

- Average cost **falls** as output increases when a firm is experiencing **internal economies of scale**.
- Average cost **rises** as output increases when a firm is experiencing **internal diseconomies of scale**.
- Firms may face **specific** economies and diseconomies of scale at the **same** output level — whether the firm is experiencing economies or diseconomies overall will depend on which is having the **greater effect**.

External Changes can cause **LRAC Curves** to **Shift**

- **External** economies of scale will cause the LRAC curve to **shift** downwards by reducing average costs at **all output levels**.
- External **diseconomies** of scale will force the LRAC curve to shift **upwards**.
- A change in **taxation** might cause the LRAC curve to shift up or down, e.g. an increase in fuel duty would cause a bus company's LRAC to shift up.
- **New technology** could cause the LRAC curve to shift down if it means firms can use factors of production more efficiently at all levels, e.g. faster computers for workers.

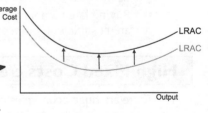

AQA ONLY

AQA Students need to know the **L-shaped LRAC Curve**

1) Some economists argue that the LRAC curve is **L-shaped**. They claim **average costs fall sharply** as **output increases**, and then either **continue** to **fall slowly** or **level off**.

2) This is based on the idea that while **some internal diseconomies of scale** will occur with **increasing output** (e.g. managerial diseconomies of scale) they'll be **offset** by **continued reductions** in **average cost** due to things like production and technical economies of scale — so the LRAC curve **won't** begin to **curve upwards**.

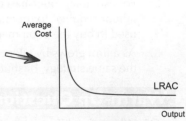

Warm-Up Questions

Q1 Explain why a short run average cost curve can't cross a long run average cost curve.

Exam Question

Q1 A firm is aiming for a particular level of output. Why might the firm **not** be able to reduce its costs to those shown on an LRAC curve for this level of output in the short run?   [6 marks]

Long run average cost — very important for thrifty marathon participants...

Make sure you know which concepts apply to short run and to long run cost curves — mixing them up is a fairly common mistake.

Returns to Scale

In the long run, the effect on output of increasing <u>all</u> of the factor inputs is described by returns to scale. **For all boards.**

Returns to Scale describe the Effects of Increasing the Scale of Production

In the **long run** firms can increase **all** of their factor inputs.
Returns to scale describe the effect on **output** of increasing **all factor inputs** by the same proportion.

INCREASING RETURNS TO SCALE

There are **increasing returns to scale** when an increase in all factor inputs leads to a **more than proportional** increase in output. E.g. **doubling** all of the factor inputs results in a **tripling** of output.

CONSTANT RETURNS TO SCALE

There are **constant returns to scale** when an increase in all factor inputs leads to a **proportional** increase in output. E.g. **doubling** all the factor inputs results in a **doubling** of output.

DECREASING RETURNS TO SCALE

There are **decreasing returns to scale** when an increase in all factor inputs leads to a **less than proportional** increase in output. E.g. **tripling** all the factor inputs results in a **doubling** of output.

Li was convinced that increasing his moustache size had led to a more than proportional increase in dating success.

Increasing Returns to Scale contribute to Economies of Scale

1) Returns to scale and economies of scale are **not** the same thing.
    — **Returns to scale** describe how much **output** changes as input is increased,
    — **Economies of scale** describe reductions in **average costs** as output is increased.
2) However, there is a link between the two ideas:
    — **Increasing** returns to scale contribute to **economies of scale**,
    — **Decreasing** returns to scale contribute to **diseconomies of scale**.
3) When returns to scale are **increasing**, long run average cost will **fall**. An increase in input leads to a **more than proportional** increase in output, so **more** output is being produced **per unit** of input.
4) When returns to scale are **constant**, long run average cost will stay the same — costs are increasing proportionally to output.
5) When returns to scale are **decreasing**, long run average cost will **rise**. **Less** output is being produced **per unit** of input.

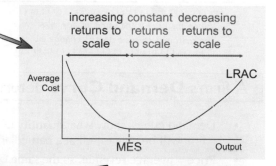

Long Run Average Costs are Minimised at the MES

*   The **minimum efficient scale of production** (MES) is the lowest level of output at which the **minimum possible** average cost can be achieved — it's the first point at which the LRAC curve reaches its minimum value. This is likely to be the **optimal** level of production.
*   There might be a **range** of production levels where LRAC is minimised, or the MES might be the **only** LRAC minimising level.
*   The MES **varies** between industries — industries with very high fixed costs (e.g. oil extraction) have a **very large MES**. This affects the whole **structure** of an industry — industries with a **large MES** will favour **large firms** more.

Matteo was wondering if he could cover up his secret bread habit by claiming his bakery had a high MES.

Warm-Up Questions

Q1 What are decreasing returns to scale?

Exam Question

Q1 Explain how returns to scale affect average costs in the long run. [6 marks]

Increasing returns to scale — put a bit more in, get a lot more out...
You need to remember what increasing, constant and decreasing returns to scale are, and how they affect long run average costs.

The Revenue of a Firm

A firm's revenue is the money it receives from selling its production output. Revenue depends on the price a firm is able to get for the quantity of its product that it's selling. So revenue is affected by the demand curve the firm faces. **For all boards.**

Revenue is the Money firms receive from Selling their Goods or Services

Total revenue (TR) is the **total amount** of money received, in a time period, **from a firm's sales**.

Total revenue is equal to the **total quantity** (Q) sold multiplied by the **price** (P). It's also called **turnover**. It can be found using the formula: **TR = Q × P**

Average revenue (AR) is the **revenue per unit sold**.

Average revenue is TR **divided** by quantity sold (so **average revenue = price**): **AR = TR ÷ Q**

Marginal revenue (MR) is the **extra revenue** received as a result of selling **the final** unit of output.

Marginal revenue is the **difference** between TR at the new sales level (TR_n) and TR at one unit less (TR_{n-1}): $MR = TR_n - TR_{n-1}$

Alicia wasn't sure why her accountant wanted to see her turn over...

Quantity sold	Price (£)	Total Revenue (£)	Marginal Revenue (£)
0	5	—	—
1	5	5	5
2	5	10	5
3	5	15	5
4	5	20	5

When the price is the same for any sales level, the marginal revenue doesn't change either.

Quantity sold	Price (£)	Total Revenue (£)	Marginal Revenue (£)
0	250	—	—
1	200	200	200
2	180	360	160
3	170	510	150
4	160	640	130
5	150	750	110
6	135	810	60

When the price has to change to increase sales, the marginal revenue will change depending on the quantity sold.

A firm's Demand Curve determines how Revenue relates to Output

- Demand curves show what **quantity** of a product a firm will be able to sell at a particular **price**.

- **Price = average revenue**, so the **same** curve shows the relationship between quantity sold and average revenue. (So the demand curve could be labelled **AR**.)

- A firm's **total revenue** is given by **quantity × price**. TR at price P_1 is shown by the shaded area on the diagram.

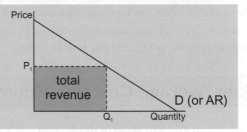

A Firm that's a Price Taker has a Perfectly Elastic Demand Curve

A firm that's a **price taker** has **no power** to control the price it sells at — price takers have to **accept** the price set by the **market**.

A price taker's demand curve will be completely flat — demand is **perfectly elastic**. If the firm **increases** the price then the quantity sold will drop to **zero**. And there's no reason to decrease the price because the **same quantity** would sell at the original **higher price**.

(There's more about price takers on p.56.)

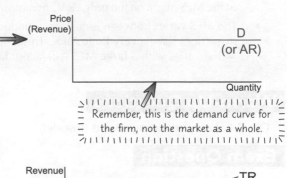

Remember, this is the demand curve for the firm, not the market as a whole.

With a Perfectly Elastic demand curve AR = MR

1) When demand is perfectly elastic the **price** is the **same**, no matter what the **output level**.

2) In this case **marginal revenue = average revenue**, because each extra unit sold brings in the same revenue as all the others.

3) When average revenue is **constant**, total revenue increases **proportionally** with sales, as in the diagram on the right.

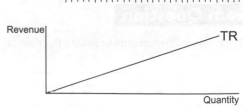

The Revenue of a Firm

A firm that's a **Price Maker** has a **Downward Sloping Demand Curve**

Price makers (e.g. monopolists — see p.62) have **some power** to set the price they sell at.
A price maker's demand curve will slope **downwards** — to increase sales the firm must reduce the price.

With a **Downward Sloping** Demand Curve **TR is Maximised** when **PED = −1**

1) If a firm's demand curve is a **straight line sloping downwards** then price elasticity of demand (PED) will **change** depending on where the firm is operating on the curve.

2) So, to **recap** what's covered on p.20:

   • At the midpoint of the demand curve PED = −1.

   • To the left of the midpoint, demand is elastic, so decreasing a product's price **towards** the midpoint will cause a **more than proportionate** increase in sales and **total revenue** will **increase**.

   • To the **right of the midpoint**, demand is **inelastic**, so decreasing a product's price **below** the price at the midpoint will cause a **less than proportionate** increase in sales and **total revenue** will **decrease**.

   • **Total revenue is maximised** when the firm is operating **at the midpoint** of the demand curve — when **PED = −1**.

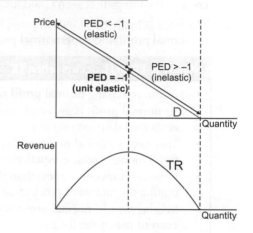

And **MR = 0** when **TR** is at its **Maximum**

1) The demand curve is also the average revenue curve.

2) So the maximum total revenue occurs at the midpoint of the average revenue curve.

3) The MR curve is always twice as steep as the AR curve.

4) When total revenue is at its maximum, MR = 0. (At the point where additional sales reduce total revenue, marginal revenue becomes negative.)

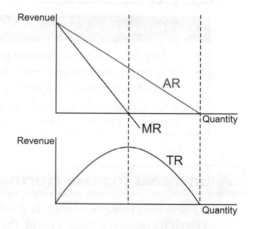

Warm-Up Questions

Q1 What is turnover?

Q2 What is marginal revenue?

Q3 Is the price of a product the marginal revenue or the average revenue for that product?

Q4 What is marginal revenue equal to when total revenue is at its maximum?

Exam Questions

Q1 The table shows information on a firm's revenue given different sales levels of its only product. Calculate the marginal revenue for each output level. [2 marks]

Q2 Explain why the average and marginal revenue curves of a price-making firm slope down, while those of a price-taking firm are horizontal. [15 marks]

Quantity sold	Price (£)	Total Revenue (£)	Marginal Revenue (£)
0	12	0	—
1	10	10	
2	8	16	
3	6	18	
4	4.50	18	
5	3	15	

Downward sloping demand curve — an economist's favourite yoga pose...

Revenue is determined by the quantity a firm is able to sell at a given price, so the shape of a firm's revenue curves depends on the price elasticity of demand the firm faces. The price elasticity of demand, and how this changes at different output levels, will be different for different firms in different markets. There's a lot going on here — make sure you've got your head round all of it.

Profit

The basic idea here is that firms need to make a profit to survive. But be warned... some of this might seem a bit weird at first, because making a profit isn't quite as simple as bringing in more money than you pay out. **These pages are for all boards.**

Economists distinguish between Normal Profit and Supernormal Profit

1) Here's the basic equation for working out **profit**: (Remember... TC consists of the **money costs** of the things that have to be paid for **and** the **opportunity costs** of the things that aren't paid for.)

> **Profit = Total Revenue (TR) – Total Costs (TC)**

2) There are actually two kinds of profit in economics — **normal profit** and **supernormal profit**.

Supernormal profit is also known as abnormal profit.

NORMAL PROFIT occurs when TR = TC

- A firm is making **normal profit** when its total revenue **equals** its total costs.
- So **normal profit** is an 'economic profit' of **zero** — i.e. a profit of zero if **all** costs are taken into account.
- This means normal profit occurs when the **extra revenue** left, on top of what's needed to cover the firm's money costs, is **equal** to the **opportunity costs** of the factors of production that aren't paid for.
- If the extra revenue is **less** than those **opportunity costs**, then the firm would have been **better off** putting the factors of production to a **different use**.
- In other words, **normal profit** is the **minimum** level of profit needed to keep resources in their **current use** in the long run.

A firm can make a 'money profit' or 'accounting profit' (i.e. receive more money than it pays out), but an economic profit of zero.

SUPERNORMAL PROFIT occurs when TR > TC

- A firm is making **supernormal profit** when its total revenue is **greater** than its total costs.
- This means the **revenue** generated from using the factors of production in this way is **greater** than could have been generated by using them in any **other** way.
- If firms in an industry are making **supernormal profit**, this will create an **incentive** for other firms to try to **enter** that industry.

There's more about this in Section 4.

A firm needs to make Normal Profit to Keep Operating in the Long Run

1) If a firm can't make normal profit it will **close** in the **long run**, because its revenue is not covering all of its costs. Even if it's making a money profit, the factors of production it's using could be used to **better effect** elsewhere.

2) However, in the **short run**, a firm has **fixed costs** that it has to pay, whether or not it produces any output. So a loss-making firm may **not** close **immediately** — it all depends on how its revenue compares to its **variable costs**.

- If a firm's total revenue is greater than its total variable costs (or if its average revenue is greater than its average variable costs), then it'll continue to produce in the short term.
- Any revenue generated above the firm's variable costs can contribute towards paying its fixed costs. If the firm stops production immediately, it'll actually be worse off.

- If a firm's **total revenue** is **less** than its **total variable costs** (or if its **average revenue** is less than its **average variable costs**), then it'll close **immediately**.
- If it **continues** to produce, it'll actually be **worse off**.

3) In the long run the firm can be **released** from its fixed costs (e.g. by no longer renting a factory) and it will shut down.

4) Shut-down points can be shown **diagrammatically**:

- In the **long run**, if the price **remains below P** (where **normal profit** is being made), then the firm should **exit the market**. The **losses** the firm is making **aren't sustainable**.
- If the price is **between P and P₁**, the firm should **continue** to produce in the **short run**.
- If the price falls **below P₁** the firm should **cease production immediately**, as its variable costs aren't being covered.

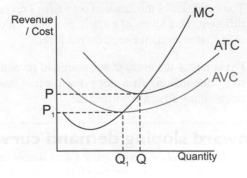

Profit

Profit is **Maximised** when **Marginal Cost = Marginal Revenue**

1) Economists generally **assume** that firms are aiming to **maximise** their **profits**.  See p.13 for more about this.
   To do this, they need to find the optimum output level at which to operate.

   - If marginal revenue (MR) is **greater** than marginal cost (MC)
     at a particular level of output, the firm should **increase output**.
     This is because the revenue gained by increasing output is **greater**
     than the cost of producing it. So **increasing output adds to profit**.

   - If marginal revenue (MR) is **less** than marginal cost (MC) at a
     particular level of output, the firm should **decrease output**.
     This is because it's costing the firm more to produce its last unit of output
     than it receives in revenue. So **decreasing output adds to profit**.

2) This means the **profit-maximising** output level occurs when **MC = MR**.
   This is known as the "MC = MR profit-maximising rule".

   > **Profits are maximised when MC = MR.**

   Religious artists aim
   to maximise prophets.

3) You can use this rule to find a firm's **profit-maximising output level** from
   a diagram showing MR and MC, as in the two examples below.

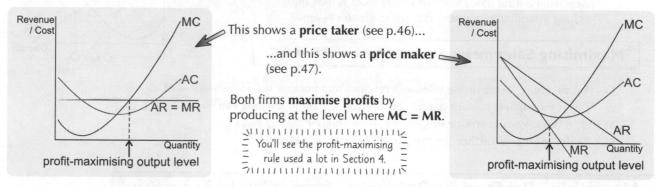

This shows a **price taker** (see p.46)...

...and this shows a **price maker**
(see p.47).

Both firms **maximise profits** by
producing at the level where **MC = MR**.

You'll see the profit-maximising
rule used a lot in Section 4.

profit-maximising output level

profit-maximising output level

Warm-Up Questions

Q1 What is supernormal profit?

Q2 State the condition for profit maximisation.

PRACTICE QUESTIONS

Exam Questions

Q1 Discuss when a firm whose average costs exceed its average revenue in the long run should close down. [4 marks]

Q2 The diagram shows the costs and revenues for a profit-maximising firm.
The most suitable action for the firm, assuming no changes in costs
or demand, would be to output at which of the levels shown?

[1 mark]

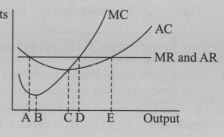

Supernormal profit — profit that wears its pants over its trousers...

Profit's a funny one — but the basic message here is that in the long run a firm needs to bring in enough revenue to cover all its costs. Sounds straightforward... but you have to remember that in economics, a firm's costs include the opportunity costs of things it's not had to pay for. So a business owner's time has to be included in a firm's costs, even if the owner doesn't take a wage from the business, for example. The upshot of this is that an 'economic profit' of zero is perfectly normal (no pun intended). I told you this was weird. Anyway, remember all that, plus all that stuff about why a loss-making firm might keep operating in the short run if it'll help it to pay its fixed costs. Also remember everything else in this book. Then you ought to do very well in your exam.

The Objectives of Firms

The objectives of firms vary — they will largely depend on who has control. Often, firms will accept some sort of compromise between different objectives in an attempt to 'keep everyone happy'. **These pages are for all boards.**

Profit Maximisation is assumed to be the Objective of a firm

1) The traditional **theory of the firm** is based on the **assumption** that firms are aiming to **maximise profit**.

2) But in reality, there are **other objectives** a firm might consider **more important**. For example, **revenue maximisation** and **sales maximisation** are other common objectives.

Aiming for Other Objectives will Reduce Profit in the Short Run

A firm aiming to **maximise profit** will operate at output level Q, where **MR = MC**.
Firms that are aiming for **other objectives** will operate at **different** output levels.

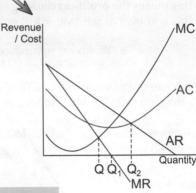

Maximising Revenue means producing where MR = 0

1) **Revenue** is maximised when **MR = 0**.
2) This happens at output level Q_1 — a higher output than Q.
3) If a firm is aiming to maximise revenue they will keep increasing output **past** the point where profit is maximised, as long as adding **more output** leads to **greater revenue**.

Maximising Sales means producing where AR = AC

1) A firm aiming to **maximise sales** will produce at an output level where **AR = AC**.
2) This is the **highest** level of output the firm can sustain in the **long run**.
3) Q_2 is the sales-maximising output level — it's **higher** than Q and Q_1.
4) If **sales increased further** the firm would be making a **loss**.

Maximising Profit might Only be an objective for the Long Run

1) **Maximising profit** in the **long run** sometimes means **sacrificing profit** in the **short run**.

2) A firm may try to **maximise sales** or **revenue** in the **short run**, e.g. a firm might maximise revenue or sales to increase its **market share**, or to gain **monopoly power** so that it can make **supernormal profits** in the long run. Or high sales might make it easier for the firm to **borrow money**.

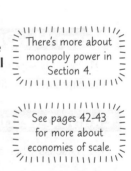

There's more about monopoly power in Section 4.

3) Some firms may even be willing to operate at a **loss** in the **short run** in order to make a **profit** in the **long run**. A firm may expect **revenue to increase** in the future, for example, once they've been in the market for a while and their **brand recognition** increases. Or a firm might expect to **reduce costs** when they're able to output at higher production levels (i.e. experience economies of scale), and so they may keep operating at a loss while they **build up** the business.

See pages 42-43 for more about economies of scale.

4) A firm's objective may be to simply **survive** in the **short run** by achieving **normal profit**. Then, when it's **established** in a market, it can try to **maximise profits**.

Alongside profit, some firms will aim to increase their growth — see pages 52-53.

Some firms have Alternative Objectives

1) Some firms might aim for something not **directly** related to profit, revenue or sales. But these objectives are usually pursued while **also** aiming to make at least **normal profit**.

2) For example, some organisations are '**not for profit**' — they don't pay out profit to their owners and their **main aim** is to 'do good' or provide some kind of benefit to the public. Other firms will focus on producing **high quality products**, at the expense of maximising profits in the short run, to **gain loyal customers**.

3) Many firms are also interested in **corporate social responsibility** (**CSR**). This involves firms operating in a way that brings **benefit** to **society**, as well as trying to make **supernormal profit** (unlike 'not for profit' firms). For example:

- A firm may try to **protect** the **environment** by using **sustainable resources**.
- A firm may **support local businesses** by using suppliers in their region.
- A firm may choose to **pay its workers above** the standard market rate.

4) A firm's CSR policies can help it **increase** its **profits** by encouraging consumers to buy from them.

The Objectives of Firms

Divorce of Ownership from Control often happens as firms Grow

1) In **small** firms, the **owner** often **manages** the company on a day-to-day basis.

2) As firms **grow**, the owners often raise finance by **selling shares** — the new shareholders become **part owners** of the firm. But the firm will actually be run by **directors**, who are appointed to **control** the business in the shareholders' interests.

3) This is known as the **divorce of ownership from control** — the owner(s) of the firm are **no longer** in day-to-day control.

4) **Directors** might have **different** objectives to the **owners**.

5) Employees and other **stakeholders** in firms may also have their own **objectives** and might have some level of **control**.

> A firm's stakeholders include everyone with an interest in or who is affected by the firm — e.g. employees, managers, suppliers, customers, etc.

- The **divorce of ownership from control** can lead to what's known as the **principal-agent problem**.

- This is where a **principal** (e.g. **shareholders**) pays for an **agent** (e.g. a **managing director**) to act in their interests, but instead the agent acts in their own **self-interest**.

- For example, a firm's shareholders will want a firm to **maximise profits** to increase the value of its shares. However, if the managing director's **pay** or **bonus** is linked to **revenue** or **sales**, then they may choose to maximise those things instead.

- Directors might also be keen to grow some aspect of the firm (e.g. sales or market share) because they **enjoy** running a large organisation, or because being in charge of a large firm will further their **career**.

- **Employees** (another example of an agent) are likely to aim to increase their own **pay or benefits** (or just to keep themselves in a job), **ahead** of aiming to make profits for the firm.

Owners can Retain Control with Accountability and Incentives

1) How much **control** the managers or directors of a firm have can depend on how **accountable** they are to the owners. By holding managers or directors accountable, **owners** can **tackle** the **principal-agent problem**.

2) Shareholders can **remove** directors by vote if they're not happy with them, but they often **lack information** that might make them do this.

3) **Accountability** means managers and directors having to **justify** what they've done in the past and **explain** their future plans and intentions.

4) Owners might also try to **encourage** directors to aim for profit maximisation by offering **incentives** which make this an attractive objective for the directors to pursue — e.g. a **bonus** linked to profits, or free or discounted company **shares**.

Sometimes people Satisfice rather than Maximise to Make Life Easier

1) **Satisficing** means trying to do **just enough** to satisfy important stakeholders, instead of aiming to **maximise** a quantity such as profits (or **minimise** something like costs). It's sometimes described as 'aiming for an **easy life**'.

2) Satisficing often arises when different **stakeholders** have different objectives, which might be **conflicting**.

3) For example, rather than maximising profit, directors might aim to make '**enough profit**' to stop shareholders getting too concerned, and paying employees '**high enough wages**' that they don't look for work elsewhere or threaten to go on strike. (This is another example of the **principal-agent problem**.)

Warm-Up Questions

Q1 Other than profit maximisation, give three other objectives firms might have.

Q2 What is satisficing?

Exam Question

Q1 Evaluate the view that all firms are aiming to maximise profit.   [25 marks]

And I thought a stakeholder was a particularly robust fork...

Traditional economics assumes firms aim to maximise profit — but in reality this often isn't the case. Especially in larger firms, the people who control the business won't be the owners and will have their own objectives, such as revenue or sales maximisation. Remember, firms can only pursue other objectives while making at least normal profit in the long run, else they won't survive.

Why Firms Grow

*A firm grows by increasing its output. It can do this by increasing its own production scale or by taking over other firms. There are lots of reasons for a firm to grow and ways in which a firm can achieve growth. **For Edexcel and OCR only.***

Growth can Increase Profit and bring Other Benefits

1) Firms usually grow to increase their **profit** — there are several ways that growth can achieve this:

> **Increasing economies of scale** — a firm might grow to reach the **minimum efficient scale** of production (MES), where long run average costs are minimised (see p.45 for more about MES).
>
> **Increasing market share** and **reducing competition** — if a firm controls a large part of the market they might gain some **monopoly power** that allows them to **set prices** and make **supernormal profits**.
>
> **Expanding into new markets** — a firm might try to sell its products in **different countries**, for example.

2) However, there are also **other reasons** why a firm might grow, such as to **achieve managerial objectives** — directors might seek the **status** of running a large firm, for example.

Internal Growth means Increasing Production Scale

1) **Internal growth** (also known as **organic growth**) is growth as a result of a firm increasing the levels of the **factors of production** it uses. For example, increasing output by building a larger factory, hiring more workers, and increasing the amount of raw materials used.

2) A key **advantage** of internal growth is that a firm has **control** over exactly how this growth occurs.

3) However, the downside is that internal growth tends to be **slow**, and it can also be **expensive**.

External Growth means Combining Firms

1) **External growth** (also known as **inorganic growth**) is growth as a result of **takeovers** and **mergers**:
   — a **takeover** is when one firm **buys another firm**, which becomes part of the first firm,
   — a **merger** is when two firms unite to form a **new company**.

2) External growth is **quicker** and may be **cheaper** than internal growth.
   It might also be the easiest way to gain **experience** and **expertise** in a new area of business.

3) External growth can happen through **horizontal integration**, **vertical integration**, or **conglomerate integration**:

> *The terms takeover and merger are often used interchangeably, but there are legal and technical differences between the two.*

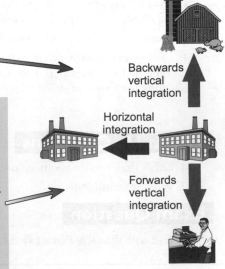

Backwards vertical integration

Horizontal integration

Forwards vertical integration

Horizontal and Vertical Integration happen between firms in the Same Market

1) **Horizontal integration** means combining firms that are at the **same stage** of the production process of **similar products** — for example, a **merger** between **two pharmaceutical companies** or between a **bookshop** and a **music shop**.

2) Firms can **increase economies of scale**, **reduce competition** and **increase market share** through horizontal integration.

1) **Vertical integration** means combining firms at **different stages** of the production process of the **same product**.
   - **Forward vertical integration** happens when a firm takes over another firm that is **further forward** in the production process (closer to the end customer). E.g. a **leather manufacturer** buying a **shoe factory**.
   - **Backward vertical integration** happens when a firm takes over another firm that is **further back** in the production process (further away from the end customer). E.g. a **book printer** buying a **paper plant**.

2) By taking over suppliers or retailers, a firm can gain more **control** of the **production process**. This might be in order to maintain higher **quality standards**, or make the overall process more **efficient**.

3) This can create **barriers to entry** (see pages 60-61) by preventing competitors from accessing suppliers or retailers.

EDEXCEL ONLY

Why Firms Grow

EDEXCEL ONLY

Conglomerate Integration happens between firms in Unrelated Markets

1) **Conglomerate integration** means combining firms which operate in completely **different markets**.
   E.g. an **educational stationery supplier** merging with a **tractor manufacturer**.

2) Conglomerate mergers allow firms to **diversify**, which means they can **spread their risk** — if one part of the new firm does badly, this can be **compensated for** by profit from another part of the firm.

3) A conglomerate merger will also allow a firm to use **profits** generated by one product to **invest** in another.

Growth will have Disadvantages

The growth of a firm can lead to some **disadvantages**, for example:

- If two firms merge there will be a duplication of staff, such as marketing, finance and human resources personnel. It's likely that some of this staff will be made redundant. Furthermore, the two firms will each have a leader — these leaders will either have to find a way to work together, or one will need to leave.

- The merged firms may have different and incompatible objectives that will need to be resolved.

- A firm can put itself in a lot of debt in order to raise the finance necessary to complete a takeover.

- The new, larger firm may suffer from diseconomies of scale.

- A firm that takes over another business may overestimate its value and pay far more for it than it's actually worth. This makes it hard for the new larger firm to make a return on the investment.

After the two catering firms merged, jokes about 'too many cooks spoiling the broth' became slightly awkward.

The growth of firms will Affect Consumers

ADVANTAGES

- A **larger firm** may benefit from **economies of scale** which could lead to **price reductions** for consumers.
- The **combined creativity** of two firms working together may lead to the production of **superior products**.

DISADVANTAGES

- Consumers will have **less choice** if two, or more, firms merge.
- The **reduction** in **competition** caused by firms merging may also lead to **higher prices** for consumers.
- Two merged firms may **produce less output** than two separate firms, which will lead to **price increases**.

Governments usually **monitor mergers** to see if they'll lead to consumers getting an **unfair deal**. For example, a merger can lead to the creation of a **monopoly**, which will have advantages and disadvantages for consumers. If a government decides that a merger **isn't fair** to consumers, then it can take action to **block** the merger — see p.94 for more.

Warm-Up Questions

Q1 What is the difference between internal and external growth?
Q2 Give three disadvantages of growth for a company.

PRACTICE QUESTIONS

Exam Question

Q1 Discuss the potential benefits of horizontal integration in a market which is experiencing declining profits. [10 marks]

Horizontal integration? I suppose that's one way of bringing firms together...

You've got to get those different types of integration clear in your head — it's very easy to muddle them up. Cover the book up and see if you can remember which way round it all goes — if it hasn't sunk in, have another read through and try again...

Business Growth and Demergers

Sometimes, after a merger, one or both firms will realise they've made a terrible mistake — this is one occasion when a demerger might happen. ***These pages are for Edexcel only.***

A **Demerger** is the **Breaking Up** of a firm into **Separate Firms**

1) If a firm is experiencing disadvantages as a result of expanding into different markets, or diseconomies of scale, it might sell off parts of its business to create separate firms. This is called a demerger.

2) The idea is to allow each new smaller firm to focus on a specific market, and make more profit than they did as part of the larger firm.

3) Sometimes a firm will sell off a particularly weak part of its business which is making little or no profit. It's likely to get a low price for this part of the firm, but it will hope that the sale will mean profits are improved for the remaining parts.

4) There are several other reasons why a firm may demerge, for example:
   * To release money to pay off business loans.
   * To release money to reinvest in the firm (e.g. to buy new equipment).
   * The hoped-for benefits of a merger didn't materialise.
   * Either in response to, or to prevent, government intervention when a firm could be classed as having monopoly power in an industry (see p.94-95). In the UK, the government can force a company to demerge if it considers it to have too much monopoly power.
   * It might be expected that there will be an increase in share price, meaning that the total value of the demerged firms will be greater than the value of the original firm. This might occur if one part of the company is performing poorly and is negatively affecting the share price of the whole firm.

Demergers have an impact on **Businesses, Workers** and **Consumers**

Businesses
* A demerged firm may become **more efficient** and be able to focus on **improving** its **production processes**.
* Any **economies of scale** will be **reduced**, but there may also be a **reduction** in any **diseconomies of scale**.
* A firm will have **greater independence** — for example, a demerged firm can negotiate its own contracts rather than relying on its parent company.
* A firm's **market value** is likely to **increase** compared to its value when it was part of a larger organisation.
* **Selling off** an **unprofitable** part of a firm is **difficult** and it may have to be sold at a **huge loss**. This could **harm** the **image** of the demerged firm and make shareholders **unhappy**.

These are just some examples — there are lots of other impacts on businesses, workers and consumers.

Workers
* There may be an **improvement** in **manager-worker relations** as a smaller, demerged firm will have **fewer employees**.
* **More jobs** might be **created** as, for example, a demerged firm may need to hire marketing, finance and human resources staff.
* Workers may **lose morale** if the situation surrounding a demerger **isn't explained clearly** to them.

Consumers
* There's likely to be **improved consumer choice** as **competition** will **increase** (see p.59 for more), and this may cause **prices** to **fall**.
* Consumers will be **less confused** as to what each company does.
* Consumers are likely to benefit from having **smaller firms** that are **more focused** on their **needs**.

"... and, if we demerge, I'll never have to see you ever again."

Business Growth and Demergers

Sometimes firms will Choose to Stay Small...

1) The **legal requirements** for small businesses can be **simpler** and **less expensive** to comply with.

E.g. small firms may not need to have their accounts audited each year.

2) Firms may also be concerned about experiencing **diseconomies of scale** if they expand — they might then choose to remain small. Some possible concerns include:

- Getting larger might mean their **relationships** with **customers** become more impersonal.
- Large firms can become **complacent** about their operations and become less focused and efficient.
- Larger firms also tend to be **less responsive** to change than smaller firms. Small firms have greater **flexibility**.

3) A firm's owners might not want the **extra work** and **risks** involved in expanding — they might prefer free time over profit.

4) Small firms have a **greater awareness** of, and **control over**, their **environmental impact**, which can be very important for some business owners.

5) Firms might want to remain small to **avoid being noticed** and taken over by larger firms.

...and sometimes firms are Forced to Stay Small

1) Firms might be **forced** to remain small if they can't raise the necessary **finance** to expand. It can be **hard** for small businesses to get **loans** as they're seen as a **risky investment** — lenders might feel there's a good chance the firm may go out of business.

2) If a firm supplies a **niche market**, it might only have a small **demand**, so may have no potential to expand its sales.

3) A firm may simply **lack** the **skills** and **expertise** to be able to expand. For example, it can require a **high level** of **entrepreneurial skill** to be able to see how a firm could expand and to carry through that expansion — many managers of a small firm **won't** have that skill.

4) Similarly, a firm may **lack** the **resources** to be able to cope with **additional regulations** and **bureaucracy** that larger firms have to deal with.

See p.92-93 for more on government regulations.

Warm-Up Questions

Q1 What is a demerger?
Q2 Give three impacts of demergers.
Q3 Give four reasons why a firm might prefer to remain small.
Q4 List four constraints on business growth.

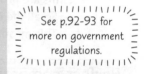

Exam Questions

Q1 A firm decides to split into two separate companies. A demerger is unlikely to lead to:
A) an increase in purchasing economies of scale.
B) a decrease in any diseconomies of scale.
C) improved consumer choice.
D) the creation of more jobs.

[1 mark]

Q2 A small, successful firm specialises in the production of ornate, handmade furniture for very wealthy customers. Explain why this firm might want to stay small.

[5 marks]

Tips on demerging — always open with "It's not you, it's me..."

Ah, break-ups — they can be a bit awkward, and sometimes lead to a little bit of embarrassment. But hey, it's not the end of the world — maybe that old economies of scale sparkle will come back. Maybe, in time, another firm will come along that'll make the heart sing again. Mmm hmm... Oh, and there's some stuff here on the constraints on growth that you should learn, too.

Perfect Competition

Perfectly competitive markets don't happen in real life... but that doesn't mean they're not important.
They show the conditions needed to achieve some really useful outcomes. ***These pages are for all boards.***

Perfectly Competitive markets have certain Characteristics

1) The **model of perfect competition** is a description of how a market **would** work **if** certain conditions were satisfied.

2) It's a theoretical thing — there are **no** real markets that work quite like this. But understanding how perfect competition works makes it easier to understand what's going **wrong** with real-life markets when they have undesirable results.

3) In a **perfectly competitive** market, the following conditions are satisfied:

- There's an infinite number of suppliers and consumers.
  - Each of these suppliers is small enough that no single firm or consumer has any 'market power' (i.e. no firm or consumer can affect the market on their own).
  - Each firm is a 'price taker' (as opposed to a 'price maker') — this means they have to buy or sell at the current market price.

  So all firms have O% concentration. See p.66 for more about concentration.

- Consumers have perfect information — i.e. perfect knowledge of all goods and prices in a market.
  - Every consumer decision is well-informed — consumers know how much every firm in the market charges for its products, as well as all the details about those products.

- Producers have perfect information — i.e. perfect knowledge of the market and production methods.
  - No firm has any 'secret' low-cost production methods, and every firm knows the prices charged by every other firm.

- Products are identical (homogeneous).
  - So consumers can always switch between products from different firms (i.e. all the products are perfect substitutes for each other).

  This also means there's no branding, since branding makes some products seem different from others.

- There are no barriers to entry and no barriers to exit.
  - New entrants can join the industry very easily. Existing firms can leave equally easily.

- Firms are profit maximisers.
  - So all the decisions that a firm makes are geared towards maximising profit.
  - This means that all firms will choose to produce at a level of output where MC = MR (see p.49).

Perfect competition leads to Allocative Efficiency... usually

1) The conditions for a perfectly competitive market ensure that the **rationing, signalling** and **incentive** functions of the **price mechanism** (see p.28) work perfectly. In particular:
   - all firms are **price takers** ('the market' sets the price according to consumers' preferences, **rationing** resources and **signalling** priorities),
   - consumers and producers have **perfect knowledge** of the market, and there are **no barriers** to entry or exit (so firms can recognise and act on **incentives** to change their output level or enter/leave a market).

   See p.60-61 and 72-73 for more on barriers to entry and exit.

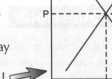

2) In perfect competition, a market's **demand curve = marginal utility (MU)**, because consumers' demand reflects what that good is worth to them and that decreases as quantity increases due to the **law of diminishing marginal utility** (see p.12).

3) Also, a market's **supply curve = marginal cost (MC)**, because producers' marginal costs increase as quantity increases due to the **law of diminishing returns** (see p.40).

4) **Allocative efficiency** occurs when a good's price is **equal** to what consumers want to pay for it, and this happens in a perfectly competitive market because the price mechanism ensures that producers supply **exactly** what consumers demand. So, **P = MC or P = MU.**

5) **Without** perfect competition, a market **can't** achieve allocative efficiency.

Allocative efficiency and externalities
Perfectly competitive markets will achieve **allocative** efficiency, **assuming** that there are **no externalities** (see p.74).
- Strictly speaking, allocative efficiency occurs when **P = MSC** (marginal social cost — i.e. including external costs to third parties).
- Perfect competition results in a long run equilibrium where **P = MPC** (marginal private cost — i.e. the cost to the firm of producing the product, **ignoring** external costs).
- But if there are **negative externalities**, say, then **MPC < MSC** — which means that **P < MSC**. This will mean that there's allocative inefficiency, and that will lead to **overproduction** and **overconsumption**.

Perfect Competition

Perfect Competition means Supernormal Profits are Competed Away

1) In perfect competition, **no firm** will make **supernormal profits** in the **long run**.

2) This is because any **short-term supernormal profits** attract new firms to the market (since there are **no barriers to entry**). This means supernormal profits are '**competed away**' in the long term — i.e. firms **undercut** each other until all firms make only normal profit.

Also, all firms are forced to become productively efficient (see next page for more information).

3) These diagrams show how this **equilibrium** is maintained in the **long run**.

- Suppose there's **high demand** for a product across an **industry** as a whole, leading to a firm making **supernormal profits**, as shown in red in the diagram.

  - The firm's **total revenue** is TR = Q × P (= the total area of the red and grey rectangles).
  - The firm's **total costs** are TC = Q × c (= the area of the grey rectangle, since c is the firm's average cost (AC) at this level of output).
  - **Subtract** TC from TR to find the firm's **profit**.
  - Here, TR > TC, so this firm is currently making a **supernormal profit** of TR – TC (= the area of the red rectangle).

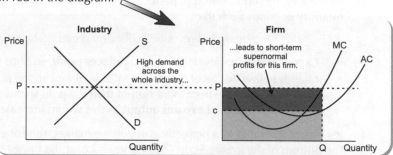

- In a **perfectly competitive** market, those supernormal profits mean other firms will now have an **incentive** to enter the market. And since there are **no barriers to entry**, they can do this easily.

- This results in a shift in the industry **supply curve** to the right...

- ...meaning the **market price falls** until **all** excess profits have been **competed away**, and a new **long run equilibrium** is reached at price P_1 (with this firm supplying Q_1).

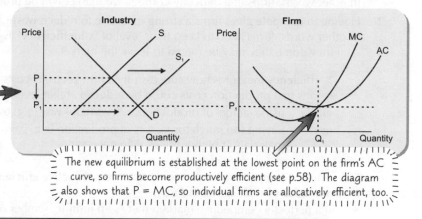

The new equilibrium is established at the lowest point on the firm's AC curve, so firms become productively efficient (see p.58). The diagram also shows that P = MC, so individual firms are allocatively efficient, too.

A firm will Leave a market if it's Unable to make a profit in the Long Run

1) If the **market price** (AR) falls **below** a firm's average unit-cost (AC), the firm is making **less** than normal profit (i.e. a **loss**).

2) There are **no barriers to exit** in a perfectly competitive market (see p.56), so in the **long run** the firm will just **leave** the market.

3) However, in the short run, there are **two possibilities**:
   - If the selling price (AR) is still **above** the firm's **average variable costs** (AVC), then the firm may **continue to trade** temporarily.
   - If the selling price (AR) falls **below** the level of the firm's **average variable costs** (AVC), then it will leave the market **immediately**.

See p.48 for more about shut-down points.

Warm-Up Questions

Q1 List the conditions needed for a perfectly competitive market.

Q2 Explain the link between perfect competition and allocative efficiency.

Q3 What would force a firm to leave a market immediately?

Exam Question

Q1 Explain, with diagrams, the long run equilibrium positions for a firm and its industry in a perfectly competitive market.

[15 marks]

My perfect competition is a prize crossword in the Sunday papers...

In practice, no market completely satisfies the assumptions behind perfect competition. However, the closer a real-life market comes to satisfying them, the more likely it is to behave in the way predicted by the theoretical model. This is tricky stuff, but it's worth taking the time to really get your head round all those diagrams before you move on.

Perfect Competition

Perfect competition sounds pretty good... I mean... it's perfect, after all.
But for the exam, you need to know very specifically what's good about perfect competition. **These pages are for all boards.**

Perfect competition leads to **Productive Efficiency**

1) **Productive efficiency** is about ensuring the **costs** of production are as **low** as they can be. This will mean that prices to **consumers** can be low as well.

2) In perfect competition, productive efficiency comes about as a **direct result** of all firms trying to **maximise** their **profits**.

3) At the long run equilibrium of perfect competition, a firm will produce a **quantity** of goods such that:

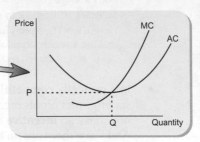

> marginal revenue (MR) = marginal costs (MC)

- Output **above** this level (MC > MR) **reduces profit**, so firms wouldn't produce it.
- Output **below** this level (i.e. MR > MC) would mean the firm would **earn** more revenue from extra output than it would **spend** in costs — so the firm would **expand output** as this would **increase profit**.

4) It's no accident that in a perfectly competitive market, this long run output level is at the **bottom** of the average-cost (AC) curve — i.e. at the lowest possible cost level. In other words, firms in a perfectly competitive market will be **productively efficient**.

5) Having to **compete** gives firms a strong incentive to reduce **waste** and **inefficiency**. In other words, firms need to keep their level of '**x-inefficiency**' as low as possible — if they don't, they may be forced to **leave** the market.

> **X-efficiency** measures how successfully a firm keeps its costs down. **X-inefficiency** (or '**organisational slack**') means that production costs could be **reduced** at that level of production. X-inefficiency can be caused by:
>
> **either** using factors of production in a **wasteful way** (e.g. by employing more people than necessary),
>
> **or**   **paying too much** for factors of production (e.g. paying workers more than is needed or buying raw materials at higher prices than necessary).

6) But perfectly competitive markets only achieve **productive efficiency** if you assume that there are **no economies of scale** in the industry.
- In a perfectly competitive market, there's an **infinite** number of firms.
- This means that each firm is **very small**, and so **can't** take full advantage of **economies of scale**.
- If there are economies of scale, then an industry made up of an **infinite number** of very **small** firms may be **less productively efficient** than if there was one very **big** firm (i.e. a monopoly — see p.63).

Perfect competition **Doesn't** lead to **Dynamic Efficiency**...

1) **Dynamic efficiency** is about **improving efficiency** in the **long term**, so it refers to the willingness and eagerness of firms:
   a) to carry out **research and development** to **improve** existing products or **develop** new ones.
   b) to **invest** in **new technology** or **training** to improve the production process and reduce production costs.

2) However, these strategies involve considerable **investment** and therefore **risk**, so they will only take place if there's adequate **reward**.

3) Firms in a **perfectly competitive** market earn only **normal profit**, so there's **no reward** for taking risks. This means dynamic efficiencies will **not** be achieved.

4) However, as long as a market is towards the 'perfect-competition end' of the spectrum shown on p.59, then firms can achieve a degree of **dynamic efficiency** without becoming too allocatively and productively **inefficient**. This is why firms do achieve some degree of **dynamic efficiency** — in real life, no market is perfectly competitive.

...but does lead to **Static Efficiency**

1) If **allocative** and **productive** efficiency are achieved at any particular point in time, this is called **static efficiency**. But static efficiency can't last forever, since **technology** and **consumer tastes** change. For example, the methods used to make cars in the 1920s might have been allocatively and productively **efficient** at the time, but they'd be hopelessly out of date now.

2) To remain allocatively and productively efficient, car makers would have needed to **invest** in new production technology and design new models at some point.

> You might also come across economic efficiency, which is similar but more general — it means resources are allocated in the best way, and waste is minimised.

Perfect Competition

In **Real Life** there's a **'Spectrum'** of different market structures

1) In a **perfectly competitive** market, all the goods produced are **identical**, so the only way for firms to compete is on **price**. ← *This means the only way firms can compete with their rivals is by selling their products at a lower price.*

2) In practice, firms usually compete in **other ways** than on price — for example, they might use:

Improved products	Better quality of service	Wider product ranges
Advertising and promotion	Nicer packaging	Products that are easier to use

3) In the real world, markets fall somewhere on a 'spectrum' of different **market structures**.

Perfect competition ← *Every real-life market lies somewhere between these two extremes.* → **Pure monopoly**
(Competition maximised) | (No competition)

4) At one extreme are '**perfectly competitive** markets', and at the other are '**pure monopolies**' (where there's no competition at all — see p.62 for more info). **Real-life** markets lie somewhere between these extremes.

5) The **closer** an actual market **matches** the description of a perfectly competitive market, the more likely it is to **behave** in the same way.

Governments often try to **Encourage Competition** in markets

1) Perfectly competitive markets lead to **efficient** long run outcomes **in theory** (e.g. the long run equilibrium is allocatively and productively efficient, and firms are forced to become x-efficient).

2) By **encouraging competition**, governments hope to achieve these same kinds of efficiencies in **real life**. For example, governments want to make sure firms: *See p.94-95 for more about competition policy.*
   (i) are forced to **produce efficiently**, reducing costs where possible,
   (ii) set **prices** at a level that's **fair** to consumers,

3) They also hope competition will encourage firms to **innovate**, leading firms to create both new **products** (giving **more choice** for consumers) and new **production processes** (allowing firms to reduce their costs further).

4) There are various **policies** a government can introduce to **increase competition** in the economy:

- Encourage **new enterprises** with **advice** and **start-up subsidies**.
- Increase **consumer knowledge** by ensuring that **comparison information** is available.
- Introduce more **consumer choice** and competition in the **public sector**. This might involve creating 'internal markets' in sectors such as health and schooling, for example. ← *An internal market is where different parts of the same organisation compete against each other. For example, groups of hospitals in the NHS now compete for patients.*
- **Privatise** and **deregulate** large monopolistic nationalised industries.
- Discourage **mergers** and **takeovers** which might **excessively reduce** the number of competing firms.
- Encourage more **international** competition — e.g. by joining the EU, countries enter into a multinational 'single market' (see page 208 for more information).

Warm-Up Questions

Q1 What is meant by x-inefficiency?

Q2 What does it mean if a firm has static efficiency?

Q3 Describe three policies a government could introduce in order to increase the competitiveness of markets.

PRACTICE QUESTIONS

Exam Question

Q1 To what extent would you expect firms in a perfectly competitive market to be dynamically efficient? [5 marks]

Economics is all about real life — and perfectly competitive markets...

I think this is all quite interesting. I mean... perfect competition doesn't happen in real life. But understanding how it works in theory lets governments come up with all sorts of policies to try to get some of the benefits anyway. That's the benefit of an economic model — real life is hard to understand, so start by trying to understand something much simpler.

Barriers to Entry

Barriers to entry are 'obstacles' a firm might face if it tried to enter a new market — e.g. anything that makes entering a new market difficult or expensive. **These pages are for all boards.**

Barriers to entry **Vary** between **Markets**

1) A **barrier to entry** is any **potential difficulty** or **expense** a firm might face if it wants to enter a market.

2) The '**height**' of these barriers determines:
   - **how long** it will take or **how expensive** it will be for a new entrant to establish itself in a market and increase the amount of competition,
   - **whether** new entrants can successfully join the market **at all**.

   High barriers to entry mean entering a market will take longer or be more expensive.

3) Barriers to entry allow firms that are **already** in the market (called '**incumbent**' firms) to make **supernormal** profits, before new entrants enter the market and compete these profits away. How long **incumbent** firms can make supernormal profits for depends upon:
   - The **height** of the barriers to entry — i.e. how long the barriers can **prevent** new firms entering the market.
   - The **level** of supernormal profit being earned — this is because the **greater** the **profits** to be made, the more effort new entrants will be willing to make to **overcome** the barriers.

4) **Perfectly competitive** markets have **no barriers** to entry whatsoever.

   They also don't have any barriers to exit — firms can leave a market whenever they choose (see p.72 for more about leaving a market).

5) In a **pure monopoly market** the barriers to entry are **total**. **No** new firms can enter, so the monopolist remains the **only** seller.

   See page 62 for monopolies.

6) As usual, in **real life** the situation often lies somewhere between the extremes of perfect competition and a monopoly. There are normally **some** barriers to entry, but they're **not** usually **total**.

Barriers to entry can be created in **Various Ways**

1) Barriers to entry come about for **various** reasons. For example:
   a) The tendency (innocent or deliberate) of **incumbent** firms to **create** or **build** barriers.
   b) The **nature** of the industry leading to barriers over which incumbent firms and new entrants have **little control**.
   c) The extent of **government regulation** and **licensing**.

2) The **overall** barrier to entry into a market might be made up of a number of individual barriers:

Barriers to entry due to incumbent firms' actions

- An **innovative new product or service** can give a firm a head start over its rivals which can be difficult for a new entrant to overcome. If the new technology is also **patented** then other firms can't simply copy the new design — it's **legally protected**.

- Strong **branding** means that some products are very **well known** to consumers. The **familiarity** of the product often makes it a consumer's first choice, and puts new entrants to a market at a disadvantage.

- A strong brand can be the result of a firm making genuinely **better products** than the competition, or can be created by **effective advertising**. The barrier to entry is the **expense** and **difficulty** a new entrant to the market would have in attracting customers away from the market leaders.

  Both create a barrier to entry.

- **Aggressive pricing tactics** by incumbent firms can **drive** new competition **out** of the market before it becomes established. Incumbent firms may be able to **lower prices** to a level that a new entrant cannot match (e.g. due to economies of scale) and drive them out of business. This is sometimes called '**predatory pricing**' (or '**destroyer pricing**' or '**limit pricing**').

  It's often hard to distinguish between healthy price competition and predatory pricing.

- Just the **threat** of a '**price war**' may be enough to deter new firms from entering a market.

Barriers to Entry

Barriers to entry can be due to the nature of an industry

- Some 'capital-intensive' industries require huge amounts of capital expenditure before a firm receives any revenue (e.g. steel production and aeroplane production require a massive investment in sophisticated manufacturing plants before any steel or aeroplanes can be sold). The cost of entering these markets is huge, so smaller enterprises may not be able to break through.

  This barrier isn't the result of any deliberate obstruction by incumbent firms.

- If investments can't be recovered when a firm decides to leave a market, then that may make any attempt to break into a market very risky and unappealing. (See p.72 for more about these 'sunk costs'.)

  The barriers to exit can act as a barrier to entry.

- If there's a minimum efficient scale of production then any new firms entering the industry on a smaller scale will be operating at a higher point on the average cost curve than established firms. This means any new entrant has higher production costs per unit, so they'd have to sell the product to consumers at a higher price.

  Some economies of scale are only available to firms operating on a large scale — see p.45 for more about minimum efficient scale of production.

Barriers to entry can be due to government regulations

- If an activity requires a licence, then this restricts the number and speed of entry of new firms coming into a market. For example, pubs, pharmacists, food outlets, dentists and taxis all require licences before they can operate. Similarly, in a regulated industry (e.g. banking), firms have to be approved by a regulator before they can carry out certain activities.

  The reasons for needing a licence may be quite reasonable, but the process of getting one slows down (and can prevent) new entrants.

- New factories may need planning permission before they can be built.

- There will also be regulations regarding health and safety and working conditions for employees that firms will need to keep to.

New entrants sometimes have their own Advantages

1) Not all new entrants to a market are small firms trying to compete against established 'giants'.

2) Sometimes the new entrants can be large successful companies that wish to diversify into new markets.

3) Their large size means they have greater financial resources, so they may be more successful in breaking into new markets.

   When Virgin Money entered the banking sector, their large resources meant they could overcome the barriers to entry — but they had to invest heavily and advertise extensively.

Entering the pencil sharpener industry caused few worries for the directors of To the Edge of the Universe plc.

Warm-Up Questions

Q1 Compare the barriers to entry in a perfectly competitive market and in a monopoly.

Q2 Describe the three main types of barrier to entry to a market.

Q3 How might the size of a potential new entrant influence its ability to break into a new market?

PRACTICE QUESTIONS

Exam Questions

Q1 Describe how branding can be used by incumbent firms to create barriers to entry to a market. [5 marks]

Q2 To what extent are barriers to entry always the result of anticompetitive behaviour by established firms? [15 marks]

A barrier to entry — what an economist calls a bouncer...

Barriers to entry change over time. For example, in the old days, if you couldn't find a publisher willing to print your new novel, there wasn't very much you could do about it — your masterpiece may have remained undiscovered forever. Nowadays though, you can easily get loads of copies printed using a self-publishing website. (There's more about this kind of thing on p.73.)

Monopolies

The word 'monopoly' is used by different people to mean slightly different things. On the next couple of pages, it means an industry with only one firm in it. (There's also a little more info on monopolies on p.85.) **These pages are for all boards.**

A **Monopoly** is a market containing a **Single Seller**

1) In economics, a **monopoly** (or 'pure monopoly') is a market with only **one firm** in it (i.e. one firm **is** the industry). In other words, a single firm has **100% market share**.

In law, a monopoly is when a firm has a market share of 25% or more.

2) Even in markets with more than one seller, firms have **monopoly power** if they can influence the price of a particular good on their own — i.e. they can act as **price makers**.

In a monopoly, the price isn't determined by 'the market'.

3) Monopoly power may come about as a result of:

   • **Barriers to entry** preventing new competition entering a market to compete away large profits (see p.60).

   • **Advertising and product differentiation** — a firm may be able to act as a price maker if consumers think of its products as more desirable than those produced by other firms (e.g. because of a strong brand).

   • **Few competitors in the market** — if a market is dominated by a small number of firms, these are likely to have some price-making power. They'll also find it easier to differentiate their products.

4) Even though firms with monopoly power are price makers, **consumers** can still **choose** whether or not to buy their products. So **demand** will still depend on the price — as always, the **higher** the price, the **lower** the demand will be.

A **Monopolist** makes **Supernormal** profits — even in the **Long Run**

This diagram shows how a firm behaves in a **monopoly market**.

1) Assuming that the firm wants to **maximise profits**, its level of output will be where **MC = MR** (see p.49) — shown by the red dot.

2) If the firm produces a quantity Q_M, the **demand** (or AR) curve shows the **price** the firm can set — P_M.

3) At this output the **average cost** (AC) of producing **each unit** is AC_M.

4) The difference between AC_M and P_M is the **supernormal** (excess) profit **per unit**. So the **total supernormal profit** is shown by the **red** area.

5) In a monopoly market, the **barriers to entry** are **total**, so no new firms enter the market, and this supernormal profit is **not competed away**.

6) This means the situation remains as it is — this is the **long run equilibrium position** for a monopolist.

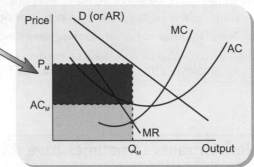

In perfect competition, a firm's marginal revenue and average revenue are the same — they both equal the equilibrium price (which is set by the market, not the firm, see p.57). In a monopoly market, this isn't true — see p.47.

Monopolies aren't **Productively** or **Allocatively Efficient**

1) The above diagram shows that MC **isn't** equal to AC at the **long run equilibrium position** for a monopoly (i.e. the firm **isn't** operating at the **lowest** point on the AC curve). This means that a monopoly **isn't productively efficient**.

2) The same diagram shows that the price charged by the firm is **greater** than MC. This means that a monopoly market is **not allocatively efficient**. Producers are being '**over-rewarded**' for the products they're providing.

3) Because of the restricted supply, the product will also be **underconsumed** — consumers aren't getting as much of the product as they want.

4) The red area shows how some of the **consumer surplus** (see p.29) that would have existed at the market equilibrium price P_C is transferred to the producer.

5) There's a **deadweight welfare loss** too. The grey area shows **potential** revenue that the **producer isn't** earning on the quantity Q_M to Q_C of the product that **consumers** would have been prepared to pay for (but which isn't produced).

Monopolies have further **Drawbacks**

   • There's no need for a monopoly to **innovate** or to respond to **changing consumer preferences** in order to make a profit, so they may become complacent.

   • Similarly, there's no need to **increase efficiency**, so x-inefficiency can remain high.

   • Consumer choice is restricted, since there are no alternative products.

   • Monopsonist power (see next page) may also be used to exploit suppliers.

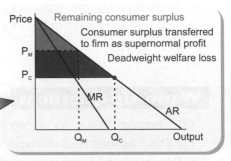

Another drawback is that playing it ruins friendships — this fight is all over who gets to play with the racing car counter.

Monopolies

Natural Monopolies have A Lot of Monopoly Power

Some industries lead to a **natural monopoly** — this can mean they have a great deal of monopoly power.

- Industries where there are **high fixed costs** and/or there are **large economies of scale** lead to **natural monopolies**.
- If there was **more than one** firm in the industry, then they would **all** have the same high fixed costs. This would lead to **higher costs** per customer than could be obtained by a single firm.
- In this case, a monopoly might be **more efficient** than having lots of firms competing. For example, the supply of **water** is a **natural monopoly** — it makes no sense for competing firms to all lay **separate** pipes.

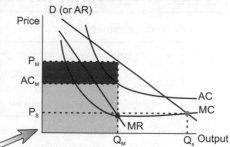

1) A natural monopoly will have **continuous economies of scale** — i.e. LRAC always **falls** as output increases (meaning MC is always below AC — see p.39). A **profit maximising** natural monopoly will **restrict output** to where MC = MR (at Q_M).

2) A government might be **reluctant** to break up a natural monopoly as this could **reduce efficiency**. However, it might want to provide **subsidies** to the natural monopoly so that it **increases output** to the point where demand (AR) = supply (MC) — this is Q_S. This will **reduce prices** to P_S (from P_M).

Monopolies have some Potential Benefits

1) A monopolist's **large size** allows it to gain an advantage from **economies of scale**. If **diseconomies of scale** are avoided, this means it can keep **average costs** (and perhaps **prices**) low. A monopolists will produce more than any individual producer in a perfectly competitive market would.

2) The **security** a monopolist has in the market (as well as the **supernormal profits**) means it can take a long-term view and **invest** in **developing** and **improving** products for the future — this can lead to **dynamic efficiency**.

3) Increased **financial security** also means that a monopolist can provide **stable** employment for its workers.

4) **Intellectual property rights** (IPRs) allow a form of legal **limited monopoly** that can actually be **in consumers' interests** because they'll benefit from better quality, innovative products.
   - There are various types of IPRs, such as **copyright** and **patents**. These allow a firm **exclusive** use of their **innovative ideas** (i.e. no one else is allowed to use them) for a **limited time**.
   - During this time, **supernormal profits** may be possible, but this is seen as the **reward** for **innovation** and **creativity**.
   - Without the **protection** of IPRs, firms would have **little incentive** to **risk** their resources investing in innovative products or processes — other firms would simply be able to **copy** those ideas (and immediately start to compete away any supernormal profits).

> IPRs are particularly important in the 'creative industries' — e.g. music, television, video games, and so on.

A Monopsony is a market with a Single Buyer

1) A **monopsony** is a situation when a **single buyer** dominates a market.

2) A monopsonist can act as a **price maker**, and drive down prices. For example, **supermarkets** are sometimes accused of acting as monopsonists when buying from their suppliers. Some people claim supermarkets unfairly use their market power to force **suppliers** to sell their products at a price that means those suppliers make a **loss**.

3) This could be seen as a monopsonist **exploiting** its suppliers. But it could be in the interests of **consumers** if the supermarkets **pass on** those low prices (by charging low prices to their **customers**).

4) If a firm is the single buyer of **labour** in a market, it can exploit its power and **lower** the wages of its employees.

Warm-Up Questions

Q1 What does it mean to say a monopoly is a 'price maker'?

Q2 Give two examples of arguments made in favour of monopolies.

Exam Question

Q1 Using a diagram, show how supernormal profit is earned in a monopoly, even in the long run. [10 marks]

Monopoly... monopsony... — it's all Greek to me...

The most important thing here is that a monopolist firm is a price maker, giving it a lot of 'market power'. There's some debate as to whether monopolies are a good or bad thing, but the UK government's current view is that competition is preferable.

Price Discrimination

An example of price discrimination would be if you and a friend went into a restaurant and had exactly the same meal... but the restaurant charged you different prices. **These pages are for all boards.**

Price Discrimination means charging Different Prices for the Same Product

1) **Price discrimination** occurs when a seller charges **different prices** to **different customers** for **exactly** the **same product**.

> - It's **not** price discrimination if the products **aren't exactly** the same.
> - So Business-class and Standard-class plane tickets are **not** an example of price discrimination, since it **costs more** to provide the comfier seats and extra legroom in Business class.

Don't confuse price discrimination with price differentiation, where a producer charges different prices for similar but different products.

2) Several **conditions** need to be satisfied for a firm to make use of price discrimination:
   - The seller must have some **price-making** power (e.g. there might be barriers to entry preventing competition). So **monopolies** (and **oligopolies** — see p.66) can price discriminate.

   Price-taking firms in a perfectly competitive market cannot practise price discrimination.

   - The firm must be able to distinguish **separate groups** of customers who have **different** price elasticities of demand (**PED**). In fact, the **more groups** that the market can be subdivided into, the **greater** the gains for the seller.

   And the cost of finding out this information needs to be lower than any potential gains.

   - The firm must be able to prevent **seepage** — it must be able to prevent customers who have bought a product at a **low price** re-selling it **themselves** at a **higher price** to customers who could have been charged **more**.

   Examples

   - **Theatres** and **cinemas** offer 'concession' prices for certain groups (e.g. students and pensioners).
   - **Window cleaners** could charge more in a smart neighbourhood than in a lower-income area.
   - **Train tickets at rush hour** cost more than the same train ticket at other times of day.
   - **Pharmaceutical drugs** may be sold at different prices in different countries.

Price discrimination transfers Consumer Surplus from Consumer to Producer

1) A **consumer surplus** is the difference between the **actual selling price** of a product and the price a consumer **would have been willing to pay**. For example, if the price of a cinema ticket was £8, but a consumer would have been willing to pay £10, then the consumer surplus is £2.

2) Price discrimination attempts to turn **consumer surplus** into **additional revenue** for the seller.

   i.e. turn consumer surplus into producer surplus.

3) There are different **degrees** of price discrimination.

First Degree price discrimination (or Perfect price discrimination)

- **First degree** price discrimination is where each **individual** customer is charged the **maximum** they would be willing to pay.
- This would turn **all** the consumer surplus into **extra revenue** for the seller. In the diagram, **total revenue** = **red** and **grey** shaded areas combined.
- However, the cost of **gathering** the required information to do this, and the difficulty in preventing **seepage**, makes this method unlikely to be used in practice.

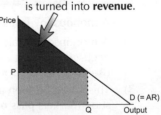

All the **consumer surplus** that would have existed at price P is turned into **revenue**.

Second Degree price discrimination

- **Second degree** price discrimination is often used in **wholesale markets**, where **lower prices** are charged to people who purchase **large quantities** (i.e. price **varies** with quantity demanded).
- This turns **some** of the consumer surplus into revenue for the seller, and encourages **larger orders**.
- In the diagram, the seller charges P_1 per unit for the customers buying quantity Q_1, and P_2 per unit for the customers buying quantity Q_2.
- If **all** customers were charged P_1, then the firm's total revenue would be the **grey** area. By charging some customers P_2, the **red** area is turned into **additional revenue** for the firm.

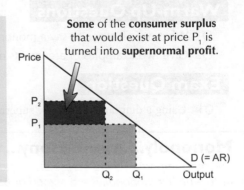

Some of the **consumer surplus** that would exist at price P_1 is turned into **supernormal profit**.

Price Discrimination

Third Degree price discrimination

- **Third degree** price discrimination is when a firm charges **different prices** for the **same product** to **different segments** of the market. These different segments could be:
  - customers of different **ages** — for example, a **leisure centre** might have different prices for adults, children and pensioners.
  - customers who buy at different **times** — for example, a **telephone company** might charge different amounts for phone calls made during **office hours** and phone calls made in the **evening**.
  - customers in different **places** — for example, a **pharmaceutical company** might sell its goods at different prices in different countries.
- For example, a seller can identify **two groups** of customers (Group A and Group B) with **different price elasticities** of demand (PED), as in these diagrams.

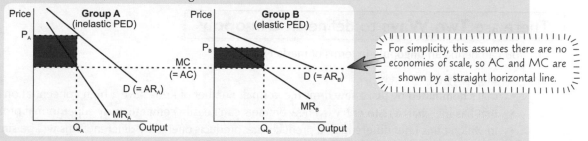

For simplicity, this assumes there are no economies of scale, so AC and MC are shown by a straight horizontal line.

- To **maximise profit**, the seller would set the price for each group at a level where **MC = MR**. This means:
  - it will charge a **higher price** to the group with a more **inelastic** PED (e.g. P_A for Group A).
  - It will charge a **lower price** to the group with a more **elastic** PED (e.g. P_B for Group B).
- The **red** areas represent the **supernormal profit** earned from each group.
  This **total** supernormal profit is **greater** than if the **same** price were charged to **everyone**.

Price discrimination is **Good** for **Sellers** and **Possibly Bad** for **Others**

Price discrimination certainly results in **increased revenue** for the seller.
Whether this is seen as **fair** or **unfair** depends on what happens to that extra revenue.

1) The use of price discrimination means that **some** or **all** of the **consumer surplus** is **converted** into revenue for the **seller** — i.e. the seller increases revenue **at the expense of** the consumer. However, the extra revenue could be used to **improve products**, or **invested** in more efficient production methods which might lead to lower prices.

2) In all cases, the **average revenue** is greater than MC — so price discrimination does **not** lead to **allocative efficiency**, because allocative efficiency occurs when P = MC (see p.56).

3) Consumers are **not** treated equally, but often the people who end up paying **more** have **higher incomes**, so are more able to **afford** those higher prices. Some people see this as **fair**, especially if the greater profits made from some customers are used to **subsidise lower prices** paid by others (e.g. train passengers **commuting** to work pay **high fares**, and profits from these customers could be used to help support **daytime** services). 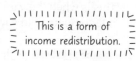 This is a form of income redistribution.

Warm-Up Questions

Q1 Explain what is meant by the term 'price discrimination', and give two examples.
Q2 What conditions are needed for a firm to use price discrimination?
Q3 Explain with the use of graphs:
  a) First degree price discrimination.   b) Second degree price discrimination.   c) Third degree price discrimination.

PRACTICE QUESTIONS

Exam Question

Q1 Discuss the extent to which price discrimination is beneficial to producers and consumers.   [10 marks]

Perfect price discrimination — where everything costs what it's worth (to you)...

This is tricky stuff — no doubt about it. But if you can get your head round what those graphs are showing, then you've gone a long way towards understanding why firms make use of price discrimination. Whether it's a good or bad thing overall is basically a matter of opinion — for a lot of people it would depend on what firms actually do with their increased revenue.

Oligopolies

It's useful to know about concentration ratios... so that's up first. After that, it's oligopolies all the way, so enjoy. **All boards.**

Concentration Ratios show How Dominant the big firms in a market are

1) Some industries are **dominated** by just **a few** companies (even though there may be many firms in that industry overall). These are called **concentrated markets**.

2) The **level** of domination is measured by a **concentration ratio**.
   - Suppose **three firms** control **90%** of the market, while another **40 firms** control the other **10%**.
   - The **3-firm concentration** ratio would be **90%** (i.e. the three largest firms control 90% of the market).
   - It's easy to calculate the **n-firm concentration ratio** of a market. For example, suppose a market is worth £45m and you wanted to find the **3-firm concentration ratio**. If the biggest three firms have revenues of £15m, £9m and £7m respectively, the 3-firm concentration ratio is: $\frac{(15 + 9 + 7)}{45} \times 100 = \mathbf{68.9\%}$

There are Two Ways to define an Oligopoly

1) You can define an **oligopoly** in terms of **market structure**:

   An **oligopoly** is a market:
   - that's **dominated** by just a **few** firms (i.e. a small number of firms have a high concentration ratio),
   - that has high **barriers to entry** (so new entrants can't easily **compete away** supernormal profits),
   - in which firms offer **differentiated** products (i.e. products offered by different firms will be **similar** but **not identical**).

2) Or you can define an **oligopoly** in terms of the **conduct** of firms (i.e. how they **behave**):

   An **oligopoly** is a market:
   - in which the firms are **interdependent** — i.e. the actions of **each** firm will have some kind of **effect** on the **others**,
   - in which firms use **competitive** or **collusive** strategies to make this interdependence work to their advantage.

Firms in an oligopoly can either Compete or Collude

1) Unlike with perfectly competitive markets and monopolies, there's **no single strategy** that firms in an oligopolistic market should adopt in order to **maximise profits**.

2) Firms in an oligopoly face a **choice** about what kind of **long-term strategy** they want to employ, and each company's decision will be affected by how the **other interdependent** firms in the market act.

3) This means that there are **different** possible scenarios in an oligopolistic market.

   Competitive behaviour

   This is when the various firms **don't cooperate**, but **compete** with each other (especially on **price**).

   The model of the prisoners' dilemma illustrates why these agreements sometimes break down — see p.69.

   So two different markets may both be oligopolies, but the behaviour of the firms involved in the two markets could be completely different.

   Collusive behaviour

   - This is when the various firms **cooperate** with each other, especially over what **prices** are charged.
   - **Formal collusion** involves an **agreement** between the firms — i.e. they form a **cartel**. This is usually **illegal**.
   - **Informal collusion** is **tacit** — i.e. it happens **without** any kind of agreement. This happens when each firm knows it's in their best interests **not** to compete... as long as all the other firms do the **same**.
   - Some firms in a collusive oligopoly might still be able to act as **price leaders**, setting the pattern for others to **follow** (i.e. if that firm changes its prices, other firms will do the same, so prices remain at **similar levels** to each other).

4) The behaviour that occurs depends on the characteristics of a **particular market**.

   Competitive behaviour is more likely when...
   - One firm has **lower costs** than the others.
   - There's a relatively **large number** of big firms in the market (making it harder to know what everyone else is doing).
   - The firms produce products that are **very similar**.
   - Barriers to entry are **relatively low**.

   Collusive behaviour is more likely when...
   - The firms all have **similar costs**.
   - There are **relatively few firms** in the market (so it's easier to check what other firms are charging, etc.).
   - **'Brand loyalty'** means customers are less likely to buy from a different firm, even when their prices are lower.
   - Barriers to entry are **relatively high**.

Oligopolies

Collusion can bring about similar outcomes to a Monopoly

1) **Collusive oligopolies** can produce results quite similar to those in a monopoly.

2) Collusive oligopolies generally lead to there being **higher prices** and **restricted output** (and **underconsumption**), as well as **allocative** and **productive inefficiency**. Firms in collusive oligopolies often have the **resources** to invest in more efficient production methods and achieve **dynamic efficiency**, but there's not always an **incentive** for them to do so. So collusive oligopolies can lead to **market failure**.

3) Because the firms in a collusive oligopoly **don't lower prices** even though they **could**, they make **supernormal** profits **at the expense of** consumers.

4) In the case where colluding firms have an **agreement** to restrict output to maintain high prices, the firms set a **price** (P_O) and a **level of output** (Q_O) that will **maximise profits** for the industry (i.e. where MC = MR for the industry). They then agree output **quotas** — the level of output each of the firms will produce. The resulting supernormal profits for one of these firms is shown in **red**.

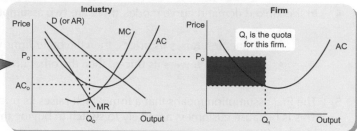

5) Firms that **collude** on **price** may still **compete** in other ways though, so the firms' **marketing policies** are very important.
   - For example, colluding firms may try to **differentiate** their products from their competitors' — either by **improving** them in some way or by trying to create a strong **brand** to attract and retain customers.
   - They could use **sales promotions** (e.g. 'loyalty' rewards for customers who make repeat purchases).
   - They may even try to find new **export markets**.

6) Other firms that try to break into the market may face **predatory pricing** tactics (see p.60 for more info). Even so, if the potential profits are large enough, they may **persevere** until they eventually establish themselves. However, they may then see that it's **not** in their interests to compete further — if so, **collusion** can re-emerge.

Oligopolies Might Not be as bad as they sound

1) Some economists argue that **collusive** oligopolies are either:
   a) **not as bad** as they're sometimes made to sound,
   b) **unstable** — i.e. they're unlikely to last for long, There's more about this 'instability' on p.69.
   c) **both** of the above.

2) They argue that **formal collusion** is quite unlikely to occur because it's usually **illegal**, and any **informal** collusion is likely to be **temporary**, because one firm will soon decide to '**cheat**', and lower its prices to gain an advantage (called **first-mover advantage** — see p.69). This kind of behaviour is likely to trigger a **price war** (and falling prices).

3) Even in a **collusive** oligopoly:
   - If firms aren't competing on **price**, then **non-price competition** might even be stronger, leading to some **dynamic efficiency**. This would be good for **consumers** if it led to product innovations and improvements.
   - Firms are **unlikely** to raise prices to **very high** levels. This is because **high prices** may provide a **strong incentive** for **new entrants** to join the market, even if the barriers to entry are high. (See p.71 for more info.)

4) **Competitive oligopolies** can achieve **high** levels of **efficiency** — these markets often work well in practice.

Warm-Up Questions

Q1 Explain the two ways you can define an oligopoly.

Q2 What is meant by formal collusion? And informal collusion?

Q3 Explain why different oligopolistic markets can produce very different outcomes.

Exam Question

Q1 Discuss the extent to which the existence of oligopolistic markets is against the interests of consumers. [10 marks]

I reckon 'Oligopoly' would be an interesting game...

Oligopolies are quite different from perfectly competitive and monopolistic markets, because there's 'more than one way to play the game and win'. This means that it's much harder to predict what's likely to happen in an oligopoly. It could work out really badly for consumers, with firms making large monopoly-style profits... or it could all turn out very differently. It'll depend on how firms think they can best further their own interests. There's more about playing the 'oligopoly game' on the next two pages.

Interdependence in Oligopolistic Markets

Interdependence makes it tricky for a firm to decide how to act, since it'll then be affected by how competing firms react. The 'models' on these pages can help you work out how firms are likely to behave. **These pages are for all boards.**

The **Kinked Demand Curve** model is used to explain **Price Stability**

1) In oligopolistic markets, each firm is affected by the behaviour of the others — the firms are **interdependent**.

2) You can understand some **outcomes** from certain oligopolistic markets by viewing the market from **each firm's perspective**.

3) For example, the model of the **kinked demand curve** illustrates why prices are often quite **stable**, even in some **competitive** oligopolies.

4) In the kinked demand curve model, there are **two assumptions**:

> - If one firm **raises** its prices, then the other firms will **not raise** theirs.
> - If one firm **lowers** its prices, then the other firms will **also lower** theirs.

5) The first assumption means that a firm which **raises** its prices will see quite a large **drop** in **demand**. This is because customers are likely to **switch** to buying their goods from **other** firms. In other words:

> When price is **increased**, demand is **price elastic**.

So it makes sense for the competing firms not to increase their prices.

This means any firm that **raises** prices will **lose out** — the **fall in demand** will more than **cancel out** the gains from charging a **higher price**.

6) The second assumption means that a firm which **lowers** its prices will **not gain** any **market share** (although the **overall size** of the market may **increase slightly**, given that **all** the firms will have lowered their prices). In other words:

> When price is **decreased**, demand is **price inelastic**.

Any competing firm not reducing its prices will lose revenue, since customers will buy elsewhere.

This means any firm that **reduces** prices will **lose out** — they **won't** gain market share but the average **price** for their products will have **fallen**.

7) The result of the above assumptions is a **kinked demand curve** — like this:

8) The outcome is that firms have **no incentive** to change prices. If they **either** raise **or** lower prices, they will **lose out** as a result.

9) The result is **price stability** for prolonged periods of time.

Note that the firms are competing here — not colluding. Each firm would reduce prices if that would help increase revenue... but it doesn't.

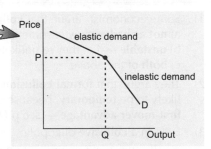

The **Kinked Demand Curve Model** describes just one possible outcome

1) The kinked demand curve model shows one type of **interdependence**.

2) This means that it **doesn't** explain the behaviour of firms in **every** oligopoly.

3) The **assumptions** in the kinked demand curve model may **not** be appropriate for every oligopoly — and if they're **not**, the model **won't** predict firms' behaviour at all well. Other oligopolistic markets will be better described using **different** models.

EDEXCEL ONLY

Game Theory can be used to understand the results of Interdependence

The behaviour of firms in oligopolistic markets can be looked at as a kind of 'mathematical game'.

> - **Game theory** is a branch of maths.
> - It's all to do with analysing situations where **two or more 'players'** (e.g. people, firms, etc.) are each trying to work out what to do to **further their own interests**.
> - The fate of each of the players depends on their **own** decisions, and the decisions of **everyone else**. So all the players are **interdependent**. This is why it's often used to analyse situations in **economics**.

Interdependence in Oligopolistic Markets

The **Prisoners' Dilemma** model can show **First-Mover Advantage**

1) The **prisoners' dilemma** model can be used to understand how **interdependent** firms might act in an oligopolistic market. In the version below there are actually **two firms** (instead of two prisoners).

- Suppose there are just **two firms** in a market, Firm A and Firm B.
- Each firm has to decide **what level of output** to produce in their oligopolistic market situation.
- For simplicity, assume that each firm has **two options**:
  - produce a **high level** of output
  - produce a **low level** of output
- Both firms **know** the **other** firm is also trying to decide what level of output to produce.
- And both firms **know** that they're **interdependent** — i.e. **both firms** will be affected by **each other's decision**.

2) The results of the firms' different choices can be summarised using a **payoff matrix**. The **coloured** figures show the profit that each firm will make for different combinations of choices.

Firm A

Firm B	Low output	High output
Low output	200 200	300 100
High output	100 300	−100 −100

For example, if Firm A outputs at a high level and Firm B outputs at a low level, then Firm A will make a profit of 300, while Firm B will make a profit of 100.

3) If the firms **cooperate** and agree to restrict output to **low levels**, then the outcome for **both** firms (a profit of 200) is **better** than if they **both** output at a **high level** (a loss of 100). This could work well for both firms... if they can **both** be **trusted**.

If they both output at a high level, they'll 'flood the market' and drive down the price until it's below the cost of production.

4) However, it's **in the interests** of each firm to stop cooperating and **raise output** — **as long as** they do this **before** the other firm decides to.

5) This is because if **one firm** decides to 'cheat' and **increase output** (to get a profit of 300), then it's actually **in the interests** of the other firm to keep producing at a **low level** and take the **reduced profit** of 100 (instead of raising output and forcing both companies to make a **loss** of 100). This is an illustration of **first-mover advantage**.

However, neither firm can be certain if (or when) the other will decide to raise output.

6) The theory of first-mover advantage shows why **cartels** can be **unstable** — every firm knows they can get an advantage if they **break** the agreement **before** anyone else does.

Being the first mover **Isn't** always an advantage

1) Being the **first mover** can give a firm an **advantage**... but it can also be a **disadvantage**.

2) **Different decisions** will make sense in **different situations** — it all depends on the numbers in the **payoff matrix** (i.e. the potential **profits** and **losses** that each firm could make in the various possible scenarios).

3) For example, suppose several firms are all deciding whether to launch a new type of product into a market.

- The 'first mover' could make a **huge profit** by winning a large market share very early.
- However, if they've **overestimated** the demand for the product, they may make **huge losses**.
- Also, competitors may be able to use a lot of the technology that the first firm has **developed**, **reducing** their **costs**, and allowing them to charge a **lower price** than the first mover.

Warm-Up Questions

Q1 Use the prisoners' dilemma to illustrate how a firm can obtain a first-mover advantage.

Exam Question

Q1 Explain how the kinked demand curve can explain price stability in some oligopolistic markets. **[15 marks]**

Unlike the prisoners, you face no dilemma — you really need to learn this...

The prisoners' dilemma gets its name because the same basic choices are usually described in terms of two prisoners who have jointly committed a serious crime. It looks so simple, but by changing the numbers in the payoff matrix you can show how all sorts of terrible outcomes (including ones that happen in real life) are actually the result of everybody acting 'sensibly'.

Monopolistic Competition

Monopolistic competition is a market structure that sits somewhere between perfect competition and monopoly.
As you might expect, it's got some of the characteristics of both structures. ***These pages are for all boards.***

Monopolistic Competition resembles a Lot of Real-life industries

1) **Monopolistic competition** (sometimes called **imperfect competition**) lies part-way along the range of market structures — between perfect competition and monopolies.

Perfect competition   Monopolistic   Oligopoly   Monopoly
competition

2) In **monopolistic competition**, the conditions of perfect competition are 'relaxed' slightly and instead become:

- Some **product differentiation** — either due to **advertising** or because of **real differences between products**.
  - This means the seller has some degree of **price-making power**.
  - So each seller's demand curve **slopes downwards**.
  - But the **smaller** the product differences, the more **price elastic** the demand for each product will be.

  Remember... if all the products were identical (as in perfect competition), a firm's demand curve would be horizontal.

- There are **either** no barriers to entry **or** only very low barriers to entry.
  - This means that if very high supernormal profits are earned, new entrants can **join** the industry fairly easily.

3) These 'relaxed' conditions are actually **more typical** of firms in **real life**. This means that the **behaviour** predicted in this model may also be more **realistic**.

The Short Run position is like a Monopoly...

In monopolistic competition, the **barriers to entry** and/or the **product differentiation** mean that **supernormal profits** can be made, but only in the **short run**.

- The **profit-maximising** level of output occurs where **MC = MR**.
- The diagram shows the **output** leading to the **profit-maximising** price (P).
- This means the firm earns **supernormal** profit.
  Here the supernormal profit is shown by the red rectangle.

  This is basically the same as for a monopoly, although because there might be similar (i.e. substitute) products available, demand is likely to be more price elastic.

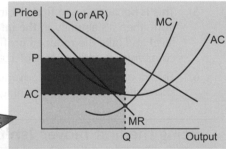

...but the Long Run position is more like Perfect Competition

1) But unlike in a monopoly, the situation shown by the above diagram **doesn't last** in the long run.

2) In monopolistic competition, the **barriers to entry** are **fairly low**, so new entrants will join the industry. These new entrants will cause the **established** firm's **demand curve** to shift to the **left** (since the overall demand is now **split** between **more** firms).

3) New entrants will **continue** to join (and the established firm's demand curve will **continue** to shift **left**) until:

- **Only normal profit** can be earned — this is where **P = AR = AC**.
  At this point the slopes of the **AC curve** and the **demand** (or **AR**) **curve** touch **tangentially** (i.e. they meet, but they don't actually cross). This is shown by the **red dot**.
- At this quantity, **MR = MC** (see the **blue dot**).

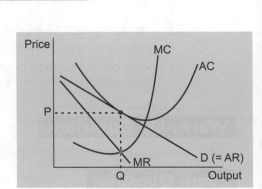

4) Since the firm is **not** producing at the **lowest point** on the AC curve, this outcome is **not productively efficient**.

5) And since the equilibrium price is **greater** than MC, this is **not allocatively efficient**.

6) But despite this, a monopolistically competitive market will generally achieve much **greater efficiency** levels than a monopoly market.

Monopolistic Competition

Prices in Monopolistic Competition are Higher than in Perfect Competition

1) The **short run** position of monopolistic competition is basically the same as in a **monopoly**. However, unlike in a monopoly, **new entrants** to the market will drive prices down until only **normal profit** is earned in the **long run**.

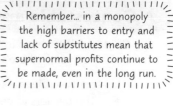 Remember... in a monopoly the high barriers to entry and lack of substitutes mean that supernormal profits continue to be made, even in the long run.

> Exactly **how long** this process takes is important.
> * If it takes a **very long** time, the market will resemble a **monopoly**.
> * But if it all happens relatively **quickly**, then the market will be more like a **perfectly competitive** market.
> * This is why firms are often willing to spend large amounts of money to try to **differentiate** their product (e.g. by **improving** it or by **advertising** to create a strong **brand**). The **longer** a firm can retain its **price-making power**, the longer it can make **supernormal** profit.

2) But unlike in **perfect competition**, in monopolistic competition the firm is **not** producing at the **lowest point** on the **AC curve**.

3) These different positions on the AC curve mean that **prices** in monopolistic competition tend to be **higher** than in **perfect competition**.

4) This is because firms in monopolistic competition need to spend money on **differentiating** their **product** (e.g. by **advertising**) and creating **brand loyalty**.

There's no need for advertising in perfect competition because consumers already have perfect knowledge. And in perfect competition, all products are identical, so there's no price differentiation.

5) Firms in monopolistic competition have also **chosen** to **restrict output** in order to **maximise profits**. This means they **don't** benefit from all the **economies of scale** that they could.

6) Prices in monopolistic competition tend to be **lower** than those charged by a **monopoly** seller.

7) Generally, monopolistic competition is felt to work **reasonably well** in practice.

Monopolistic competition **Doesn't** usually lead to **Dynamic Efficiency**

1) The length of time it takes for new entrants to force **all** firms in monopolistic competition to only make **normal profit** is the length of time an **incumbent** firm can make **supernormal profits**.

2) These supernormal profits are reward for risky **production investment** or **product innovation**.

3) However, the **lack** of barriers to entry mean that firms are unlikely to invest huge amounts of money on new innovations — so there's likely to be less **dynamic efficiency** in a monopolistically competitive market.

4) In the **long run**, the **absence** of supernormal profit will mean there **won't** be much money available for investment.

Warm-Up Questions

Q1 Describe the conditions that give rise to monopolistic competition.

Q2 Using a graph, explain:
    a) the short run position for a firm in monopolistic competition.
    b) the long run equilibrium position for a firm in monopolistic competition.

Q3 Compare price levels in monopolistic competition with price levels in:
    a) a perfectly competitive market.
    b) a monopoly.

PRACTICE QUESTIONS

Exam Question

Q1 Explain how the long run outcome in monopolistic competition differs from that in a monopoly market.   [12 marks]

Monopolistic competition does what it says on the tin...

Monopolistic competition is what the name suggests... a sort of halfway house between a monopoly and perfect competition. You don't get all the drawbacks of a monopoly (drawbacks for a consumer, that is), but you don't get all the benefits of perfect competition either. It's actually a good description of many real-life markets too, so you need to know all about it.

Contestability

*To decide whether a market is contestable, you need to think about what the market <u>could</u> be like...
not necessarily what it's like right now.* **These pages are for all boards.**

A **Contestable** market is **Open** to **New Competitors**

1) **Contestability** refers to **how open** a market is to **new competitors** (i.e. **potential** competition),
even if currently there's little **actual** competition.

> In a **contestable** market:
> * The barriers to **entry** and **exit** are **low**. So if **excess profits** are made by **incumbent** firms, new firms will enter.
> * **Supernormal** profits can **potentially** be made by new firms (at least in the short term).

2) These factors mean that incumbent firms always face the **threat** of increased competition. Increased competition is
more likely if the incumbent firms make **large supernormal** profits, as new entrants will want some of those profits.

3) This means incumbent firms have an **incentive** to set prices at a level that **won't** generate **vast** supernormal profits.

High Barriers to Entry or Exit mean Low Contestability

It's the **low barriers to entry** that make potential competition a **genuine threat** to incumbent firms.
So anything that makes barriers **higher** makes a market **less contestable**. Barriers to entry are **high** if:

1) There are **patents** on key products or production methods.
   * Patents give a firm **legal protection** against other firms **copying** its products or production methods.
2) **Advertising** by incumbent firms has already created **strong brand loyalty**.
3) There's a threat of **limit pricing** (i.e. **predatory pricing**) tactics by the incumbent firms.
   * If new entrants fear a **'price war'**, then they may decide not to enter the market.
   * This would be particularly difficult for new entrants if the incumbent firms
   had **lower costs** as a result of having been in the market for longer.
4) **Trade restrictions** are present (e.g. tariffs or quotas) — these don't allow new foreign
entrants to compete in domestic markets on equal terms with the incumbent firms.
5) Incumbent firms are **vertically integrated** (see p.52).
   * This could mean that access to supplies of **raw materials** or **distribution networks** is difficult for new firms.
6) **Sunk costs** (a barrier to exit) are high.
   * Costs are 'sunk' if they **cannot be recovered** when a firm leaves an industry.
   * These costs might include **investment** in specialised equipment, or **expenditure** on advertising.
   * If these sunk costs are high then the **cost of failure** is high, and potential
   new entrants may be **deterred** from even entering the market.

Patents can protect products and processes.

Hit-and-Run tactics can be used in contestable markets

1) The **low** barriers to **entry** and **exit** in a contestable market can mean that new entrants will '**hit and run**'.

> **Hit-and-run tactics**
> * This means **entering** a market while **supernormal profits** can be made...
> * ...and then **leaving** the market once prices have been driven down to **normal-profit** levels.

2) As long as the **profit** made while in the market is **greater** than the entry and
exit costs, it's worthwhile for a firm to compete... even for a **short time**.

Firms can reduce their sunk costs by leasing equipment rather than buying it.

The contestability of a market affects the **Behaviour** of **Incumbent Firms**

1) In a **contestable** market, it's the **threat** of increased competition (as well as the **actual** competition
from firms already in the market) that affects how incumbent firms **behave**. For example, incumbent
firms will know that high supernormal profits (which will maximise **short-term profits**) are likely to
attract **new entrants**, and that these new entrants are likely to **drive down** prices.

2) So it might make more sense for the incumbent firms to sacrifice some short-term profits, and set **lower
prices** to **avoid** attracting new entrants. This may be the best way to maximise profit in the long run.

3) **Incumbent** firms have an interest in **creating** high barriers to entry if they can.

Contestability

AQA ONLY

4) This could involve heavy spending on **advertising**, or making it clear they would be prepared to engage in **predatory pricing** if new firms entered the market. (Though firms have to be careful not to break any laws on predatory pricing.)

5) But in the **long run**, firms in contestable markets will move towards **productive** and **allocative efficiency**, because supernormal profit is **competed away** and firms must settle for **normal profit**.

Technological Change can have a Big Impact on a Market's Structure

1) Barriers to entry to an industry are **not** fixed for all time. **Technological change** can **raise** or **lower** barriers to entry.

2) **Technological change** occurs through **invention** and **innovation**, e.g. the invention of **new products** and **services**, or **new production methods**.

3) Technological change can have an **impact** on:
   - the **structure** of a **market** (see 'creative destruction' below),
   - **production methods**, e.g. the machinery used to produce goods,
   - the **consumption** of **goods** and **services**, e.g. e-books have changed the way books are consumed.

Invention is making something new. *Innovation* is changing a product or process that already exists.

4) **Invention** and **innovation** can lead to:
   - improvements in **capital equipment** (e.g. factories, roads), leading to **improvements** in the **quality** of **goods** produced,
   - **barriers to entry** (see p.72) being **reduced** or **increased** — for example, **cheaper production methods** may **reduce** barriers to entry into a market, but **increases** in the **levels** of **capital** required to produce the latest products may **increase** barriers to entry,
   - a level of **monopoly power** (see p.62) for the **first firm** which utilises the new invention or innovation,
   - improvements in **labour productivity** and **efficiency**, e.g. due to more effective machinery,
   - **larger economies of scale**.

New Technology can also lead to Creative Destruction

1) **Creative destruction** is an **important process** in market economies. It's the idea that markets are **constantly evolving** and **changing** due to **innovation** and the **invention** of new products and production methods. This can even lead to the **destruction** of **existing markets** and the **creation** of **new ones**.

2) The destruction of existing markets causes **job losses**, but in the long run, **new jobs** will be **created** in the **new markets** and society benefits from the **improvement** of goods and services.

3) **Technological change** is likely to lead to creative destruction. A new or incumbent firm may develop a good or service that's **much better** than the **existing one**, and this can **alter** the market's **structure**.

For example, the development of the **railways** in Britain during the **19th century** meant that firms began to **transport freight** by rail rather than by canal — **destroying** the **monopoly power** of the **canal owners**. In turn, the development of **motorways** and **lorries** destroyed the monopoly power that the railway owners had gained over the transport of freight.

For technological change to lead to creative destruction it needs to cause a significant change to a market, not just a tweak to an existing product.

4) In this way, technological change can lead to firms being **put out of business**. Even big firms that **seem** unchallengeable are **vulnerable** to changes in technology, as innovative new entrants will be **attracted** to markets where **large supernormal profits** are being made. However, this means large incumbent firms also have an **incentive** to keep inventing and innovating (which is **good for consumers**) to keep barriers to entry high.

Warm-Up Questions

Q1 What does contestability mean? What are the characteristics of a contestable market?

Q2 What are sunk costs? Why do high sunk costs make a market less contestable?

Q3 Describe one way in which incumbent firms can create barriers to entry in an industry.

PRACTICE QUESTIONS

Exam Questions

Q1 Discuss the effect of high contestability on the behaviour of incumbent firms. [10 marks]

Q2 How might technological change affect the barriers to entry of a market? [6 marks]

A contestable market is open for businesses...

Some people think that a market's contestability is more important than its actual structure. They say that just the _threat_ of new competition is enough to make people act as though the competition _already exists_. Right, that's this section ticked off. Bye!

Externalities

The price mechanism isn't perfect — this section shows you how markets fail and what governments do to try to stop this happening. Externalities are an important cause of market failure, so you need to learn about them really well. **For all boards.**

AQA ONLY

Market Failure occurs when a market Allocates Resources Inefficiently

1) A market **fails** when the **price mechanism** (i.e. the forces of supply and demand)
   fails to allocate scarce resources **efficiently** and **society suffers** as a result.

2) Market failure is a **common problem** and **governments** often **intervene** to try to prevent it (see p.86-97).

Market failure can be Complete or Partial

1) When there's **complete** market failure, **no market exists** — this is called a **'missing market'**.

2) **National defence** is an example of a **missing market** as there's **no market** which allocates national defence. This means that **governments** need to intervene and provide it.

3) When the market functions, but either the **price** or **quantity supplied** of the good/service is **wrong**, then there's **partial failure**.

4) The provision of **health care**, if left completely to market forces, is an example of **partial failure**. If health care was left to market forces, then some people **wouldn't** be able to **afford** the treatment they needed. As a result, **governments** might **intervene** and provide **free** health care.

Externalities affect Third Parties

1) **Externalities** are the effects that producing or consuming a good/service has on people who **aren't** involved in the making, buying/selling and consumption of the good/service. These people are often called **'third parties'**.

2) Externalities can either be **positive** or **negative**. **Positive externalities** are the **external benefits** to a third party and **negative externalities** are the **external costs** to a third party.

3) Externalities can occur in **production** or **consumption**. For example:

- A **negative externality** of producing steel could be **pollution** that harms the local environment.

- A **positive externality** of producing military equipment could be an **improvement** in **technology** that benefits society.

- A **negative externality** of consuming a chocolate bar could be **litter** that's dropped on the street.

- A **positive externality** of someone training to become a **doctor** (remember — the training is being **consumed**) could be the **benefit** to **society** that this brings.

Market Failure occurs because Externalities are Ignored

1) A **private cost** is the **cost of doing something** to either a consumer or a firm. For example, the cost a firm pays to make a good is its private cost and the price a consumer pays to buy the good is their private cost.

2) **External costs** are caused by **externalities**, e.g. if you dropped an empty crisp packet then that creates an **external cost** to the council who have to employ someone to sweep it up.

3) **Adding** the **private cost** to the **external cost** gives the **social cost**. The social cost is the **full cost** borne by **society** of a good or service.

4) A **private benefit** is the **benefit gained** by a consumer or a firm by doing something. For example, the private benefit a consumer might get from purchasing a skiing holiday is their enjoyment of the experience.

5) **External benefits** are also caused by **externalities**, e.g. a factory that **invests** in new equipment may create the **external benefit** of needing less electricity, which reduces its impact on the climate.

6) **Adding** the **private benefit** to the **external benefit** gives the **social benefit**. The social benefit is the **full benefit** received by **society** from a good or service.

7) **Market failure** occurs because in a free market the price mechanism will only take into account the **private costs** and **benefits**, but **not** the **external costs** and **benefits**.

Externalities

Externalities can be shown using Diagrams

1) Here's an example of **negative externalities** from **production**.

2) The **marginal private cost** (**MPC**) is the cost of **producing** the **last unit** of a good.

3) The **marginal social cost** (**MSC**) = the **marginal private cost** + the **external cost**.

4) So, the **difference** between the **MPC** and the **MSC curves** is the **external cost** of production — the **negative externalities**.

5) If the **MPC** and **MSC curves** are **parallel** then external costs per unit produced are **constant**. If the curves **diverge** then external costs per unit increase with output.

6) An example of why the curves might diverge is **pollution** — the **external costs** per unit created by pollution can **increase** as output increases.

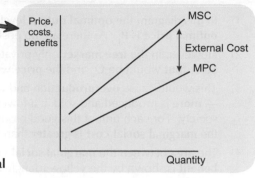

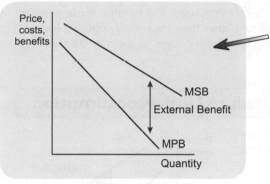

7) Here's an example of **positive externalities** from **consumption**.

8) The **marginal private benefit** (**MPB**) is the benefit to someone of **consuming** the **last unit** of a good.

9) The **marginal social benefit** (**MSB**) = the **marginal private benefit** + the **external benefit**.

10) The **difference** between the **MPB** and the **MSB** curves are the **external benefits** — the **positive externalities**.

11) Again, if the **MPB** and **MSB curves** are **parallel** then external benefits per unit are **constant**. If they **diverge** then external benefits per unit increase with output.

12) An example of when the curves might diverge is **vaccination** — the more people that are vaccinated, the **greater** the **protection** for **unvaccinated** people.

The Equilibrium Point may be Different to the Socially Optimal Point

1) When **supply** and **demand** are equal there's **equilibrium** in the free market.

2) In a free market consumers and producers only consider their **private costs** and **private benefits** — they **ignore** any **social costs** or **benefits**. As a result, the **MPC** curve can be seen as the **supply curve** of a good or service and the **MPB** curve can be seen as the **demand curve**.

3) So, **equilibrium** occurs when **MPC = MPB**. On the diagram this is where output is Q_e and price is P_e.

4) However, the **socially optimum level** of output is where **MSC = MSB**, because this includes the **external costs** and **benefits** to society.

5) This means that the **socially optimum level** of **output** is Q_1 and the **socially optimal price** is P_1. This level of output and price will give society the **maximum** benefit of any **positive externalities** and still cover the cost of any **negative externalities**.

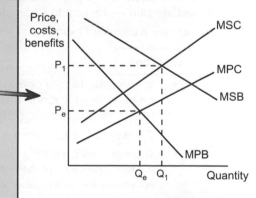

Warm-Up Questions

Q1 What are private costs?

Q2 On an externality diagram, where is the socially optimal level of output?

PRACTICE QUESTIONS

Exam Question

Q1 Use a diagram to explain why the socially optimal level of output might be different to the output at the equilibrium point.

[6 marks]

Socially optimal point — when all your friends think you're cool...

You've got to learn these diagrams for negative and positive externalities — it's very likely that they'll come up in the exam and you may even need to draw one. So it's worth spending a bit of time practising how to make one. Don't forget to label it.

Externalities

Right, so let's get down to some examples of all this. **For all boards.**

Ignoring **Negative Production Externalities** leads to **Overproduction**

1) In this diagram the **optimal output level** of this good is Q_1 and the **optimal price** is P_1. As there are no positive externalities, MPB = MSB.

2) However, in the **free market** only private costs are considered. So **output** would be Q_e and the **price** would be P_e.

3) This would cause **overproduction** and **underpricing** of this good — **more** is produced and sold at a **lower** price than is **desirable** for society. For each unit of this good produced between Q_1 and Q_e the **marginal social cost** is **greater** than the **marginal social benefit**.

4) The **area** between the **marginal social cost** and **marginal social benefit** is shown by the yellow triangle **ABC**. This is the area of **welfare loss** — the loss to society caused by **ignoring externalities**.

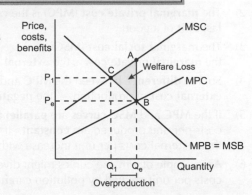

> **A chemical factory** may **ignore** the **externalities** it produces, such as the release of harmful waste gases into the atmosphere. If this happens then **output** from the factory will be **higher** than the **socially optimal level** (where MSC = MSB) and that will lead to a **welfare loss** to society (e.g. problems caused by the harmful waste gases).

Ignoring **Positive Consumption Externalities** leads to **Underconsumption**

1) In this diagram the **optimal level** of **output** for this good is Q_1 and the **optimal price** is P_1. As there are no negative externalities, MPC = MSC.

2) In the free market only **private benefits** are considered. So **output** would be Q_e and the **price** would be P_e.

3) This would cause **underconsumption** and **underpricing** of this good — **less** is consumed and sold at a **lower** price than is **desirable** for society. For each unit of this good consumed between Q_e and Q_1 the **marginal social benefit** is **greater** than the **marginal social cost**.

4) The **area** between the **marginal social benefit** and **marginal social cost** is shown by the green triangle **DEF**. This is the area of potential **welfare gain** — the gain to society **lost** by **ignoring externalities**.

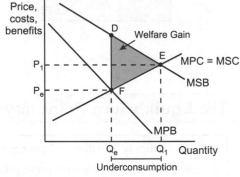

5) Here are a couple of examples of services with **positive consumption externalities**:

Education:

- In a **free market** the **positive externalities** of **education** will be **ignored** by suppliers of education. Their choices are based on **profit maximisation**.

- The positive externalities will also be ignored by **students/parents**, who will **only** consider the **benefits** to **themselves/their children** — e.g. that a good education will help someone get a better/higher-paid job.

- There are many positive externalities of education — for example, the better educated the workforce the **more productive** they are, which in turn **increases** a **country's output**. Furthermore, increasing education levels has other **social benefits** such as reduced crime levels and a happier population.

Health care:

- In the **free market**, **providers** and **consumers** of **health care** will only consider the **private costs** and **benefits**. The decisions they make will **ignore** any **positive externalities**.

- There are many positive externalities of health care — for example, a healthier workforce will be **more productive** and take less time off work, which will in turn **increase** a country's **economic output**. There are also **social benefits** to receiving health care — for example, society as a whole will benefit if people have an improved sense of personal well-being and increased life expectancy.

6) In the free market, both of these services are **underconsumed** and **potential welfare gain** to society is **lost**.

Externalities

Ignoring **Negative Consumption Externalities** leads to **Overconsumption** ⟵

1) In this diagram the **optimal level** of **output** for this good is Q_1 and the **optimal price** is P_1 (assuming MPC = MSC). The marginal private benefit is **larger** than the marginal social benefit.

2) In the free market only **private benefits** are considered. So **output** would be Q_e and **price** would be P_e.

3) This would cause **overconsumption** and **overpricing** of this good — **more** is consumed and sold at a **higher** price than is **desirable** for society. For each unit of this good consumed between Q_1 and Q_e the **marginal social cost** is **greater** than the **marginal social benefit**.

4) The **area** between the **marginal social cost** and **marginal social benefit** is shown by the yellow triangle **KLM**. This is the area of **welfare loss** — the loss to society caused by **ignoring externalities**.

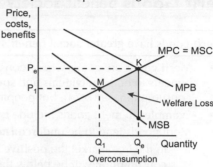

Example | Drivers will **ignore** the **negative consumption externalities** associated with driving their cars, such as pollution and congestion. This will result in the usage of cars being **higher** than the **socially optimal level**, causing a welfare loss to society (e.g. traffic jams reducing the productivity of workers).

Ignoring **Positive Production Externalities** leads to **Underproduction** ⟵

1) In this diagram the **optimal level** of **output** for this good is Q_1 and the **optimal price** is P_1 (assuming MPB = MSB). The marginal private cost is larger than the marginal social cost.

2) In the free market only **private costs** are considered. So **output** would be Q_e and **price** would be P_e.

3) This would cause **underproduction** and **overpricing** of this good — **less** is produced and sold at a **higher** price than is **desirable** for society. For each unit of this good consumed between Q_e and Q_1 the **marginal social cost** is **lower** than the **marginal social benefit**.

4) The **area** between the **marginal social cost** and **marginal social benefit** is shown by the green triangle **PQR**. This is the area of potential **welfare gain** — the gain to society lost by **ignoring externalities**.

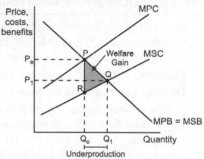

Example | Employers will **ignore** the **positive production externalities** associated with paying to **train** their employees, such as the benefit to society of having a more highly skilled workforce. This means resources **won't** be allocated to training employees to the **socially optimal level**, causing a **potential welfare gain** to society to be **lost**.

A lack of **Property Rights** can cause **Negative Externalities** ⟵

1) The **absence** of **property rights** can result in **production** and **consumption externalities**, and **market failure**. For example, a factory that emits waste water into a nearby river wouldn't be held accountable for this pollution if no one had property rights over the river and took responsibility for it.

2) **Extending property rights** would mean that these externalities could be **accounted for**. For example, a water company with property rights over a river can allow, charge for, or refuse permission for others to pollute the river. (For more on the extension of property rights, see page 96.)

3) The absence of property rights generally leads to the **overuse** (or **misuse**) of **scarce resources**, and **environmental damage**.

Warm-Up Questions

Q1 Give an example of a negative production externality.

Q2 What will happen if the positive production externalities of staff training are ignored?

PRACTICE QUESTIONS

Exam Question

Q1 Use a diagram to show how the underconsumption of education in the free market leads to the loss of a potential welfare gain to society.

[12 marks]

Unlike the free market — don't ignore externalities...

... you can pretty well guarantee they'll pop up at some point in the exam. Externalities are 'the' classic reason for market failure, so you'll need to know them well and be able to reproduce the diagrams from memory. So get practising.

Merit and Demerit Goods

Classifying merit and demerit goods involves looking at the social and private benefits and costs. Some things are pretty universally agreed on, but a lot of it comes down to judgement. ***These pages are for AQA and OCR only.***

Merit Goods benefit society but Demerit Goods do the opposite

Merit goods have greater social benefits than private benefits

- **Merit goods** are goods whose consumption is regarded as being **beneficial** to **society**. They provide benefits to both **individuals** and **society** as a whole (due to the **positive externalities** that result from their consumption, see p.74), but people are usually **unaware** of the **full benefits** that merit goods provide.
- **Examples** of merit goods include **health care** and **education**.
- Merit goods tend to be **underconsumed** for two main reasons:
  - i) In the free market the **positive externalities** that merit goods provide are **ignored**, and **production** and **consumption** will be **below** the **socially optimal level**. For example, producers and consumers **won't** consider the **wider benefits** to society of a **good education**, such as having a **more productive workforce**.
  - ii) Due to **imperfect information** (see p.82 for more), consumers **don't always realise** the **full benefits** that merit goods provide. For example, people might not have enough information on how serious their **health problems** might be, so their **demand** for health care **isn't as high** as it should be and health care is **underprovided**.
- Not all merit goods will be welcomed by all potential consumers, and they can be **rejected** — for example, the offer of free vaccinations may be refused.

Demerit goods have greater social costs than private costs

- **Demerit goods** are goods whose consumption is regarded as being **harmful** to the people that consume them, but people are usually **unaware** (or **don't care**) about the harm that the demerit goods can cause. Demerit goods also have a **harmful effect** on **society** due to the **negative externalities** that result from their consumption, see p.74.
- **Examples** of demerit goods are **cigarettes** and **heroin**.
- Demerit goods tend to be **overconsumed** for two main reasons:
  - i) In the free market the **negative externalities** that demerit goods cause are **ignored**, and **production** and **consumption** will be **above** the **socially optimal level**. For example, producers and consumers **won't** consider the **wider disadvantages** to society of **cigarettes**, such as smoking-related health issues putting a strain on health care services.
  - ii) Due to **imperfect information**, consumers **don't always realise** the **harm** that demerit goods cause. For example, people might not have enough information on how a **harmful drug** might affect their health, so their **demand** for the drug is **higher** than it should be and the drug is **overprovided**.

1) Sometimes it's **hard to say** which goods should be classified as merit or demerit goods. Whether a good fits into one of these classifications is usually a **value judgement** — based on people's **opinions** and not on **economic theory** or **facts**.

2) For example, some people consider **contraception** to be a **merit** good, but **others** don't.

3) **Not all** goods with **positive externalities** are merit goods, e.g. planting flowers in a garden may have positive externalities, such as providing pollen for bees or an attractive sight for passers-by, but flower seeds are unlikely to be seen as merit goods whose consumption should be encouraged for the benefit of society.

4) **Not all** goods with **negative externalities** are demerit goods, e.g. driving a car can cause negative externalities (like pollution), but driving a car isn't seen as being harmful to an individual in the way that taking a drug might be.

The market Underprovides merit goods and Overprovides demerit goods

Merit goods generate Positive Externalities

1) If it's left to the free market then price and quantity demanded of a merit good will be at P_e and Q_e respectively, where the MPB curve **crosses** the MPC/MSC curve. The **market equilibrium** is below the **socially optimal** level of consumption (Q_1) — where MSC = MSB.

2) The area **ABC** is the potential welfare gain **lost** by underconsuming/underproducing the merit good.

3) To increase consumption to the socially optimal level of Q_1 the government could introduce a **subsidy** (see p.88) to bring the price down to P_2.

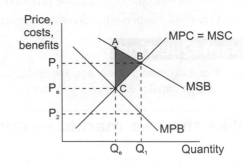

Merit and Demerit Goods

Demerit goods generate Negative Externalities

1) Again, if it's left to the free market then the price and quantity demanded of a demerit good will be at P_e and Q_e respectively, where the MPC/MSC and the MPB curves cross. The **market equilibrium** is above the **socially optimal** level of consumption at Q_1 — where MSC = MSB.

2) The area **DEF** is the **welfare loss** caused by overconsuming/overproducing the demerit good.

3) To decrease consumption to the socially optimal level of Q_1 the government could introduce a **tax** (see p.86-87) to bring the price up to P_2.

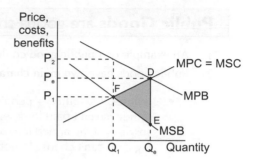

Short-term decision-making can affect the Consumption of goods

When individuals take a **short-term** approach to decision-making, it can lead to the **underconsumption** of **merit** goods and the **overconsumption** of **demerit** goods.

1) People **often** only consider the **short-term benefits** or **costs**. Individuals can **fail** to see the need to make **provision** for the **future** and for **potential changes** in their circumstances. A good example of this is paying into an old-age pension.

2) The **long-term** private benefits of **merit goods** are **greater** than their **short-term** private benefits and the **long-term** private costs of **demerit goods** are **greater** than their **short-term** private costs.

3) The **short-term benefits** of paying towards a pension (knowledge that you are saving for your old age) are **less** than the benefits of **receiving** that pension when you retire.

4) The **short-term costs** of buying cigarettes are much **less** than the **long-term** costs, e.g. serious smoking-related illness.

Go on... just think about the short-term benefit.

Governments can Intervene in markets for merit and demerit goods

1) The **failure** of the free market to supply the **socially optimal levels** of merit and demerit goods is the **main reason** why governments **intervene** to affect their supply. Governments can **directly provide** certain goods or services (see p.91) or they can uses **taxes** and **subsidies** (see p.86-88) to decrease or increase consumption of certain goods or services to the **socially optimal level**.

2) Governments have **a lot of information** regarding the **costs** and **benefits** of goods/services to both individuals and society as a whole, and can **use** this information to make decisions that benefit the whole of society.

Warm-Up Questions

Q1 What is a merit good and why does the consideration of merit goods involve value judgements?

Q2 How can imperfect information affect the supply of demerit goods?

Exam Question

Q1 Explain why a free market will underprovide merit goods. [6 marks]

The optimal level of fake tan consumption is 'just' before orange...

It can be tricky to get your head around these concepts, so make sure you take the time to do so. The key thing to remember is that for merit goods social benefits exceed private benefits and for demerit goods the private costs are less than the social costs.

Public Goods

The under-provision of public goods is an important example of market failure and it's one of the main reasons for government intervention to correct market failure. **These pages are for all boards.**

Public Goods are goods that are consumed Collectively

1) An example of a **public good** could be a flood defence scheme or street lighting.

2) Public goods have **two main characteristics**:

- **Non-excludability** — people **cannot** be **stopped** from consuming the good even if they **haven't** paid for it, e.g. you couldn't stop an individual benefiting from the services of the armed forces. (Public goods are also said to be **non-rejectable**, e.g. you can't choose to not be protected by the armed forces — they'll do it anyway.)

  - **Non-rivalry/non-diminishability** — **one person** benefiting from the good **doesn't** stop **others** also benefiting, e.g. more people benefiting from flood defences doesn't reduce the benefit to the first person to benefit. This means that public goods have **zero marginal cost** — there's no additional cost to extending the good to one more person.

3) Some other examples of public goods include **firework displays** and **lighthouses**.

Private Goods are the Opposite of public goods

1) **Private goods** are **excludable** (you can stop someone consuming them) and they **exhibit rivalry**.

2) For example, biscuits are a private good — if you eat a biscuit you **stop** anyone else from eating it.

3) Unlike public goods, people have a **choice** as to whether to consume private goods — biscuits can be rejected.

4) **Most** goods are private goods — anything from **bread** to a **university education**.

This is roughly what it looks like when goods exhibit rivalry.

Some Public Goods can take on the Characteristics of Private Goods

1) Some goods are **pure public goods**, e.g. lighthouses. Others can exhibit the characteristics of a public good — but **not fully**. These are known as **non-pure** (or **quasi**) **public goods**.

> For example, **roads** appear to have the characteristics of a public good — often they're **free** for everyone to use (non-excludable) and one person using a road **doesn't prevent** another person from using it too (non-rivalrous). However, **tolls** can make a road **excludable** by excluding those who don't pay to use the road, and **congestion** will make a road exhibit **rivalry** as there's a limit to the number of people who can benefit from the road at any one time.

2) **New technology** can **change** a good that once had the characteristics of a **public** good into a **private** good.

> For example, 'analogue' television broadcasting has some characteristics of a **public good** — if you own a TV and an aerial then TV broadcasts are **non-rivalrous** and **non-excludable**. However, the **invention** of **digital technology** has meant that channels can be **encrypted** to ensure that if people want a certain channel, they have to **pay for it**.

Public Goods

Public Goods are Under-provided by the free market

1) The **non-excludability** of public goods leads to what's called the **free rider problem**.

2) The free rider problem means that once a public good is provided it's **impossible** to **stop** someone from **benefiting** from it, even if they **haven't** paid towards it. For example, a firm providing street cleaning **cannot** stop a free rider, who has **refused** to pay for street cleaning, **benefiting** from a clean street.

3) The **price mechanism cannot** work if there are free riders. Consumers **won't** choose to pay for a public good that they can get for free because other consumers have paid for it.

4) If everyone decides to **wait and see** who will provide and pay for a public good, then it **won't** be provided.

5) It's also **difficult** to set a **price** for public goods because it's **difficult** to **work out** their **value** to consumers.

6) **Producers** will tend to **overvalue** the benefits of a public good in order to **increase** the **price** that they charge. **Consumers** will **undervalue** their benefits to try to get a **lower price**.

7) These problems mean that firms are **reluctant** to supply public goods, and the problems will cause **market failure**. As a result, governments will usually have to intervene to provide the public good (see p.91).

> **Positive externalities** are a form of public good. They're consumed by those who **don't** pay for them, so they're an example of the **free rider problem**.

AQA students — No market exists for externalities, so they're an example of a missing market.

Some Parts of the Environment are Public Goods

1) Parts of the environment are often considered to have the characteristics of **public goods**. For example, the air is a **public good** which **isn't** bought or sold on a market — it's **non-excludable** and **non-rivalrous**.

2) Both **clean air** and **dirty, polluted air cost** the **same** (i.e. nothing) — so if clean air becomes **scarce** (as a result of pollution) its price **won't rise** and **deter** people from 'using it up' (e.g. by polluting it).

3) The non-excludability of clean air leads to the **free rider problem**. The **benefits** of **not polluting** the air, or **cleaning** the air afterwards, **aren't restricted** to those who have 'paid' for the clean air by choosing **not** to pollute, or choosing to **clean** the air. Therefore, in the free market, it's **unlikely** that anyone will either choose not to pollute, or to clean up the pollution they make.

4) This is an example of the economic theory known as the **tragedy of the commons** — the idea that people acting in their **own best interests** will overuse a **common resource** without considering that this will lead to the **depletion** or **degradation** of that resource.

Resource depletion is the reduction of available natural resources due to their overuse. Resource degradation occurs when natural resources are made less productive by human activity. For example, if land is farmed intensively the soil may become less fertile, which means crops won't grow as well.

5) The tragedy of the commons can explain a lot of the **causes** of **environmental market failure**. **Governments** will usually have to **intervene** to prevent the destruction and degradation of common resources, e.g. through **taxation** or **subsidies**, **legislation** or **government spending**.

Warm-Up Questions

Q1 What does non-excludability mean?

Q2 What does non-rivalry mean?

Q3 Briefly explain what is meant by the free rider problem.

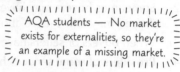

PRACTICE QUESTIONS

Exam Question

Q1 Which of the following reasons explains why is it unlikely that there will be a market-provided flood defence system for an area prone to flooding?
A) There is insufficient knowledge to build an adequate flood defence system.
B) Flooding is important for farming.
C) Individuals may be charged for their usage of the flood defence system.
D) The existence of the free rider problem.

[1 mark]

Free riders — a big problem for waves in Australia, California, Newquay...

The difference between public goods and private goods is straightforward and it's easy to see why market failure is caused by people not paying for public goods. If it's left to the market, no one would put up street lamps or provide flood defences.

Imperfect Information

Perfect information will hardly ever actually exist. Unsurprisingly, this leads to another example of market failure. **For all boards.**

Symmetric Information means Everyone has Equal and Perfect Knowledge

1) In a **competitive market** it's assumed that there's **perfect information**. That means that **buyers** and **sellers** are assumed to have **full** knowledge regarding **prices**, **costs**, **benefits** and **availability** of products.

2) **Perfect** information which is **equally** available to **all** participants in a market is known as **symmetric information**.

3) Assuming that buyers and sellers are **rational** in their behaviour, this symmetric information will allow the **efficient allocation** of resources in and between markets. However, symmetric information **rarely** exists, e.g. **buyers** often don't have the **time** or **resources** to obtain full information on prices before **buying** a product.

Asymmetric Information involves a Lack of Perfect Information in a market

1) Usually **sellers** have **more** information on a product than **buyers**. For example, a used car salesman will have more information about the history of a car they're selling than a prospective buyer.

2) Sometimes **buyers** may have more information than **sellers**. For example, an antiques collector (buyer) may know more about the value of an antique than the person selling it.

3) When **buyers** or **sellers** have **more information** this is known as **asymmetric information**, and information is **imperfect**.

4) **Providers** of **some** services have a lack of information because the thing they provide a service for is **unpredictable**, e.g. health service providers don't know **when** someone will become ill and with **what** health problem.

5) **Moral hazard** is another possible result of asymmetric information. This happens when people take **risks** because they won't suffer the **consequences** themselves if things go wrong. For example, an individual could buy **home insurance**, but then behave **recklessly** (for example not locking their doors), safe in the knowledge that they're covered. This can happen because the insurance provider **lacks information** about how the individual is acting.

Information Failure causes Market Failure

1) **Imperfect information** means that **merit** goods (e.g. education, health care and pensions) are **underconsumed** and **demerit** goods (e.g. tobacco and alcohol) are **overconsumed** (for more on merit and demerit goods see p.78-79). There are many reasons why **imperfect information** affects the **consumption** of merit and demerit goods, for example:

   - Consumers may not know the **full personal benefit** of a merit good. They may not realise that a good education could lead to improved future earnings, or that a regular medical check-up might improve their lifespan.
   - Consumers may **lack** the **information** to decide which good or service is right for them.
   - Consumers may not have the information on how **harmful** a demerit good, such as alcohol, can be.
   - **Advertising** for a demerit good may withhold or 'gloss over' any health dangers.

2) Due to **information failure**, merit goods tend to be **underprovided** and demerit goods are **overprovided**, causing a **misallocation of resources** and **market failure**. There are many reasons why **imperfect information** affects the **provision** of merit and demerit goods, for example:

   - Pension providers have a greater knowledge of the pension schemes available than their clients — this can lead to them selling unnecessary schemes or more expensive schemes than may be needed.
   - Doctors have a greater knowledge of medicine — they may persuade their clients to purchase more expensive care than is required.
   - Information on a good/service may be too complex to understand, e.g. the technical differences between computers may be confusing to a consumer, so they might struggle to work out which is best for their needs.

Warm-Up Questions

Q1 What is symmetric information?
Q2 What is asymmetric information?

Exam Question

Q1 Describe how imperfect information can lead to the overprovision of a demerit good. [4 marks]

You won't find imperfect information in this book...

Don't get confused by all the different names on this page. Make sure you get your head around what perfect information is — when it exists there's symmetric information in a market and when it doesn't there's usually asymmetric information.

Inequity

Equity is another word for fairness, so inequity means 'unfairness'. Some people think that big differences in income and wealth between people is unfair and that this is an example of a market failure. **This page is for AQA and OCR.**

Consumption by an Individual depends on Wealth and Income

1) **Income** is the amount of money received over a **set** period of time, e.g. per week or per year.
2) Income can come from **many sources** — e.g. **wages**, **interest** on bank accounts, **dividends** from shares and **rents** from properties.
3) Wealth is the **value** in money of **assets** held — **assets** can **include** property, land, money and shares.
4) The **greater** an individual's income and wealth, the **more** goods and services they're **able** to purchase.

Income and Wealth are not distributed Equally in a market economy

1) Many people view **differences** in income and wealth as **unfair**, especially if they're **significant**.
2) In economies with **high** levels of **inequality** of income and wealth distribution (e.g. Sierra Leone), there can be people who are **starving** whilst others have **very high** levels of income and wealth.
3) Inequality is **caused** by several things, such as **wage differentials** (see p.106), **discrimination** (see p.110-111) and **regressive taxes** (see p.169). Generally speaking, people who are **born** into a **poor family** will **remain poor** because they **won't** have the **income and wealth needed** to **improve** their **situation**.
4) This is because inequality can lead to **differences** in **access** to **resources**. For example, people with **very low** income or wealth may **not** be able to **afford** vital resources and services, such as **education**. As a result, a lack of education may well mean these people will **continue** to have low income or wealth as they will struggle to get a good job. People with higher income and wealth will be able to afford the **best education**, and improve their prospects of high income in future.

   This market failure is 'normative' — it's based on opinion, not fact.

5) Some economists argue that the **unequal** distribution of income and wealth is a **consequence** of **market failure**, because the free market has led to this **inequitable** (unfair) distribution of income and wealth. As a result, they say that **redistribution** of income and wealth would lead to an **allocation** of **resources** that would **increase** the benefit to society, and society's **overall** 'happiness'.
6) The argument for this is that the **benefit** to a poor person from an **additional** £1 of income would be **greater** than the **loss** to a rich person who paid £1 extra in tax.
7) Inequality is also a **cause** of **market failure**. If, for example, some people **don't** have the income and wealth to be able to pay for things that they **need** (such as merit goods, like education), then resources **won't** be **allocated efficiently**.

Governments might try to Distribute income and wealth more Equally

1) Correcting this market failure requires **government intervention** — see p.167 for some examples.
2) The level of redistribution undertaken by governments is a **political decision** based on **value judgements** — it's up to them how much they redistribute income and wealth.
3) Some people argue that redistributing income **reduces** the **incentive** for individuals and firms to work hard. These incentives are needed to encourage **efficiency** within the market, and not having them may cause **greater market failure**.

Warm-Up Questions

Q1 What is income?
Q2 What is wealth?
Q3 Why might the redistribution of income and wealth be considered as undesirable?

PRACTICE QUESTIONS

Exam Question

Q1 Explain why the unequal distribution of income and wealth is considered a market failure. [4 marks]

I'd love it if the government would distribute some more income my way...

This market failure is more opinion-based than the others — not everyone agrees that inequality of income and wealth is a market failure. Whether you agree or not, you need to know why a government may act to redistribute income and wealth.

Immobile Factors of Production

*Hang in there — just a few more pages on market failure to go. Immobile factors aren't just things which can't physically move — they also include things such as an individual with little training or education. **This page is for AQA only.***

Factors of Production can be Immobile

1) An **immobile** factor of production is one that can't easily be **moved** to another area of the economy.

2) **Land** is an immobile factor of production — it cannot be moved from one location to another. **Land** can also be immobile because, for example, it may only be good for **one type** of agriculture (e.g. land on which rice is grown may not be suitable for growing wheat).

3) A lot of **capital** is **mobile** (e.g. computers) — it can be moved from one location to another, but some is **immobile** because of its **size** (e.g. a steel foundry) or its **specialist nature** (e.g. a nuclear reactor).

4) Land and capital can become immobile by **human action** — e.g. a farmer may **choose** not to change the crops he grows on his land **despite** changes in climate.

Labour Immobility can be Geographical or Occupational

Labour is mobile if workers are able to move from one job to another — this movement could be between **occupations** or between **geographical areas**. However, there are several reasons why labour can be immobile:

Reasons for geographical immobility:

- **Large** house-price, rent and cost-of-living differences **between** areas can make it **very difficult** for workers to **move location** to obtain work.
- There may also be **high costs** involved in **moving** houses.
- A **reluctance** to leave family and friends.
- A **dislike** of change.
- **Imperfect information** about the jobs **available** in different areas.

The most significant factor in the UK affecting geographical mobility is the high house prices in the South-East — the area of highest employment opportunities.

Reasons for occupational immobility:

- Lack of **training**, **education** and **skills** required to do a **different job**.
- Lack of **required** qualifications or **required** membership of a professional body (e.g. doctors have to be **registered** with the General Medical Council).
- Lack of **work experience**.

Occupational immobility will cause structural unemployment (see p.150).

Immobile Factors of Production cause Market Failure

1) Immobile factors of production mean there's often **inefficient** use of **resources** — resources are often **unused** or **underused**. This **inefficiency** in the **allocation** of resources means there's **market failure**.

2) There's a limit to how much a **government** can tackle immobile factors of production. Governments can't **move land** and most of them can't **force workers** to **relocate**.

3) However, governments can take some action to **improve labour mobility**. For example:
- To improve **geographical** mobility governments could offer **relocation subsidies** or **mortgage relief** to make moving to a particular area **more affordable** for workers. Governments could also offer incentives to **encourage** the **construction** of housing in areas where it's needed to provide homes for workers.
- To improve **occupational** mobility governments could provide more **training programmes** to increase people's skills.

Warm-Up Questions

Q1 Give three examples of immobile factors of production.
Q2 What are the two types of labour immobility?

PRACTICE QUESTIONS

Exam Question

Q1 How can immobile factors of production lead to market failure? [4 marks]

A traffic light — a good example of a geographically immobile worker...

The stuff on this page isn't too complicated — some things that are needed for production can't be moved, whether that's land, labour or capital. This means that these resources might not be used to their full potential, causing market failure.

Market Failure in Monopolies

Monopolies can cause market failure through inefficiency and by restricting consumer choice. **This page is AQA only.**

Learn the difference between **Monopolies** and **Monopoly Power**

1) A **pure monopoly** is a market with only **one supplier**. However, markets with **more than one** supplier will **also** be referred to as a **monopoly** if **one** supplier **dominates** the market.

2) **Monopoly power** is the ability of a firm to **influence** the price of a particular good in a market. For example, a firm with monopoly power can **control** the **supply** of a good to **influence** its **price** — the firm is able to be a **'price maker'**. This can happen when there's a pure monopoly but also in markets where there's more than one firm.

3) Firms providing **essential** goods or services with no substitutes have the **greatest** monopoly power. The more **inelastic** the **demand** for a product is, the **greater** the monopoly power tends to be.

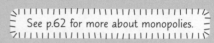
See p.62 for more about monopolies.

Monopolies cause **Market Failure** and the **Misallocation** of **Resources**

1) The diagram shows the supply and demand curves of a market. The **market equilibrium** would be at **point M**, where supply is Q_c and price P_c.

2) However, in a **monopoly** situation there's only one firm in the market, so it could misallocate resources by **restricting supply** to Q_m and force the **price** up to P_m.

3) This is a **market failure** which causes a **welfare loss** of **KLM** — there are fewer units available for consumers to buy (Q_m to Q_c are no longer available). The area of P_cP_mKL, which would've been part of the consumer surplus, is **added** to the **firm's profits**.

4) By **restricting output** monopolies can **fail** to exploit some **economies of scale**. This means that **productive efficiency isn't achieved** and the firm isn't producing output at the lowest point on its average cost curve (see below).

5) Monopoly firms can also experience **higher costs of production** than firms that exist in a **competitive market** — this can be because **monopolies** have less of an **incentive** to innovate to make production methods as efficient (and cost-effective) as possible. They may also have **no incentive** to **cut costs** as they're **price makers**.

6) Furthermore, market failure will be caused by the **effect** monopolies have on **consumers**. Consumer choice is **restricted** because there are fewer products to choose from, and monopolies **won't** necessarily **react** to the **wants** and **needs** of consumers because they can set their own prices.

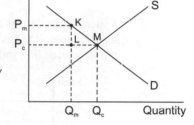

Monopolies can bring **Benefits** to an **Economy**

1) In some markets the most **efficient** way of allocating resources is to have **one** producer who's able to exploit **economies of scale** and achieve productive efficiency. If the market consisted of lots of **small producers** they wouldn't be able to **collectively** achieve the **same level** of economies of scale or **productive efficiency**.

2) As **large firms** can exploit **large economies of scale**, they can pass on these cost savings to their customers, who are able to take advantage of **low prices**. This will also help their **international competitiveness**.

3) Monopolies can use their **profits** for research into **new** production methods and products. This could lead to **innovation** and **better products** being made available for customers.

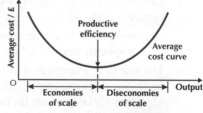

Warm-Up Questions

Q1 What is a pure monopoly?

Q2 In what ways might a monopoly lead to a misallocation of resources?

Exam Question

Q1 With the use of a diagram, explain how a firm with a monopoly can cause market failure. [8 marks]

I start every day with 100% pure, freshly-squeezed monopoly...

The basic thing to take on board here is that monopolies can cause market failure. Not surprising really when they can restrict output and stop resources being allocated properly. Don't skim over the diagrams — you need to understand what they show.

Taxation

Governments use taxes to offset or reduce negative externalities caused by certain goods/services. **For all boards.**

Governments use **Indirect Taxes** to affect the **Supply** of some goods/services

1) **Indirect taxes** can be imposed on the purchase of **goods or services**.
There are **two types** of indirect tax: **specific** and *ad valorem*:

> **Specific** taxes — these are a fixed amount that's charged per unit of a particular good, no matter what the price of that good is. For example, a set amount of tax could be put on bottles of wine regardless of their price.

> *Ad valorem* taxes — these are charged as a **proportion of the price** of a good. For example, a 20% tax on the price of a good would mean that for a £10 product it's £2 and for a £100 product it's £20.

There are also direct taxes. These are imposed on individuals or organisations. For example, income tax is paid by people who earn an income.

2) Indirect taxes **increase costs** for **producers** so they cause the **supply curve** to **shift** to the **left**.
The two types of indirect taxes **affect supply curves in different ways**, as shown in the diagrams below:

A specific tax causes a parallel shift of the supply curve. The tax is the same fixed amount at a low price (P_1) and a high price (P_2).

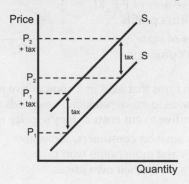

An *ad valorem* tax causes a **non-parallel shift** of the supply curve, with the biggest impact being on higher price goods. The tax is a **smaller amount** at a **low price** (P_1) compared to a high price (P_2).

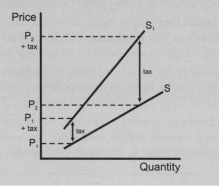

Governments **Tax** goods with **Negative Externalities**

1) Governments often put extra **indirect taxes** on goods that have **negative externalities**, such as petrol, alcohol and tobacco.

2) Governments may use **multiple** indirect taxes on **one** item, e.g. in the UK **cigarettes** have a **specific tax** (called **excise duty**) and an *ad valorem* tax on their **retail** price.

3) The aim of this taxation is to **internalise the externality** that the good produces, i.e. make the producer and/or consumer of the product **cover the cost** of its **externalities**. The taxes make **revenue** for the government which can be used to **offset** the effects of the **externalities** — e.g. the revenue generated from a tax on alcohol could be used to pay for the additional police time needed to deal with alcohol-related crime.

4) Another example of a specific tax used in the UK is **landfill tax**. The tax aims to **offset** the impact of landfill on the environment:

James desperately wanted to see where all the non-recyclable rubbish went.

- Local authorities or firms that **dispose** of waste at **landfill** sites are charged an **environmental tax**. The tax is set at an amount which attempts to **reflect** the **full social costs** of using landfill — i.e. the external cost linked to the burying of waste in landfill, such as pollution released from landfill sites.

- The tax should **encourage recycling**, which in turn will **reduce** the **negative externalities** caused by landfill that harm the environment.

- However, the tax has led to an **increase** in fly-tipping by firms to **avoid** having to **pay** the tax. (Fly-tipping is the **illegal dumping** of **waste** on land that isn't designated for waste disposal, e.g. farmland and roadsides.)

Taxation

The **Total Amount** of **Tax Paid** can be shown on a diagram

1) The diagram shows the effect of an *ad valorem* tax — the **supply** curve moves **up** from S to S_1.

2) In the diagram, the **total tax paid** is ACP_1P_2. This is made up of the total tax paid by the **consumer** (BCP_1P) **plus** the total tax paid by the **producer** ($ABPP_2$). The part of the tax paid by the **consumer** is equal to the rise in price from **P** to P_1. The part of the tax paid by the **producer** is equal to the difference between P_2 and **P**.

3) The **amount** of tax passed on to the **consumer** will depend on the **price elasticity** of demand — if demand for a good is **price inelastic**, most or all of the extra **cost** is likely to be **passed on** to the consumer. If demand for a good is **price elastic**, then the **producer** is much **more likely** to take on most of the **extra cost**.

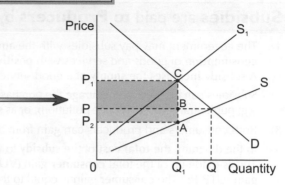

There's more detail on how indirect taxes affect producers and consumers on page 31.

There are **Advantages** and **Disadvantages** to this kind of tax

Advantages

1) The **cost** of the negative externalities is **internalised** in the **price** of the good — this **may reduce** demand for the good and the level of its production, **reducing** the **effects** of the negative externalities.

2) If demand **isn't** reduced, there's still the benefit that the revenue gained from the **tax** can be **used** by the government to **offset** the externalities — e.g. tax on **cigarettes** could be used for funding government services to help people to **stop smoking**.

Disadvantages

1) It can be **difficult** to put a **monetary value** on the 'cost' of the **negative externalities**.

2) For goods where **demand** is **price inelastic**, the demand **isn't reduced** by the **extra cost** of the tax.

3) Indirect taxes usually **increase** the cost of **production**, which **reduces** a product's international competitiveness.

4) Firms may choose to **relocate** and sell their goods abroad to **avoid** the indirect taxation. This would **remove** their contributions to the economy, such as the **payment** of **tax** and the **provision** of **employment**.

5) The money raised by taxes on demerit goods **might not** be spent on **reducing** the effects of their externalities.

Warm-Up Questions

Q1 Describe the difference between a specific tax and an *ad valorem* tax.

Q2 Sketch a diagram to show how the supply curve shifts when an *ad valorem* tax is introduced on a good or service.

Q3 Give one advantage and one disadvantage of indirect taxes on goods with negative externalities.

Exam Question

Q1 The diagram shows the impact of an indirect tax imposed on a demerit good. The revenue received by the government would equal:

A) £2000

B) £400

C) £1600

D) £800

[1 mark]

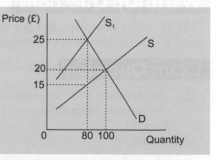

I think it's time for a government intervention — they really need help...

There are two types of indirect tax that you need to know about. Remember, they both cause the supply curve to shift, but in a slightly different way. On the diagram at the top of this page make sure you understand that the cost of the tax can be split into the parts paid by the consumer and producer. If you're doing Edexcel there's a bit more detail you need to know (see p.30-31).

Subsidies

The government can intervene in a positive way — by giving subsidies to producers or consumers. ***This page is for all boards.***

Subsidies are paid to Producers by the government

1) The government may pay subsidies with the aim of **encouraging** the **production** and **consumption** of goods and services with **positive** externalities — e.g. merit goods. A subsidy **increases** the **supply** of a good/service, so the **supply curve** shifts to the **right**.

2) Subsidies can be used to **encourage** the purchase and use of goods/services which **reduce** negative externalities, e.g. public transport (to reduce pollution), or as **support** for firms to help them become more **internationally competitive**.

3) Both consumers and producers can **gain** from a **subsidy**.

4) In the diagram, the **total cost** of the **subsidy** to the government is VTP_2P_1. This is made up of the total **consumer** gain ($VUPP_1$) **plus** the total **producer** gain (UTP_2P). The **consumer** gain is equal to the fall in price from **P** to P_1. The **producer** gain is equal to the difference between **P** and P_2.

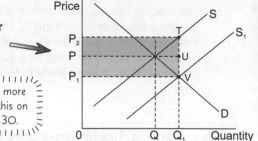

5) The **subsidy** results in the price of the good/service **falling** from **P** to P_1, and the **quantity** demanded **increasing** from **Q** to Q_1.

6) The **proportion** of the subsidy producers and consumers benefit from depends on the **elasticity** of the **supply** and **demand** curves.

There's more about this on page 30.

7) Sometimes **subsidies** might be given **directly** to **consumers** instead.

There are Advantages and Disadvantages to Subsidies

Advantages

1) The **benefit** of goods with positive externalities is **internalised**, i.e. the cost of these externalities is covered by the government subsidy, so the **price** of the goods is **reduced** from what it would be in the absence of the subsidy.

2) Subsidies can **change preferences** — producers will supply goods with positive externalities and consumers will consume them and receive the benefits from them. Also, making a merit good **cheaper** by the presence of a subsidy makes it **more affordable** and **increases demand** for it.

3) The **positive externalities** are **still** present. For example, if a subsidy is paid for **wind farms**, the wind farms will still **reduce pollution** levels.

4) Subsidies can support a domestic industry until it **grows** to the point that it can exploit **economies of scale** and become **internationally competitive**. (Though this could encourage inefficiency — see below).

Disadvantages

1) It can be difficult to put a monetary value on the 'benefit' of the positive externalities.

2) Any subsidy has an opportunity cost — the money spent on it might be better spent on something else.

3) Subsidies may make producers inefficient and reliant on subsidies. The subsidy means that producers have less incentive to reduce costs or innovate.

4) The effectiveness of subsidies depends on the elasticity of demand — subsidies wouldn't significantly increase demand for inelastic goods.

5) The subsidised goods and services may not be as good as those they're aiming to replace. For example, imported goods may be better quality than the domestically produced alternatives a subsidy is promoting.

Warm-Up Questions

PRACTICE QUESTIONS

Q1 Give one advantage and one disadvantage of subsidies for goods with positive externalities.

Exam Question

Q1 The diagram shows the impact of a subsidy on a merit good. Government expenditure on the subsidy would equal:
A) GFJ
B) OLFC
C) ACFJ
D) EFG

[1 mark]

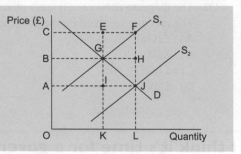

Subsidise your heating bills — move in with your next-door neighbour...

Subsidies can act as an incentive to producers or consumers, or they can help a company to be internationally competitive.

Price Controls

Setting minimum and maximum prices can have a big effect on supply and demand. **This page is for all boards.**

Governments can set a **Maximum Price** for a good or service

1) A maximum price (or price ceiling) may be set to **increase consumption** of a merit good or to make a **necessity** more **affordable**. For example, a government may set a maximum rent price to keep the cost of renting a property affordable.

2) If a maximum price is set **above** the market equilibrium price, it will have **no impact**.

3) If it's set **below** the market equilibrium, it will lead to **excess demand** and a **shortage** in **supply** of Q_1 to Q_2. The excess demand cannot be cleared by market forces, so to prevent shortages the product needs to be rationed out, e.g. by a ballot.

4) A good's price elasticity of **supply** and price elasticity of **demand** will have a **big** effect on the **amount** of excess demand.

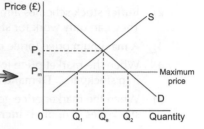

Governments can set a **Minimum Price** for a good or service

1) **Minimum** prices (or price floors) are often set to make sure that **suppliers** get a **fair** price. The European Union's Common Agricultural Policy (CAP — see p.100) involves the use of a **guaranteed minimum price** for many **agricultural** products.

2) If a minimum price is set **below** the market equilibrium price, it will have **no impact**.

3) If it's set **above** the market equilibrium price, it will **reduce** demand to Q_1 and **increase** supply to Q_2, leading to an **excess supply** of Q_1 to Q_2.

4) To make a minimum price for a good work the government must **purchase** the excess supply at the **guaranteed** minimum price. The goods bought by the government will either be **stockpiled** or **destroyed**.

5) Government **expenditure** would then be ABQ_2Q_1.

6) A good's price elasticity of supply and price elasticity of demand will have a **big** effect on the **amount** of excess supply.

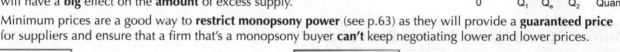

7) Minimum prices are a good way to **restrict monopsony power** (see p.63) as they will provide a **guaranteed price** for suppliers and ensure that a firm that's a monopsony buyer **can't** keep negotiating lower and lower prices.

Maximum Prices	Minimum Prices
Advantages: • Maximum prices can help to increase **fairness**, by allowing **more** people the **ability** to purchase certain goods and services. • They can also be used to **prevent** monopolies from **exploiting** consumers. **Disadvantages:** • Since demand will be **higher** than supply, some people who **want** to buy the product **aren't** able to. • Governments **may** need to introduce a **rationing** scheme to **allocate** the good, e.g. through a ballot. • Excess demand can lead to the creation of a **black market** for a good.	**Advantages:** • Producers have a guaranteed **minimum income** which will encourage **investment**. • **Stockpiles** can be used when supply is **reduced** (e.g. due to bad weather) or as **overseas aid**. **Disadvantages:** • Consumers will be paying a **higher** price than the market equilibrium. • Resources used to produce the **excess** supply could be used elsewhere — there's an **inefficient** allocation of resources. • **Government spending** on a minimum price scheme could be used in **other areas** — schemes may have a **high opportunity cost**. • **Destroying excess goods** is a **waste of resources**.

Warm-Up Questions

Q1 Give two disadvantages of guaranteed maximum prices and two disadvantages of minimum prices.

Exam Question

Q1 Use a diagram to show how the setting of a maximum price for a good can result in excess demand. [8 marks]

The government egg stockpile is huge — I think it's time for a crackdown...

What a terrible yolk... anyway, moving on... setting a maximum or minimum price for something means that the market forces can't determine the price of a good or service — minimum and maximum pricing acts to restrict the price that can be charged.

Buffer Stocks

Governments might use buffer stocks to reduce market failure in agriculture. ***This page is for OCR only.***

Buffer Stocks are used to try to **Stabilise** commodity prices

1) **Prices** in **commodity markets**, especially for agricultural products, can be **very unstable**.
2) **Buffer stock** schemes aim to **stabilise** prices and **prevent** shortages in supply. They can **only** work for **storable** commodities — e.g. wheat.
3) A **maximum** price (price ceiling) and **minimum** price (price floor) for a commodity are set by a government.
4) When the market price for a product goes **below** the price **floor**, the government **buys** it and stores it in stockpiles. **Demand** is **increased** and the price is brought up to an **acceptable** level.
5) When the market price goes **above** the price **ceiling**, the government **sells** the product from its **stockpiles**. Supply is **increased** and the price is **brought down** to an **acceptable** level.

- For example, the **quantity supplied** (Q_1) in a **good** year (when levels of production have been high) is shown by the supply curve S_1, so its **market price** would be P_1.
- This price is **below** the **minimum** price, so to **prevent** this price fall, the government would **purchase** a quantity of Q_3 to Q_1 of the good at the set **minimum price**. Supply would be **reduced** and the market price would **rise** to the set **minimum** price.
- The goods **bought** by the government would be **added** to its stockpile.
- The **quantity supplied** (Q_2) in a **poor** year is shown by the supply curve S_2. The **market price** would be P_2.
- The government would **sell** Q_2 to Q_4 from its stockpile, at the set **maximum** price. Supply is **increased** and the market price would **fall** to the set **maximum** price.
- If the market price is **between** the set minimum and maximum, no action is taken.

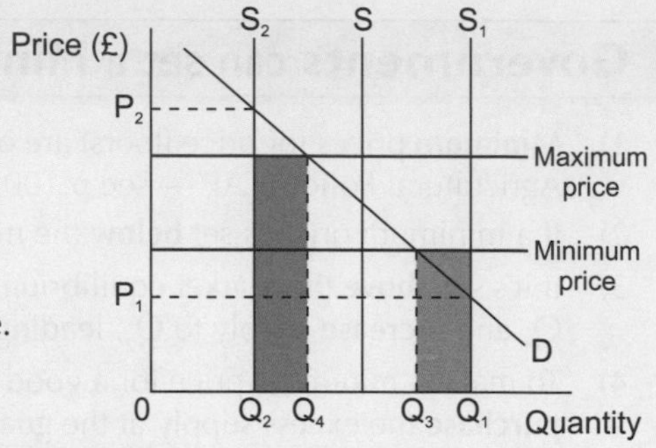

Buffer Stocks often **Aren't Successful**

In theory, the **income** from **selling** the product at the set **maximum** price should pay for **purchases** at the set **minimum** price and the **running** of the scheme. However, buffer schemes often don't work for a number of reasons:

- If the **minimum** price is set at **too high** a level, the scheme will **spend excessively** purchasing stocks to **maintain** this minimum price.
- If there's a **run** of **good** or **bad** harvests, then the scheme may **buy excessively** or **run out** of stock.
- **Storage** and **security** of the stockpiles can be **expensive**.
- Some commodities will **deteriorate** and go to waste over time, causing **losses** for the scheme.
- Producers may **overproduce** because they will get a **guaranteed minimum price**. This can lead to massive **stockpiles** and a **waste** of **resources**.

PRACTICE QUESTIONS

Warm-Up Question

Q1 Give three reasons why buffer stock schemes might not be successful.

Exam Question

Q1 A buffer stock scheme for wheat production is being used. In a year when supply is shown by the supply curve S_1 the price per bushel received by farmers will be:

A) P_1
B) P_2
C) P_3
D) P_4

[1 mark]

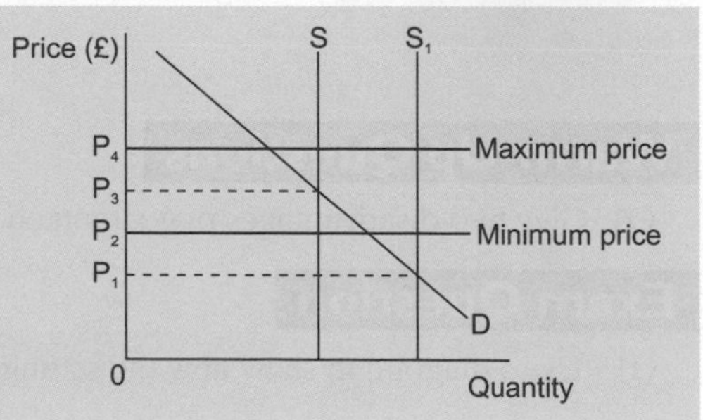

I tried to stabilise prices with butter stocks — it was a tasty, tasty mess...

Buffer stocks involve maximum and minimum prices at the same time (wowser) — make sure you know how they work.

State Provision

State provision is where the government provides certain goods or services. It's often referred to as 'government expenditure' as it involves governments spending money to provide things, and they have to decide which things to provide. **For all boards.**

Governments **Directly Provide** some goods and services

The state provided Viv with all the latest medical equipment — unfortunately, she was a chef.

1) Governments use **tax revenue** to pay for **certain** goods and services so that they're **free**, or **largely free**, when consumed. Examples in the UK **include** the NHS, state education, waste disposal and the fire and police services.

2) **Public goods**, such as **defence** and **street lighting**, are also **provided** by the state.

3) State provision can come **directly** from the government, e.g. state schools and the army, or alternatively, governments can **purchase** the good or service from the **private sector** and provide it to the **public** for **free**, e.g. in some areas **community health services** are **purchased** from private companies and then **provided free** to NHS patients.

State Provision is a way to Overcome market failure

1) Governments might provide certain things to **increase** the **consumption** of merit goods, such as **education** and **health**.

2) **Free provision** of services can help to **reduce inequalities** in access, e.g. due to differences in **wealth**.

3) It can also **redistribute** income — most of the money to **pay** for the services comes from taxing **wealthier** citizens.

4) The **level** of state provision is a **value judgement** made by the government — it's up to the government to decide the **amount** of a good/service that they **provide**. This decision is likely to be based on **how important for society** they think it is that they provide the good/service.

State Provision has several Disadvantages

1) State provision may mean there's **less incentive** to operate efficiently due to the absence of the **price mechanism**.

2) State provision may **fail** to respond to **consumer demands**, as it lacks the motive of **profit** to determine **what's supplied**.

3) The **opportunity cost** of state provision of a good or service is that **other** goods or services **can't be supplied**.

4) State provision can **reduce** individuals' **self-reliance** — they know the good or service is there for them if they need it.

Health Care is a Merit Good that's sometimes Provided by Governments

1) The government funds the NHS so that **society benefits** from the **positive externalities** of **health care**. For example, the consumption of health care can contribute to a healthier, happier population and reduce the number of days people take off work due to sickness.

2) However, there are **drawbacks** to the **state provision** of health care by the NHS. These include:

   • Demand for health care in the UK has increased dramatically since the NHS was introduced. Because the NHS is **free at the point of delivery**, this has led to **excess demand** and problems like long waiting lists.

   • Hospitals and clinics can be **wasteful** of **resources**, such as money wasted on unused prescriptions.

   • The NHS may not always respond to the **wants** and **needs of patients** — e.g. local NHS officials might relocate medical services against the wishes of the population in their area for cost-saving reasons.

   • The NHS can **reduce patients' self-reliance**. For example, it can remove the incentive for patients to deal with medical issues themselves — patients might visit their doctor or hospital with problems which could be treated at home with medicines they could buy in a shop (e.g. colds or sore throats).

Exam Question

Q1 Describe the possible disadvantages of state provision of health care. [6 marks]

My bedroom is a state — it'll take some serious intervention to sort it out...

There are different reasons for state provision of goods and services. For example, the government might want to encourage the consumption of a merit good, or make a certain good or service accessible to everyone no matter how much they earn.

Privatisation, Regulation and Deregulation

Governments can reduce market failure by increasing efficiency or competition in markets. They can intervene in a market to achieve this, e.g. regulation, or they can reduce their involvement in a market, e.g. privatisation and deregulation. **All boards.**

Privatisation can Improve Efficiency

There's information on public ownership/nationalisation on p.97.

1) A **publicly owned** firm/industry is owned by the **government**. The firm/industry will usually act in the **best interests** of consumers — so **prices** tend to be **low** and **output** tends to be **high**. This is possible as they **don't** have to make **profits**.

2) However, publicly owned firms/industries tend to be **inefficient** because they **lack competition** and that can lead to **market failure**. Governments may decide to **increase** competition through **privatisation**.

3) **Privatisation** is the **transfer** of the **ownership** of a firm/industry from the **public** sector to the **private** sector.

4) Some economists believe this will lead to a **more efficient** firm/industry, because it'll be open to **free market competition**. Private firms have **shareholders**, so they'll usually need to **maximise** their **profits** to keep the shareholders happy.

5) Privatisation covers a number of different things, for example:

- The **sale** of public (nationalised) firms — e.g. the Royal Mail was **privatised** through the **sale** of **shares**.
- **Contracting out** services — a government pays a **private firm** to carry out work on its behalf, e.g. **cleaning** government-owned buildings, such as **hospitals** or **schools**.
- **Competitive tendering** — private firms **bid** (or **compete**) to gain a **contract** to provide a service for the government. Firms will compete on **price** and the **quality** of the service offered.
- **Public Private Partnerships (PPPs)** — a private firm works **with** a government to build something or provide a service for the public. An example of a PPP is a **Private Finance Initiative (PFI)** — a private firm is **contracted** by the government to **run** a project. For example, in the UK, some hospitals or schools are **built** by a **private** firm, then the government **leases** the buildings from the firm (usually for a long period of time).

PPP Example

In 2010, **Marks & Spencer** agreed a five-year partnership with **Somerset County Council Waste Partnership** for Marks & Spencer to provide **funding** (up to £250 000 per year) for the council to **collect waste** from **roadsides** in the county. This funding has enabled the county council to **improve** its **recycling services**, and Marks & Spencer has benefitted from the collection of **recyclable plastic** that can be used for its products.

Advantages	Disadvantages
Increased competition **improves** efficiency and **reduces x-inefficiency** (see p.58).	A privatised **public** monopoly is likely to become a **private** monopoly — so extra measures, e.g. deregulation (see p.93), need to be taken to avoid this (see p.94).
Improves resource allocation — privatised firms have to react to **market signals** of supply and demand.	Privatised firms may have **less focus** on **safety** and **quality** because they have **more focus** on reducing **costs** and increasing **profits**.
PFIs enable the building of **important facilities** that the government might not be able to **afford** to build.	The new private firm might need **regulating** (see below) to prevent it from being a **private monopoly** — this adds **cost** for **taxpayers**.
PFIs means **lower taxes** in the **short run** because the government won't pay for the new facility immediately.	A PFI will often **cost more** in the long run than it's worth — so it adds to **government debt** and may **not** represent value for money.
The government **gains revenue** from **selling** firms.	PFIs mean **higher taxes** for **future generations** to pay for the cost of the government leasing the facility.

Government Regulation comes in Various forms

1) **Regulations** are rules that are enforced by an authority (e.g. a government) and they're usually backed up with **legislation** (i.e. laws) — which means that legal action can be taken against those that break the rules. They can be used to **control** the activities of producers and consumers and try to **change** their **undesirable behaviour**.

2) Regulations are used to try to **reduce** market failure and its impacts. They can **help** in a number of areas:

- **Reducing** the use of **demerit** goods and services — e.g. by **banning** or **limiting** the sale of such products.
- **Reducing** the power of **monopolies** — e.g. using a regulating body to set rules such as **price caps**.
- Providing some **protection** for consumers and producers from **problems** arising from **asymmetric information** — e.g. the Consumer Rights Act **protects consumers** against firms supplying **substandard** goods.

Privatisation, Regulation and Deregulation

3) With appropriate legislation, firms or individuals who **don't** follow the regulations can be **punished**, e.g. with **fines**.

4) For example, laws, like the **Clean Air Act** and the **Environmental Protection Act**, have been created to **limit** the **damage** caused to the environment by economic activity and to **enforce minimum environmental standards** in major industries.

Regulations can be **Difficult** to **Set**

1) It can be difficult for a government to work out what is 'correct'. For example, a government might set the level of acceptable pollution by firms **too low** or **too high**.

2) There's a need for regulation in **some** areas to be **worldwide** rather than in just one country. For example, regulations to **control** greenhouse gas **emissions** might be **more effective** if they were enforced worldwide — regulations in **one country** may reduce its emissions, but this could be **offset** by an increase in emissions **elsewhere** in the world.

3) Following excessive regulations can be **expensive** and may force firms to **close** or to **move** to a different country.

4) **Monitoring** compliance with regulations can be **expensive** for a government, and if the **punishment** for **breaking** regulations isn't harsh enough, then they may **not** be a **deterrent** and **change behaviours**.

Some regulations are set to **Encourage** the use of **Renewable Energy**

1) The UK government introduced **Renewables Obligation Certificates** (ROCs) to **encourage** the use of power generated from **renewable** energy sources (e.g. wind and hydroelectric power).

2) Electricity **suppliers** were given a set **minimum percentage** of power that had to come from **renewable** sources.

3) Companies who **generated** the renewable energy were issued with ROCs which linked to the **amount** of renewable energy they **generated**. They then **sold** these certificates on to **suppliers**.

4) **Suppliers** that **fell short** of the **target percentage** of **power from renewable sources** had to pay a **financial penalty**. The money **raised** from these penalties was **distributed** between the suppliers who **did** reach the **target**.

Deregulation is basically the **Opposite** of **Regulation**

1) Deregulation means **removing** or **reducing** regulations. It removes some barriers to entry, so it can be used to **increase competition** in markets, particularly **monopolistic** markets, and tackle market failure.

2) Deregulation is often used **alongside/as part of** privatisation — privatising an industry effectively removes the legal barriers to entry that prevent other firms entering the market. **Additional** deregulation to reduce barriers to entry further can then be used to help prevent the privatised public monopoly from becoming a private monopoly.

3) Examples of deregulation in the UK include the deregulation of **directory enquiries**. BT, which was a **private** firm at the time, provided the directory enquiries service — it was deregulated to allow **other firms** to enter the market.

Advantages	Disadvantages
Improves resource allocation — removing regulations means the market becomes **more contestable**, so new firms are more likely to **enter** the market. The **threat** of **competition** from new firms, or the actual **entry** of new firms into the market, means prices **fall** closer to marginal cost (MC) and output **increases**.	It's difficult to deregulate some **natural monopolies**, e.g. utilities. These require **large infrastructures**, e.g. the water industry needs a **pipe network**. These infrastructures are **expensive** to build and maintain, and there's only a need for **one** of them.
It can be used alongside the **privatisation** of a public monopoly to prevent the privatised firm from becoming a **private** monopoly.	Deregulation can't fix other **market failures** such as negative externalities, consumer inertia or immobile factors of production.
Improves efficiency by **reducing** the amount of 'red tape' and **bureaucracy**.	Deregulation might mean there's **less safety** and **protection** for consumers.

Consumer inertia is resistance to change by consumers — e.g. it's seen as too much effort to change energy suppliers.

Warm-Up Questions

Q1 Explain two advantages of privatisation.

Q2 What is meant by regulation?

Exam Question

Q1 Evaluate privatisation as a method to improve efficiency in an industry made up of a single public monopoly. [15 marks]

Competitive tendering — seeing who's best at pounding a steak...

Privatisation and deregulation can increase competition and improve efficiency, and regulation can reduce other market failures.

Competition Policy

Make sure you know all about monopolies and oligopolies (see Section 4) before you read these pages. Monopolies can reduce the efficiency of a market and cause market failure, so governments may discourage their formation. **For all boards.**

Competition Policy aims to Increase Competition in a market

1) Governments often choose to **intervene** in **concentrated markets** where monopoly power is causing **market failure**. For example, if a monopoly exists and prices are **above** the market equilibrium price, there's a **misallocation** of resources and a **deadweight welfare loss** (see p.62) — i.e. there's market failure.

2) The intention of the government is to **protect** the **interests** of **consumers** by **promoting competition** and **encouraging** the market to function more **efficiently**. The government can do this through the use of **competition policy**.

Governments often want to Prevent Monopolies from forming

The **European Commission** and the UK's **Competition and Markets Authority (CMA)** both monitor competition to look out for **unfair** monopolistic behaviour. Things they look out for include:

1) **Mergers** — they monitor mergers and takeovers so they can **prevent** those that aren't **beneficial** to the **efficiency** of the market or to **consumers**. They may choose to **stop** a merger that would give a firm **too high** a market share (e.g. over 25%) and make it a **monopoly**, or that would give a firm **too much** monopoly power.

2) **Agreements** between firms (e.g. **cartels**, **collusive oligopolies**) — often, agreements involving **price fixing**, **splitting** markets or **limiting** production are **anti-competitive**, cause market **inefficiency** and are **unfair** to consumers.

3) The **opening** of markets to **competition** — this is when markets that were **controlled** by a government are **opened** up to competition. For example, if a **government-owned** transport service is **privatised**, the government might want to ensure the **existing** firm is open to free market competition and doesn't **dominate** the market as a private monopoly.

4) **Financial support** from governments (European Commission only) — if a government in **one EU country** gives financial support to firms in a market, this may give them an **unfair advantage** over firms in other EU countries in that same market.

The European Commission and the CMA can **block mergers** and **impose fines** on firms **guilty** of anti-competitive behaviour.

Some Markets have their own Regulating Bodies

1) Regulatory bodies are particularly common in **monopolistic** or **oligopolistic** markets. Here are some UK examples:

2) These bodies have varying **responsibilities** — these might include regulating prices, monitoring safety and product standards, and encouraging competition.

- OFWAT regulates the **water** industry.
- OFCOM regulates the **communication** industries.
- OFGEM regulates the **gas** and **electricity** markets.

3) Regulating bodies can be at risk of **regulatory capture** (see p.99).

Competition Policy is generally seen to be Useful and Effective

1) The **effectiveness** of competition policy is greatly affected by the **information** available to the European Commission or the CMA — they'll need to decide whether behaviour in different markets is **anti-competitive** or **unfair** to the **consumer** based on the information they have.

2) If the information available to the government is **reliable**, then it should be able to intervene in the market in a way that will **improve** efficiency, allocate resources **more effectively** and **improve** fairness to the consumer. If the information is **imperfect** then this could lead to **government failure**.

3) Competition policy and its implementation (e.g. through regulations) have **costs** — but in general, these costs are seen to be **outweighed** by the **benefits**. If the costs **outweigh** the benefits, this is an example of **government failure** (see p.98).

Governments can Intervene in various ways

There are many ways a government can **intervene** in a market to try to increase **competition**.

Privatisation can introduce Competition into a market where there's a Public Monopoly

1) A **publicly** owned monopoly can be **privatised** to open it up to competition and force it to respond to **market signals**.

2) However, privatisation alone **won't** increase competition, as the **public monopoly** may just become a **private monopoly**. There could also be an **increase** in **prices** and a **reduction** in **output**, as a **private** monopoly is **less likely** to act in the best interests of consumers. So, other steps need to be taken **alongside** privatisation, such as **deregulation** (see page 93), to **increase** competition and **protect consumers**.

Competition Policy

Regulation can be used to Control or Prevent Monopoly Power

1) Governments might use **regulation** (see p.92-93) to **prevent** a firm from gaining **monopoly** power, or to **increase** competition by **reducing** the monopoly power a firm already has.

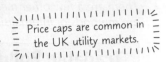
Price caps are common in the UK utility markets.

2) For example, a government or regulating body might introduce **price caps** (or **price ceilings**) to stop firms from charging prices that are considered to be **too high**. Price caps put a **maximum** on the **price increase** that firms can charge their customers. Here are **two types** of price cap:

   - **RPI – X** means firms must make **real price cuts**. RPI is **inflation** (see p.124) and X is the **efficiency improvements** the government or regulating body **expects** firms to be able to make. So for example, if the **RPI** (inflation) was **3%** and **X** was **1%**, firms could only increase their prices by up to **2%**.
   - **RPI – X + K** is commonly used in the **water industry**. K is the amount of **investment** firms will need to make in order to achieve efficiency improvements. In this case, the firm can charge **higher prices** to **offset** the cost of efficiency improvements.

   Price caps **limit** price rises, making a market **fairer** to consumers. They also provide an **incentive** for firms to **increase efficiency** (the more efficient they are, the more profit they keep), and consumers **benefit** from **improved services**.

3) Alternatively, the government or a regulator could **monitor** prices to ensure they stay **reasonable** and **fair** to consumers.

4) Governments may introduce regulations to ensure **quality standards**, such as in **food production** or **construction**.

5) Governments can regulate profits by imposing **windfall taxes** on what it decides are **excessive profits** — this means the government will tax those profits at a **higher rate**. Windfall taxes can help to **prevent** firms from gaining too much **monopoly power**, but it **reduces** their **incentive** to **improve efficiency** (as the extra profits might be taxed).

6) Setting **performance targets** can also help to maintain competition, but they need to be combined with some sort of **penalty**, e.g. a **fine**, if a firm **doesn't** reach its target. Examples of performance targets include:

   - Firms might be given certain **standards** of **customer service** they need to achieve.
   - NHS departments might be given targets for the **number of patients** they should treat.

   There are **disadvantages** to performance targets. Health and safety, quality of service and any other areas of a business which aren't included in targets might be **overlooked** in order to reach performance targets.

Here are a couple of examples of **regulation** in markets by the **UK government** and the **EU**:

Payment Protection Insurance (PPI)

- PPI is insurance that's used to repay debt should the borrower be unable to do so, e.g. due to illness. In the UK there was little competition in the PPI market, a high level of rejected claims and a lot of cases of selling unnecessary cover.
- The market was investigated by the Competition Commission (now the CMA) who produced a list of requirements for firms selling PPI, such as providing information about the right to cancel and costs. The aims were to prevent future mis-selling, help consumers make informed decisions, and increase competition in the market.
- These requirements have increased competition, and successful reclaims of mis-sold insurance have risen since the investigation.

Mobile Phone Roaming Charges

- Roaming charges are charges for data usage, calls or texts, made or received, when abroad. The European Commission has monitored these charges since 2007 and found that a lack of competition led to excessively high charges.
- The European Commission has used price caps to significantly reduce data roaming charges, and charges for calls and text messages.
- All telecommunications providers in member states must comply with these price caps. Firms can offer lower prices than the caps to compete with each other.

Deregulation can also be used to Increase Competition

1) **Deregulation** (see p.93) an make a market more **contestable**, so it's easier for **new** firms to **enter** the market.

2) This **increases** competition, causing the **price** to **fall** closer to marginal cost, and **output** to **increase**.

Deregulation is usually used alongside privatisation to make sure that a public monopoly doesn't become a private one (see previous page).

Warm-Up Questions

Q1 Why might governments want to discourage monopolistic behaviour?

Q2 Briefly discuss the effectiveness of competition policy.

PRACTICE QUESTIONS

Exam Question

Q1 Explain what a body such as the Competition and Markets Authority (CMA) does to monitor competition. [10 marks]

Price cap — the latest economic fashion accessory...

Competition policy is all about encouraging competition and stopping behaviour that's likely to prevent a contestable market.

Other Methods of Intervention

*There are a few other methods of government intervention covered here. Pollution permits and the extension of property rights are methods of internalising negative externalities so that they're accounted for by the market. **These pages are for all boards.***

Tradable Pollution Permits are used to try to Control pollution levels

1) Governments may try to **control** pollution by putting a **cap** on it. The government will set an **optimal level** of pollution and **allocate** permits that allow firms to emit a **certain amount** of **pollution** over a period of time (usually a year).

2) Firms may **trade** their permits with other firms, so if a firm can keep its emissions **low**, it can **sell** its permits to other firms who want to **buy** permits to allow them to **pollute more**.

3) Tradable pollution permits use the **market mechanism** — pollution is given a **value** and firms can **buy** and **sell** permits.

4) The **EU emissions trading system (ETS)** is a tradable pollution permit scheme, with permits called **emissions allowances**. These allowances (of greenhouse gas emissions) are **distributed** between the EU's **member** governments, who in turn **allocate** these allowances to **firms**.

5) Firms will be **fined** if they **exceed** their allowances, but they can **trade** allowances between themselves, so firms can buy **extra allowances** to cover any **extra emissions**.

Sure, the pollution was bad, but at least they all had a day out at the beach.

6) Each year the number of allowances available is **reduced**. This gives firms an **incentive** to **lower their emissions** (e.g. by investing in technology to cut emissions) — if they don't then they might have to buy more allowances.

7) Firms in the ETS are allowed to invest in **emission-saving schemes** outside of the EU to **offset** their own emissions. For example, a German firm could invest in **low-carbon power production** in India to offset some of its emissions in Germany.

ADVANTAGES

- These schemes are a good way of trying to **reduce** pollution to an **acceptable** level, as they **encourage** firms to become **more efficient** and **pollute less**.
- Firms causing low levels of pollution will **benefit** from these schemes — they'll be able to **sell** permits, allowing them to **invest more** and **expand**.
- Governments can use any **revenue**, e.g. from fines, to **invest** in other **pollution reducing** schemes.
- These schemes **internalise** the externality of pollution.

DISADVANTAGES

- The **optimal pollution level** can be difficult to set. If the level is set too **high**, firms have **no incentive** to **lower** their emissions. If the level is set too **low**, new firms might not be able to **start up** at all, or existing firms might choose to **relocate** to somewhere they're **less restricted** (**harming** a country's **economic growth**). So, setting the optimal pollution level at the **wrong** level can lead to **government failure**.
- The pollution permit scheme creates a **new market** — there might be **market failure** within this new market.
- **High** levels of pollution in specific areas may still exist, and this would still be **harmful** to the environment.
- There are **administrative costs** involved in such schemes, to both **governments** and **firms**.

The Extension of Property Rights uses the Market Mechanism

AQA ONLY

1) As was discussed on p.77, the **absence** of **property rights** can lead to **market failure**. **Extending property rights** is a way of **tackling** this market failure.

2) Owners of the rights can **charge** consumers and producers for using the property and **sue** if permission hasn't been granted. This means that **negative externalities** are **internalised** by the extension of property rights as a **value** has been put on the property (so its use will be determined by the forces of **supply** and **demand** — the **market mechanism**). For example, if a chemical company pollutes a river then it must increase its prices so that it can afford to pay compensation to the river's owner, or find a way to reduce its pollution.

3) The **money raised** by charging polluters can be used to **reduce** the **effects** of any **negative externalities**.

4) An extension of property rights could **improve** management of **resources** so they'll **last longer**. It could also mean negative externalities are **more carefully monitored** and **regulated**.

There are several Problems associated with Extending Property Rights

1) It can be **difficult** for a **government** to **extend property rights**. For example, EU rules allow boats from one EU country to fish in the waters of another EU country, stopping the allocation of property rights over these waters.

2) **Externalities** can affect **more than one country**. For example, deforestation in Malaysia could have impacts for the whole world by contributing to climate change, but the UK can't extend property rights to Malaysia.

Other Methods of Intervention

3) The **high costs** of **suing** an individual or company that infringes property rights can put off organisations from taking action to uphold those rights.

4) It's **difficult** for the owner of a property to **put a value** on its **use**.

5) There are often difficulties in **tracing** the **source** of **environmental damage**. For example, a chemical leak into a river could kill fish in a fish farm a great distance from the source of the leak — the property rights holder for the fish farm may not have the information available to demand compensation from the firm responsible.

Governments Intervene to help consumers make Well-Informed Decisions

1) Governments try to provide **information** on the **full costs** and **benefits** of goods and services. This information is given to try to help consumers make **rational choices** and prevent market failure caused by consumers and producers having **asymmetric information**. **Examples** of government-provided information include:

- School and hospital performance league tables.
- Advertising campaigns encouraging healthy eating.
- Compulsory food labelling for most foods.
- Health warnings on cigarette packets.

2) The **provision** of information will impact on the **demand** for the goods. Governments will try to **increase demand** for goods/services that they think will be **beneficial** to people and society (these will usually be **merit goods**) and **reduce demand** for goods/services that they think will be **harmful** to people and society (these will usually be **demerit** goods).

3) The **effectiveness** of government information provision is often questioned. For example, the **growing obesity problem** in the **UK** suggests that government **healthy eating campaigns** aren't having a significant impact on the public.

Governments could Nationalise some industries

1) There are several **advantages** of **nationalisation** as it can give governments the **control** to do lots of different things:
   - Governments can ensure a nationalised industry **better provides** the **goods** and **services** the country **needs**.
   - Governments can **set** the **output** and **prices** of an industry at a level that **most benefits society**.
   - Nationalised industries can be more easily **regulated** so that they act in the **best interest** of **consumers**.
   - Governments can pay **public sector workers** a **fair wage** (which they may not receive if they were employed privately).
   - A nationalised industry will have **greater economies of scale** than an industry populated by several private firms.
   - A nationalised industry can pay suppliers **fair prices** (which a private monopoly is less likely to do).

2) However, nationalised industries tend to be **inefficient** because they're **not** driven to **reduce costs** and **make profit**. There's also **little incentive** for a nationalised firm to **act prudently** (leading to the risk of '**moral hazard**', see p.82), as the firm will know that the government and tax payers will **bail them out** if they get into trouble.

Promoting Small Businesses can Increase Competition

1) Governments may choose to increase competition by **promoting small businesses**. This is likely to involve providing **tax breaks** or **subsidies** for **small firms**, or helping entrepreneurs get the **investment** they need to start a new business.

2) Reducing **regulations** and '**red tape**' (see p.98) is also a good way to encourage new, small businesses to start up.

3) Increasing competition in this way should lead to **greater choice** and **lower prices** for **consumers**.

Warm-Up Questions

Q1 Explain briefly how the ETS acts as an incentive for firms to cut their emissions.

Q2 Describe two problems linked to extending property rights.

Exam Questions

Q1 Evaluate the effectiveness of using tradable pollution permits to reduce greenhouse gas emissions. [15 marks]

Q2 Explain how governments can address the problem of asymmetric information to correct the market failure associated with the consumption of cigarettes. [6 marks]

'That's right Sir, without a permit I can't allow you to pollute that... or that...'

Tradable pollution permits are a clever way of using the market mechanism to solve a problem as they create a new market for pollution that should provide incentives for firms to reduce emissions. Extending property rights is another form of intervention that uses the market mechanism. By internalising negative externalities into a market through the extension of property rights, a government can ensure that these negative externalities are paid for, or create an incentive for them to be reduced.

AQA & EDEXCEL

Government Failure

Government failure is when government intervention causes a misallocation of resources in a market. **For all boards.**

Government Intervention can cause the Misallocation of Resources

1) Government intervention can lead to **resources** being **misallocated** and a **net welfare loss** — this is **government failure**.

2) Government failure is often an **unintended consequence** of an intervention to correct a market failure.

3) When looking at government failure in a market you should consider it in relation to the market failure it was attempting to correct. For example:

- Local authorities can charge for some forms of non-household waste disposal, e.g. some county councils charge for the disposal of DIY waste. This is an attempt to force waste producers to internalise the externalities of waste disposal.

- However, there's evidence that this has led to an increase in fly-tipping. This fly-tipping produces negative externalities for local residents (e.g. the visual pollution caused by discarded items) and requires resources to be allocated to clear up the fly-tipping.

- In this instance the intervention that aimed to reduce the negative externalities linked to waste disposal has resulted in the production of other unintended negative externalities.

Government Intervention may cause Market Distortions

Government interventions can **cause** market distortions rather than **removing them**. There are several examples of this:

- **Income taxes** can act as a **disincentive** to working hard — if you increase your earnings by working hard then you'll have to pay more income tax.

- **Governmental price fixing**, such as **maximum** or **minimum prices**, can lead to the **distortions** of **price signals**. For example, producers will **overproduce** a product if they'll receive a **guaranteed minimum price** for it and flood the market with **surplus goods**. Without the minimum price, the price signals given by the price mechanism would **stop** large surpluses from occurring.

- **Subsidies** may encourage firms to be **inefficient** by removing the **incentive** to be efficient.

Government Bureaucracy can Interfere with the way markets work

1) Governments have lots of **rules and regulations** — often referred to as **'red tape'**. These usually exist in order to **prevent market failure**.

2) The enforcement of these rules and regulations by government officials is known as **bureaucracy**. Excessive bureaucracy (e.g. too many regulations slowing down a process unreasonably) is seen as a form of **government failure**.

3) Red tape can interfere with the forces of **supply and demand** — it can prevent markets from working **efficiently**. For example, **planning controls** can create **long delays** in construction projects. If these delays affect housing developments then this could restrict supply for the housing market.

4) In general, lots of red tape could mean that there are **time lags** so governments can't respond quickly to the **needs** of **producers** and/or **consumers**. This might result in a country having a **competitive disadvantage** to countries that are able to respond more quickly.

5) Bureaucracy can lead to a **lack of investment** and **prevent** an economy from operating at **full capacity**.

Conflicting Policy Objectives are a source of Government Failure

1) A government's effort to achieve a certain **policy objective** may have a **negative impact** on another. For example, if a government introduces **stricter emission controls** for industry this would contribute towards its **environmental objectives**. However, this could **increase costs** for firms and **reduce their output** — causing unemployment and a fall in economic growth.

2) Politicians are also constrained by what is **politically acceptable**. For example, it's unlikely that the UK government would ban the use of private cars to reduce greenhouse gases because of the idea's **political unpopularity**.

3) Governments often favour **short-term solutions** because they're under pressure to solve issues **quickly**. For example, increasing the capacity of the UK road network will help with short-term congestion, but may increase road usage (and congestion) in the long term.

Government Failure

Government Failure can be caused by Inadequate Information

1) **Imperfect** or **asymmetric information** can mean it's **difficult** to **assess** the extent of a **market failure**, and that makes it hard to put a **value** on the **government intervention** that's **needed** to correct the failure. For example, an incorrect valuation of a market failure might lead to taxes or subsidies being set at an inefficient level.

2) Governments may not know how the population **want resources** to be **allocated**. Some economists would argue that the **price mechanism** is a better way of allocating resources than government intervention.

3) Governments don't always know how **consumers** will **react**. For example, campaigns to **discourage under-18s drinking alcohol** may lead to alcohol being viewed as desirable and **increase drinking** by this age group.

Administrative Costs can also be a cause of Government Failure

1) Government measures to correct market failure, such as policies and regulations, can use a **large amount of resources** — this can result in **high costs**. For example, the maintenance costs of a scheme to offer farmers a minimum price for a product can be substantial.

2) Some government interventions require **policing**, which can also be **expensive**. For example, for pollution permit schemes the emissions of the firms included in the scheme must be monitored to check they aren't exceeding their allowances.

Pollution permits are discussed on p.96.

There are some other causes of Government Failure

Some other reasons for government failure are:

- **Regulatory capture** — firms covered by **regulatory bodies**, such as utility companies, can sometimes **influence** the decisions of the regulator to ensure that the outcomes **favour** the **companies** and not the consumers. For example, a regulated industry might pressurise their regulatory body into making decisions that benefit them.

- It takes **time** for governments to work out where there's market failure, and then devise and implement a policy to correct it — meanwhile, the problem may have changed.

- Government policies can be affected by issues outside of its control known as **'external shocks'** — e.g. a major oil leak would impact on the effectiveness of anti-pollution policies.

Bjorn had everything he needed to capture a regulator.

Warm-Up Questions

Q1 What is government failure?

Q2 Give an example of how a government intervention can lead to a market distortion.

Q3 List three causes of government failure.

PRACTICE QUESTIONS

Exam Questions

Q1 A government banned the sale of a legal substance which has effects similar to some illegal drugs and can be hazardous to health. Which one of the following situations would be considered a government failure?
A) Public opinion of the government improved as the ban demonstrated a strong concern for public health.
B) Consumption of the substance fell dramatically and there were fewer hospital admissions due to its use.
C) The cost of imposing the ban was greater than the net benefit generated by it.
D) The public became more aware of the dangers of the substance.

[1 mark]

Q2 A government has increased the level of tax on cigarettes. A neighbouring country has a lower rate of tax on cigarettes. Explain how this intervention could lead to a government failure.

[6 marks]

It's taken time for me to develop my policy on blue cheese — I'm not a fan...

There are a few potential causes of government failure. This gives you an insight into how tricky it can be for governments to implement something that effectively sorts out a market failure. Maybe we should be a bit kinder to governments when they get it wrong... Anyway, conflicting policy objectives, inadequate information and administrative costs are key causes to remember.

Examples of Government Failure

To see the consequences of government failure it's useful to look at some examples of it in different markets. **For all boards.**

The **Common Agricultural Policy (CAP)** was set up to help farmers

1) The main aim of the CAP is to **correct market failure** caused by **fluctuating prices** for agricultural products. By correcting these fluctuations it aims to provide a **reasonable**, **stable income** for farmers.

2) To achieve its aim the CAP uses measures such as subsidies and buffer stocks (see p.90 for buffer stocks). Another measure is import restrictions on goods from outside the EU — for example, **tariffs** are placed on **imported goods** to allow the guaranteed minimum price level to be maintained.

3) The CAP has had **some success** in stabilising prices and farmer incomes, but it has also caused several **problems**:

- The CAP **encourages increased output** as farmers are guaranteed a **minimum price** for all that they produce. Increased output can lead to **environmental damage** from a greater use of intensive farming methods and chemical fertilisers.

- The **minimum prices** have also led to an **oversupply** of agricultural products, which have to be **bought** and **stored** by government agencies at **great expense**. Governments have **sold these stocks** at a low price **outside of the EU** — negatively affecting farmers outside the EU who **cannot compete** with such **low prices**.

- There are large amounts of **wasted food products** when perishable goods have to be **destroyed**.

- The increased food prices caused by the CAP are particularly **unfair** on **poorer households** who spend a larger proportion of their income on food. It can be argued that the **welfare gains to farmers** brought about by the CAP are **smaller** than the size of the **welfare loss to consumers**.

- There's a **cost to the taxpayer** of getting rid of excess agricultural produce (either by destroying it or by selling it for a very low price). This is because the produce disposed of in this way achieves a **lower price** than was paid to the producer for it by the EU.

- The CAP can cause **conflicts** with **other countries** as it can make exports from non-EU countries **less competitive**, e.g. as products from non-EU countries can be subject to import tariffs. Also, there's **conflict between countries** within the EU about how much of the CAP budget they should each receive.

4) The CAP has resulted in **distortions** in agricultural markets — it has encouraged **oversupply**, leading to a **misallocation of resources**. This misallocation of resources causes a **net welfare loss to society**, as does the high opportunity cost of running the policy.

5) In recent years prices have **moved closer** to the **market price** as part of the EU's reforms of the CAP, but there are still problems with the policy.

Governments may intervene in **Housing Markets** by setting **Maximum Rents**

1) Price controls, such as maximum rents, are used by governments to **protect tenants** from **excessive rental charges**.

2) The downside of the control of rent prices is that it can cause **shortages** of rental properties. This can be shown using a diagram:

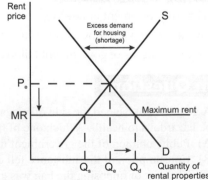

- Introducing a maximum rent would **decrease** the **rent price** from P_e to **MR**. This would cause the demand for rental properties to increase from Q_e to Q_d and supply to fall from Q_e to Q_s.

- This could cause a shortage of rental properties of Q_s to Q_d because there's an **excess demand** for them — only some individuals demanding a rental property will get one (Q_s).

3) The problems caused by maximum rents are an example of government failure:

- The **excess demand** for rental properties could lead to a **shortage** of available properties and cause a **black market** to develop. In a black market people are likely to end up paying more than the maximum rent level, so they won't gain any benefit from the government's maximum rent level. Also, landlords operating illegally on the black market may not offer a good service to their tenants.

- A **shortage** of rental properties can also impact the supply of **workers**. People might not be able to find somewhere to rent near to where they work — this could affect the ability of firms to attract new staff in areas where shortages are particularly bad.

Examples of Government Failure

Governments may provide **Subsidies** to **Public Transport**

1) Bus and train journeys may be **subsidised** to **reduce car usage** and **pollution levels**.

2) Subsidies **don't always** lead to **increases** in **passenger numbers** — bus transport is often viewed as an **inferior good** so even if it's cheaper, demand might not increase. Individuals may also find travelling by car **preferable** for reasons of privacy or convenience.

> As incomes rise, demand for inferior goods fall — see p.21.

3) The allocation of resources to public transport services that don't increase their usage and don't cause a reduction in pollution can be seen as a **misallocation of resources** and will lead to a **net welfare loss**. Underused public transport services may actually contribute to higher overall emissions as people aren't using their cars less.

Road Congestion Schemes aim to **Reduce Externalities** linked with **Traffic**

1) Road congestion schemes are a method of **reducing** the **external costs** linked to **road congestion** and the **pollution** (air and noise) that it creates. These schemes are also called **road pricing**.

2) The schemes work by **charging users** to travel on roads in areas where **congestion** is a **problem**.

3) Ideally the charge needs to be set at a level that will result in the **socially optimal level of traffic**. However, working out what this charge is could be very difficult.

4) Getting the charge wrong has impacts on the effectiveness of road congestion schemes:
   - If the price is set **too low** then it will have a limited impact on traffic levels.
   - If the price is set **too high** then too few cars will use the area covered by the charge. This will result in **reduced trade** for businesses within the congestion charge area, an **under-utilisation** of the road space in the congestion charge area, and may also cause congestion in **other areas**.

5) Road congestion charges may **unfairly** impact on **poorer motorists** in an area and put them off using their cars.

Fishing Quotas were introduced to help make fishing more **Sustainable**

1) Fishing quotas were introduced by the EU in an attempt to make sure **fish stocks** remain **stable** in European waters. They aim to **prevent overfishing**, which can have severe negative impacts on fish populations, by setting **limits** on the amount of fish that can be caught.

2) The system of fishing quotas has been **heavily criticised** and has a few key problems:

   - Fish stocks are **depleting** even with quotas in place. This could indicate that the quotas have been **set too high** and **overfishing** is still taking place.
   - Fishing boats that exceed their quotas often throw large amounts of dead fish back into the sea — these dumped fish are known as **discards**. As well as damaging fish stocks, these discards are also wasteful.
   - There has been **poor monitoring** of fish catches. This could mean that fishing boats have been overfishing and it hasn't been detected.

3) Problems with EU fishing quotas have led to a need for **reform**. One change is called a **landing obligation**. This means that everything fishermen catch must be kept on board and be counted against their quotas — they aren't allowed to discard any fish. This landing obligation is difficult to police — it would be a huge task to check that every fishing boat hasn't discarded any fish at sea.

Warm-Up Questions

Q1 Use a diagram to show how setting maximum rent prices can lead to a shortage of rental properties.

Q2 Give two reasons for subsidising public transport.

Q3 Describe one problem linked with fishing quotas.

Exam Questions

Q1 It has been decided that the level of funding available for farm subsidies is to be reduced over the next 5 years. Explain two advantages of reducing the subsidies paid to farmers. [4 marks]

Q2 Evaluate the arguments for and against a nationwide system of road pricing in major cities. [10 marks]

I reckon my washing-up quota is set too high — I wish I had a dishwasher...

So, there are quite a few examples of government failure. Thankfully most governments will be trying to correct these failures, although doing this is easier said than done — it's not straightforward to iron out problems with big policies like the CAP.

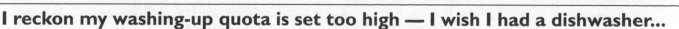

Labour Demand

Labour is important — without it firms can't produce goods and services. Although maybe in the future robots will run firms totally by themselves... imagine that. But for now they can't, so learn these pages. **These pages are for all boards.**

The **Demand** for **Labour** is a **Derived Demand**

1) The **demand** for labour comes from **firms** and the **supply** of labour comes from the **economically active population**.

2) When firms demand workers it's because they need them to make the goods that are being demanded by their customers. So the demand for labour is **driven** by the demand for the goods that this labour would produce — this is **derived demand**.

3) When demand for these goods **increases**, so does the demand for labour. When demand for goods **decreases**, the derived demand for labour also decreases, resulting in unemployment.

> The **economically active population** is the people in an economy who are **capable of**, and **old enough to**, work (regardless of whether they're employed or unemployed).

Firms will **Only Demand Workers** if they will **Make Money** by employing them

1) Firms demand labour in order to make **revenue** from selling the goods/services that the labour produces.

2) The **marginal productivity theory** says that the demand for any factor of production (e.g. labour or land) depends on its **marginal revenue product** (**MRP**).

3) The **marginal revenue product of labour** (MRP$_L$ — sometimes you'll just see this referred to as MRP) is the **extra revenue gained** by the firm from **employing one more worker**.

4) MRP$_L$ is calculated by multiplying the **marginal physical product of labour** (MPP$_L$, which is the output produced by the additional worker) by the **marginal revenue** (MR, price per unit).

> This theory looks at the marginal revenue from increasing one factor of production (e.g. labour), but keeping the rest constant.

5) Firms will **only hire workers** if they **add more** to a firm's **revenue** than they add to its **costs**. Here's an example:

> If an **extra worker** produced **10 units per hour** that were sold for £12 each, the MRP$_L$ would equal **£120** (10 × £12). As long as the worker costs less than this to employ (per hour), it's **profitable** to employ the extra worker.

6) The **cost** of hiring **one additional worker** is called the **marginal cost of labour** (MC$_L$). In a **perfectly competitive** labour market the MC$_L$ is **equal to** the **wage** paid to the additional worker.

7) In a perfectly competitive market the firm cannot influence the wage — the wage (W) on the diagram is the **market equilibrium wage** (the wage where supply equals demand in that market). If you compare the wage to the MRP$_L$, this indicates the quantity of labour a firm needs to use to be most **cost-effective**.

- When MRP$_L$ is equal to the market equilibrium wage (MC$_L$), the firm has the **optimum number** of workers (Q) to maximise profits.

- When MRP$_L$ is **greater than** the wage, a firm could increase its profits by employing more workers — the firm is employing too few workers (Q$_1$).

- When MRP$_L$ is **less than** the wage, workers are adding more to costs than they are to revenue, so the firm is employing **too many workers** (Q$_2$).

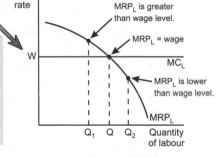

The **MRP$_L$** curve is the **Same Shape** as the **MPP$_L$** curve

1) Remember, MRP$_L$ = MPP$_L$ × MR. This means that the values that make up the **MRP$_L$** curve are the same as the ones that make up the **MPP$_L$** curve **multiplied** by the **MR** (which is assumed to be constant).

2) As the values on the MPP$_L$ curve are multiplied by the **MR** to form the MRP$_L$ curve, the curves are the **same shape**.

3) The MPP$_L$ curve is **downward sloping** because of the **law of diminishing returns** (see p.40). In other words, as each new worker is employed the amount of **additional output** that's produced **falls**.

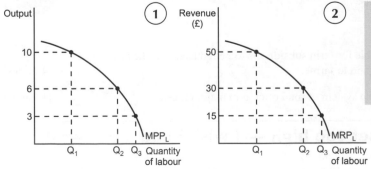

- The diagrams show the **MPP$_L$** and **MRP$_L$** curve of the same firm.

- By looking at these two diagrams it's possible to work out the **MR**. To get a revenue of **£50** at Q$_1$ on diagram 2, output at Q$_1$ on diagram 1 (**10**) must have been multiplied by **5** — so the MR is **£5**.

> The MPP and MRP curves are sometimes shown with an initial upward slope because MPP (i.e. the average output per unit of labour) can increase at lower levels of employment.

Labour Demand

A firm's Demand for Labour is affected by Productivity

1) Generally, a firm's demand for labour will decrease if wages rise. However, this depends on whether the wage increase is accompanied by an increase in **productivity** (the output per worker per hour).

2) Higher levels of productivity reduce **unit labour costs**. Unit labour costs are the labour costs per unit of output.

3) So, if wages **increase** but are accompanied by an **equivalent increase** in worker **productivity**, this means that the **unit labour cost** stays the **same** and **demand** for labour is **unaffected**. For example:

> If a worker's **wage** was **£10** per hour and they iced **10** cakes per hour, the **wage cost per cake** would be £1. If they got a **10% wage rise** (to £11) and had a **10% rise** in productivity (to 11 cakes per hour), the wage cost per cake would still be **£1**.

4) High **unit labour costs** suggest there's low productivity and this would **reduce** a country's **international competitiveness**.

5) If a firm's unit labour costs are **reduced** as a result of an **increase** in labour productivity, it'll become **more competitive** — unless the increase is due to something which will improve the labour productivity of **competing** firms too, such as new technology, in which case its **relative** competitiveness **won't** change.

6) International competition may mean the unit labour cost in a **particular industry** is too high in **some** countries for them to be competitive and production in that industry will **stop** (see p.213 for more on competitiveness).

The MRP$_L$ curve is also the Demand curve for Labour

> This is because it shows the quantity of labour demanded at each wage rate.

Anything that affects the MRP (or MPP and MR) will **shift** the **demand (MRP$_L$) curve** for labour. Examples include:

- A change to the **price of goods** sold (**MR**) — if demand falls for a firm's product and its price falls, this would decrease the firm's demand for labour and the MRP$_L$ curve would shift to the **left**.

- Factors that affect **labour productivity** — e.g. if **new technology** or **training** increases the productivity of workers, this would increase the demand for labour and cause the MRP$_L$ curve to shift to the **right**.

- Increases to the **costs of labour** — the cost of labour doesn't only include wages. It also includes costs such as training, uniforms, safety equipment, and National Insurance contributions. If any of these labour costs increased, this would decrease the demand for labour and the MRP$_L$ curve would shift to the **left**.

Demand for labour can be Elastic or Inelastic

> You might see elasticity of demand for labour referred to as **wage** elasticity of demand for labour.

1) **Elasticity of demand for labour** measures the **change in demand** for labour when the **wage level** changes. It's calculated by dividing the percentage change in the quantity of labour demanded by the percentage change in the wage rate.

2) When demand for labour is **elastic**, small wage changes can cause **large** changes in the quantity of labour demanded. When it's **inelastic** even large wage changes only cause **small** changes to the quantity of labour demanded.

3) There are several factors that can influence the elasticity of demand for labour:

- The demand for labour is always **more elastic** in the **long run** as firms can make plans for the future to replace labour (or take on more). In the **short run**, changes are more difficult to make, so demand for labour is **more inelastic**.

- If labour can be **substituted easily** by capital (e.g. machines), then the demand for labour will be **elastic**.

- If **wages** are a **small proportion** of a firm's **total costs** then the demand for labour will be **more inelastic** — this is because a wage increase will have **little impact** on total costs. If wages are a **large proportion** of a firm's total costs then demand for labour will be **more elastic** — even small wage increases will have a **large impact** on total costs.

- It's important to consider the **price elasticity of demand** (PED) of the **product** being made. The more **price elastic** the demand for the product is, the more elastic the **demand for labour** will be. In this situation, when **wages rise** firms **aren't able** to pass the increase in costs (higher wages) to consumers by **increasing prices**. If they did, their sales would decrease by a **greater proportion** than the increase in price — so overall their **sales revenue** would **fall**.

Warm-Up Questions

Q1 Define MRP$_L$.
Q2 Why are the MPP$_L$ curve and the MRP$_L$ curve the same shape?

PRACTICE QUESTIONS

Exam Question

Q1 State and explain two factors that could increase the demand for labour. [6 marks]

They said my job could be done better by a machine — they were right...

For this topic it's important to learn the difference between MRP$_L$, MPP$_L$ and MC$_L$. Remember that demand for labour is linked to the demand for the good or service the labour produces (it's a derived demand) and also the PED of the good or service.

Labour Supply

Unsurprisingly this topic is all about labour supply... more surprising is that it's not all about the wage that workers get paid. There's more to work than just getting paid — a well-stocked biscuit tin is a big perk... **These pages are for all boards.**

Labour Supply can refer to an Individual or an Occupation

1) An **individual's labour supply** is the total number of **hours** which that person is willing to work at a given wage rate. In the **short run** the supply of labour depends on an **individual's decision** to choose between **work** or **leisure** at a given wage rate.

2) For an **occupation**, the labour supply is the number of **workers** willing to work in that occupation at a given wage rate.

3) As the **wage rate** for an occupation **rises**, the quantity of labour supplied **increases**:

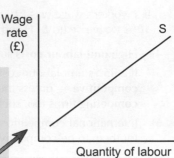

- Usually, **individuals** are prepared to work **more hours** as the wage rate increases. However, there'll be a **limit** to how many hours an individual will be prepared to work, even if wages continue to rise.
- Although **individual** workers have a **limit** to the amount of labour they're **willing** to supply, high wages will attract **more workers** to an occupation and **increase** the labour supply.
- This means that the **supply curve** for labour in an occupation **slopes upwards**.

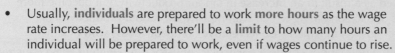

The Supply of Labour can be influenced by Job Satisfaction

1) The supply of labour in the **long run** is determined by **pecuniary** (monetary) and **non-pecuniary** (non-monetary) factors. These factors determine the welfare gained by working, which is known as the **net advantage**.

2) The net advantage of a job can be divided into **two types** of benefits:

Pecuniary benefits: this is the welfare a worker gains from the **wage** they receive (or more specifically, what's bought with it).

Non-pecuniary benefits: this is the welfare a worker can gain from **non-wage benefits** of their job. Examples of these benefits include:

- flexible working hours
- employee discount
- a generous holiday allowance
- convenience of job location
- training available
- opportunities for promotion
- job security
- perks of the job (e.g. a company car)

'Job satisfaction' (see below) is a non-pecuniary benefit.

Firms offering non-pecuniary benefits can **encourage workers** to **supply more labour** at a given wage rate. So they can effectively cause the position of the labour supply curve to shift.

3) When a worker enjoys their job (has high job satisfaction) they're **more willing** to accept a **lower wage** (low pecuniary benefits) because they gain **high non-pecuniary benefits** from their job.

4) People are likely to gain **low non-pecuniary benefits** from unpleasant or boring jobs with low job satisfaction. Everything else being equal, workers doing these jobs will want a **higher wage** to **compensate** for the low non-pecuniary benefits they receive.

There's more about other factors affecting wages on *pages 106-107.*

Other factors can affect the Supply of Labour to a Particular Job or Industry

Factors that affect the supply of labour include:

- The size of the **working population** in an area or the country as a whole. For example, if there's an ageing population with a large proportion of people in retirement then there may be insufficient workers to meet demand for labour.

The working population is the same as the economically active population (see p.102).

- The **competitiveness of wages** — workers may pick the job that will pay them the highest wage. Firms/industries that pay poor wages may struggle to attract enough labour.

- The **publicising of job opportunities** — it may be difficult to attract sufficient workers to a particular job/industry if jobs are not advertised effectively.

Changes in these factors will shift the market supply curve for labour.

Labour Supply

The quantity of labour supplied depends on the **Elasticity** of the labour supply

1) The main determinant of the elasticity of labour supply is the level of **skills and qualifications** needed for a job.

Low-skilled jobs

1) In **low-skilled jobs** the supply of labour tends to be **elastic**. This means that a small rise in the wage rate causes a proportionately larger rise in the quantity of labour supplied. This is because there's a **large pool** of low-skilled workers and many may be unemployed and looking for work (i.e. very willing to work).

2) It's also important to remember that most low-skilled jobs tend to have **similar wage rates**. If one low-skilled job increases its wage rate, even by a small amount, low-skilled workers from other occupations will be attracted quickly.

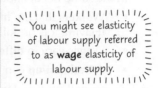
You might see elasticity of labour supply referred to as **wage** elasticity of labour supply.

Skilled jobs

1) The supply curves for **skilled jobs** such as doctors, pilots and lawyers tend to be **inelastic**, particularly in the short run. This can be explained by looking at the following example.

2) If there was a **shortage** of doctors in the UK, a rise in the wage rate would not be enough to increase the supply in the **short run** as it takes several years to train to become a doctor. Increasing wage rates would have the effect of persuading more people to choose medicine at university (in order to become doctors), but this would only have an effect in the **long term**.

Net migration of doctors from other countries into the UK could increase supply in the short run — see below.

2) The **mobility of labour** is also another important factor that affects the elasticity of labour supply.

- If workers are **occupationally mobile** (they can move from one occupation to another quickly), then wage rises will cause **greater** increases in the supply of labour — labour supply will be more **elastic**.

- If workers are **geographically mobile** (they can move locations to where the jobs are), then wage rises will cause **greater** increases in the supply of labour — labour supply will also be more **elastic**.

Rhonda and Clare were thinking about relocating to Lapland for work.

Net Migration of Labour can Increase the supply of labour

1) The EU supports the **free movement of labour** between its member states (see p.208).

2) **Net migration of workers** to a state can **increase** the **supply of labour** and help alleviate shortages of skilled workers (see p.121).

3) It can also help with the increased demand for **seasonal workers**, for example in agriculture and construction.

Warm-Up Questions

Q1 What is the opportunity cost of work?

Q2 List four non-pecuniary factors that may determine the supply of labour.

Q3 Why is the supply of low-skilled workers elastic?

PRACTICE QUESTIONS

Exam Question

Q1 Discuss, giving examples, factors which could affect the elasticity of labour supply. [15 marks]

A fisherman couldn't catch any fish — must be net migration...

Labour supply is all about the number of hours people are willing to work. If you have a job that you love then you might want to spend loads of time at work. Then again, you might change jobs if you see one advertised that offers better pay.

Wages

Right, there are a few diagrams to learn here (I know, sorry). A key thing to notice is that things are different depending on whether the labour market is perfectly or imperfectly competitive. ***These pages are for all boards.***

Market Forces can determine wages in a Labour Market

1) **Wage differentials** are the differences in wages between different groups of workers, or between workers in the same occupation. There are many reasons why these differentials exist, for example:
   - Workers that are **highly skilled** tend to be paid more, e.g. if they're highly trained or have high-level qualifications. (Having lots of skills or experience to offer an employer is known as having **high human capital** — see p.6.)
   - Wages vary in **different regions** and between **industries** — in some locations/industries workers will earn more.
   - A **trade union** can influence the wage rate paid to a group of workers (see p.108-109).

2) Wages will probably be **higher** if demand is high and inelastic, and supply is low and inelastic. Wages tend to be **low** when demand is low and elastic, and supply is high and elastic. This can be seen in the examples below:

Lawyers	Office cleaners
• **Lawyers** are paid **high wages**. • Demand for lawyers is **high** because they have a high MRP (marginal revenue product, see p.102) — in other words they're able to make lots of revenue for their firm. • Demand is also **inelastic** because lawyers are **not easily replaced** — few people have the right skills and experience. • Supply will be **low**, especially in the short run, as it takes a long time to train to become a lawyer, and not everyone has the abilities to become one.	• **Office cleaners** are paid fairly **low wages**. • Demand for cleaners is relatively **low** compared to the supply. The MRP for cleaners is low — this means demand for them is low as cleaners don't contribute greatly to the revenue of their employer. • Supply will also be **high** and **elastic** as there are no long training periods involved. Many people can do the job as no specific skills or qualifications are needed.

> Generally, when people talk about wages they mean **nominal** wages — i.e. the **amount** of money that people are paid. Economists also talk about **real** wages, which take **inflation** into account and represent the actual purchasing power of people's wages.

Wages are made up of Transfer Earnings and Economic Rent

1) In a labour market, **transfer earnings** can be seen as the **minimum payment** that's required to keep labour in its **current occupation** — i.e. the minimum pay that will stop a worker from switching to their next best paid job. The **size** of this transfer payment **differs** between workers.

2) Workers are often paid in **excess** of their transfer earnings — the excess above transfer earnings is called **economic rent**.

3) This means that a worker's **wages** can be **divided** into **two parts**: transfer earnings and economic rent. For example, a worker earns £400 per week. In his next best job he'd earn £350 per week. So his weekly wage is made up of £350 transfer earnings and £50 economic rent.

4) Transfer earnings and economic rent can be shown using a diagram like the one below:

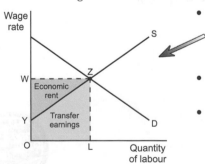

   - In this market the **equilibrium wage rate** is **W**. A worker who's paid this wage supplies their labour at the margin because if the wage was **reduced**, the worker would look for **alternative employment** and **leave** this labour market. For the marginal worker the **wage** rate is **equal to** their **transfer earnings**.
   - The area under the supply curve below the equilibrium point (OYZL) is equal to the **transfer earnings** of workers in this market.
   - The total earnings of all the workers in the market is equal to OWZL. **Economic rent** is equal to the part of this area which isn't accredited to transfer earnings — the triangle above the supply curve (YWZ).

5) The **elasticity** of the labour supply curve has a significant impact on the **proportion** of the total earnings that makes up **transfer earnings** and **economic rent**. This is shown on the diagram to the right.

   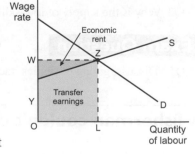

   - As the **supply curve** becomes more **elastic**, the proportion of the total earnings that's economic rent **decreases** and the proportion that's transfer earnings **increases**.
   - The **opposite** occurs if the **supply curve** becomes more **inelastic**.

6) For occupations where the supply of labour is **elastic**, the earnings of each worker will be **mainly transfer earnings**. The opposite is true for occupations that have an **inelastic** supply of workers (their earnings will be mainly **economic rent**).

Wages

In a **Perfectly Competitive Labour Market** firms are **Price Takers**

The diagrams show the **equilibrium wage rate** and **level of employment** for a perfectly competitive **labour market** and an **individual firm** within it:

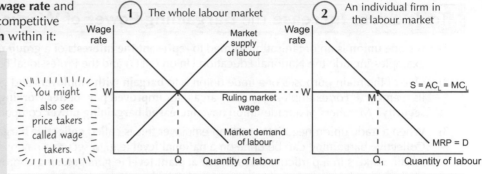

- In diagram 1 the **ruling market wage** (W) is determined by the forces of demand and supply.

- Individual firms have no power to influence the wage level so they're forced to accept the ruling market wage, i.e. firms are **price takers** — see diagram 2.

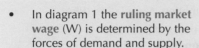

You might also see price takers called wage takers.

- The ruling market wage is also the **individual firm's labour supply curve**. This curve is **perfectly elastic** because the wage rate is **set by the market** and the firm can **hire as many workers as it wants** at this wage rate (W). Notice that the supply curve is also the **average cost of labour** (AC$_L$) curve (total wages divided by number of workers is equal to the wage rate) and the **marginal cost of labour** (MC$_L$) curve (the cost of employing one more worker is equal to the wage rate).

- In diagram 2, the firm decides to use the quantity of labour Q$_1$ because at Q$_1$ it **maximises profits** (MRP = MC$_L$ at point M, which is where a firm has the optimum number of workers — see p.102). (In a perfectly competitive market the MC$_L$ is **equal to** the **ruling wage**, so a firm will take on labour up to the point at which **MRP** is **equal to** the **wage rate** (W).)

- Remember, this is only a **theoretical model** as perfectly competitive labour markets don't exist in the real world. However, it's still useful to compare this model with real markets, which are all **imperfectly competitive** to some extent (see below).

A **Monopsony Labour Market** is an example of an **Imperfect Market**

1) This example shows the difference that **imperfections** can make to a labour market.

2) A **monopsony** means there's only **one buyer** in a market. In a **monopsony labour market** there's a **single employer**, so workers have only one choice of employer to work for.

3) A monopsonist employer can pay a wage that's **less than** a **worker's MRP** and **less than** what would've been paid in a **perfectly competitive labour market** (wages are **relatively** lower than in perfect competition). Monopsonist employers can also **drive down** the **level of employment** below the level that would exist in a perfectly competitive labour market.

4) The wages and employment levels in a monopsony labour market can be shown using the diagram below:

- The **marginal cost of labour** (MC$_L$) curve is **above** the average cost of labour (AC$_L$) curve, so the cost of employing one more worker is **more** than the average cost. MC$_L$ is above AC$_L$ because each time an extra worker is hired, not only does the firm have to pay that worker a **higher** wage to attract them, but the firm also has to **increase** existing workers' wages to the **same** level.

- The **average cost of labour** (AC$_L$) curve shows the number of workers that are prepared to work for the monopsonist at different wage levels — so the AC$_L$ curve is also the **supply curve**.

- Firms will hire the number of workers that **maximise their profits** (where MRP$_L$ = MC$_L$). This is at **T**, and the number of workers hired is **Q$_1$**. The **wage paid** is **W$_1$** — the supply curve clearly shows that Q$_1$ workers will accept W$_1$ wage.

- Unlike in a perfectly competitive market (where wages would be **W$_c$** and the labour supplied **Q$_c$**), this wage is **lower** than the **MRP** of labour. The monopsonist could pay a **higher** wage than W$_1$, but it doesn't need to as Q$_1$ workers will work for W$_1$. This means that monopsonists are **price makers**.

Warm-Up Questions

Q1 List three factors which might contribute to wage differentials.

Q2 Describe briefly what is meant by firms in a perfectly competitive labour market being 'price takers'.

Exam Question

Q1 Using a diagram, explain how wages and employment levels are determined in a monopsony labour market. [8 marks]

If you've got big skills it probably means you can pay big bills...

Wage differentials exist both between workers in the same occupation and between different groups of workers. As lovely as the diagrams are, they aren't just there to look pretty or to fill space — you need to understand what each one is showing.

Trade Unions

Trade unions are formed when workers come together and try to get a better deal from their employers. They can mean that workers get a higher wage, but it's not all good news and Margaret Thatcher wasn't a big fan. **For AQA and OCR only.**

Trade unions **Increase** the **Bargaining Power** of **Workers**

1) A **trade union** is an organisation formed to **represent the interests** of a **group of workers**. Examples include the National Education Union (NEU) and the Professional Footballers Association (PFA).

2) One of the main purposes of a trade union is to **bargain with employers** and get the best outcome for its members. For example, they can bargain for **improved pay**, **better working conditions** and **job security**. Members of a trade union have **increased bargaining power** compared to **individual workers**.

3) When a trade union negotiates with an employer this is called **collective bargaining**. Collective bargaining can be done on a **national level** (e.g. to secure a pay rise for all workers in a particular industry) or at **plant level** (e.g. negotiating improved working conditions for employees at an individual workplace).

4) **Productivity bargains** can be made, which is where unions agree to specific changes that'll **increase productivity** in return for **higher** wages or **other benefits** for its members. For example, **performance-related pay agreements** may be negotiated. This is when workers get pay increases that are linked to the quality of their work and their productivity.

> When looking at the effects of trade unions you should assume a '**closed shop**', i.e. every worker is a trade union member. This limits the available labour supply and means that firms can only pay the wage rate agreed by the trade union.

5) Trade unions can also have a role in making sure workers are safe at work by making sure any laws about working conditions are adhered to. For example, they will make sure workers have **sufficient breaks** and their place of work meets **health and safety requirements**.

6) Trade unions can also help to protect their members from **discrimination** (see p.110-111).

Trade union **Membership** in the UK was at its **Peak** in the **Late 1970s**

1) Trade unions are **most powerful** when they have **huge membership** — the more members a union has, the more influence it can have. At their peak in 1979, the trade unions in the UK were **very powerful** and had around 13 million members.

2) During the **1980s**, when Margaret Thatcher was the Prime Minister, the Conservative government acted to **reduce the power of trade unions** — e.g. by making it more difficult for trade unions to go on strike. The government at the time saw **weakening** the **trade unions** as a supply-side policy that would help make UK industry **more flexible** and **competitive**.

3) In addition, there was a big decline in the **large manufacturing industries** (e.g. shipbuilding) in the 1980s and 90s, which had huge trade union membership. This **de-industrialisation** meant that there was a shift in employment towards jobs in the **service sector** where unions tend not to exist — so union membership **fell sharply**.

4) Modern trends in the economy have also **reduced** union membership further. Workers on **flexible contracts** and **part-time workers** (both of which are becoming more common in the economy) are **less likely** to **join a union**.

5) Since the **mid 1990s** trade union membership has remained **fairly stable**, between 6 million and 7 million members.

Trade Union Wage Negotiations may result in Unemployment

1) Trade unions can **cause labour market failure** by **forcing wages up** to a level **higher** than the **market equilibrium wage** — causing a **surplus of labour** (i.e. **unemployment**). Some of a firm's income is redistributed to the workers and its **costs of production increase**.

2) The effect of **trade union wage negotiations** in a **perfectly competitive labour market** can be seen on the diagram below:

- **Without trade union action** firms would pay the **equilibrium wage rate** (W_e) and the level of employment would be L_e.
- When the trade union forces the wage rate up to W_t this means firms can't employ workers for less than this wage. This results in a **kinked supply curve** (shown in red). At W_t the quantity of labour employed **falls** to L_1.
- At this higher wage rate (W_t) there's an **oversupply of workers** — there's **insufficient demand** for the number of workers willing to work, so there's unemployment (L_1 to L_2), and this is labour market failure.
- The **level of unemployment** caused by the wage increase depends on the **elasticity** of the labour demand curve.

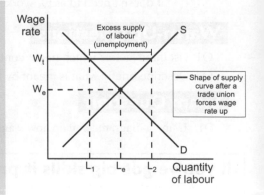

Trade Unions

Pay Rises negotiated by trade unions May Not lead to Unemployment

1) Trade unions can help to increase the wages of their members without causing unemployment. To do this the **productivity** of trade union members must **increase** — this would **increase demand** for workers from firms and help **prevent** the situation of an **excess supply** of labour described on the previous page.

2) Trade unions can help persuade their members to agree to **more efficient working practices** which **increase worker productivity**. This is good for firms as a **more productive workforce** may **increase** their **profits**. Workers will benefit from higher wages and trade union membership won't be reduced by unemployment.

3) When workers become **more productive** a firm's **MRP** (demand) curve **shifts** to the **right**. Firms can afford to pay wages that are equal to a worker's MRP (see p.102), so if a trade union can help raise the MRP of workers, then an increased wage can be justified.

In Monopsonistic Labour Markets trade unions can Increase Wages and Jobs

1) A monopsonistic employer pays workers a wage that's lower than their MRP (see p.107). If a trade union was involved it could **increase** the **wage rate** whilst maintaining the same level of employment, or even increasing it.

2) When a trade union enters a monopsonistic labour market this is an example of a **bilateral monopoly**. This is when there's a **single buyer** and a **single seller** — so in this case there's a single buyer of labour (the monopsonist) and a single seller (the trade union).

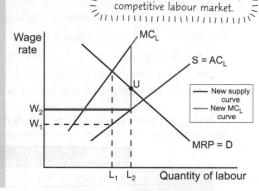

Remember, a monopsonistic labour market is an imperfectly competitive labour market.

- W_1 is the wage that the monopsonist would have paid its workers **without a union** (check p.107 to recap why).
- The presence of a union may increase wages to W_2. In doing this it will change the shape of the **supply/average cost of labour (AC_L) curve**, and that'll then change the shape of the marginal cost of labour (MC_L) curve.
- The **profit maximising** level of workers is still where the MC_L curve crosses the marginal revenue product (MRP) curve. This is now at **point U**, giving a **new increased level of employment** of L_2.
- The union has managed to **increase wages** from W_1 to W_2, and **increase employment** from L_1 to L_2.

3) The presence of the trade union in the market means that the **wage rate** and **level of employment** have been brought **closer** to the levels that they'd be at in a **free market**. The trade union has had a positive impact on the labour market.

Trade Unions are Less Likely to cause Market Failure Today

1) Government legislation has **reduced** the **power** of **trade unions**. They're **less likely** to cause **market failure** (e.g. by increasing unemployment) because they have **less influence**.

2) Trade unions have made big changes in the workplace though. In return for **higher pay** and **better working conditions** firms have benefited from a **more productive** and **flexible workforce**. Don't forget that the increased productivity of workers may drive an **increased demand** for workers and lead to a **reduction** in the level of **unemployment**.

Warm-Up Questions

Q1 Describe what a trade union is.

Q2 Describe the trend in trade union membership in the UK since the 1970s.

Q3 Draw a diagram to show how a trade union can increase wages and the level of employment in a monopsonistic labour market.

Exam Question

Q1 Discuss the extent to which trade unions cause labour market failure. [20 marks]

"We want better pay! When do we want it? NOOOOOOOOOOOOOOOW..."

Ah, trade unions — makes me think of miners going on strike, but that's not the only thing trade unions do. Of course they're linked to some strike action in the UK, particularly in the 1970s, but they also have an important role in protecting workers' rights and negotiating for a fair wage. Learn the theory about how trade union action might create jobs or increase unemployment.

Discrimination

Workers can be discriminated against for reasons that aren't related to their ability to do a particular job — this is pretty unfair. But first up on this page is wage discrimination, which is a bit different. **These pages are for AQA and OCR only.**

Wage Discrimination can result in Lower Wage Costs for firms

1) **Wage discrimination** is **similar** to **price discrimination**.

2) Wage discrimination takes place when **employers** with **monopsony power** pay **different wage rates** based on different workers' **willingness to supply labour**. This can be shown by the diagram below:

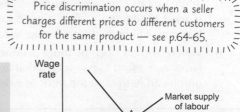
Price discrimination occurs when a seller charges different prices to different customers for the same product — see p.64-65.

- **Without wage discrimination** all workers in a competitive market are **paid W$_e$** — the market equilibrium price.
- The **total wage cost** for firms is OW$_e$AL$_e$.
- When employers start to pay the **minimum** each worker is prepared to work for (i.e. their transfer earnings — see p.106), the total wage cost is **reduced** to OBAL$_e$ (the green area shown on the diagram).
- **Employers gain** while **workers lose out**.

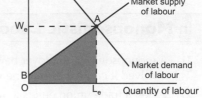

3) Wage discrimination shouldn't be confused with **labour market discrimination**. This is a different concept based on workers being discriminated against depending on differences between them, such as **gender** and **race** — see below.

4) Wage discrimination is common in professions where employees **negotiate** their own pay and conditions — some people will be able to negotiate a **higher wage** than others for the **same job**.

5) In general, there are some categories of workers who are **more likely** to be prepared to work for **lower** wages, e.g.:
- **Young** workers may be more interested in **gaining experience** than earning a high wage.
- **Part-time** workers may be willing to work for **lower** wages if they're not the **main** wage earner in their **household**.
- Some **immigrants** will accept **lower** wages if they're higher than the wages they could earn in their country of origin.

Wage Discrimination has Advantages and Disadvantages

	Advantages	Disadvantages
Workers	• As employers' wage costs will be reduced, it can **increase** demand for labour, providing **more jobs**.	• Can lead to the **exploitation** of vulnerable workers, who could be **forced** to accept low wages. • Could force wages **down** for **all** workers in a market.
Employers	• **Reduces** the cost of wages, which can lead to higher profits.	• Can require **additional administration** (e.g. it takes extra paperwork to pay workers in the same job different wages). • Can lead to **industrial unrest** if workers know about the **differences** in wages.
Economy	• Could **increase** employment levels through increased demand for labour.	• Could lead to increases in **inequality**, so **benefits** may be required to 'top up' low wages.

Labour Market Discrimination is a Cause of Labour Market Failure

1) Labour market discrimination is when a **specific group of workers** is **treated differently** to other workers in the same job.

2) Workers can be discriminated against because of their **race**, **gender**, **sexuality**, **religion**, **disability**, **age**, etc. Here are two examples of labour market discrimination:

Racial discrimination can occur when employers only want to work with and employ people from a **particular ethnic background**. They're prepared to pay a price for this — the **loss in productivity** from not employing a worker that's perhaps the most suited for the job.

The **gender pay gap** is where average pay rates are lower for women than for men. Part of this pay gap is thought to be due to **discrimination by employers** that are prepared to pay male employees more than female employees for doing the **same job**.

3) In the UK this sort of discrimination is **against the law**. The Equality Act of 2010 replaced all previous anti-discrimination laws and made discrimination **illegal** in the UK.

4) Discrimination can be one cause of the **unequal distribution of wealth and income** (see p.165), and can lead to a **misallocation of resources**, **reduced efficiency** and **increased costs**.

Discrimination

Workers suffering from Discrimination tend to Earn Less

1) Workers who suffer from discrimination are generally forced to accept **lower wages**.

2) Discrimination can also mean that some workers find it more difficult to find a job. They may resort to accepting a **lower-paid job** that they're **overqualified for**. This is unfair to them and is also a **misallocation of resources**.

3) In addition, workers who are the victims of discrimination may be **put off** from going for **promotions**, which can leave them in low-paying jobs with **limited career prospects**.

Employers who Discriminate can incur Increased Costs

1) Employers who are influenced by their own prejudices believe that the **marginal revenue product** (MRP) of the discriminated group of workers is **lower** than it really is. This means that they demand **fewer** of these workers.

2) When demand falls the MRP/demand curve **shifts left**, which means that **wages go down** for the discriminated group.

3) By discriminating like this, firms have **fewer workers to choose from**. By ignoring workers who may have been more suited to a job and more efficient, they **increase** their **costs of production**. Increased costs may lead to **increased prices**.

4) This discrimination can be shown by the diagrams on the right.

   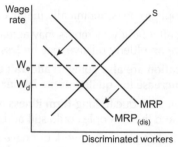 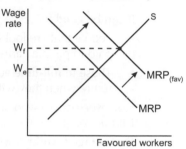
   Discriminated workers   Favoured workers

   - For discriminated workers, **MRP** is **lower** than the level in the free market and this results in a **lower wage rate** (W_d).

   - For favoured workers employers believe their **MRP** to be **greater** than it really is. This shifts the MRP curve to the right, **increasing** the **wage rate** for these workers (to W_f).

5) Employers that **don't discriminate** have access to a **greater supply** of labour.

   - As the **demand** for discriminated workers is **reduced** in firms that **discriminate**, there are **more workers** available to supply their labour to firms that **don't discriminate**.

   - The **supply curve** for these firms **shifts right** and the **wage rate decreases**. This means discriminated workers could lose out again.

Discrimination leads to Increased Costs for the Government and Economy

1) The government may need to increase **welfare payments** to support **discriminated workers**.

2) Discriminated workers working for **unfairly low wages** will also reduce the government's **tax revenues**, which would be higher if these workers were paid fairly.

3) If discriminated workers aren't in a job that's well suited to them (e.g. if they're overqualified), their levels of **productivity** can **fall**. When **output** and **efficiency** (both allocative and productive) **fall**, a country may **lose international competitiveness**. This could negatively affect the country's **balance of payments**, reducing the **sale of exports**, and this in turn may cause **unemployment**.

Warm-Up Questions

Q1 Define wage discrimination.

Q2 Workers can be discriminated against because of their age. List three other forms of labour market discrimination.

Q3 Explain how discrimination can lead to increased costs for governments.

Exam Questions

Q1 Explain the impact of labour market discrimination on workers' wages and productivity. [8 marks]

Q2 Use a diagram to explain how firms that discriminate against workers can experience increased costs. [8 marks]

Wanted: hard-working, driven discrimination joke. Please apply to CGP at...

Discrimination is another type of labour market failure. There are two types of discrimination you need to know about. Wage discrimination is where workers are paid different wages depending on their willingness to supply labour. Discrimination in the labour market is when workers are discriminated against because of things like their age or ethnicity — this is illegal in the UK.

Imperfections

There are many imperfections that can exist in labour markets (often called labour market failure).
These imperfections have various impacts on labour markets. **These pages are for all boards.**

Not all **Economic Inactivity** is **Labour Market Failure**

1) People are classed as **economically inactive** if they're
   not working and also **not looking for work**.

2) Economically inactive people are considered by economists
   as a **waste** of a **scarce resource** (labour).

3) People are economically inactive for several reasons:

Economic inactivity suited
Geoffrey just fine.

   - They **care** for sick, elderly or young people (unpaid).
   - They're in **full-time education**.
   - They have a **long-term illness** or **disability**.
   - They're **choosing not to find a job** or have **given up**.

4) It can be **good** for some people to be economically inactive. For example:
   - People that are looking after family members may actually save the government money. For example, the benefits
     paid to people caring for an elderly relative may be **less expensive** than the cost of providing a professional carer.
   - Those in **full-time education** are also going to **add value** to the economy in the
     future when they will **increase** the **quality** of the **labour force**.

5) However, people who are inactive due to **long-term illness** or **disability**, but are still **able** to work, represent **market failure**.
   Labour is a scarce resource and these people could still add to an **economy's output** if work can be found for them.

6) **Discouraged workers** who have tried to find work but have **given up** are also a waste of scarce labour in exactly the
   same way. Discouraged workers are also more likely to suffer from depression, which can add to **health care costs**.

All labour markets suffer from **Imperfect Information**

1) **Imperfect information** is another source of labour market failure.

2) Perfect information would exist if **workers knew everything** about every **job** and **employers knew everything** about
   every potential **worker**. Using this information workers and employers would find their **ideal job** and **employees**.

3) Of course, the **real world isn't perfect**:
   - Many **workers** end up in jobs that **aren't the best fit** for them (e.g. that don't utilise their skills fully and keep
     them motivated) and/or **don't pay enough**. Or, they might end up with **no job** at all.
   - **Employers** end up with workers that aren't as **productive** as they could be, which increases their **costs of
     production** and makes their goods **less competitive**.

4) Imperfect information increases **frictional unemployment** (see p.151). When people
   are between jobs they need to **spend time researching** to find the **right job**. If they
   had the benefit of **perfect information** their task would be **simpler**.

Skill Shortages increase the **Costs of Production** for firms

1) A shortage of anything **drives up** its **price**. Therefore shortages of skilled labour drive
   up the **wage costs** for **firms**, which in turn **increases** their **costs of production**.

2) A shortage also means that firms may be forced to **employ workers** who **don't** have the **desired
   level** of **qualification/experience** for the job, and this will **reduce productivity** and **quality** levels.

3) **Training** can increase employee skills and make them **more productive**, but employers
   can be **reluctant** to **provide it** as they often worry about other firms **poaching**
   their **newly-trained employees** without incurring the costs of this training.

4) **Encouraging** the **immigration** of workers with certain **skills** is one
   way of tackling skills shortages — see page 121.

Imperfections

Unemployment exists when labour Supply is Greater Than labour Demand

1) Unemployed workers are a **waste of scarce resources** — unemployment means an economy isn't making use of all its resources effectively. However, in an economy there's always some level of unemployment, and unemployment actually helps to **keep wages down**.

2) For example, if everyone in an economy had a job and an employer wanted to hire a worker, they would have to offer them a **higher wage** than their current job. A firm could offer better **non-pecuniary benefits** (e.g. a health care package, greater career progression opportunities — see p.104) instead, but this would still **increase** the firm's **costs**.

3) Unemployment only becomes a **serious market failure** if it's at a **high level** and persists for a **long period** of time.

4) If the level of **unemployment benefit** is **too high**, i.e. the replacement ratio (the ratio of how much a person would earn if they were **unemployed** to how much they'd earn if they were **employed**) is too high, this can cause **unemployment**. This means that people can be better off by **choosing not to work** (**voluntary unemployment**) and claiming unemployment benefit rather than **working** for a **low wage** — this is called the **unemployment trap**.

The unemployment trap is different to the poverty trap, which is covered on p.166.

Some people are More Geographically Mobile than others

1) **Geographical immobility** of labour is when workers aren't able to (or are reluctant to) **move to different locations** to find the best jobs for themselves. When this happens they end up either **unemployed** or in jobs that **aren't suited to them** — so there's a misallocation of resources and market failure occurs.

2) There are a number of reasons behind geographical immobility. They include:
   - People make **friends** and have **family** that they don't want to move away from.
   - It's **expensive** to **move house**. Not only does it cost to buy a house, but it costs to sell your house too.

3) Geographical labour immobility can lead to labour **shortages** in one area and labour **surpluses** in another. This can then be followed by **regional wage differences** — **high** wages in the areas with **shortages** and **low** wages in the areas with **surpluses**.

Occupational immobility is when it's Difficult to Switch Jobs

1) **Occupational immobility** is when workers **aren't able** to **move** from **one occupation to another** with ease.

2) In an ideal world workers would be able to **transfer their skills** from one job to another or **retrain** with ease, but in reality this **often isn't the case**. When workers have **specific skills** they aren't always able to use them in another job.

3) Occupational immobility can be affected by age. **Younger workers** are **more likely to retrain**, but older workers may lack the confidence or motivation to do so.

4) Some occupations also require **high-level qualifications** and particular **personality traits**. For example, not everyone is cut out for the years of academic study required to become a vet and not everyone can cope with the sight of blood.

5) Occupational immobility can contribute to **unemployment**, and may mean **skills shortages** (see previous page) are harder to fix. For example, if the labour of **skilled workers** in a particular occupation started to be replaced by machines, those workers **may not** be able to easily transfer their skills to other occupations and many could become **unemployed**.

Warm-Up Questions

Q1 Describe three reasons why people can be economically inactive.

Q2 Explain how a shortage of skilled labour can increase a firm's costs of production.

Q3 Why is some unemployment desirable in an economy?

PRACTICE QUESTIONS

Exam Question

Q1 Explain the likely impacts of a high level of occupational immobility on an economy. [4 marks]

Keep economically active — revise economics whilst jogging...

I don't know about you, but I always take a revision guide on a jog... OK, that's a lie, but seriously, getting a grip on labour market imperfections is important — they're the reasons why perfectly competitive labour markets don't really exist. Mind-blowing stuff.

Labour Market Characteristics

Barriers to entry impact the overall structure of the labour market, and incentives play important roles in economies as they have significant impacts on workers and firms. **These pages are for OCR only.**

Barriers that stop people Changing Jobs create Segmented Labour Markets

1) In theory, if there were **no barriers** to entry and exit, workers would move from low wage jobs to high wage jobs until **everyone** had the **same wage**. However, in reality there would still be **some wage differentials** because **not everyone** has the motivation and talent to do a **high-paying job** (such as a surgeon).

2) In fact some people in **vocational jobs**, like **nursing**, aren't motivated by money (e.g. they choose to do their job mainly because they love doing it), so they wouldn't get a job in a **different profession** to earn **higher wages**. They might, however, move to a **different nursing job** with **higher pay**.

3) In reality, **barriers** to entry and exit **do exist** and they prevent the free movement of workers between all of the different jobs that are available — this is what causes **segmented labour markets** to exist. Rather than one labour market, there are **many** distinct labour markets, which are sub-markets of the labour market.

Howard quickly realised that the barrier to exit might be more of a problem.

4) The **main barrier** to entry in segmented labour markets is **qualifications/skill levels** — this **limits supply** and **increases wages** of particular groups of workers. The existence of these barriers might lead to **market failure** because the forces of demand and supply can't act to equalise wages — i.e. the market equilibrium wage can't be the same across a segmented labour market.

5) Barriers aren't all bad though. Making sure workers in **highly-skilled occupations** have the **necessary skills** is crucial to **keeping people safe** — no one wants an unqualified dentist. So, **minimum qualifications** make sure the **right people** are doing the right job — making the market **more efficient**.

Incentives can be given to either Workers or Firms

1) **Incentives** are given to people to encourage them to work (instead of claiming unemployment benefits), which will increase the **participation rate** and the **labour supply**. For example, people who are **looking** and **applying** for jobs or who are in work but earning **low incomes** can claim **Universal Credit**. Those who are eligible are paid a certain amount of money depending on their **earnings** (and other criteria). If a person has a low income then will they receive less Universal Credit than if they had no income, but overall they will **earn more** (through their **combined** income and Universal Credit). This encourages people to find work.

> The participation rate is the percentage of the working age population (aged 15 and above) that are in work or actively seeking work in an economy — it's the proportion of economically active people in the population.

2) Incentives can also be given to **firms** with the aim of **increasing** the number of available jobs. For example, Employment Allowance means that firms who **should** pay up to £3000 in National Insurance contributions for their employees **don't** actually have to pay anything at all. This benefits **smaller** firms by **reducing** their costs and it also leads to **job creation**, but many of these jobs are low-paid.

3) A national minimum wage (NMW) (see p.116) can be an incentive for **migrants** to move to a country if it's **higher** than wages they would be paid in their country of origin — see p.121 for more on migration.

Labour Market Characteristics

Demographic changes to the population and the labour market also have effects on the economy.

Demographic Changes can be a Major Concern for Governments

1) **Demographic changes** are changes in the **composition** of a population. This might be changes in the **proportion** of people who are of working age (e.g. between 15 and 65) or in the **gender** split of a population.

This population may be, for example, the population of a labour market, or the entire population of a country, or the population of a particular region.

2) The UK has an **ageing population**, which means that a **large proportion** of the population is **over 60**. This is also the case for **many other developed** countries.

3) This demographic change is causing several big **problems**:

- The UK government pays a **state pension** (a certain amount of money per week) to workers once they reach the state pension **age** and have made a **minimum** number of years of National Insurance contributions — so an **ageing** population means state pensions are a **growing cost** for the government.

- The NHS is used **more** by older people, so an ageing population puts a **strain** on many of its services and **increases** the cost to the government.

- There's a **reduction** in the working age population, a **reduction** in labour supply and an **increase** in the **dependency ratio**. As a **greater proportion** of the population is **not** working, there are **fewer** people paying **taxes** to help the government to fund pensions and the NHS.

A dependency ratio tells you how many people are either too young or too old to work, relative to the number of people of working age.

4) These problems are **unlikely** to resolve themselves soon, as life expectancy is increasing. The government needs to take action to tackle the problems caused by an ageing population (see p.118-121 for more on how governments might intervene).

5) The **impacts** of an ageing population on the labour market can include:

- **Wage increases**, particularly for **younger** workers who will be more **scarce**.
- A **greater proportion** of the working population being **older**, e.g. over 50.
- **Increased** participation in labour markets by those over 65.
- Changes in **employment patterns** — e.g. **more** jobs caring for the elderly population.
- The need for **more immigration**, particularly of young, skilled workers.
- **Tax** increases to cover the costs of the **increasing number** of elderly people, e.g. to pay for health care and pensions.

6) Other demographic changes have different impacts on the labour market. For example, increased **female participation** in a labour market can increase the **supply** of labour and lead to a **fall** in wages.

Warm-Up Questions

Q1 Give an example of how barriers to entry and exit in the labour market can be a good thing.

Q2 How could a national minimum wage incentivise migration of labour?

Q3 Give three possible impacts of an ageing population on the labour market.

Exam Questions

Q1 Explain how barriers to entry and exit can result in segmented labour markets.

[8 marks]

I like my labour markets like I like my chocolate — segmented...

There are lots of things that can have an impact on labour markets or change their structure. Remember that a lot of things that seem like they'll be bad for the economy, e.g. barriers to entry and exit, or an ageing population, often have at least a few positive effects too. Being able to consider both the advantages and disadvantages of something will help you to get marks in your exam.

Minimum, Maximum and Living Wages

There are lots of ways governments can influence or restrict wages — these pages cover a few of them. For example, in the UK, the government sets a minimum wage that workers are to be paid per hour. **These pages are for all boards.**

EDEXCEL ONLY

Governments Intervene in the labour market to Correct Market Failure

1) Governments intervene to **correct labour market failure** because it causes several problems, such as **unemployment** or **very low** wages.

2) There are many ways governments can intervene in the labour market — several are covered on the following pages. One of the main ways the government can intervene is by **influencing** wages.

Public Sector Wages allow governments to Intervene in the labour market

1) The money to pay public sector workers comes from the **government**, so governments have a big **impact** on public sector wages. This means that governments **should** be able to ensure that public sector workers are paid **decent**, **fair** wages.

2) However, in the UK the government went through a period of **reducing** public sector spending. This led to job **losses**, pay **cuts** and **freezes** in pay increases for many public sector workers. The government **clashed** with trade unions over these changes, leading to **strikes**.

3) Restricting pay can cause a **recruitment crisis** in the public sector — if wages are restricted **too much**, more people will look for work in the **private** sector instead and it can be difficult to **retain** high-quality workers.

4) The government is a **monopsony employer** in the public sector (see p.107 for more on monopsony employers), but trade unions can act to **increase** public sector wages and employment by creating a **bilateral monopoly** (see p.109).

The National Minimum Wage (NMW) aims to make wages fairer

1) The NMW sets a legal **minimum hourly rate of pay** for different age groups. A NMW was first introduced by the UK government in 1999 to stop firms setting wages so low that their employees couldn't afford a decent standard of living. It aims to prevent the exploitation of workers due to the **payment** of **unfairly low wages**.

2) By increasing the pay of the poorest workers a NMW leads to a **more equitable distribution** of **income**.

3) A NMW helps to **encourage people to work**. For example, having a minimum wage might encourage workers to **get a job** instead of **claiming benefits**, as it improves the replacement ratio (see p.113).

4) In addition, increasing the number of people in work **increases** the **participation rate** (see p.114), which is good for the economy and **increases** the **labour supply**.

> In 2016, the UK government introduced a higher minimum wage for workers aged 25 and over called the National Living Wage (NLW).
> Don't confuse this with the 'living wage', which is calculated by the Living Wage Foundation (see p. 117).

EDEXCEL & AQA

It can be argued that introducing a NMW leads to Unemployment

1) Using supply and demand diagrams it could be argued that **increasing the wage rate** would lead to a **contraction** in **demand** for **labour**. This can be seen in the diagrams below:

> This is similar to when trade unions negotiate a pay rise — see the diagram on p.108.

- Introducing a minimum wage that's higher than an industry's equilibrium wage (W_e) would **raise** the **wage rate** from W_e to NMW. This would cause the supply of labour to increase from Q_e to Q_2 and demand to fall from Q_e to Q_1.
- This could cause unemployment of Q_1 to Q_2 because there's an **excess supply of labour**.
- Introducing a minimum wage when the demand and supply of labour is fairly **elastic** (diagram 1) results in **greater unemployment** than when the demand and supply of labour is more **inelastic** (diagram 2) — the **difference** between Q_1 and Q_2 is **larger** in diagram 1.

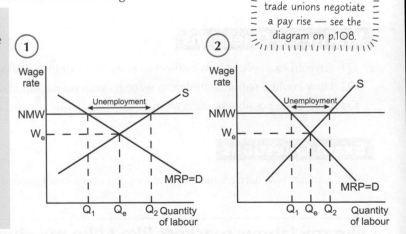

2) Unemployment caused by the introduction of a NMW would be an example of government failure. However, there's evidence to suggest that having a NMW **hasn't caused** a significant **negative impact** on the **level of employment** in the UK.

3) A NMW can be used to help **tackle inequality** and **poverty** — there are other ways of doing this too (see p.167).

Minimum, Maximum and Living Wages

Introducing a NMW can have a number of **Advantages** and **Disadvantages**

Advantages

- Introducing a NMW may help those on **very low incomes** and **reduce the** level of **poverty** in a country.
- A NMW may also **boost the morale** of workers as they'll receive better wages. Happier workers tend to be **more productive**, so output may increase as a result.
- A NMW means there's **greater reward** for doing a job that pays the NMW. It gives people more **incentive** to get a job rather than be unemployed.
- The government's **tax revenue** is likely to be **greater** if a NMW is introduced.

How beneficial a NMW is may depend on the level it's set at.

Disadvantages

- A NMW can **increase wage costs** for firms. This might mean they have to **cut jobs**, resulting in increased **unemployment**.
- A NMW could decrease the **competitiveness** of **UK firms** compared to firms in other countries that have lower wage costs.
- UK firms may have to **pass on** increased wage costs to consumers by **increasing** their **prices**, and this could contribute to **inflation**.
- There are **doubts** about whether introducing a NMW really **decreases poverty**. This is because many of the poorest members of society, such as the elderly and disabled, are **not in work** (so aren't able to benefit from an increased wage rate).

If you got an exam question about what would happen if the NMW was increased, then you could use these advantages and disadvantages too.

The '**Living Wage**' covers the **Basic Cost** of living

1) The '**living wage**' is an hourly wage independently worked out by the Living Wage Foundation. It's a wage that'll cover an individual's **basic cost of living** in the UK and it's **higher** than the current NMW (and NLW). There are two different rates — one for London and one for the rest of the UK.

2) It's **not compulsory** for employers to pay the living wage, but the government **encourages** it. **Over 1000** UK employers, such as Barclays and Google™, have **voluntarily** committed to pay their employees **at**, or **above**, the 'living wage'.

3) Most of the **advantages** and **disadvantages** of a NMW (see above) apply to the 'living wage' too — and the NMW diagram on the previous page shows what effect a 'living wage' may have on employment levels.

A government can set a **Maximum Wage**

1) A **maximum wage limits** a worker's wage rate. To be effective it must be set **below** the **market equilibrium wage rate**, which will **reduce** wages in that market (to W_m) and **increase** demand for labour (to Q_2).

2) The possible **benefits** of a maximum wage include:

- **Rises** in wages **above** increases in productivity can cause **inflation**, so setting a maximum wage can **limit** how much prices can rise and help to **prevent** the wage-price spiral (see p.152).
- A maximum wage could **limit** the level of **inequality** in a country (especially if there's also a **minimum** wage).
- A maximum wage could **reduce** a firm's **labour cost** and **increase** their **willingness** to **hire more workers** (they'll demand Q_2 on the diagram).

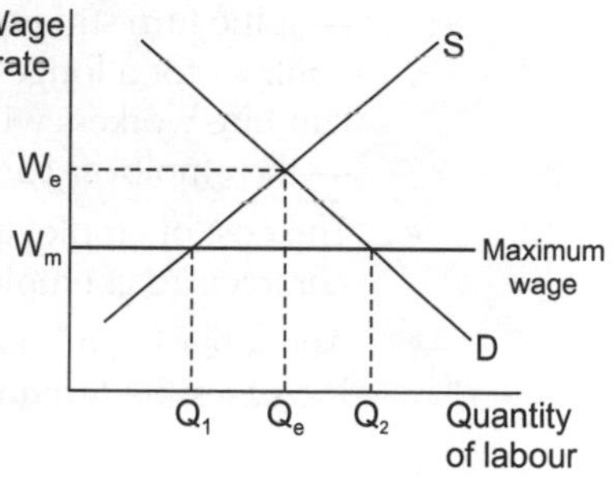

Graph: Wage rate (y-axis) vs Quantity of labour (x-axis). Supply curve S and Demand curve D intersect at equilibrium W_e, Q_e. A horizontal line at W_m below W_e is labelled "Maximum wage". Points Q_1, Q_e, Q_2 marked on x-axis.

3) There are arguments **against** a maximum wage too:

- Some believe it's **unfair** to **not** reward greater effort or ability with higher income.
- The possibility of **higher pay** and **pay increases** provides **motivation** to work harder.
- If only **some** countries had a maximum wage, people who could earn **higher** wages in **other** countries might move abroad (on the diagram, labour **beyond Q_1** could get higher wages abroad). Similarly, if **one industry** had a maximum wage and **another didn't**, then people would train to work in the industry **without** a maximum wage.

Warm-Up Questions

Q1 Give two benefits of a national minimum wage.

Q2 What is a 'living wage'?

Exam Question

Q1 Discuss the implications for an economy of introducing a national minimum wage. [15 marks]

My maximum wage is three ice lollies and a sherbet lemon...

A minimum wage is a classic example of intervention in the labour market, but it's worth remembering that it's not all positive. Bear in mind that a government can set the minimum wage at a level where it's a 'living wage' (i.e. covers the basic cost of living).

Labour Force Flexibility

Flexible labour and wages are useful for an economy — flexibility makes it easier for an economy to respond to changes and therefore to recover when things aren't going too well. **This page is for Edexcel and OCR only.**

Labour Force Flexibility is Good for the economy

1) **Government intervention** to improve the **flexibility** of the labour force will help to **reduce** labour market immobility.

2) A **flexible labour force** is one where workers can **transfer between activities** quickly in response to changes in the economy. For example, a worker in a flexible labour force would be able to retrain or transfer their skills to another job easily if something badly affected the industry they were employed in.

3) Governments can act to increase the flexibility of the workforce:

The flexibility of Demar's labour was high — by day he was just an ordinary accountant, but by night he used his numerical competence to fight crime.

- To **increase** the **flexibility** of workers, governments can **promote** or **subsidise training** and **education schemes** that help workers gain **skills and knowledge** that are attractive to employers. They can also **provide training** directly, e.g. skills training to the unemployed.

- Recently, there have been changes to the UK education system, such as an **increase** in **apprenticeships** and **vocational education**, and **restructuring** of the exam system. These schemes should improve labour market flexibility by helping young people to **develop skills** they need to get a job. It takes **time** for the effects of these changes to be seen, so it'll be a while before anyone can **assess** whether they've been **successful or not**.

- The UK government has also increased flexibility by **reducing** the **power** of **trade unions**, which can cause inflexibility in the labour market (e.g. by negotiating for longer working contracts).

4) For **employers**, a flexible workforce is one that can be hired and fired easily. Laws that make it **easy** to hire and fire workers encourage employers to **take on more workers**. This is because firms know they can change the size of their workforce quickly (and therefore cheaply) in response to changes in the market.

5) Different types of **contract** (such as short-term and zero-hour) can also make workers more flexible for employers:

- **Short-term** contracts allow firms to hire a worker for a **certain length of time** (e.g. six months) — if the firm still needs the worker towards the end of the contract they can extend the contract for a longer period (or not) to suit their needs. **Zero-hour** contracts are where firms can hire workers without guaranteeing them a definite number of hours of work per week — the employer can offer these employees a number of hours that suits the firm's needs.

- The cost of employing staff on short-term and zero-hour contracts is **less** than **full-time** contracts (e.g. employees on zero-hour contracts don't need to be given sick pay).

- An increasing number of part-time workers and increasingly flexible working times in the UK also increases the **temporal flexibility** of labour (the ability to change the number of hours worked).

6) Zero-hour contracts are **popular** with **governments** because they **reduce unemployment figures**, but they can **cause problems** — workers on these contracts **don't** have a **guaranteed income**, so it's hard for them to manage their finances.

Wage Flexibility is an important characteristic of a Flexible Labour Force

1) **Wage flexibility** refers to the ability of real wages to **change** in response to changes in **demand for and supply of labour**.

2) **Performance-related pay** and **regional pay awards** are examples of uses of flexible wages. (Regional pay awards are used to account for variations in living costs in different regions, e.g. workers in London are usually paid higher wages than workers elsewhere in the UK because it's more expensive to live there.)

3) Wage flexibility can be an important feature during a **recession** — **wage cuts** and **pay freezes** can be accepted by workers as an alternative to losing jobs.

4) Governments can improve wage flexibility by **scrapping** the **NMW** and **limiting trade union power**.

Pensions and a Changing Workforce

Ageing populations (see p.115) make paying out pensions very expensive, so governments have to make changes to try to make the system more sustainable. Often, making multiple changes is the best way of combatting the problem. **OCR only.**

Governments might be forced to make Changes to Pensions

1) As **more people** are **living longer** (see p.115 for more on ageing populations), governments may need to **change** the way that state pensions work to ensure that they can continue to afford to pay pensions to an **increasing number of people** for an **increasingly long time**.

2) There are a number of methods governments can use, which include:

- **Raising** the **state pension age** — this will mean that on average pensioners will have fewer years claiming the state pension. The justification behind this is that because people are **living longer**, they should **work longer** before starting to claim a pension. In the UK the **state pension age** for men and women will increase to 67 by 2028. It's predicted to rise further in future years.

- **Increasing** the **contributions** necessary to **qualify** for a state pension. In the UK to **qualify** to receive the state pension you need to have paid **National Insurance contributions** for a **certain number of years** — this is paid by workers when they earn a certain amount. Pension reforms may see the **number of years** of necessary contributions **increase**.

- **Decreasing** the amount **paid out**. This means people would need to do more **planning** and **saving** for retirement while they're **working**, so they have enough money to live on when they retire. This is why the UK government made it **compulsory** for **employers** to enrol workers on a **workplace pension** (although workers can opt out), so that retirees have extra income in addition to the amount they'll receive from their state pension.

In April 2015 there was a big change in Pension Legislation

1) Approximately 18 million people aged **55 and over** were given more **flexibility** in how they can **use** and **withdraw** their private pension savings.

2) Changes were made to **pension tax rules** and certain parts of **pension legislation**.

3) For example, people now have the option to withdraw their **entire** pension fund and use or invest it as they choose, instead of having to accept a **regular** payment (e.g. monthly or annually).

4) This change in legislation aims to **increase choice**. However, it's likely to also lead to an **increase** in **spending** — e.g. by people withdrawing money from their pension savings to spend straight away. This could boost the economy because **more** spending may increase demand in an economy, creating **economic growth** and leading to **more** employment and **higher** wages. On the other hand, this growth might only be **short term**, and less spending later on could **restrict future growth**. It may also mean there's a risk that pensioners **run out of money** later in retirement, so rely more on the state, e.g. to provide **care**.

Changes to some laws will affect the Workforce size and Participation Rates

1) The pension age is currently planned to **increase** to 68 by 2046 — this will **increase** the size of the workforce, and **may** raise the participation rate (see p.114 for more on participation rates).

2) Since 2015, people **must** remain in some form of training or education until they're **18**. This has caused a **reduction** in the size of the workforce, but the **long-term** benefits of a **better educated**, **better paid**, **more productive** and **more flexible** workforce are likely to **outweigh** this drawback.

3) Childcare can be **expensive** and its cost can contribute to situations where working means people are **worse off** than if they don't work — e.g. the income someone would receive from their working wages, minus the cost of childcare, may be less than the income they'd receive if they stayed at home with their children and claimed benefits. So, **increasing** state provision of childcare (or childcare subsidies) is likely to **increase** participation rates (especially of women).

4) **Incentives** to workers and firms can help to increase participation rates — see p.114 and p.120.

Warm-Up Questions

Q1 List two ways that a government could reform pensions as the population ages.

Q2 List three ways that a government might try to increase the number of people in the workforce.

Exam Question

Q1 Analyse the different methods that governments can use to increase labour force flexibility. [8 marks]

As a contortionist, the flexibility of my labour is considerable...

It's a government's dream to have a highly flexible workforce that can do all sorts of different jobs, although it doesn't seem easy to switch from being a builder to a surgeon. Then again, there's plenty of time to retrain before you can claim your pension...

Taxes, Benefits and Legislation

Taxes and benefits are another way the government can intervene in the labour market, and sometimes intervention comes from the EU, e.g. through legislation, regulation and directives. **This page is for OCR only.**

Taxes and Benefits can affect the Level of Employment and Wage Rates

Governments can **increase** the **incentive to work** to address the market failure that's caused by economic inactivity in the labour force. They can do that by **lowering income taxes** and **benefit payments**.

Income Tax

1) **Lowering marginal tax rates** (see p.172) means workers get to **keep more** of their earnings. This acts as an **incentive** to **work more** and can **increase** the **labour supply** in the economy.

2) At the moment, workers in the UK have a **tax-free allowance** — this means they pay **no tax** on the first part of their earnings (for 2019/2020, workers won't have paid tax on the first £12 500 they earn). Recent government policy has seen the size of the tax-free allowance **increase**. This increases people's **incentive to work** and increases **equity**.

There's more on taxation on page 169.

Benefits

1) Lowering benefits **increases the gap** between **income** earned in **work** and income **without work** (from benefit payments) — i.e. it **reduces** the replacement ratio. This gives people a **greater incentive** to work, **increasing** the **participation rate** and **labour supply**.

2) Lowering benefits will reduce the effect of the **unemployment trap** (see p.113) and cut **voluntary unemployment**.

3) Recent changes to benefit legislation include:

- A **benefits cap** for working-age people claiming certain benefits — the aim is to **prevent** people from being **better off** not working than working.

- The introduction of **Universal Credit** from 2013 — a number of benefits, such as income-based Jobseeker's Allowance, are **combined** into **one benefit**. It's paid to people **looking** for work and those on **low** incomes. The aims of Universal Credit include making it **easier** for people to **move** into work and **reducing** the number of working people in **poverty**. (It's being introduced gradually — it is expected to be completed by 2024.)

The government Legislates and Regulates in labour markets

1) The government implements **legislation** and **regulation** in labour markets for a number of reasons, for example to stop **unsafe** practices and to prevent employees from being **exploited**.

2) **Legislation** involves putting **specific laws** in place, e.g. the UK has legislation on **flexible working hours** — everyone now has the **right** to request flexible working hours.

3) **Regulations** are **rules**, which are often put in place so that government legislation is met.

4) Many businesses complain that **current levels** of EU and UK legislation and regulation, including those in the labour market, are **too high** and impact on **jobs** and **growth** — e.g. rules on maternity and paternity leave. However, the **European Commission** (see p.208) works to reduce the **burden** of regulations for small (and medium) businesses.

5) EU directives are different to legislation — they're **sets of instructions** issued to EU member states. They describe **particular objectives** that need to be achieved within these states. A directive could affect **all member states**, or it could affect a **single member**.

6) Authorities within member states covered by the directive must act to deliver the objectives by a **certain date**.

7) **How** each member state accomplishes this (i.e. how they make changes through legislation or regulation to deliver the objectives of the directive) is **up to them**. This gives member states some **flexibility** over this process.

An EU directive would have been helpful when Jemma and Ling were trying to find the Eiffel Tower.

Migration

Immigration can have positive and negative impacts on economies. This means that, depending on an individual country's situation, a government might want to encourage or discourage immigration. ***This page is for OCR only.***

Migrant Workers increase the Labour Supply of a country

1) Migrant workers that are young, skilled and flexible will generally have a **positive effect** on the economy — these workers will **earn** and **spend** money, which **increases aggregate demand** and grows the economy.

2) Migrant workers can **fill skills gaps** in the economy. For example, the NHS has many nurses and doctors from foreign countries who have helped to do this.

3) This means sometimes governments will implement policies which **encourage** immigration — e.g. Canada's Federal Skilled Worker Program allows foreign workers from 347 different occupations to apply for **permanent** residency if they meet certain **criteria**.

4) **Free movement of workers** between the EU member states has allowed workers to migrate to different EU countries. For example, there was an influx of workers into the UK from Eastern European countries that became members of the EU (such as Poland) — part of the reason for this was the higher wages in the UK.

5) In the UK, there has been a **net inward migration** of working-age people in recent years, from **EU** and **non-EU** countries. This helps the UK to **cope** with the problem of an **ageing population** (see p.115).

6) As migrant workers increase the supply of labour available, it's possible that migrant workers entering a labour market could **depress** the **market wage rate**. This is thought to be especially true of low-skilled workers, such as farm labourers:

- **Before immigration** the wage rate of farm workers was W_1.
- When migrant workers expand the labour supply it **shifts** the **supply curve** to the right (from S to S_1).
- At this level of supply (S_1), there is an **excess supply** of farm labourers at W_1. The **wage rate falls** until it clears the market, which it does at W_2.
- The increased supply of farm labourers has resulted in the **wage rate falling** from W_1 to W_2.

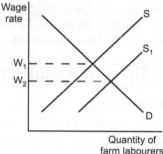

Governments might try to Reduce Immigration

1) In recent years UK governments have **tried to reduce** immigration, particularly of **low-skilled** workers. This is because the **high level** of migration to the UK is believed to be **unsustainable**. The government is more supportive of **skilled** migrants coming to the country, as they can contribute **more** to the UK economy.

2) The **effectiveness** of government policies to reduce immigration has been limited by a number of factors. For example, the EU **restricts** its **member states** on the rules it can implement on immigration — **freedom of movement** of EU citizens to any EU member nation is an **important principle** of the EU and is written into its treaties. This was one of the reasons that **immigration control** was widely discussed in the lead-up to the UK's **2016 referendum** on its EU membership.

3) The UK made some **changes** to its policies to **limit** immigration — for instance:

- It placed a **cap** on the number of **skilled worker visas** available to non-EU workers.
- **Restrictions** on certain welfare benefits were brought in to make the UK **less attractive** to migrants — e.g. EU migrants **couldn't** claim benefits, such as Jobseeker's Allowance (JSA), during their first **three** months in the UK.

Warm-Up Questions

Q1 Briefly explain how income tax and benefits can affect the level of employment in an economy.

Q2 Give one change in UK immigration policy.

Exam Question

Q1 Explain, using a diagram, how an influx of migrant workers can depress the market wage rate. [4 marks]

Wearing pink on a Friday — an unlikely objective of an EU directive...

You'll be pleased to know that that's it for the labour market. Don't run off for a celebratory cuppa just yet though — make sure you've got your head round these pages first. They're full of lovely, important government intervention stuff...

Measuring Economic Growth

Instead of looking at individual markets, firms or people, macroeconomics looks at the economy as a whole — that includes the government, all firms, all individuals, other countries etc. **These pages are for all boards.**

There are **Four** main **Macroeconomic** indicators

These four **main** macroeconomic indicators can be used to measure a country's **economic performance**:

1) The rate of **economic growth**.   3) The level of **unemployment**.
2) The rate of **inflation**.   4) The state of the **balance of payments**.

Governments use these indicators to **monitor** how the economy is doing.

GDP is a measure of **Economic Growth**

1) Economic growth can be measured by the change in **national output** over a period of time. The national output is **all** the **goods** and **services** produced by a country.

2) Output can be measured in **two** ways:

1. Volume	**2. Value**
Adding up the **quantity** of goods and services produced in one year.	**Calculating** the value (£billions) of all the goods and services produced in one year.

National output is **usually** measured by **value** — this is called the **Gross Domestic Product (GDP)**.

3) GDP can also be calculated by adding up the total amount of **national expenditure** (aggregate demand, see p.132) in a year, or by adding up the total amount of **national income** earned in a year. This means that, in theory, national output = national expenditure = national income (see p.130-131 for more on the **circular flow** of income).

Economic Growth is usually measured as a **Percentage**

1) The **rate** of economic growth is the **speed** at which the **national output** grows over a period of time.

2) Over the course of **several years**, the speed of this growth is **not** usually constant. Here are a few useful terms:

- Long periods of high economic growth rates are often called **booms**.
- If there's **negative** economic growth for **two consecutive quarters** (a 'quarter' is just a 3-month period of time — a quarter of a year), this is called a **recession**. A **long** recession is often referred to as a **slump**.
- An **economic depression** is worse than a recession — it's a **sustained** economic downturn which lasts for a **long** period of time (e.g. several years).

> *Remember — a slowdown in the rate of economic growth means growth is still rising, but more slowly. It doesn't mean economic growth is negative — output isn't falling.*

3) Over one year, a country's GDP may **increase** or **decrease**. This simply measures the **change** in the amount of goods and services produced between one year and the next. The change in GDP can be shown in **two** ways — as a **value** (£billions), or as a **percentage**.

4) To **measure** the rate of economic growth over time as a percentage, use this formula:

$$\frac{\text{Change in GDP (£billions)}}{\text{Original GDP (£billions)}} \times 100 = \text{Percentage change}$$

5) Some GDP growth may be due to **prices rising** (inflation, see p.124). **Nominal GDP** is the name given to a GDP figure that **hasn't** been adjusted for inflation. This figure is **misleading** — it'll give the impression that GDP is **higher** than it is.

6) Economists **remove** the effect of inflation to find what's called **real GDP**. For example, a 4% increase in the **nominal GDP** during a period when **inflation** was 3% means **real GDP** only rose by about 1%. The other 3% was due to rising prices.

GDP Per Capita can indicate the **Standard of Living** in a country

1) GDP can be used to give an indication of a country's **standard of living**. This is done by **dividing** the total **national output** by the country's population to get the national output **per person** — GDP per capita. Here's the formula:

$$\frac{\text{Total GDP}}{\text{Population size}} = \text{GDP per capita}$$

> *'Per capita' just means 'per head' or 'per person'.*

2) In theory, the **higher** the **GDP per capita**, the **higher** the **standard of living** in a country.

3) Economists also use the indicators **Gross National Income (GNI)** and **Gross National Product (GNP)**:

4) **GNI** is the GDP **plus** net income from abroad — this **net** income is any income earned by a country on investments and other assets **owned abroad**, **minus** any income earned by foreigners on investments **domestically**.

5) **GNP** is similar to GNI — it's the **total output** of the **citizens** of a country, whether or not they're **resident** in that country.

6) GNI and GNP per capita can be also be used to **compare living standards** between different countries. They are calculated in a **similar** way to GDP per capita — by **dividing** the **total** GNI or GNP by the country's population.

Measuring Economic Growth

Purchasing Power Parity is used in comparisons of Living Standards

1) When using **GDP per capita** (or **GNP** or **GNI per capita**) to compare **living standards** in countries that use **different currencies**, the **exchange rate** might not reflect the **true worth** of the two currencies — so comparing GDP per capita in this way might not give an **accurate** picture.

2) To **overcome** this problem, comparisons are usually carried out using the principle of **purchasing power parity** (PPP).

3) **Purchasing power** is the **real** value of an amount of money in terms of what you can **actually** buy with it. This can **vary** between countries — for example, in a **less developed** country, e.g. Malawi, $1 will buy **more** goods than in a **more developed** country, e.g. Canada.

4) Using **PPP** in comparisons of countries' living standards involves **adjusting** the GDP per capita figures to take into account the **differences** in purchasing power in those countries, with the results usually expressed in US dollars. This makes for a **more accurate** and **easier** comparison.

Using GDP to make Comparisons has Limitations

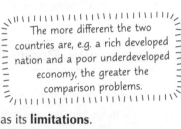
The more different the two countries are, e.g. a rich developed nation and a poor underdeveloped economy, the greater the comparison problems.

1) **GDP** and **GDP per capita** are used to **compare** the economic performance and the standards of living in **different** countries:
   - A **high GDP** would suggest a country's **economic performance** is **strong**.
   - A **high GDP per capita** suggests that a country's **standard of living** is **high**.

2) Using the GDP and the GDP per capita to make comparisons between countries has its **limitations**. There are **several** things that GDP and GDP per capita figures might **not** take into **account**:

   - The extent of the **hidden economy** — economic activity that **doesn't** appear in official figures.
   - **Public spending** — some governments provide **more benefits**, such as unemployment benefits or free health care, than others. For example, two countries might have **similar** GDP per capita figures, but one country might **spend** much more money **per person** on providing benefits that improve the standard of living.
   - The **extent** of income inequality. Two countries may have **similar** GDP per capita, but the distribution of that income between rich and poor **may** be very different.
   - **Other** differences in the standard of living between countries, such as the number of hours workers have to work per week, working conditions, the level of damage to the environment, and different spending needs (e.g. cold countries spend **more income** on heating to achieve the **same level** of comfort that exists in warm countries).

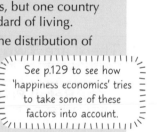
See p.129 to see how 'happiness economics' tries to take some of these factors into account.

Index Numbers represent percentage changes

Index numbers are useful for **making comparisons** over a period of time. The first year is called the **base year** — the index number for this year is set at **100**. Changes up **or** down are expressed as numbers above or below 100. For example:

- A 3% **rise** in real GDP over one year would mean the index rose to **103** in year 2.
- A 2% **fall** in real GDP over one year would mean the index fell to **98** in year 2.
- An index number of **108** in year 4 means an 8% rise from the **base year**.

Warm-Up Questions

Q1 What are the four main macroeconomic indicators?

Q2 What is the difference between nominal and real national output figures? Why is this important?

Q3 What is meant by purchasing power parity? When is it used? Why is it important?

Q4 What can index numbers be used to show?

Exam Question

Q1 Why might comparing the GDP per capita of two countries fail to provide an accurate comparison of their standards of living? [8 marks]

I thought GDP wrote revision guides? No? GCP? PCG? Oh, forget it...

There are two key facts on these pages — GDP is the value of all the goods and services produced in a country in a year. Economic growth is measured as the percentage change in GDP over time. You'll need to learn the rest of this stuff too though. Sorry.

Measuring Inflation

Inflation is always being mentioned on the news — it's a key figure which is used to help measure how the economy is doing. **These pages are for all boards.**

There are **Two Ways** to **Define Inflation**

1) Inflation is the sustained **rise** in the **average price** of **goods** and **services** over a period of time. Keep in mind that:
   - The prices of some goods may be rising **faster** than the average.
   - Some prices may be rising **more slowly**.
   - Some prices may even be **falling**.

2) Inflation can also be seen as a **fall** in the **value** of money. This means that:
   - A **fixed** amount of money (e.g. £10) buys **less** than before.
   - The **purchasing power** of money has fallen (for more on purchasing power, see p.123).

Inflation can be **Positive** or **Negative** (or 0)

1) **Inflation** (or positive inflation) is when the **average price** of goods and services is **rising**.

2) Sometimes the **average price** will actually be **falling**. This is called **negative inflation**, or **deflation**.

3) Other times, a country may experience **hyperinflation**. This is when prices rise **extremely quickly** and money rapidly **loses** its value.

4) If the rate of inflation is **slowing down**, e.g. from 6% to 4%, this is called **disinflation**. Prices are still rising but at a **slower** speed.

There are **Two** main **Measurements** used for **Inflation**

The **Retail Price Index** (RPI)

1) **Two** surveys are carried out to **calculate** the RPI.

2) The first survey is a survey of around 6000 households, called the **Living Costs and Food Survey**.

3) This is used to find out **what** people spend their money on, e.g. petrol, apples, haircuts. The survey also shows what **proportion** of income is spent on these items. This is used to work out the relative **weighting** of each item (this will be important in a second) — for example, if **20%** is spent on transport, then a 20% **weighting** will be given to transport.

4) The second survey is based on **prices** — it measures the **changes** in price of around **700** of the most **commonly** used **goods** and **services** (these goods and services are often referred to as the 'basket of goods').

5) The items are chosen **based on** the Living Costs and Food Survey. What is in the basket **changes** over time, because technology, trends and tastes change (see the diagram below for some examples). This ensures that the basket always **reflects** what the **average household** might spend its money on.

6) The price **changes** in the second survey are **multiplied** by the **weightings** from the first survey. These are then converted to an **index number** (see p.123 for more on index numbers). So **inflation** is just the **percentage change** to the index number over time — e.g. if the index number **rises** from 100 to 102, then **inflation** is 2%.

> The weightings are important because the larger the proportion of a household's income that's spent on an item, the larger the effect a change in the price of that item will have on average spending.

Goods added to the basket → Goods removed from the basket

Daily disposable contact lenses | Ebooks | Honey | Blueberries

The basket of goods

Local newspapers | Disposable cameras | Analogue radios | Boiled sweets

Measuring Inflation

The **Consumer Price Index** (CPI)

The CPI is calculated in a **similar** way to the RPI, but there are **three main** differences:

1) Some items are **excluded** from the CPI, the main ones being:
   - Mortgage interest payments
   - Council tax
2) A slightly **different formula** is used to calculate the CPI.
3) A **larger** sample of the population is used for the CPI.

These differences mean that the CPI **tends** to be a little **lower** than the RPI — the **exception** is when **interest rates** are very low. However, they both tend to follow the same **long-term** trend.

The CPI is the **official** measure of inflation in the UK. Many other countries collect data on inflation in a **similar** way to the CPI, so it's often used for **international comparisons**.

The **CPI** and **RPI** have **Limitations**

The RPI and CPI can be really **useful**, but they also have their **limitations**:

1) The RPI **excludes** all households in the top 4% of incomes. The CPI covers a **broader range** of the population, but it **doesn't** include mortgage interest payments or council tax.
2) The information given by households in the Living Costs and Food Survey can be **inaccurate**.
3) The basket of goods only changes **once** a year — so it might miss some short-term changes in spending habits.

The RPI and CPI are important for **Government Policy**

The RPI and CPI are used to help determine **wages** and **state benefits**.

See pages 152-153 for more on inflation.

1) **Employers** and **trade unions** use them as a starting point in wage negotiations.
2) The **government** uses them to decide on increases in **state pensions**, and other welfare **benefits**.
3) Some benefits are **index-linked** — they rise **automatically** each year by the **same** percentage as the chosen index.

They're also used to measure changes in the UK's **international** competitiveness.

1) If the rate of inflation measured by the CPI is **higher** in the UK than in the other countries it trades with, then UK goods become **less** price competitive, as they'll **cost more** for other countries to buy.
2) So — **exports** will **fall**, and **imports**, which will be made relatively **cheaper** by domestic inflation, will **increase**.

Warm-Up Questions

Q1 In what two ways can inflation be defined?

Q2 Describe what happens to prices during a period of:
   a) Negative inflation
   b) Hyperinflation
   c) Disinflation

Q3 In what ways is the RPI different from the CPI?

Q4 Aside from measuring inflation, give an example of a use of RPI/CPI.

Exam Question

Q1 Explain three limitations of the RPI as a measure of inflation. [6 marks]

Revision can be a bit deflating, but try to stay positive...

And there I was thinking inflation was just blowing up a balloon. The RPI and the CPI are two different measures of inflation — make sure you know what they are, the key differences between the two, and some examples of what else they're used for.

Measuring Unemployment

There are two main ways of measuring unemployment — each has its advantages and disadvantages. **For all boards.**

There are **Two** ways of **Defining Unemployment**

1) The **level** of unemployment is the **number** of people who are looking for a job but cannot find one.

2) The **rate** of unemployment is the number of people out of work as a **percentage** of the **labour force**.

The **rate** of unemployment is used when making **comparisons** between countries, as different countries have different **population sizes**.

The labour force is all the people who are willing and able to work. This includes those working and those looking for work.

There are **Two** ways of **Measuring Unemployment**

1) The Claimant Count

The claimant count is the **number** of people claiming unemployment-related benefits from the government. This includes people who claim Jobseeker's Allowance (JSA), Universal Credit and smaller groups of additional claimants. There are **advantages** and **disadvantages** of using the claimant count to measure unemployment:

Advantages:
- This data is **easy** to obtain — you just count the number of people claiming the unemployment-related benefits.
- There's **no** cost in collecting the data as it's recorded when people apply for the benefits.

Disadvantages:
- It can be **manipulated** by the government to make it seem **smaller** — for example, a change in the rules (e.g. **raising** the school leaving age to 19) could reduce the **number** of people who could claim benefits, which would make it **seem** that unemployment was falling.
- It **excludes** those people who **are** looking for work but are **not** eligible to (or choose not to) claim any benefits.

2) The Labour Force Survey

The International Labour Organisation (ILO) uses a **sample** of the population. It asks people who **aren't** working if they're **actively seeking** work. The **number** of people who answer 'yes' (whether they're claiming benefits or not) are added up to produce the **ILO unemployment count**. There are **advantages** and **disadvantages** to using this figure:

Advantages:
- It's thought to be **more accurate** than the claimant count.
- It's an **internationally** agreed measure for unemployment, so it's easier to make **comparisons** with other countries.

Disadvantages:
- It's **expensive** to collect and put together the data.
- The sample may be **unrepresentative** of the population as a whole — making the data **inaccurate**.

The figure from the Labour Force Survey tends to be **higher** than the claimant count because certain groups of people are **excluded** from the claimant count. For example, some people **can't claim** any benefits because they have a **high earning** husband/wife, or they might have too much money in **savings**.

Unemployment comes at a **Cost** to the **Whole Economy**

See p.150-151 for more information on unemployment.

Governments want to keep track of **unemployment figures** for a number of reasons:

1) A **high** rate of unemployment suggests that an economy is doing **badly**.

2) Unemployment will lead to **lower incomes** and **less spending**. This will have an impact on **companies** too — they might sell **fewer goods**, or need to **cut prices** and make **less profit**.

3) Unemployment means there's **unused** labour in the economy, so **fewer** goods and services can be **produced**.

4) It also means the government has **extra costs**, such as **welfare benefits**, and **less revenue** because **less tax** is paid.

Measuring the Balance of Payments

The balance of payments is all about the money coming into and going out of the country. **This page is for all boards.**

The **Balance of Payments** refers to **International Flows** of money

The balance of payments records:

- The flow of money **out** of a country, e.g. to **pay** for **imported** goods.
- The flow of money **into** a country, e.g. **payments** from **exported** goods.

If goods are exported, they leave the country and money moves the other way, i.e. into the country to pay for them. For imports, it's the opposite.

It's the **value** of **exports** and **imports** that's calculated in the balance of payments, **not** the **volume**.
So if **prices change**, but **volume** remains the **same**, then the **value** of exports and imports will **change**.

There are **Four** sections to the **Current Account**

The **main** part of the balance of payments you need to know for your exam is the **current account**, which records the **international exchange** of goods and services. It consists of **four** sections:

See p.154-157 for more about the balance of payments.

1) **Trade** in **goods**, often called 'visible trade' — so goods will either be **visible imports** or **visible exports**. Examples: cars, computers, food.

2) **Trade** in **services**, often called 'invisible trade'. These can be **imported** or **exported** too. Examples: tourism, insurance, transport.

3) **International** flows of **income** earned as salaries, interest, profit and dividends. Examples: interest on an account held in a foreign country, dividends from a company based abroad.

4) **Transfers** of money from one person or government to another. Examples: foreign aid, transfer of money to or from a family member who lives in another country.

The balance of payments **Isn't** always **Balanced**

1) The flows of money coming **into** a country **may not** balance the flows of money **out**.
   - If the money flowing **in** exceeds the money flowing **out**, there's a **surplus**.
   - If the money flowing **out** exceeds the money flowing **in**, there's a **deficit**.

2) In recent years, the UK has had a **deficit** in its balance of payments. Although the UK has usually had a **surplus** in **invisible trade**, it has also had a **large deficit** in **visible trade**.

3) A deficit **isn't** necessarily a bad thing — but it might be a sign that a country is **uncompetitive**.

4) Governments want to **avoid** a large, long-term deficit — this **would** cause bigger problems, for example job losses (see p.156).

Tom had always been good at balancing anything.

Warm-Up Questions

Q1 Give two negative effects unemployment has on an economy.

Q2 For each of the items below, identify where it would appear in the current account of the balance of payments and whether it is a flow into or out of the UK.

Item 1   A British car company increases its sales to the Far East.

Item 2   Dividends from shares in an American company paid to a British shareholder.

Item 3   A British family holidaying in Spain who pay for a taxi in Madrid.

Exam Questions

Q1 Name the two main measures of unemployment, giving one advantage and one disadvantage of each.   [4 marks]

Q2 Explain what a surplus and a deficit are on the current account of the balance of payments.   [4 marks]

Labour Force be with you...

There's a lot on these two pages — definitions, advantages, disadvantages... You'll need to understand it all before you move on.

Measuring Development

No one is perfect — not even economists (shocking, I know). It's impossible to get a truly accurate measure of economic performance, so sometimes economists include development to try to get a better overall impression. There are lots of ways to consider development — take a look at these pages to get an idea of some of them. ***These pages are for all boards.***

Looking at **Development** can give a **Fuller** picture

1) Measurements of **growth** or **unemployment** are used to work out the **standard of living** in a country, but often those figures **don't** tell the full story. A **better** way to look at a country's standard of living is to measure its **economic development**.

2) Measuring the economic **development** of a country means trying to work out the **level** of social and human **welfare**, sometimes called the **quality of life**.

3) To **measure** development, economists need **more indicators** than just economic growth, inflation levels and unemployment rates, to be able to get a **fuller picture** of the quality of life in a country.

4) This is especially important when **comparing** the economies of two very **different** countries, e.g. a **rich, economically developed** country, such as the UK, and a **poor, less economically developed** country, such as Niger.

The **Human Development Index** considers a **Broader** range of **Indicators**

1) The **Human Development Index** (HDI) was developed by the United Nations to measure and rank countries' levels of **social** and **economic** development.

2) The HDI includes **social indicators** to give a fuller picture of the quality of life in a country.

3) The HDI combines indicators in **three** equally weighted sections:

- **Health** (as measured by life expectancy).
- **Education** (as measured by average and expected years in school).
- **Standard of living** (as measured by real GNI per capita, using the principle of purchasing power parity, PPP).

4) These figures are used because they are:
- Fairly **standard** around the world.
- Relatively **easy** to collect.

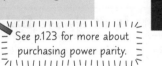
See p.123 for more about purchasing power parity.

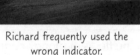
Richard frequently used the wrong indicator.

The HDI is used in different **Ways**

1) The HDI can be used to **measure** changes in **development levels** over time in a country.

2) It can also be used to **compare** the levels of development **between** countries.

3) Countries are either **ranked** in order with country number 1 being the highest...

4) ...or the HDI is given as an **index** with a range between 1 and 0.
- Above 0.8 indicates a **high** level of human development.
- Between 0.8 and 0.5 suggests a **medium** level of human development.
- Below 0.5 shows a **low** level of human development.

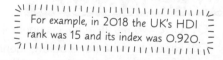
For example, in 2018 the UK's HDI rank was 15 and its index was 0.920.

The HDI has its **Critics**

1) A **long life expectancy** is **not** the same as a **high quality of life** (e.g. someone with a long life expectancy might have to work **long hours** in **unpleasant conditions**, or they might not have much **freedom**, etc.).

2) Measuring the average number of years people spend in school doesn't measure the **quality** of teaching or how well people learn what they're taught.

3) Using GNI-per-capita figures can lead to **inaccurate comparisons** — for example, GNI per capita **doesn't** include the hidden economy, and this tends to make up a **larger proportion** of the economy in **less developed** countries.

4) The HDI figure alone doesn't measure the extent of **inequality** in a country — a country with a **satisfactory** HDI rank might have a few **very wealthy** people and a **large** number of **very poor** people.

Measuring Development

There are **Other** ways to **Measure Development**

1) One way of measuring development is finding the **percentage** of adult male labour working in **agriculture**.
   - Agricultural work is very hard and **workers** are often paid **very little**.
   - The **economic output** from agriculture is **generally** quite **low** too.
   - As countries become more developed they tend to use **more machinery** for farming and employ **fewer workers**.
   - As a result, countries with a **high percentage** of the population working in agriculture generally have **low** levels of **economic development**.

2) Another measure of development is the number of **mobile phones** per thousand of the population.
   - Mobile phones improve **communication** and **trading**, which can lead to **greater** economic development.
   - A **large** number of mobile phones indicates that **wages** are **high** enough for people to **afford** to pay for them.

3) Some other indicators to measure a country's development are:
   - Levels of **disease** and **malnutrition**.
   - **Newspapers** bought per thousand of the population.
   - **Energy consumption** per head (electricity and gas).
   - Levels of political and social **freedom**.
   - Levels of **environmental** impact and sustainability.
   - **Access** to **clean** water.

A **Country's Development** affects the **Three Sectors** of its **Economy**

1) The **structure** of a country's economy is based around **three sectors**: **primary** (e.g. mining, agriculture and fishing), **secondary** (e.g. construction and manufacturing) and **tertiary** (e.g. teaching, banking and tourism).

2) **Less developed economies** often have a **large** primary sector.

3) As an economy becomes **more developed** and **wealthier**, production and consumption **increase** and the **secondary sector** will **grow**. This **increases** the use of **natural resources**, and **increases negative externalities**, such as pollution. The growth of the secondary sector can lead to the **mechanising** of the **primary sector,** as machinery can be used to provide more resources.

4) The **continuation** of a country's development will eventually result in its economy becoming **dominated** by the **tertiary sector**. Tertiary sector industries often require **fewer natural resources**, and they may **produce less pollution.** However they will begin to **import** goods, which means the pollution is likely to have **moved** to another country.

'Happiness' can be linked to **Economic Growth**

1) **'Happiness economics'** tries to measure any factor that is associated with **increased** (or **decreased**) levels of **subjective well-being** (i.e. how satisfied people say they feel with their lives) — this might include things like **political freedom** or **family relationships**.

2) 'Happiness' is tricky to measure, but many economists claim that **'psychological surveys'** can give a reliable measure of how happy and satisfied people are with their lives.

3) The UK's Office for National Statistics (ONS) now runs a **Measuring National Well-being** programme. It records statistics concerning, for example, people's **health**, **relationships**, **education** and **finances**, along with those people's **own assessment** of their **personal well-being**. The aim is to help the government devise **policies** that achieve **better outcomes** in those areas that are particularly important to people.

> This is different from traditional economics, which concentrates on financial measures.

EDEXCEL ONLY

Warm-Up Questions

Q1 What is economic development?

Q2 What are the three sections to the Human Development Index? Give two uses of this index.

Q3 Name the three sectors of an economy and give an example of a job in each one.

Exam Question

Q1 Evaluate the likely accuracy of using the Human Development Index as a way of measuring a country's standard of living.

[12 marks]

Clap along if you feel like happiness economics is the way to improve policy...

Remember — generally in economics, no single measure or statistic is ever likely to be perfect. You'll need to learn the specific uses/limitations of the Human Development Index and be aware of other measures that could be considered as well.

The Circular Flow of Income

Before you learn about the joys of aggregate demand and supply, you'll need to know about the circular flow of income. It explains the link between national output, national income and national expenditure. **These pages are for all boards.**

Income Flows between Firms and Households

1) In simple terms, an **economy** is made up of **firms** and **households**.

2) Firms **produce** goods and services, and **all** of these **goods** and **services** make up the **national output**.

3) The **households** in a country **provide** the labour, land and capital that **firms** use to produce the national output. The money **paid** to households by firms for these **factors of production** is the **national income**.

4) Households **spend** the money they get from the national income on the goods and services (outputs) that firms create — the **value** of this spending is the **national expenditure**.

5) So, all of this creates a **circular flow of income**, which can be shown by the formula:

> National **output** = National **income** = National **expenditure**

6) This **flow** of income can also be shown as a **diagram**:

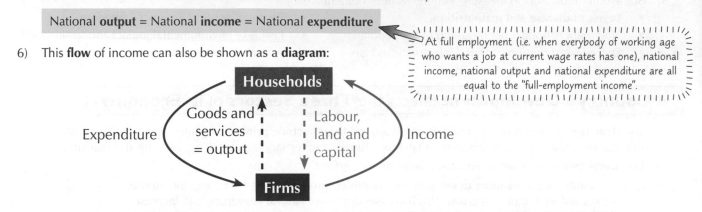

At full employment (i.e. when everybody of working age who wants a job at current wage rates has one), national income, national output and national expenditure are all equal to the "full-employment income".

There are actually two flows here:
- A **physical flow** (shown by **straight arrows**) of **'real things'** — i.e. goods, services, labour, land and capital.
- A **monetary flow** (shown by **curved arrows**) — i.e. the **money** that **pays for** the 'physical things'.

There are Injections into and Withdrawals from the flow of income

1) The **circular flow** suggests that as long as **households** keep spending what they earn, and **firms** keep using their revenues to produce more goods using the same inputs, then national output (and national income) **won't change**.

2) However, an economy's circular flow of income is **affected** by **injections** and **withdrawals** (or leakages).

3) **Injections into** the circular flow of income come in the form of **exports**, **investment** and **government spending** — these go directly to **firms**.

4) **Withdrawals** come in the form of **imports**, **savings** and **taxes** — these withdrawals can be made by **households** or **firms**.

These are injections or withdrawals of money into or out of the monetary flow.

5) **Injections** and **withdrawals** can be shown in a circular flow like this:

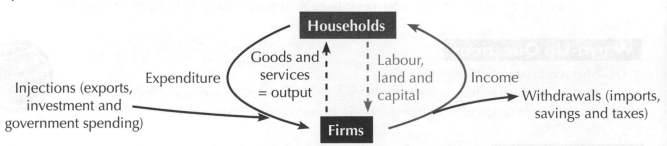

- If **injections** and **withdrawals** are **equal**, then the economy is in **equilibrium**.
- If **injections** into the circular flow are **greater** than **withdrawals**, this means that **expenditure** is **greater** than **output** — so firms will **increase output**. As a result national output, income and expenditure will all **increase**.
- If **withdrawals** from the circular flow are **greater** than **injections**, this means that **output** is **greater** than **expenditure** — so firms will **reduce output**. As a result national output, income and expenditure will **decrease**.

The Circular Flow of Income

Injections have a Multiplier Effect on the circular flow

1) When an **injection** is made into the circular flow, the **actual change** in the **national income** is **greater** than the **initial** injection — this is called the **multiplier effect**. Take a look at the following **example**:

- The government gives a firm £50 million to **invest** in new machinery. The money is used to pay households for land, labour and capital, so it's an **injection** of £50 million of **new income** into the circular flow.

- £12 million of this income **leaks** out of the circular flow as withdrawals (savings, tax and imports), but the **remaining £38 million** is **spent** on goods and services, so all £38 million goes to firms as **expenditure** — increasing **output**.

- Another £10 million **leaks** out of the circular flow as withdrawals from firms (savings, tax and imports), but the remaining £28 million is paid by firms as **income** to households.

- The cycle will continue, with households and firms **spending** some of the money and the rest **leaking** out of the circular flow, until there's nothing left of the **initial** investment.

- So the **original £50 million** has gone **round** the circular flow **multiple** times, though some of it has **leaked away** at each stage. This means the **total effect** of the initial investment on national **output**, **income** and **expenditure** is £50m + £38m + £28m + ... etc. — it's actually much **more** than £50 million.

The multiplier effect works on all kinds of things.

2) The **size** of the multiplier effect depends on the **rate** at which money **leaks** from the circular flow — e.g. the **bigger** the leakages, the **quicker** the money will **leave** the circular flow and the **smaller** the multiplier effect will be.

AQA and OCR students also need to know about how the multiplier interacts with the accelerator process — this is covered on p.141.

3) So, if **lots** of money is being spent on **imports** (or used as savings or tax), then the **multiplier effect** will actually be quite **small** because the injection will **quickly** leak out of the circular flow.

Wealth is Different to Income

1) Wealth is the total **value** of all the **assets** owned by individuals or firms in an economy.

2) Assets can include **actual money**, e.g. savings, and **physical items**, e.g. houses or cars.

3) Unlike income, which is a **flow** of money, wealth is a **stock** concept — you can think of it as a **stockpile** of **resources**. These resources **aren't** currently being **used** in the circular flow of income, but they **could** be at some point.

4) Although income and wealth are **different** things there's a **correlation** between them. For example, it's likely that an individual with a **high income** will also have **high wealth**, because they'll be able to **purchase** more **expensive** assets and have **more money** to save.

Warm-Up Questions

Q1 What are the three injections into the circular flow of income?

Q2 What are the three withdrawals from the circular flow of income?

Q3 Give a definition of wealth.

Exam Question

Q1 Comment on the potential multiplier effect on the circular flow of income of a large increase in government spending on the NHS.

[6 marks]

My assets include good looks, charm and modesty...

If there are no injections or withdrawals, or if injections = withdrawals, then national output, national income and national expenditure are all equal. If injections and withdrawals aren't balanced, this will lead to a change in the national income. It can be a bit tricky to get your head around, but you should be able to use the diagrams to help you figure out what's going on.

The Components of Aggregate Demand

Here's another delightful economics term — aggregate demand. 'Aggregate' is basically just a fancy economics way of saying 'total' — so aggregate demand means the 'total demand' in an economy. **These pages are for all boards.**

Aggregate Demand is the Total Spending on goods and services

1) **Aggregate demand** (AD) is the **total demand**, or the **total spending**, in an economy over a given period of time.
2) So aggregate demand is made up of all the **components** that **contribute** to spending/demand in an economy.
3) It's calculated using the **formula**:

> **AD = Consumption (C) + Investment (I) + Government spending (G) + (Exports (X) – Imports (M))**

Consumption and Saving are affected by a number of factors

1) Consumption (sometimes referred to as consumer spending or consumer expenditure) is the **total** amount spent by **households** on goods and services. It **doesn't** include spending by **firms**.
2) An **increase** in **consumption** will mean an **increase** in **AD** — a **reduction** in **consumption** will mean a **reduction** in **AD**.
3) Consumption is the **largest** component of aggregate demand — it makes up about **65%** of AD in the UK.
4) This means that **changes** in the level of **consumption** will tend to have a **big impact** on aggregate demand.
5) Savings are made **instead of** consumption — so income can be consumed **or** saved.
6) When consumption is **high**, saving tends to be **low**, and **vice versa**.
7) Here are some of the **main factors** affecting consumption and saving:

- **Income** — generally, as disposable income **increases**, consumption will **rise**. The **rate** at which **consumption** rises is usually **lower** than the **rate** at which **income** increases because households tend to **save** more as well.

  Disposable income is money available to spend after income tax and National Insurance have been paid.

- **Interest rates** — **higher** interest rates lead to **less** consumer spending. Consumers **save** more to take **advantage** of the higher rates and they're **less likely** to **borrow** money or **buy** things on **credit** because it's more expensive. Consumers may also have **less money** to spend if interest rates on **existing** loans and mortgages increase.

- **Consumer confidence** — when consumers feel **more confident** about the **economy** and their own financial situation, they **spend more** and **save less**. Confidence is **affected** by a **number** of factors. For example, in a **recession** consumers are usually **reluctant** to spend because their **confidence** in the economy is **low** — they might, for example, be worried about **losing** their jobs. This reluctance can **continue** even after a **recession**.

- **Wealth effects** — a **rise** in household **wealth**, e.g. due to a rise in **share** prices or **house** prices, will often lead to a **rise** in **consumer spending** and a **reduction** in **saving**. This is because of consumer **confidence** — if house prices rise **faster** than **inflation**, home owners will feel more **confident** in their own finances.

- **Taxes** — **direct tax increases** lead to a **fall** in consumers' disposable income, so they spend **less**. **Indirect tax increases**, e.g. an increase in VAT, **increase** the cost of spending, so consumers tend to **reduce** their consumption. A **reduction** in direct or indirect taxes will lead to an **increase** in consumer spending.

- **Unemployment** — when unemployment **rises**, consumers tend to spend **less** and save **more**. (People still in employment will tend to replace spending with saving, as they become more worried about **losing** their jobs.) A **fall** in unemployment means **more** people have money to **spend**, and consumers are **less** worried about losing their jobs, so consumer spending **increases**.

Don't confuse Saving and Investment

1) It's important to realise that **investment** and **saving** are **different** things.
2) **Savings** tend to be made by **households**, whereas **investments** tend to be made by **firms**.
3) For example, **savings** made by a household might be money put into a **savings bank account** each month. An **investment** made by a firm could be money paid to **build** a new office.

The Components of Aggregate Demand

Investment is made by Firms

1) **Investment** is money spent by **firms** on **assets** which they'll use to **produce** goods or services — this includes things such as **machinery**, **computers** and **offices**.

> - **Gross investment** includes **all** investment spending.
> - **Net investment** only includes investment that **increases productive capacity**.
> - E.g. if a firm has 3 old trucks, but replaces these with 5 new trucks, the **gross** investment is '**5 trucks**', but the **net** investment is '**2 trucks**'.

2) Firms **invest** with the **intention** of making **profit** in the future.

3) Investment makes up **about 15%** of AD in the UK.

4) There are **several** factors that **affect** investment:

Risk

1) The **level** of **risk** involved will affect the **amount** of investment by firms.

2) If there's a **high risk** that a firm **won't** benefit from its investment then it's unlikely that the firm will invest. For example, when there's **economic instability** (see p.148 for more on this), **less investment** will be made.

Government incentives and regulation

1) **Government incentives** such as subsidies or reductions in tax can affect the **level** of **investment**. For example, a **reduction** in corporation tax might **encourage** firms to invest, because they'll have **more funds** available to do so.

2) A **relaxing** of **government regulations** might **reduce** a firm's costs and make it **more likely** to invest.

Interest rates and access to credit

1) Firms often **borrow** the money they want to **invest**. This means that when **interest** rates are **high** or firms are unable to **access credit** (i.e. they're unable to borrow money), **investment** tends to be **lower**.

2) **High** interest rates would **reduce** how **profitable** an investment would be (since interest charges on loans will be **higher**).

3) High interest rates will also mean there's a **greater** opportunity cost of investing **existing** funds instead of putting them into a **bank account** with a high interest rate.

Technical advances

Firms need to **invest** in **new technology** to stay competitive. Investment will **rise** when **significant technological advances** are made.

> Investment also depends on how quickly national income is changing — this leads to an effect called the accelerator process (see p.141).

Business confidence and 'animal spirits'

1) The more **confident** a business is in its **ability** to make **profits** (because **demand for exports** is high, for example) the **more** money it's likely to **invest**.

2) But 'business confidence' depends partly on the general **optimism** or **pessimism** of the company's managers. Keynes recognised that **not all** investment decisions are based purely on **reason** and **rational thinking**, and that **human emotion, intuition** and '**gut instinct**' are also important factors. He called these factors '**animal spirits**'.

Warm-Up Questions

Q1 What is the formula for aggregate demand?

Q2 What is the difference between saving and investment?

Q3 What is 'business confidence' and how does it affect investment?

PRACTICE QUESTIONS

Exam Questions

Q1 How might high taxes and high interest rates affect the level of consumption? [6 marks]

Q2 Describe three factors which might affect the level of investment in an economy. [6 marks]

Take it from me — Investment gets SO annoyed if he's mistaken for Saving...

Each component of aggregate demand is affected by multiple factors. These pages have described the things that affect consumption (the biggest component) and investment. You'll see similar ideas popping up on the next couple of pages too.

The Components of Aggregate Demand

*You've seen the things that affect two of the components of aggregate demand (consumption and investment) — here are a couple of pages on the factors affecting the other two components (government spending and net exports). **For all boards.***

Government Spending doesn't include Transfers of Money

1) The **government spending** component of aggregate demand is the money spent by the government on **public** goods and services, e.g. education, health care, defence and so on.

2) Only money that **directly contributes** to the **output** of the economy is included — this means that **transfers** of money such as **benefits** (like the Jobseeker's Allowance) or **pensions** are **not** included.

3) Government spending is quite a **large** component of aggregate demand, so changes in government spending can have a big **influence** on aggregate demand.

Government Spending doesn't have to be Equal to Revenue

1) A government **budget outlines** a government's **planned** spending and revenue for the next year. Governments will usually have either a budget **deficit** or a budget **surplus**.

> *Most of a government's revenue comes from taxation.*

- If government spending is **greater than** its revenue, there will be a **budget deficit**.
- If government spending is **less than** its revenue, there will be a **budget surplus**.

2) Governments use **fiscal policy** (see p.168-171) to alter their **spending** and **taxation** to **influence** aggregate demand.

- If aggregate demand is **low** and economic growth is **slow**, or even negative, then a government may **overspend** (causing a budget **deficit**) in order to **increase** aggregate demand and **boost** economic growth.
- If aggregate demand is **high** and the economy is experiencing a **boom**, a government might **increase taxes** and **spend less** (causing a budget **surplus**) to try to **reduce** aggregate demand and **slow down** economic growth.

The government budgetigar's planned spending on seeds would cause another deficit.

3) An **imbalance** in the budget will affect the **circular flow of income** — a **budget surplus** will indicate an **overall withdrawal** from the circular flow, but a **budget deficit** will indicate an **overall injection** into the circular flow.

4) An imbalance in the budget is fine in the **short run**, but in the **long run** governments will try to **balance** out any **surpluses** and **deficits**. A long-term **surplus** might mean the government is **harming** economic growth by choosing **not** to spend, or by keeping taxes **too high**. A long-term **deficit** is likely to mean a country has a large national **debt**.

5) Sometimes governments will **balance** the **budget** so that government spending will be **equal** to revenue. This should have little **effect** on aggregate demand.

An Export from one country is Always an Import to another

1) **Exports** are **goods** or **services** that are produced in one country, then sold in another. Imports are the opposite — they're goods and services that are brought **into** a country after being **produced elsewhere**.

2) Exports are an **inflow** of money to a country, and imports are an **outflow** — so exports are an **injection** into the circular flow of income and imports are a **withdrawal**.

3) Exports minus imports (X – M) make up the **net exports** component of aggregate demand.

4) If the amount spent on imports **exceeds** the amount received from exports (as it does in the UK), **net exports** will be a **negative** number.

The Components of Aggregate Demand

There are many Factors that will Affect Imports and Exports

Several factors will affect the **net exports** component of aggregate demand:

There's more on exchange rates on p.210-212.

The exchange rate

A change in the **value** of a currency will affect net exports in **different ways** in the **long** and **short run**:

- In the **long run** — if the **value** of a currency **increases**, **imports** become relatively **cheaper** and **exports** become relatively **more expensive** for foreigners. As a result, **demand** for **imports (M)** rises and **demand** for exports **(X) falls**. So a **strong** currency (i.e. a currency with a high value) will **worsen** net exports **(X – M)** in the **long run** and reduce aggregate demand, but a **weak** currency will have the **opposite effect** and **improve** net exports.
- In the **short run** — demand for imports and exports tends to be quite price **inelastic**. For example, some goods **don't** have close substitutes, e.g. oil, while others might **have substitutes**, but there's a **time lag** before countries will **switch** to them — so in the short run demand **won't change** much. This means that **initially** when the value of a currency **increases**, net exports will actually **improve** (increase) because the **overall value** of exports **increases** and the **overall value** of imports **decreases**.

Changes in the state of the world economy

- The higher a country's **real income**, the more it tends to **import**. So **net exports fall** as real income rises.
- The state of the **world economy** also affects exports and imports. For example, the USA exports lots of goods to Canada. If Canada goes through a period of **low** (or negative) **growth** then **exports** from the USA to Canada will **decrease**. Assuming imports are unaffected, this means a **worsening** in the USA's net exports. Similarly, if Canada experiences **high growth rates**, exports from the USA are likely to **increase** — **improving** net exports.

Degree of protectionism

In the short run, tariffs and quotas (see p.202) can increase net exports by reducing imports. However, industries that are protected from international competition have few incentives to become more efficient, so will often export less in the long run. Also, in the long run, other countries may retaliate by introducing their own tariffs and quotas.

Non-price factors

These include things such as the **quality** of goods. For example, advancements in technology in a country that lead to the production of **higher quality** goods would be likely to cause an **increase** in exports from that country, because people are willing to **pay more** for something if it's really good. This would mean an **improvement** in **net exports**.

Net exports tend to make up a **small percentage** of aggregate demand, so changes in net exports have a **minor impact** on AD.

Warm-Up Questions

Q1 What does the government spending component of aggregate demand consist of?

Q2 What will cause a budget deficit?

Q3 Define 'imports' and 'exports'.

Q4 What 'non-price factors' may lead to an improvement in net exports?

PRACTICE QUESTIONS

Exam Questions

Q1 Which of the following pairs of government policies is most likely to lead to an increase in aggregate demand?
A) Increase government spending and increase taxes.
B) Decrease government spending and increase taxes.
C) Increase government spending and decrease taxes.
D) Decrease government spending and decrease taxes.

[1 mark]

Q2 Explain two factors which could increase the demand for a country's exports.

[10 marks]

Apparently net exports have nothing to do with fishing...

That's all the components of aggregate demand. It's important that you know what the components of aggregate demand are, what affects them, and how important each component is to the overall aggregate demand. But that's not all you need to know about aggregate demand, not by a long shot — turn the page and be wowed by the majestic aggregate demand curve.

Aggregate Demand Analysis

*Aggregate demand is the total demand in an economy — so the AD curve is similar to the normal demand curve. Sometimes a change in AD will cause a movement along the AD curve, other times the curve will shift. **These pages are for all boards.***

The **Aggregate Demand Curve** is similar to the normal **Demand Curve**

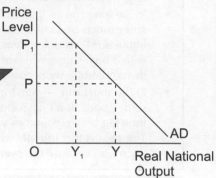

1) The aggregate demand curve uses **different** axes to the normal demand curve (p.16) — along the x-axis is **national output**, and up the y-axis is **price level**.

2) The price level represents the **average** level of prices in an economy — in the UK this price level is likely to be the **Consumer Price Index** (see p.125).

3) The aggregate demand (AD) curve slopes **downwards** — the **lower** the price level, the **more** output is demanded. **Lower** prices mean consumers can buy **more** goods/services with their money.

4) A **change** in the **price level** will cause a **movement along** the AD curve — for example, if the price level **rose** from P to P_1, the total (aggregate) demand would **fall** from Y to Y_1.

5) A rise in the price level will cause output to fall because:

- Domestic **consumption** will be **reduced** — things become **more expensive**, so people can purchase **fewer** goods and services.

- The **demand** for **exports** will be **reduced** — domestically produced products become **less competitive**.

- The **demand** for **imports** will **increase** — if prices **haven't** risen abroad, imports will become **cheaper** in comparison.

The **AD Curve** can **Shift**

Aggregate demand can **increase** or **decrease**, causing the AD curve to shift **right** or **left**.

The **AD Curve** might **Shift** to the **Right**

1) The AD curve will **shift** to the **right** if there's a **rise** in consumption, investment, government spending or net exports that **hasn't** been caused by a change in the price level. For example:

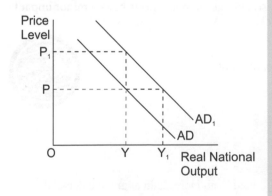

- A **reduction** in income tax will cause an **increase** in consumers' disposable income. This tends to lead to an **increase** in consumption, so there will be an **increase** in aggregate demand and a **shift** of the AD curve to the right from **AD** to AD_1 (see the diagram to the left).

- If a government changes its fiscal policy (see p.168) and decides to **increase** its spending **above** any increase in its revenue, then this is an **injection** into the circular flow of income. It will cause an **increase** in aggregate demand and a **shift** of the AD curve to the **right**, e.g. from AD to AD_1.

- A **weak** currency will make **exports cheaper** and **imports more expensive**. This will lead to a **rise** in **net exports**, so there will be an **increase** in **aggregate demand** and a **shift** of the AD curve to the **right**, e.g. from AD to AD_1.

2) The outward shift of the curve means that at a **given price level**, **more output** can be produced — but also, a **given** amount of **output** will have a **higher** price level. For example, if there's an increase in aggregate demand from AD to AD_1 — at price level P, there's an increase in output from Y to Y_1, and at output Y, the price level increases from P to P_1.

3) Labour is a **derived demand** — an **increase** in AD means **output increases**, so the **demand** for labour **increases**. **More** jobs are created so that the **extra** output can be **produced**, and there will be an **increase** in **employment** levels.

Aggregate Demand Analysis

The AD Curve might Shift to the Left

1) The AD curve will **shift** to the **left** if there's a **fall** in consumption, investment, government spending or net exports that **hasn't** been caused by a change in the price level. For example:

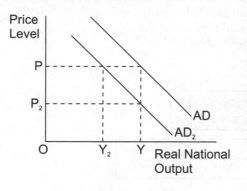

2) The inward shift of the curve means that at a **given price level** (P), **less output** (Y₂) can be produced — but also, a **given** amount of output (Y) will have a **lower** price level (P₂). There will also be a decrease in **employment** levels.

- A **rise** in **interest rates** will lead to a **reduction** in **consumer spending** because people will choose to **save** more. Higher interest rates also lead to a **reduction** in **investment** because borrowing the money to invest becomes **more expensive**. Both of these factors lead to a **reduction** in **aggregate demand**, and a **shift** of the AD curve to the **left**, e.g. from AD to AD₂ (see the diagram to the left).

- A **strong** currency will make **exports more expensive** and **imports cheaper**, so there will be a **fall** in **net exports**. This will lead to a **reduction** in **aggregate demand** and a **shift** of the AD curve to the **left**, e.g. from AD to AD₂.

The Multiplier Effect leads to a Larger Increase in aggregate demand

1) When there's an **injection** into the economy (e.g. as a result of increased government spending), the **AD curve** will **shift** to the **right**.

2) However, when money is **injected** into the circular flow of income, the **value** of the **initial** injection is **multiplied** — this is the multiplier effect that was introduced on p.131. One person's **expenditure** becomes someone else's **income**, so the money goes round the circular flow **multiple** times until it's all **leaked** out.

3) The effect is that the AD curve shifts **even further** to the right — and the bigger the **multiplier**, the greater the **shift**.

> For example, if a government **injects** money into **health care**, the money might be used for **wages**. Some of this money would then be spent by **consumers** — **increasing consumption**. This would create a **second** increase in AD, and the cycle will continue until all the money from the initial injection has **leaked out**.

The multiplier is sometimes called the 'national income multiplier'.

4) The overall **size** of the **multiplier** will depend on the **size** of the **leakages** from the circular flow of income, but it's **very difficult** to measure in practice. This is partly because there are **time lags** and the multiplier effect of government spending can take **years** to fully show up in the economy — e.g. the **full** benefits to the economy of government spending on improving transport links may only appear **years** later.

5) Measuring the size of the multiplier is also made difficult because, like everything else in the economy, it's **changing all the time**.

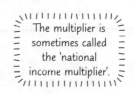

See p.179 for more about how this creates difficulties for governments aiming to achieve economic growth.

6) This makes it very difficult for any government to **accurately control** AD.

Warm-Up Questions

Q1 What causes a movement along the AD curve?

Q2 What would be the likely effect on aggregate demand of a rise in interest rates?

Exam Question

Q1 Discuss the effect of an increase in government spending on aggregate demand. Refer to the multiplier effect in your answer.

[10 marks]

There's more to come about AD curves — so I 'ope you 'aven't 'AD enough...

There can be movements along the aggregate demand curve, and shifts of the curve itself — make sure you understand the difference between the two. You also need to know the effect the multiplier will have on AD.

Aggregate Demand Analysis

These pages are about people's propensity (i.e their willingness or natural tendency) to either spend or save. There's a little bit of maths, but if you can divide two numbers, then you'll be okay. **This page is for all boards.**

Average Propensity to Consume or Save shows what happens to incomes

1) **Spending** and **saving** are both really important in an economy, and they're basically **opposite** processes. Money that's **spent** continues to circulate round the economy, while money that's **saved** is withdrawn from the circular flow described on p.130.

2) The '**average propensity**' formulas below tell you the **proportion** of the **total national income** that's either **spent** or **saved**.

$$\text{Average propensity to consume (APC)} = \frac{\text{consumption}}{\text{total income}} = \frac{C}{Y}$$

$$\text{Average propensity to save (APS)} = \frac{\text{amount saved}}{\text{total income}} = \frac{S}{Y}$$

The Marginal Propensity to Consume affects the size of the Multiplier

1) In Economics, '**marginal propensity**' is often **more important** than '**average propensity**'.

2) The **marginal propensity to consume** (**MPC**) is the proportion of any **extra** income that's **spent** on the **consumption** of goods and services. Similarly, the **marginal propensity to save** (**MPS**) is the proportion of **extra** income that's **saved**.

$$\text{Marginal propensity to consume (MPC)} = \frac{\text{Change in consumption}}{\text{Change in income}} = \frac{\Delta C}{\Delta Y}$$

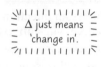
Δ just means 'change in'.

$$\text{Marginal propensity to save (MPS)} = \frac{\text{Change in saving}}{\text{Change in income}} = \frac{\Delta S}{\Delta Y}$$

3) MPC and MPS are important, since the **size** of the **multiplier** will depend on **how much** of an injection of money into the circular flow is **spent** by those who receive it, and how much is **saved**.

4) Money that's **saved** does **not** contribute to another person's **income**. This means that the **more likely** people are to **spend** their money, the **greater** the **multiplier effect**.

5) So if the MPC is **low**, the multiplier will be **small**, because any increase in income will only lead to a **small increase** in **consumption**. The rest of the increase in income will be **saved**.

6) Generally, people with **lower incomes** tend to have **higher MPCs**. The MPC also tends to be **higher** in **less developed** countries, so the multiplier will be **bigger**.

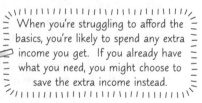
When you're struggling to afford the basics, you're likely to spend any extra income you get. If you already have what you need, you might choose to save the extra income instead.

Learn the Formula for calculating the Multiplier from the MPC

There's a simple formula for working out the **multiplier** if you know the **MPC**: ⇒

$$\text{Multiplier} = \frac{1}{1 - \text{MPC}}$$

Example: If every extra £1 of income earned in a country results in an extra 60p being spent on goods and services produced in that country, then:
    a) Find the marginal propensity to consume (MPC).
    b) Find the value of the multiplier for that economy.
    c) What will be the total increase in national income after an injection of an extra £50m?

a) If 60p out of every extra £1 of income is spent, then:

$$\text{Marginal propensity to consume (MPC)} = \frac{\text{Change in consumption}}{\text{Change in income}} = \frac{\Delta C}{\Delta Y} = \frac{0.6}{1} = \mathbf{0.6}$$

b) $\text{Multiplier} = \frac{1}{1 - \text{MPC}} = \frac{1}{1 - 0.6} = \frac{1}{0.4} = \mathbf{2.5}$

c) Total increase in national income = size of injection × multiplier = £50m × 2.5 = **£125m**

Aggregate Demand Analysis

If you're doing Edexcel or OCR then you also need to be able to find the multiplier from the marginal propensity to withdraw —
this is basically the opposite of the marginal propensity to consume, so nothing too tricky here. ***This page is for Edexcel and OCR.***

The **Marginal Propensity to Withdraw** can also be used to find the **Multiplier**

1) There's also another approach to working out the multiplier. Instead of looking at what proportion of extra income is **spent**, you can instead look at the proportion of extra income that's **withdrawn** from the economy.

2) The extra income can be **withdrawn** from the economy by:
   (i)   being **saved**,
   (ii) being paid to the government in **taxes**,
   (iii) being used to **import** goods from abroad.

3) The **marginal propensity to withdraw** (**MPW**) is the **proportion** of any **new income** that's withdrawn from an economy. MPW can be broken down in the following way:

$$MPW = MPS + MPT + MPM$$

where: • **MPS** = marginal **propensity to save**, the **proportion** of any **new income** that's saved.
   • **MPT** = marginal **propensity to tax**, the **proportion** of any **new income** that's paid as taxes.

You might see "marginal tax rate" instead of marginal propensity to tax.

   • **MPM** = marginal **propensity to import**, the **proportion** of any **new income** that's used to import goods.

Learn the **Formula** for calculating the **Multiplier** from the **MPW**

1) Since extra income must **either** be spent **or** withdrawn:

$$MPC + MPW = 1$$

2) This means you can also use the formula below to find the **multiplier**:

$$\text{Multiplier} = \frac{1}{MPW}$$

Because if MPC + MPW = 1, then MPW = 1 − MPC.

- The **multiplier** will be relatively **big** if **marginal tax rates** (i.e. the tax paid on the last £1 you earn) are **low**.
- This is because **low** marginal tax rates (i.e. a small value of **MPT**) means a small value for **MPW**, which means that the multiplier is **big**.

See p.132 for other factors that affect saving, consumption and the size of the multiplier.

Warm-Up Questions

PRACTICE QUESTIONS

Q1 What is the average propensity to consume for an economy?
Q2 Define what is meant by marginal propensity to consume.

Exam Question

Q1 Increased government spending results in an injection of £100 million into the economy. The marginal propensities to save (MPS), tax (MPT) and import (MPM) are given by MPS = 0.3, MPT = 0.4 and MPM = 0.1.
   Find the total rise in national income that results from this injection.   [4 marks]

Formulas seem to be multiplying all over these pages...

Don't complain... these pages aren't as hard as they look. I realise there's a fair bit of maths going on, but it's really not that bad. If you want to complain about all the three-letter abbreviations though, that's fine with me. By the way, don't go thinking that, because working out a multiplier looks quite easy in theory (the formulas are pretty simple after all), finding the value in practice must be pretty simple too — it isn't. See page 137 for some of the practical difficulties.

Aggregate Supply

Remember, 'aggregate' means total. So you can probably work out what aggregate supply is. **These pages are for all boards.**

There are **Two Types** of AS curve

1) **Aggregate supply** is the **total output** produced in an economy at a given price level over a given period of time. There are **two types** of **aggregate supply curve** you need to know about.

2) The first type is the **short run aggregate supply (SRAS) curve.** **Short run** aggregate supply (SRAS) curves slope up from left to right. They show that with an **increase** in the **price level**, there's an **increase** in the amount of **output** firms are willing to supply.

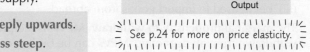

- If SRAS is **price inelastic**, the SRAS curve slopes **steeply upwards**.
- If SRAS is **price elastic**, the SRAS curve would be **less steep**.

See p.24 for more on price elasticity.

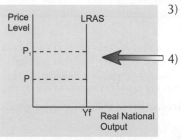

3) In the **long run**, it's assumed that an economy will move towards an equilibrium where **all resources** are being used to **full capacity** (so the economy is running at its full **productive potential**). This is shown by the **long run aggregate supply** (LRAS) curve.

4) The LRAS curve is **vertical**. An increase in the price level (e.g. to P_1) **won't** cause an increase in output because the economy is running at full capacity, so it **can't** create any more output.

These are actually 'classical' or 'neo-classical' AS curves. You also need to know about 'Keynesian' AS curves — these are on p.141.

Changes in **Costs of Production** cause the **SRAS** curve to shift

1) The SRAS curve will **shift** if there's a **change** in the **costs** of production.

2) A **reduction** in the **costs** of production means that at the **same** price level, **more output** can be **produced**, so the SRAS curve will shift to the **right**.

3) For example, a **reduction** in the price of oil might shift the curve from SRAS to $SRAS_1$ — so at price level P, **output** would **increase** from Y to Y_1.

4) **Changes** in things such as wage rates, the taxes firms pay, exchange rates and efficiency levels will cause **shifts** of the SRAS curve.

5) A sudden **decrease** in aggregate supply (leading to a price increase) could also be caused by **supply-side shocks**, such as **natural disaster** or **war**.

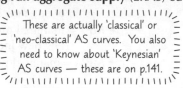

Changes in **Factors of Production** cause the **LRAS** curve to shift

1) Long run aggregate supply is **determined** by the **factors of production** — the LRAS curve will **shift** if there's a **change** in the factors of production which affects the **capacity** of the economy.

2) An **improvement** in the factors of production **increases** the **capacity** of the economy, and will shift the LRAS curve to the **right**, e.g. from LRAS to $LRAS_1$. This **increases** output (in other words, there's **economic growth**) from Yf to Yf_1 — the **same** price level now corresponds to a **higher** level of output.

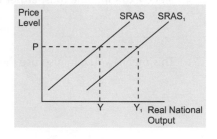

3) E.g. **investment** that leads to **advances** in **technology** and **more efficient** production will **increase maximum** output.

4) Other examples of **improvements** in the factors of production which might **shift** the AS curve to the **right** are:

- An **improvement** in education and skills — better education and training should lead to **more productive** individuals, i.e. the **output** per person will **increase**, so **maximum** output is increased.
- **Demographic changes** — e.g. skilled workers **migrating** to a country can increase the economy's capacity.
- A **supply of new resources** — new resources may mean the **maximum** output of the economy can be increased.
- **Improvements** in health care — if the **overall** health of workers **improves**, they're likely to have **less** time off work and retire at an **older** age. This means the **productivity** and **size** of the economy's labour force **increases**.
- Changes in **government regulations** — e.g. the removal of unnecessary rules and 'red tape'.
- An **increase** in competition — greater competition in an economy will cause inefficient firms to **close** and be **replaced** by more efficient firms — **increasing** an economy's **capacity**.
- Promoting **enterprise** — e.g. by providing **economic incentives** or **guidance** for people starting new businesses.
- Increasing **factor mobility** — e.g. with training schemes to reduce **occupational labour immobility** (see p.113).

5) A **deterioration** in the factors of production that **reduces** an economy's capacity will cause the LRAS curve to shift to the **left**, e.g. if there's a massive **reduction** in the **supply** of oil then the **maximum** possible output will be **reduced**.

Aggregate Supply

AQA ONLY

Banks can play a part in determining the Position of the LRAS curve

1) Firms often **borrow** money from **banks** to **invest**, usually so that they can **increase** their output — e.g. a firm might borrow money to invest in **new machinery**.

2) If a country has a **strong** banking system then this will help its economy to **grow**. It will mean there's **more money** available for investment in the economy, and this should lead to an **increase** in the **productive potential** (capacity) of the economy.

3) So **improvements** in a country's banking system will **shift** the LRAS (and the SRAS) curve to the **right**.

An exam question might refer to the 'institutional structure of the economy' — the banking system is part of this. See p.182 for more info.

AQA & OCR

A Rise in Demand might cause an 'Accelerated' increase in investment

1) One way businesses determine whether investment is needed is to look at the **current rate of change** of national income. So if national income is **growing rapidly**, then businesses will **invest heavily**.

2) This is called the **accelerator process** (or the **accelerator effect**). Firms will make 'accelerated' investment in **capital goods**, expecting to **increase output** and make **profit** in the future.

3) This is likely to occur when the economy is going through a **recovery**, or at the start of a **boom**. These are the times when **demand** will be rapidly increasing and firms will need to invest to meet this demand.

4) The multiplier (see p.131) and the accelerator work together. For example:
   • During a recovery, **AD** will be **growing**.
   • This leads to firms **increasing** their levels of **investment** — which leads to **another** increase in AD.
   • This increase in AD is then '**multiplied**', making the growth in national income **more rapid**...
   • ...which leads to even more '**accelerated**' investment.

5) The accelerator process and multiplier effect can both also happen **in reverse** — for example, during a recession, there's likely to be a **fall** in **demand** and a **fall** in **investment**, which will then have a **reverse multiplier effect**.

6) This can lead to a constant **cycle** of output first rising and then falling.

This explanation of the business cycle (see page 145) is called the multiplier-accelerator model.

The Keynesian LRAS curve is L-Shaped

Not everyone agrees that the LRAS curve is vertical. **Keynesian economists** argue that the LRAS curve actually looks like this.

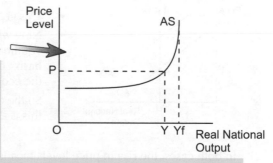

• At **low** levels of output, aggregate supply is **completely elastic** (where the curve is horizontal) — this means there's **spare capacity** in the economy, so **output** can **increase** without a rise in the **price level**. For example, if there's a lot of **unemployment** in an economy, firms will be able to employ **more** workers and **increase** output, **without** increasing price levels.

• When the curve begins to **slope upwards** this shows that the economy is experiencing **problems** with supply (known as supply bottlenecks), which are causing **increases** in **costs**. For example, this might be due to a **shortage** of **labour**, or a **shortage** of certain **raw materials**.

• The curve becomes **vertical** when the economy is at **full capacity** (Yf) — here, aggregate supply is **completely inelastic**. All resources are being used to their **maximum potential** and output **can't** increase any more.

Warm-Up Questions

Q1 Give an example of a change that would shift an SRAS curve to the right.

Q2 Explain the main differences between a classical LRAS curve and a Keynesian one.

Exam Question

Q1 A shift of the LRAS curve to the right might be caused by:
   A) a reduction in wages.   B) the discovery of a new raw material.
   C) a reduction in taxes.   D) a drop in interest rates.   [1 mark]

NB: if you aren't an economy, running at full capacity isn't a good idea...

Remember — a deterioration in the factors of production will shift the LRAS curve to the left, but an improvement in the factors of production will shift it to the right. You should know and understand the changes which would cause these shifts.

Macroeconomic Equilibrium

You've seen AD and AS on their own... now it's time to see how they work together to create a macroeconomic equilibrium. ***These pages are for all boards.***

Macroeconomic Equilibrium occurs where AS = AD

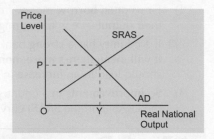

1) **Macroeconomic equilibrium** occurs where the AD and AS curves **cross**, e.g. at price level P and output Y on this SRAS curve.

2) A **shift** of either curve will **move** this equilibrium to a **different** point, but shifts of AD and AS curves affect things in **different ways**.

   In particular, the government's four macroeconomic indicators (see Section 8) are affected differently by shifts in the AS and AD curves.

An Increase in AD alone can only increase output in the Short Run

1) The effect of a **shift in AD** on the equilibrium point depends on the **slope** of the **AS curve**. This means the effects of an increase in AD can be quite different in the **short** and **long run**.

   Because the SRAS curve slopes upwards, while the LRAS curve is vertical.

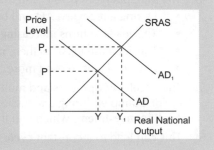

- This graph shows an **SRAS curve** along with an **AD curve**.
- When there's an **increase** in aggregate demand and the AD curve shifts from AD to AD$_1$, the **new** equilibrium point will be at price level P$_1$ and output Y$_1$.
- There's been an **increase in output**, which will lead to an increase in **derived demand**, so more **jobs** are created and unemployment is **reduced**.
- But there's also been a **rise in prices** — this is 'demand-pull' inflation.
- A **decrease** in AD will have the **opposite** effect — **output** will be **reduced** and there will be an **increase** in **unemployment**, but **price levels** will **fall**.

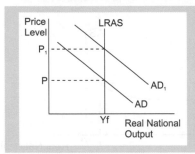

- This graph shows an **LRAS curve** along with an **AD curve**.
- Now when the AD curve shifts from AD to AD$_1$, the **new** equilibrium point will be at price level P$_1$, but the **output hasn't changed** (and **unemployment** can't fall) — because the economy is already running at **full capacity**.
- So the only effect is that **prices rise** — again, this is an example of 'demand-pull' inflation.

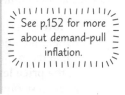

See p.152 for more about demand-pull inflation.

2) In both cases, the **rise** in price levels means there will possibly be a **worsening** of the balance of payments (see p.153).

3) In general, to improve **all four** macroeconomic policy indicators at the **same time**, there needs to be an **increase** in **LRAS**. See p.143 for more information.

   However, Keynesian economists would say that this is only sometimes true — see p.143.

The amount of Spare Capacity can Limit the effect of the Multiplier

If **supply** is already **struggling** to keep up with demand, then the **multiplier effect** after an increase in AD will probably be quite **small** — the economy just **won't** be able to cope with any further large increases in demand.

When aggregate supply (AS) is very **elastic**, there is a **lot** of spare capacity in the economy. In this case, after an initial injection shifts the AD curve, the **multiplier** can take effect to give a **large rise** in **output**.

When aggregate supply (AS) is very **inelastic**, there is much less spare capacity in the economy. The same initial shift in AD cannot be multiplied in the same way — there's a **smaller rise** in **output** (but a **large rise in prices**, i.e. inflation).

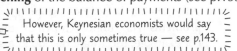

Macroeconomic Equilibrium

Shifts in AS affect All Four macroeconomic indicators in the Same Way

A shift of the AS curve will either improve or worsen **all four** indicators at the **same time**.

- For example, an **increase** in AS, shown by a shift to the right from SRAS to SRAS$_1$, will lead to an **increase** in the **capacity** of the economy. This will result in an **increase** in output — so there's **increased** economic growth. There will be **more jobs**, reducing **unemployment**. The **price level** will tend to **fall** and the economy will become **more competitive** internationally, **improving** the balance of payments.
- On the other hand, a **decrease** in AS would **worsen** the state of all four macroeconomic indicators.

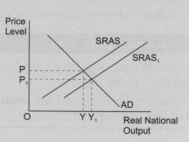

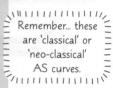

Remember... these are 'classical' or 'neo-classical' AS curves.

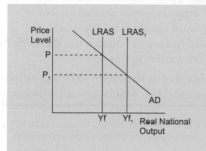

- If **LRAS** increases, then you get similar results.
- For example, if long run aggregate supply shifts from LRAS to LRAS$_1$, then in the long run **output** is **increased**, the **price level falls**, the balance of payments will potentially **improve** and the economy remains at **full employment**.
- So a **shift** of the LRAS curve will also tend to cause **all four** macroeconomic policy indicators to **improve** or **worsen** at the **same time**.

Keynesian AS curves mean changes in AS and AD have Different Effects

With a Keynesian LRAS curve (see p.141), the effects of an increase in AD can be slightly different.

- If AD increases from AD$_1$ to AD$_2$, the effects are the same as those described on p.142 — there's an **increase in prices** but **no increase in output**. This corresponds to an economy that's already operating at **full capacity**.
- If AD increases from AD$_3$ to AD$_4$, then there's an **increase in output** but **no increase in prices**. This corresponds to an economy deep in depression.
- If AD increases from AD$_5$ to AD$_1$, then there are **increases** in **both output and prices**. This corresponds to an economy operating **just under** full capacity.

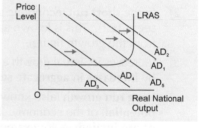

With a **Keynesian LRAS** curve, the effects of an increase in AS can also be slightly different.

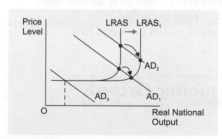

- If AS increases from LRAS to LRAS$_1$, there is a change in the macroeconomic equilibrium if AD is at **either** AD$_1$ **or** AD$_2$.
- However, if AD is at AD$_3$, then there is **no change** in the equilibrium.
- This is why Keynesian economists say that there is **little point** in aiming to **increase AS** during a **depression** — the macroeconomic equilibrium will **not** be affected and there will be **no increase** in **output** or **employment**.

Warm-Up Questions

Q1 Explain why an increase in AD cannot increase output in the long run.

PRACTICE QUESTIONS

Exam Question

Q1 Describe the possible effects on an economy of a shift to the right of the short run aggregate supply curve. [8 marks]

All the curves on these pages are making me blush...

Not everyone agrees about how an economy works. That's bad news for you, because you need to know all the theories.

Economic Growth

The government is in charge of the national economy. Sounds like fun, I know... but an economy is a tricky thing to manage and everyone hates you when you get it wrong. **These pages are for all boards.**

There are **Four Main Objectives** of **Government Macroeconomic Policy**

Governments have **four main macroeconomic objectives** they're trying to achieve:

1 Strong economic growth

1) Governments want economic growth to be **high** (but not **too** high).

2) In general, economic growth will **improve** the **standard of living** in a country.

2 Keeping inflation low

1) In the UK, the government aims for **inflation** of **2%**.

2) The **Monetary Policy Committee of the Bank of England** uses **monetary policy** (see pages 173-175) to try to achieve this target rate.

3 Reducing unemployment

1) Governments aim to **reduce unemployment** and move towards **full employment**.

2) If **more** people are employed then the economy will be **more productive**. **Aggregate demand** will also **increase** as more people will have a **greater income**.

4 Equilibrium in the balance of payments

1) Governments want **equilibrium** in the balance of payments, i.e. they want **earnings** from **exports** and other **inward flows** of money to **balance** the **spending** on **imports** and other **outward** flows of money.

2) This is **more desirable** than a **long-term deficit** or **surplus** in the balance of payments — which can cause problems.

Governments often have **other** objectives too. For example, they may want to:

- Balance the **budget** (see p.134),
- Protect the **environment** (see p.158),
- Achieve greater **income equality** (see p.158).

The relative importance that governments attach to all these objectives changes over time. See Section 11 for some examples.

There are **Different Types** of **Economic Growth**

1) **Economic growth** is an **increase** in the **productive potential** of an economy.

2) In the **short run**, economic growth is measured by the **percentage change** in real national output (real GDP — see p.122). This is known as **actual** (real) growth (this just means that the **effect** of **inflation** has been **removed** from the growth figure).

3) Increases in actual growth are usually due to an **increase** in **aggregate demand**, but they can also be caused by **increases** in **aggregate supply**. Actual growth doesn't always increase — it tends to **fluctuate up** and **down**.

4) **Long run** growth (also known as **potential** growth) is caused by an **increase** in the **capacity**, or **productive potential**, of the economy. This usually happens due to a **rise** in the **quality** or **quantity** of **inputs** (the **factors of production**) — for example, more **advanced** machinery or a more **highly skilled** labour force.

5) Long run growth is shown by an **increase** in the **trend rate** of growth. The **trend rate** of growth is the **average rate** of economic growth over a period of both economic **booms** and **slumps**. It **rises smoothly** rather than fluctuating like actual economic growth, so the **actual rate** of growth often doesn't **match** the **trend rate**.

6) **Increases** in long run growth are caused by an increase in **aggregate supply**.

A **Production Possibility Frontier (PPF)** can show **Economic Growth**

1) **Short run** and **long run** economic growth can be shown with a **PPF**.

2) Short run growth is shown by a **movement** from, say, point A to point B, while the PPF itself remains **fixed**.

3) Long run growth **occurs** if there's an **increase** in the **capacity** of the economy — this would make the PPF shift **outwards** to PPF₁.

See p.8-9 for more about PPFs.

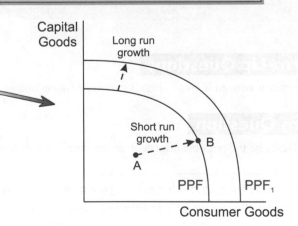

Economic Growth

The Economic Cycle has Different Phases

1) The actual growth of an economy **fluctuates** over time. These **fluctuations** are known as the **economic cycle**.

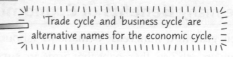

'Trade cycle' and 'business cycle' are alternative names for the economic cycle.

2) A **boom** is when the economy is **growing quickly**. Aggregate demand will be **rising**, leading to a **fall** in **unemployment** and a **rise** in **inflation**.

3) A **recession** is when there's **negative economic growth** for at least **two consecutive quarters**. Aggregate demand will be **falling**, causing **unemployment** to **rise** and a **fall** in **price levels**.

4) During a **recovery** the economy begins to **grow again**, going from **negative economic growth** to **positive economic growth**. Aggregate demand will be **rising**, so **unemployment** will be **falling** and **inflation** will be **rising**.

5) **Long run** growth is shown by an **increase** in the **trend rate** of growth. The trend rate of growth is the **average rate** of economic growth over a period of both economic **booms** and **slumps**.

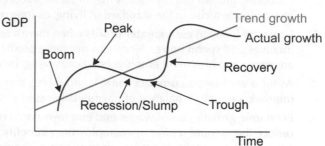

Levels of investment tend to match the rate of change of GDP (see p.141). This means that investment will be greatest when the red line is steepest.

Output Gaps can occur during periods of Boom or Recession

1) A **negative output** gap (also called a **recessionary gap**) is the **difference** between the level of **actual output** and **trend output** when actual output is **below** trend output.
   - A negative output gap will occur during a **recession** when the economy is **under-performing**, as some resources will be **unused** or **underused** (including labour, so **unemployment** may be high).
   - A negative output gap also usually means **downwards pressure** on **inflation**.

2) A **positive output** gap (also called an **inflationary gap**) is the **difference** between the level of **actual output** and **trend output** when actual output is **above** trend output.
   - A positive output gap will occur during a **boom** when the economy is **overheating**, as resources are being fully **used** or **overused** (so **unemployment** may be low).
   - A positive output gap also usually means **upwards pressure** on **inflation**.

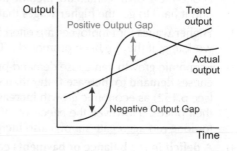

An output gap can also be thought of as the difference between actual output and productive potential.

3) During a **recovery** an economy will go from having a negative output gap to having a positive output gap as actual output **rises above** trend output.

In practice, output gaps are difficult to measure accurately.

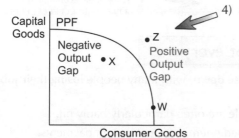

4) An output gap can be shown on a **PPF**. For example, in this diagram:
   - Point W shows the economy operating at **full capacity** — all available resources are being used.
   - Point X is **inside** the PPF. This shows that some resources are **not** being used **fully** — there's a **negative output gap**.
   - Point Z is **outside** the PPF, meaning the economy is producing a level of output that is 'beyond its potential' — this may happen if workers are working **excessively long hours** or machines are being **overused**. In this case there's a **positive output gap**.

5) An output gap can also be shown using AS and AD curves. For example, in this diagram:
   - Point W shows the economy operating at its full **productive potential**, using all available resources (i.e. it's on the LRAS curve).
   - Point X shows the equilibrium of SRAS$_1$ and AD$_1$ to the **left** of the LRAS curve. In other words the economy has the **potential** to supply at a **greater level**. The distance between Y$_1$ and Y$_f$ is a **negative output gap**.
   - Point Z shows the equilibrium of SRAS$_1$ and AD$_2$ to the **right** of the LRAS curve. The distance between Y$_2$ and Y$_f$ is a **positive output gap**.

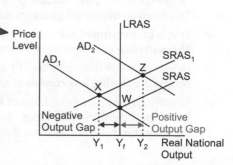

Economic Growth

We're not done yet with economic growth... or recessions. **These pages are for all boards.**

There are many Benefits of Economic Growth

1) **Economic growth** will **increase demand** for labour, leading to a **fall** in **unemployment** and **higher incomes** for individuals.

2) Economic growth usually means that firms are **succeeding**, so employees may get **higher wages**. This will also produce a **rise** in the **standard** of **living**, as long as prices **don't** rise more than the increase in wages.

3) **Firms** are likely to earn **greater profits** when there's economic growth, as consumers usually have **higher incomes** and **spend more**. Firms can use these profits to **invest** in better machinery, make **technological advances** and **hire** more employees — causing an **increase** in the **economy's productive potential**.

4) As firms are likely to **produce more** when there's economic growth then this can **improve** a country's **balance of payments** because it will sell **more exports**.

5) **Economic growth** causes wages and employment to **rise**, which will **increase** the **government's tax revenue** and **reduce** the amount it pays in **unemployment benefits**. The government can use this **extra revenue** to **improve** public services or the country's infrastructure **without** having to **raise taxes**, which is good for individuals.

6) Economic growth will **improve** a government's **fiscal position** (see p.168) because if it receives greater tax revenues and spends less on things like unemployment benefits then this will **reduce** the government's need to **borrow money**.

7) There might be some **benefits** to the **environment** brought about by economic growth, e.g. firms may have the resources to **invest** in **cleaner** and **more efficient** production processes.

Unfortunately, there are some Costs of Economic Growth

1) Economic growth can create **income inequality** — **low-skilled workers** may find it hard to get the **higher wages** that other workers are benefiting from.

2) **Higher wages** for employees are often linked to an **increase** in their **responsibilities** at work (e.g. if they've been promoted). This can **increase stress** and **reduce productivity**.

3) Economic growth can cause demand-pull inflation (see p.152) because it causes **demand** to **increase faster** than **supply**. It can also cause cost-push inflation (see p.152) as economic growth **increases** the **demand** for **resources**, pushing up their prices. However, the effects of inflation will be **reduced** if **aggregate supply** (or long run aggregate supply) also **increases**.

4) A **deficit** in the **balance of payments** can be created because people on **higher incomes** buy **more imports**. Furthermore, **firms** may **import more resources** to increase their production to meet the higher levels of demand.

In moments of quiet reflection, Suki often worried about the increased stress and reduced productivity that could arise as a result of employees' higher wages.

5) **Industrial expansion** created by economic growth may bring **negative externalities**, such as pollution or increased congestion on the roads, which **harm** the **environment** and **reduce** people's quality of life.

6) **Beautiful scenery** and **habitats** can be **destroyed** when **resources** are **overexploited**.

7) **Finite resources** may be **used up** in the creation of economic growth, which may **constrain** growth in the **future** and threaten future living standards.

See p.149 for more about sustainable economic growth.

A Recession is Bad News for Most people... but not everyone

1) A recession (period of negative growth) will usually see many firms **close down**, with many people **losing their jobs**. This means **unemployment** usually **increases**.

2) Other firms may **stop hiring** new employees — this means **young people** are often particularly badly hit.

3) **Government spending** tends to **increase** — for example, due to increased unemployment benefit payments. At the same time, the amount of **tax** a government receives usually **falls**. This leads to **increased government borrowing** and a **budget deficit** (see p.134).

4) Levels of **investment fall** — e.g. firms might reduce the amount they spend on research and development. This can have consequences for the **long run productive potential** of the economy.

5) However, some firms can benefit at times of recession — e.g. **discount retailers** can often attract more customers if people are feeling **less confident** about their economic prospects.

6) Recessions can also force firms to **face up** to their **inefficiencies**. In good times, firms might be able to **get away with** being **inefficient** in some areas. But they may need to **cut costs** to survive a recession. This can **benefit** the firm in the **long run** if it emerges from the recession **more efficient** than it was before.

Economic Growth

Short Run economic growth can be created by Increasing Aggregate Demand

1) A rise in **aggregate demand** (**AD**) will create **short run** economic growth. When **AD** rises the **AD** curve **shifts** to the **right**.

2) An increase in AD will be caused by **demand-side factors**. For example:

   - **Lowering** interest rates **encourages** investment and **increases** consumption.
   - **Increasing** welfare benefits **increases** government spending and consumption.

3) How much the AD curve shifts depends on:
   - people's **marginal propensity to consume**, **MPC** (see p.138),
   - how big the **multiplier effect** is (see p.131).

4) The higher the MPC and the **bigger** the **multiplier**, the **greater** the shift to the right of the AD curve.

5) In the diagram, national output has **increased** from Y to Y_1.

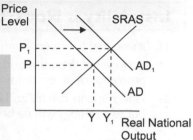

There's a lot more detail about the effects of increasing AD and AS in Section 9. The policy conflicts that can result are dealt with on pages 160-161.

Short Run Aggregate Supply Increases also create Short Run growth

1) A **rise** in **short run aggregate supply** (**SRAS**) will also create short run economic growth. When SRAS **rises** the SRAS curve **shifts** to the **right**.

2) Any factor which **reduces production costs** will cause an **increase** in SRAS. Here are some examples:

   - A fall in the price of oil will reduce production costs and increase SRAS.
   - A fall in wages will reduce production costs and increase SRAS.

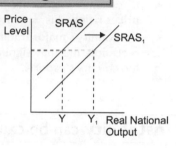

There are several ways to create Long Run Economic Growth

1) **Long run** economic growth is the result of **supply-side factors** that increase the **productive potential** of the **economy**.

2) The **productive potential** of a country can be **increased** by **raising** the **quantity** or **quality** of the **factors of production**, for example:

   - Through **innovation** — e.g. new technology.
   - **Investing** in more **modern** machinery (i.e. improving **capital stock**).
   - **Raising** agricultural **output** by using genetically modified (GM) crops.
   - **Increasing** spending on **education** and **training** to improve **human capital**.
   - **Increasing** the **population size**, e.g. by encouraging immigration, to increase the size of a country's **workforce**.

Capital stock is the stuff that's used to make goods, e.g. machines, factories, computers, etc.

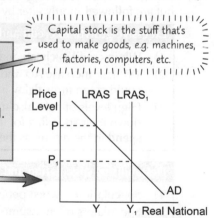

3) An **increase** in productive potential **shifts** the LRAS (or AS) curve to the right.

4) A **government** can also help to create long run economic growth by creating **stability** in a country — see p.148 for more information.

Warm-Up Questions

Q1 Describe what is meant by an 'output gap', and how it can be shown on a PPF.

Q2 List three examples of costs of economic growth.

Exam Question

Q1 Explain how economic growth might contribute to an improvement in the standard of living in a country.   [8 marks]

How to make long run economic growth — chase after it dressed as a bear...

There's lots to learn on these four pages — make sure you understand the difference between long and short run growth. Also, economic growth might sound like a good thing, but in the exam you might be asked to write about its costs — so learn 'em.

Economic Instability

*All governments aim to maintain steady and stable growth. But many economies suffer from cycles of 'boom and bust'
— where the economy alternates between good times and bad times.* **This page is for AQA only.**

Instability is Not Good for an economy

1) It's normal for an economy to go through regular ups and downs — this is the **economic cycle**.

2) However, if these ups and downs are **particularly large** or **particularly frequent**, this can cause problems for an economy.

3) Governments can try and **control** these ups and downs to a **certain extent**... but some things will be beyond their control.

See also p.159.

Economies can suffer from Demand-side Shocks or Supply-side Shocks

1) An economy might start to shrink or grow because it's affected by a **demand-side shock** (which can cause **aggregate demand** to rise or fall) or by a **supply-side shock** (which can cause **aggregate supply** to rise or fall).

2) These shocks can be **domestic** or **global**.

Examples of demand-side shocks:

- If consumer confidence is **boosted**, e.g. due to **house prices rising**, this will **increase consumer spending**.

- If a country's **major trading partners** go into a **recession**, this may significantly reduce demand for the country's **exports**.

Examples of supply-side shocks:

- A **poor harvest** reduces the supply of food, increases its price, and **reduces** the economy's **capacity**.

- The discovery of a major **new source** of a raw material will greatly reduce its price and increase its supply — **increasing** the **capacity** of the economy.

Instability can be caused by 'Animal Spirits'

1) According to classical economic theory, economic agents (e.g. people, firms, governments) always act **rationally**.

2) In fact, people often seem to act very **irrationally**. Keynes used the term **animal spirits** (see p.133) to describe how human behaviour is often guided by **instincts** and **emotions**, rather than economic realities.

3) For example, the following are common **danger signs** for an economy — they often start to **emerge** during a **boom**, but are **followed** shortly after by a **bust**, and are created (at least partly) by animal spirits.

Excessive growth in credit and levels of debt

1) When **credit** is **cheap** and **consumers** are feeling **confident**, they often **spend** more and **accumulate debt**.

2) This can **increase AD** and lead to **higher inflation**. This inflation can lead to **higher interest rates**, which could mean firms **delay** investment projects and become more **cautious**, storing up problems for an economy.

3) High levels of debt also mean that if consumers **lose confidence** for any reason, they're likely to greatly slow down their spending for fear of not being able to pay off their loans. It also means they'll have **less money to spend** in the future, as they'll be spending money repaying debts (including interest).

Destabilising speculation and asset price bubbles

1) **Speculation** is when people buy assets (e.g. houses, shares, etc.) and hope to sell them for a profit later.

2) Speculators often assume that an **increase** in the price of an asset means that its price will **continue** to increase in the **future** — this prompts further **buying** of the good and further **price increases**, leading to **further** buying and **further** price increases, and so on.

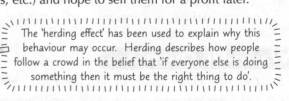

The 'herding effect' has been used to explain why this behaviour may occur. Herding describes how people follow a crowd in the belief that 'if everyone else is doing something then it must be the right thing to do'.

3) This behaviour can lead to **asset price bubbles** — where prices increase way beyond the asset's **'true value'**.

4) Eventually the bubble **bursts** and asset prices start to **fall**. When this happens, people's optimism and confidence can disappear. If people start to **fear** they'll **lose money**, they may start to **sell** the assets... leading to **further** price decreases, and **further** selling, and so on.

5) **Property** and **shares** are often affected by asset-price bubbles, and the effects of a sudden fall in UK house prices, for example, can be dramatic. As people feel **less wealthy** and **less confident**, they start to **save** instead of spend, and this can lead to a **downward spiral** in the economy.

Economic Instability

Sustainable growth is in part about being able to expand the economy every year. **This page is for all boards.**

Sustainable Growth is Difficult to Achieve

1) **Sustainable economic growth** means making sure the economy **keeps growing** (now and in the future), **without** causing **problems** for future generations (there's more on sustainability on p.225). Sustainable growth relies on a country's ability to:

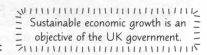
Sustainable economic growth is an objective of the UK government.

- **Expand output** every year.
- Find a **continuous supply** of raw materials, land, labour and so on, to continue production.
- Find **growing markets** for the increased output, so it's always being bought.
- **Reduce negative externalities**, e.g. pollution, to an acceptable level so they don't hamper production.
- Do all of the above things at the **same time** as many **other** countries who are pursuing the **same objectives**.

2) It's **very difficult** for a country to do all of these things at the same time, so sustainable growth is **hard** to achieve.

3) To be able to achieve sustainable growth, countries will need to **develop renewable** resources. Non-renewable resources will **run out** and, for growth to be sustainable, a **continuous supply** of raw materials is **necessary**.

4) Countries will also need to **innovate** to create **new technologies** that **reduce negative externalities**, such as pollution, and the **degradation** of resources, such as land or rivers, **without** stopping output from expanding.

5) A country that achieves **sustainable** growth will gain **long-term** benefits to society — it can more easily **plan ahead**, since it can be more confident about its long-term economic prospects.

You need to know about the UK's Recent Macroeconomic Performance

1) It's **important** for the exam that you've got some idea of the **UK's recent macroeconomic performance**.

2) You should keep an eye on the **news** and look for any **important developments** about the **UK's economy** — e.g. there might be a rise in interest rates or a large fall in unemployment. Here are a few **general points** to get you started:

- From **2000** until **2008** the UK enjoyed **continuous GDP growth** of, on average, **just under 3%** each year. However, in 2008 the UK went into a **recession** that lasted for **several months** and was followed by a long, **slow recovery**.

- During the recovery the UK economy went through **short bursts** of growth followed by **slow-downs** — it almost went **back** into a **recession** in **2012**. From **2013 onwards**, the UK has had much more **consistent GDP growth** and, by **2014**, **GDP returned** to the level it was **just before** the recession — suggesting that the **recovery** is **complete**.

- Between **2000** and early **2015** the rate of **inflation** in the UK, as measured by the **Consumer Price Index** (**CPI**), has been quite **steady** — generally inflation has been **between 0.5** and **3%**.

- There have been **some exceptions** to this steady level of inflation. On a **couple** of occasions, inflation rose to about **5%**, **well above** the government's target of **2%**. This happened just at the **start** of the **recession** in **2008** and **again** in **2011**. Inflation then **fell** again and remained between 0 and 3% for some time.

- **Unemployment** in the UK remained **quite low** between **2000** and **2008** — **between** about **1.4** and **1.7 million**.

- Between **2008** and **2011** unemployment **rapidly rose**, reaching about **2.7 million** (an **unemployment rate** of **8%**). Since then unemployment has **fallen**, but, by January 2015, it was still **higher** than it was at the start of 2008.

- The UK has had a **current account deficit** in its **balance of payments** for the **whole period** between **1984** and **2014**. The deficit was at its **largest** during this period towards the **end of 2014**.

- The UK economy is dominated by its **service sector**, which accounts for roughly three quarters of GDP. **Manufacturing** now accounts for around a tenth of GDP.

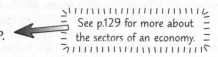
See p.129 for more about the sectors of an economy.

Warm-Up Questions

Q1 Give an example of a demand-side shock and a supply-side shock.

Q2 Explain how 'animal spirits' can lead to an asset price bubble.

PRACTICE QUESTIONS

Exam Question

Q1 Explain why asset price bubbles can be destabilising for an economy. [8 marks]

Sustainable growth is the Holy Grail of economics...

Right, there's a lot of stuff here, but it's important. Basically, everyone wants sustainable growth, but it's easier said than done. Make sure you know the UK's recent macroeconomic performance so you can slip some useful points into your answers.

Unemployment

*Make sure you properly understand the easy stuff on this page — it'll definitely help when you get to the trickier stuff that's coming up in a bit. **These pages are for all boards.***

Governments want Full Employment

1) Governments aim for **full employment**, which is where everybody of working age (excluding students, retirees, etc.), who wants to work, can find employment at the **current** wage rates.

See p.126 for more info about unemployment.

2) Full employment **doesn't mean** everyone has a job — in most economies there will **always** be people **between jobs**.

3) Governments **want** full employment because this will **maximise production** and **raise standards of living** in a country.

4) If there's **unemployment** in an economy then it **won't** be operating at **full capacity**, so it'll be represented by a point **within** the **PPF curve** (e.g. point A). At **full employment** the economy can **operate** at **full capacity**, so it can be represented by a point **on** the PPF curve (e.g. point B).

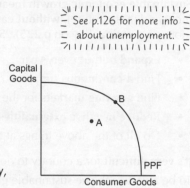

5) **Under-employment** would also mean an economy is not operating at full capacity, and it will be represented by a point **within** its PPF curve. Under-employment is when someone has a job, but it's not a job that utilises that person's **skills**, **experience** or **availability** to the best effect. For example, a qualified accountant serving drinks in a pub might count as under-employed, as might someone who could only find **part-time** employment when they actually wanted a **full-time** position.

Economic Growth and the Time of Year affect Unemployment

1) Labour is a **derived** demand — an employer's demand for labour is derived from **consumers'** demand for goods/services. So when demand in the economy is **low** (e.g. when there's negative economic growth), unemployment will **rise** — but when demand is **high**, unemployment will **fall** (e.g. when there's positive economic growth).

2) **Cyclical** unemployment (or demand-deficient unemployment) usually happens when the economy is in a **recession** — when aggregate demand falls, employment will **fall** too. A country suffering from a **negative output gap** (see p.145) is likely to have cyclical unemployment too.

Recessions don't bother Clive — he has cyclical employment.

3) **Seasonal unemployment** occurs because demand for labour in certain industries **won't** be the **same** all year round. For example, the **tourism** and **farming** industries have 'peak seasons' where the need for labour is much higher than at other times of year. **Retailing** is also affected by seasonal unemployment (many shops will be particularly busy at Christmas, for example).

4) **Seasonal** unemployment tends to be **regular** and **predictable**, and it only affects **certain industries**. **Cyclical** unemployment, on the other hand, can affect **any** industry.

Structural Unemployment is made worse by Labour Immobility

1) Structural unemployment is caused by a **decline** in a certain **industry** or **occupation** — usually due to a **change** in **consumer preferences** or **technological advances**, or the availability of **cheaper alternatives**. It often affects **regions** where there's a decline in **traditional manufacturing** (e.g. shipbuilding or the steel industry) and it's made worse by **labour immobility**:

- **Occupational** immobility occurs when some occupations may decline over time, but the workers in these occupations **don't** have the skills required to be able to do the jobs that are available.

- **Geographical** immobility is where workers are unable to **leave** a region which has high unemployment to go to another region where there are jobs. This might be because they can't **afford** to move to a different region, or they have **family ties**.

See p.113 for more on labour immobility.

2) If a **region** is affected by structural unemployment then it could also suffer from the **negative multiplier effect** — unemployment will lead to less **spending**, and so cause **more** unemployment in the region.

3) The **problem** of structural unemployment may become **more common** in the future:

- **Technological change** in both products and production methods is **accelerating quickly**. This will **speed up** the **decline** of out-of-date industries and **reduce** the number of workers needed to make products.

- Consumer spending is **more likely** to change as consumers are better **informed** (through the internet and social media) than ever before — making them more likely to **switch** to **lower priced** or **higher quality** goods.

Unemployment

Frictional Unemployment is caused by the Time it takes to find a New Job

1) **Frictional** unemployment is the unemployment experienced by workers **between** leaving one job and starting another.

2) Even if an economy is at **full employment**, there will be **some** frictional unemployment. There will always be some employees **changing jobs** — maybe because their contract has run out or because they want to earn higher wages.

3) The **length** of time people spend looking for a **new** job (the 'time lag' between jobs) will depend on several things:
   - In a **boom** the number of job vacancies is much **higher**. So frictional unemployment is likely to be **short term**.
   - In a **slump** frictional unemployment could be much **higher** as there will be a **shortage** of jobs.
   - **Generous welfare benefits** will give people **less incentive** to look for a new job, or they can mean people can afford to **take their time** to look for a good job — so the time spent between jobs **may** increase.
   - The **quality** of **information** provided to people looking for jobs is important too. If people **don't know** what jobs are available or what skills they need to get the job they want, then they're likely to **remain unemployed** for **longer**.
   - **Occupational** and **geographical** labour immobility (see p.113) will also affect the length of time between jobs.

Real Wage Unemployment is caused by wage increases Above the equilibrium

- **Real wage unemployment** is caused by **real wages** being pushed **above** the **equilibrium level** of employment (where labour demand **equals** labour supply). It's usually caused by **trade unions** negotiating for **higher wages** or by the **introduction** of a **national minimum wage**.
- Introducing a **national minimum wage (NMW) above** the **equilibrium wage rate (W$_e$)** would cause the **supply** of labour to **increase** from Q$_e$ to Q$_s$ and demand to fall from Q$_e$ to Q$_d$. This would then cause **unemployment** of Q$_s$ to Q$_d$, due to the **excess supply**.
- However, a **rise** in **productivity** or in **consumer spending** would increase the **demand for labour** (causing the **labour demand curve** to **shift** to the **right**) and this would **reduce** the **size** of the **increase** in **unemployment**.

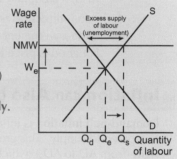

Migration may affect unemployment during a Recession

1) **Migration** of **workers** into a country increases the **supply** of **labour**.

2) When the economy is **strong**, **national income** should increase as a result of migration — especially if the **skills** and **knowledge** of the migrant workers is **different** from the mix of skills of the country's **native population**. There's little evidence from the UK that migration during a **boom** increases unemployment among the native population.

3) During a **recession**, unemployment among **native** workers (especially **low-skilled** workers) may increase, especially if migration levels are particularly **high**. However, even these effects **weaken** over time.

There are several Costs and Consequences of Unemployment

1) The unemployed will have **lower incomes**, which means that they'll spend less and this could **reduce** firms' **profits**.

2) Unemployment will mean **less** income tax revenue for governments, and **less** consumer spending will reduce their indirect tax revenue. The government will also have to **spend** more on unemployment **benefits**.

3) Areas with high unemployment can have high **crime** rates, and reduced incomes can cause people to have **health problems**.

4) Workers who are unemployed for a **long** time may find that their skills and training become **outdated**. This will **reduce** their **employability** and make it **more** likely that they'll stay unemployed.

Warm-Up Questions

Q1 Briefly explain why unemployment will rise during a recession.

Q2 What might cause a region to be affected by structural unemployment?

Exam Question

Q1 Explain how high unemployment may affect a country's economic growth. [8 marks]

Structural unemployment — when buildings have no work to do...

Most unemployment is involuntary (i.e. people want to work but can't find a job), but some types can be voluntary — e.g. frictional unemployment would be voluntary if someone left their job and wanted to take time off before finding a new one.

Inflation

Inflation can rise because of higher costs and increased consumer demand. **These pages are for all boards.**

Inflation can be caused by **Cost-Push Factors**

1) **Cost-push inflation** is inflation which is caused by the **rising cost** of **inputs** to production.

2) Rising costs of inputs to production force producers to **pass on** the **higher costs** to **consumers** in the form of **higher prices**, which causes the **aggregate supply curve** to shift to the left (from AS to AS₁). For example:

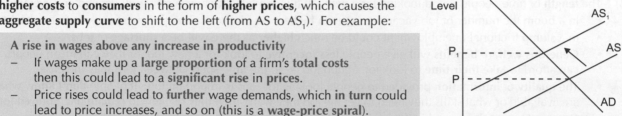

- **A rise in wages above any increase in productivity**
  - If wages make up a **large proportion** of a firm's **total costs** then this could lead to a **significant rise** in **prices**.
  - Price rises could lead to **further** wage demands, which **in turn** could lead to price increases, and so on (this is a **wage-price spiral**).
- **A rise in the cost of imported raw materials**
  - If the **world prices** of inputs **rise** then, in the short run, **producers** will pay the **higher** cost and set higher prices. This is how price increases in **world commodity markets** can lead to **higher domestic inflation**.
  - Also, if a country's currency decreases in value then producers will have to pay more for the **same imports**.
- **A rise in indirect taxes**
  - If the government raises indirect taxes (see p.86), this will increase costs and, in turn, prices.
  - If a good is **price inelastic** then **more** of the cost of the **tax** will be passed on to the **consumer**.

Inflation can **Also** be caused by **Demand-Pull Factors**

Demand-pull inflation is inflation caused by **excessive growth** in **aggregate demand** compared to supply. This growth in demand **shifts** the **aggregate demand curve** to the **right** (from AD to AD₁), which allows sellers to **raise prices**. It could be caused by:

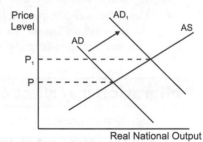

- **High consumer spending or high demand for exports**
  - High consumer spending could be caused by **high levels** of **confidence** in **consumers' future employment prospects** (e.g. during a period of low unemployment). **Low interest rates** encourage **cheap borrowing** and greater **spending**.
  - **High foreign demand** for **exports** could be caused by rapid economic growth in **other countries**.
- **The money supply growing faster than output**
  - If the **amount of money** in the economy is **not matched** by the **output** of goods and services (sometimes termed 'too much money chasing too few goods'), this can lead to a rise in prices. This might be the case, for example, when **interest rates** are **low** and consumers are spending more.
  - Monetarist economists believe that **excess money** is the **biggest** cause of inflation (see below).
- **Bottleneck shortages**
  - If **demand** grows **quickly** at a time when labour and resources are already being **fully used**, then increasing output may lead to **shortages** (i.e. there may be a positive output gap). These shortages will cause **prices** to **rise** and firms' **costs** to **increase**.
  - Price rises caused by shortages (e.g. a rise in wages for skilled labour) in **one area** of the **market** may be **copied** by other markets (e.g. higher wages for low-skilled labour), leading to more **general inflation**.

AQA & OCR →

Fisher's Equation of Exchange

1) The **quantity theory of money** is based on Fisher's equation of exchange.

> money supply × velocity of money = price level × aggregate transactions
> **MV = PT**

2) On the left-hand side is **M** (= the **total amount of money** in the economy) and **V** (= the **speed** at which money is spent). On the right-hand side is **P** (= the **price level**) and **T** (= the **total** amount of **transactions** in the economy).

3) Monetarists argue that, in the **short run**, **V** and **T** are **unlikely to change**, so any increases in **P**, the price level, will be directly caused by an **increase to M**, the money supply. Both sides of the equation are assumed to be equal to each other, so any increase in the **money supply** (M) will create the **same percentage increase** in the **price level** (P).

4) To **avoid inflation**, monetarists believe that the **money supply** needs to be strictly **controlled**.

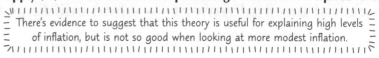

There's evidence to suggest that this theory is useful for explaining high levels of inflation, but is not so good when looking at more modest inflation.

Inflation

There are several Costs and Consequences of Inflation

1) Inflation will cause the **standard of living** of those on **fixed**, or **near-fixed**, **incomes** to **fall**. This will have the **biggest impact** on those in **low income employment** or on **welfare benefits**.

2) A country's competitiveness will be **reduced** by **inflation** as exports will cost **more** to buy and imports will be **cheaper**. If **exports fall** and **imports rise**, then this could create a **deficit** in the **balance of payments** and **increase unemployment**.

3) Inflation **discourages saving** because the value of savings falls. This makes it **more attractive** to spend (creating demand-pull inflation) **before** prices rise further.

4) A **reluctance** to **save** creates a **shortage** of funds for **borrowing** and **investment**, which means that it's harder for firms to make improvements, e.g. buy new machinery. If **interest rates** go up to reduce inflation, this will also **reduce investment**.

5) Inflation creates **uncertainty** for firms as rising costs will **reduce investment** — harming future growth.

6) Inflation can cause **shoe leather costs**, which are the costs of the **extra time** and **effort** taken by consumers to search for **up-to-date** price information on the goods and services they're using, and **menu costs**, which are the **extra costs** to firms of **altering** the **price information** they provide to consumers.

7) An extreme case is **hyperinflation**, where inflation grows very quickly to very high levels (e.g. **several hundred percent** or more). It's often the result of governments creating **too much** money (e.g. because of a war or some other crisis).

Deflation Isn't a good thing

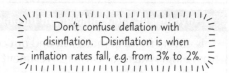
Don't confuse deflation with disinflation. Disinflation is when inflation rates fall, e.g. from 3% to 2%.

1) When the **rate of inflation** falls **below 0%** it's called **deflation**. Although there are many costs and consequences of inflation, deflation **isn't** very good either.

2) Deflation is often a sign that the economy is **doing badly**, as it's usually caused by **falling aggregate demand** and **increased unemployment**.

3) However, deflation can also be caused if firms' **costs fall** (e.g. because of new technology) and these **benefits** are then **passed on** to consumers in the form of **lower prices**.

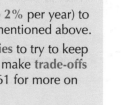
However, if the economy is healthy and people feel generally confident, deflation may not cause problems.

4) Deflation can cause **big problems**. For example, if consumers think that prices are falling then they may choose **not** to spend in the hope that prices will **fall further**.

5) **Less spending** and **lower prices** will also mean **lower profits** for firms and reduced economic growth.

Inflation of 2% is Acceptable

- In the UK, the Bank of England and the government consider **low and stable inflation** (up to 2% per year) to be **acceptable**. **Excessive inflation** (above 2%) is undesirable and can cause the problems mentioned above.

- The government uses a **combination** of **monetary policy**, **fiscal policy** and **supply-side policies** to try to keep the rate of inflation at 2% (see Section 11). However, to achieve this the government has to make **trade-offs** between their **inflation target** and their **other three** main economic objectives (see p.160-161 for more on the conflicts between objectives).

- Some economists, called **monetarists**, believe that bringing down inflation in the **short run** will **help** the government in the **long run** to achieve the other main economic objectives.

Warm-Up Questions

Q1 What is cost-push inflation?

Q2 Give two possible causes of demand-pull inflation.

Q3 How might deflation be damaging to an economy?

Exam Question

Q1 The UK government aims to keep inflation at 2%.
Evaluate the reasons why the UK government might want to keep inflation at this rate. [12 marks]

I inflated by an unacceptable 2% over Christmas...

The diagrams aren't here just to look pretty — they should help you to understand what's going on. You'll need to know reasons for cost-push and demand-pull inflation, and why the UK government wants to keep inflation at around 2%.

The Balance of Payments

In Section 8 (p.127), you'll have seen a bit about the balance of payments — I imagine you've been eagerly waiting to find out more, so here are some pages just for you. I know, I'm too good to you. **These pages are for all boards.**

The BOP records All Financial Transactions of a country with other countries

1) The **balance of payments** (**BOP**) records **all** flows of money **into** and **out of** a country.
2) The UK BOP is made up of the **current account**, the **capital account** and the **financial account**.

> You don't need to know about the capital and financial accounts in great detail, but there's a bit more info about them on p.157.

There are Four sections of the Current Account

1. Trade in goods

1) Trade in goods measures **imports** and **exports** of **visible** goods — e.g. televisions, apples, potatoes, books.
2) The UK's **biggest** goods exports include things such as **machinery**, **mechanical appliances** and **pharmaceuticals**.
3) The UK's **biggest** goods imports also include **machinery** and **mechanical appliances**, along with **mineral fuels** (e.g. coal) and **oils**.

2. Trade in services

1) Trade in services measures **imports** and **exports** of **services** such as insurance or tourism.
2) Some of the UK's biggest **exported** services are **banking** and **insurance**.
3) The UK's biggest **imported** services include **tourism** (e.g. holidays abroad).

3. Investment and employment income (or 'primary income')

This covers flows of money **in** and **out** of a country resulting from **employment** or **earlier investment** — e.g.:

- Deposits in **foreign banks** receive **interest payments**.
- Businesses set up **overseas** by a UK company will earn **profits** for the UK **parent company**.
- Shares bought in **foreign firms** will bring **dividend payments** to the UK shareholder — the shares themselves **won't** appear on the current account.
- **Salaries** paid to UK residents working abroad.

4. Transfers (or 'secondary income')

1) Transfers are the **movements** of money **between** countries which **aren't** paying for goods or services and aren't the result of investment.
2) Transfers include **payments** made to family members **abroad** and **aid** paid to or received from **foreign countries**.

Add up the Individual Balances to find the overall Current Account Balance

		£ million	£ million
Trade in Goods			
	Export of goods	306 765	
	Import of goods	419 364	
	Balance		-112 599
Trade in Services			
	Export of services	209 127	
	Import of services	130 261	
	Balance		78 866
Investment income			
	Credits	157 675	
	Debits	172 639	
	Balance		-14 964
Transfers			
	Credits	19 296	
	Debits	46 458	
	Balance		-27 162
Current balance			**-75 859**

> Subtract imports from exports to get the balances for trade.

> Subtract debits from credits to get the balances for investment income and transfers.

> Add up the balances for the individual sections to find the overall balance. Remember, a positive balance is a surplus, and a negative balance is a deficit.

Recent data on the **UK's balance of payments** shows:

- A **large deficit** on the balance of **visible** trade — the UK **imports more** goods than it **exports**.
- A small **surplus** on the balance of **invisible** trade — the UK **exports** slightly **more** services than it **imports**.
- A **surplus** on flows of **investment income** — the UK receives more payments from investment than it pays out.
- A **deficit** on transfers — for example the UK makes **foreign aid payments**, amongst other things.

As a result, the UK has a **large deficit** on its current account, and it has had a deficit **every year** since 1984. This means that the UK's current **macroeconomic policy** includes having to deal with a balance of payments **deficit**.

The Balance of Payments

There are usually **Many Causes** of a BOP **Surplus** or **Deficit**

A country might experience a **current account deficit** if:

1 **There are high levels of consumer spending (low savings rate)**

- When there's **economic growth**, consumers and firms **buy** more **imports**.
- If the **income elasticity of demand** for imports is **high** then there will be a **greater increase** in imports.

2 **It's struggling to compete internationally**

- Countries that **can't compete** internationally will see a **reduction** in exports.
- Some countries (especially more developed countries) may not be able to **compete** with **low** costs of **production** in other countries, e.g. **newly industrialised** nations.
  - When the costs of production in a country rise **faster** than in **competitor** countries — e.g. due to higher labour costs, production inefficiencies, a **fall** in labour productivity etc., then exports will **fall** and imports will **rise**.
  - Other countries may **struggle** to **compete** with countries that have access to more **advanced** technology or more **efficient** methods of production, which can **lower** costs and **improve** the **quality** of the products they make.
  - If the country has **structural problems**, e.g. labour immobility, this could be making domestic products and exports **more expensive**.
- A **rise** in the value of a currency will make goods **more expensive** to foreign buyers, so **exports** will **fall**. At the same time, foreign goods will be **cheaper** to buy, so **imports** will **rise**.
- If inflation **rises** exports will **fall** because they'll become **more expensive** and **less competitive** in **foreign** countries. Imports will **rise** because it'll become **cheaper** for consumers and firms to buy **imports** rather than domestic products.

> ⎮⎮⎮⎮⎮⎮⎮⎮⎮⎮⎮⎮⎮⎮⎮⎮⎮⎮⎮
> The UK's large deficit in visible trade is partly caused by a lack of competitiveness in its manufacturing industries.
> ⎮⎮⎮⎮⎮⎮⎮⎮⎮⎮⎮⎮⎮⎮⎮⎮⎮⎮⎮

3 **It has to deal with external shocks**

- If there's a **rise** in the world prices of imported **raw materials**, e.g. oil, timber or metals, and the **demand** for these materials is relatively **price inelastic**, then a country will end up **paying more** for these imports — at least in the **short run**.
- An **economic downturn** in countries to which a country **exports** can cause a sudden **reduction** in the amount of **exports** that are demanded.
- The imposition of **trade barriers** (see p.202) on goods by a trading partner could mean a sudden reduction in the number of **exports** made to that country.

Ellie was suffering from a different kind of external shock.

A country might experience a **current account surplus** if:

1) It's been experiencing a **recession** — sometimes domestic producers will **struggle** to sell products domestically, so they'll focus their efforts on competing in **international** markets instead. There may be a **fall** in imports too as a result of an **overall reduction** in spending.
2) Its domestic currency has a **low value** — this will make exports **cheaper** and imports **more expensive**.
3) **High interest rates** are causing **more** saving and **less** spending.

Warm-Up Questions

Q1 Describe the four sections of the balance of payments current account.

Q2 Explain the term 'external shock', with reference to an economy's balance of payments.

PRACTICE QUESTIONS

Exam Question

Q1 In recent years the UK economy has had a balance of payments deficit. Explain why. [8 marks]

Deficit? No, it can hear perfectly well...

You've got to learn what the four sections of the current account are and how a balance of payments deficit might be caused. Make sure you can see how the BOP links to other aspects of the economy, e.g. exchange rates and economic growth.

The Balance of Payments

I know what you're thinking... the balance of payments is basically the best thing ever.
Luckily there are two more pages all about it. **These pages are for all boards.**

There can be **Consequences** of a **BOP Surplus** or **Deficit**

Consequences of a BOP deficit

1) A balance of payments **deficit** could indicate that an economy is **uncompetitive**.

2) A deficit **isn't always** a bad thing — it might mean that people in that country are **wealthy** enough to be able to afford **lots of imports**. A deficit may also allow people to enjoy a **higher** standard of living, as they're importing the things they want and need. But, a **long-term deficit** is likely to cause problems.

3) The consequences of a deficit include a **fall** in the value of a currency, leading to **higher import prices** — at least in the **short run**. This can lead to an increase in **inflation**.

4) A balance of payments deficit may also lead to **job losses** domestically — for example, if more goods are being **imported**, that may mean fewer goods need to be produced **domestically**, so **unemployment** may increase.

Consequences of a BOP surplus

1) **Surpluses** can show that an economy is **competitive**.

2) However, if a country has a **surplus** for a **prolonged** period of time, e.g. Japan, they may experience **stagnation**. This means that, for example, due to **low domestic demand**, they'll experience **low**, or even **negative, economic growth** — which also has the potential to lead to **other** problems, such as **high unemployment**.

3) A large surplus on a current account may also be a result of an economy's **overreliance** on **exports**.

4) If a surplus is created by a country having an **undervalued currency**, this will create **inflationary pressures** — the price of **imported components** for use in **production** will **rise**, meaning a **rise** in the **costs of production** and therefore a **rise** in the **price level**.

Governments often try to **Correct Imbalances** in the **BOP**

1) Governments might try to correct a **BOP deficit**:

   - They might use **policies** to **reduce** the price of **domestic** goods — this should **increase** exports and **reduce** imports. For example, a government might use **supply-side policies** to remove **structural** problems (see p.176 for more).

     These are expenditure-switching policies — they switch consumer spending away from imports, towards domestically produced goods instead.

   - Governments might impose **restrictions** on **imports** — for example, a government might impose **tariffs** on **imports** to make them **relatively** more expensive (compared to domestic goods) for **domestic consumers**. This might cause **inflation** if demand for imports is too **price inelastic**.

   - They may **devalue** (fixed exchange rate systems) or **depreciate** (floating exchange rate systems) the **currency** (see p.210) — this will make exports **cheaper** and imports more **expensive**. For this to be **successful**, the Marshall-Lerner condition must hold (see p.212).

   - Governments might use **fiscal** or **monetary policy** to reduce spending in the economy (see p.168-175 for more) — however, as well as **reducing imports**, it's likely to also **reduce domestic demand** and harm economic growth.

     These would be examples of expenditure-reducing policies.

2) Governments might try to correct a **BOP surplus** — for example, they might **raise** the value of their currency. This will **reduce** the demand for **exports** and **increase** the demand for **imports**. However, this is likely to result in a **reduction** in output and has the potential to cause a **rise** in unemployment.

3) When the governments of **major economies** try to correct imbalances in their BOP, it can have **global impacts**:

   - **Supply-side policies** to correct deficits may lead to an **increase** in **world trade** and **growth**.

   - **Restrictions** on imports can lead to **trade wars**, **reducing** international trade and leading to **lower** global efficiency. Restrictions might also break **WTO rules** (see p.202).

   - If a government's attempts to reduce its BOP deficit lead to a **fall** in exports from **developing** countries, this may have many **negative** consequences. For example, **economic growth** in those developing countries will be **limited**, leading to a **rise** in **unemployment**. **Reduced** economic growth in developing countries has the potential to **hold back** global improvements in **efficiency**.

The Balance of Payments

The **Capital** and **Financial** accounts show **Asset Transfers**

1) The **capital** account includes **transfers** of **non-monetary** and **fixed** assets —
the most important part of this is the flow of non-monetary and fixed assets
of **immigrants** and **emigrants**, e.g. when an immigrant comes to the UK,
their assets become part of the UK's **total assets**.

2) The **financial** account involves the movement of financial assets. It includes:
- **Foreign direct investment** (FDI) (see p.194).
- **Portfolio investment** — investment in financial assets, such as **shares** in overseas companies.
- **Financial derivatives** — these are **contracts** whose value is based on the value of an asset, e.g. a foreign currency.
- **Reserve assets** — these are financial assets held by the **Bank of England** to be used as and when they're **needed**.

3) **Income** from the financial account, e.g. in the form of interest, is recorded in the **current account**.

4) The current account **should balance** the capital and financial accounts, e.g. a deficit of £5bn on the current account
should be offset by a surplus of £5bn on the capital and financial accounts. However, due to **errors** and **omissions**,
the current account and capital and financial accounts often **don't** balance, so a **balancing figure** is needed.

There are both **Short-term** and **Long-term** capital and financial flows

1) **Long-term** flows are due to things such as FDI and portfolio investment. They're usually quite **predictable**
as, for example, FDI is often made when a country gains a **comparative advantage** in producing
something, which tends to happen over a **long** period of time.

2) **Short-term** flows (sometimes called '**hot money**' — see p.174 for more)
are based on **speculation** and people/firms trying to **quickly** make
money — e.g. by **moving** money from one currency to another
expecting to make a profit through **changes** in **exchange rates**.

Private financial flows come from individuals and firms, and official financial flows go to and from governments and other official organisations (e.g. the EU).

International economies are more **Interconnected** than ever before

1) **International trade** and **capital flows** mean that many firms and governments
have **interests** and **investments** in lots of different countries.

2) This allows those firms and economies to **grow**
in ways that wouldn't be possible otherwise.

Private individuals may also invest and trade internationally.

3) However, it also means that economies are now **dependent** on each other much more than ever before.
For example, a **banking crisis** in one country can now cause **economic problems** in many different countries
— e.g. if **foreign** firms or governments have **borrowed** or **lent** money to banks that have **collapsed**.

4) Similarly, if one country enters a **recession**, then this might cause **problems** for countries that **trade** with it (see p.195).

5) These connections mean that **global trade imbalances** carry a serious risk. For example, the USA
currently has a very large **current account deficit**, while China has a very large **surplus**.
If the USA imposed **tariffs** to try and **reduce** their deficit, then other countries could **retaliate**
with their own tariffs, **harming trade** and **damaging economies**.

Warm-Up Questions

Q1 Briefly explain the difference between the current, capital and financial accounts
of the balance of payments.

Q2 List four methods a government might adopt to remove a persistent trade deficit.

PRACTICE QUESTIONS

Exam Question

Q1 The US has a current account deficit on its balance of payments, and it imports a lot of goods from China.
Evaluate the possible benefits to the US balance of payments current account of a rise in the value of the
Chinese renminbi.

[15 marks]

As the Chancellor often reminds us — "Hip hop, the BOP don't stop"...

*Phew — there's quite a lot to learn on the balance of payments, but don't let it overwhelm you. Just keep in mind
that a balance of payments deficit can bring some pretty undesirable consequences if it gets out of control.*

Other Economic Policy Objectives

Governments have lots of other objectives for the economy. Here are another four objectives they might try to achieve — but remember that different governments will have different priorities. **These pages are for Edexcel and OCR.**

Governments try to **Distribute Income** more **Equally**

1) In any economy, there is a wide **range** of **earnings**. Earnings **depend** on a number of things, including:
   - **Labour skill** — training and education raises a person's **labour productivity** and, usually, their **pay rate**.
   - **Market forces** in the **labour** market — **shortages** or **surpluses** of various kinds of labour **influence** the **wage rate**, e.g. a **shortage** of electricians may **increase** an electrician's wage, a **surplus** may **reduce** it.
   - **Geography** — in **less** prosperous parts of the country, **earnings** are **lower**.
   - **Level** of **responsibility** — in general, the greater the **authority** and **responsibility** of a job, then the **higher** the **pay**.

2) Governments may want to **distribute** income more **equally** to **increase** overall **welfare** or **reduce** poverty so there's a better overall **standard of living**. Governments may also consider **too much** inequality in society to be **unfair**.

   There's more about inequality and poverty on p.165.

3) The redistribution of income can also **benefit** the **economy**. **High** earners tend to **save** more of their income and **low** earners tend to **spend** most or all of it — so income redistribution will **increase overall** consumer spending, and **raise** aggregate demand, output and employment.

4) The government can redistribute income by **reducing** the **net income** (take-home pay) of **high earners** and **increasing** the **net income** of people with **no** or **low incomes** — this can be done by:
   - **Tax** — especially income tax.
   - **Welfare payments** — paid to those on no, or low, incomes.

5) However, redistributing income carries a **risk**, as some income differences are **beneficial**:

   - The **reward** of **higher wages** acts as an **incentive** to hard work, training and risk-taking — so **too little** inequality would mean these **incentives** are **lost** and people will not work as hard.
   - **Wealth creation** can produce **employment** and **income opportunities** for others.
   - **Spending** by people with **high incomes** (e.g. on luxury goods that might not be purchased by those on lower incomes) creates **jobs** for others.

Governments try to **Protect** the **Environment**

Environmental protection has become **more important** to governments. Two of the **main** factors governments recognise are:

1 Damage/pollution to the environment

The role of the government is to:
1) **Identify** environmental damage caused by firms/individuals, e.g. **carbon emissions** from factories or cars.
2) Measure the **cost** of this damage.
3) Use **financial penalties** or certain **restrictions** or **bans** to **reduce** environmental damage and provide an **incentive** for firms/individuals to **decrease** the damage they cause. These might include:
   - Non-market policies — outright bans or limits on **polluting practices**.
     For example, **banning** cars which produce **unacceptable** levels of **carbon dioxide**.
   - Market policies — influencing the **cost** of polluting and therefore changing the behaviour of firms/individuals. For example, **tradable pollution permits** (see p.96) — these put a **restriction** on the **amount** of pollution a firm can produce, but firms are allowed to buy/sell permits between themselves.

2 Depletion of finite resources caused by continued economic growth

1) Some governments feel it's necessary to use **non-renewable resources**, such as oil and copper, more **wisely** to either **avoid** a future without them, or just to make them last for **longer**.
2) For example, governments might want to **encourage** the **development** and **use** of **renewable** energy resources, so that non-renewable resources such as coal and oil can either be **replaced** or will last for **longer**. They might try to achieve this by giving **financial incentives** to firms to develop or use **renewable** energy.

Other Economic Policy Objectives

Governments try to ensure Economic Stability

1) Economic growth tends to fluctuate up and down (this is called the economic cycle — see p.145). This involves periods of **high** growth (booms) followed by periods of **low** or even **negative** growth (slumps, recessions or depressions).

2) If the fluctuations are **frequent** or particularly **big** then there will be economic instability. This will:

   • **Discourage** firms from planning any long-term investment, which **harms** the economy in the **long run**.

   • **Discourage** foreign firms from making **investments**, which means that the country **misses out** on extra **money** being brought **into** the economy and the **creation** of **new jobs**.

3) Governments try to reduce the fluctuations in growth and **avoid** both slumps and booms. They try to do this through a combination of **fiscal** and **monetary** policies (see p.168-175 for more on these).

4) Governments also try to avoid **volatility** in the rate of inflation, unemployment and exchange rates — big **fluctuations** in any of these will also discourage investment and make it hard for governments and firms to plan for the future.

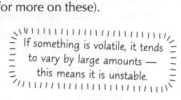
If something is volatile, it tends to vary by large amounts — this means it is unstable.

5) Economic stability will also depend on how **politically stable** a country is. If governments are **corrupt** or **cannot** enforce the **rule of law** on their people then the country's economy will be unstable too.

Governments try to improve Productivity

• Improving a country's **productivity** will help **future economic growth**.

• Governments don't have much **control** over the **productivity** of **private** companies — but there are ways in which they can encourage improvements. For example, they might offer financial help to firms so they can buy **more efficient** equipment, or they could introduce **regulations** to **increase** competition between firms so that they're **forced** to improve their **productivity**.

• In the public sector, the government has more **direct control** over productivity. For example, the **UK government** could improve the NHS's productivity by **introducing** procedures that might be **cheaper** and/or more **effective**.

• Governments can also improve the **productivity** of society in **general**. For example, the government could increase **spending** on **schools** and **improve education**, which will help to develop a **better trained** and more **productive** labour force.

Governments use supply-side policies to improve productivity. See p.176-177 for more.

Warm-Up Questions

Q1 List three factors which might cause one person to earn more than another.
Q2 In what ways could a government redistribute income?
Q3 Why might a government encourage the use of renewable energy resources?
Q4 In what ways could fluctuations in economic growth damage an economy?
Q5 How could a government encourage improvements in productivity of private companies?

Exam Question

Q1 Explain with examples how a government might try to alter the behaviour of firms that damage the environment.

[8 marks]

Financial penalties — a cause for dread for any England fan...

So you've learnt all about the big four macroeconomic objectives — here's another four objectives to have a think about. Not all governments have these objectives, but you should learn the principles behind them. It's also worth remembering that governments might not choose a policy that's best for a country economically — they might choose one that's the most popular with voters.

Conflicts Between Economic Objectives

Here's a bit about what governments want to do and the problems they face in doing it.
These pages are for all boards.

Governments make **Trade-offs** between their objectives

1) Remember... most governments have the same four **main macroeconomic objectives** (see p.144):
   - Strong economic growth,
   - Reducing unemployment,
   - Keeping inflation low,
   - Maintaining an equilibrium in the balance of payments.

2) They may also have **other objectives** (see p.158-159), such as:
   - A more equal distribution of income and wealth,
   - Protecting the environment,
   - Maintaining economic stability,
   - Improving productivity and international competitiveness.

3) However, trying to achieve **one** of these objectives may make it **more difficult** to achieve **another** — in other words, there may be **conflicts** between **policy objectives**.

4) In the short run, governments decide which objectives they think are **most important** and **accept** that these decisions may have an adverse effect on their other objectives — i.e. they make **trade-offs** between their objectives.

5) Governments may have to use **short-term policies** to correct **sudden problems**, such as major unemployment caused by a severe recession. In a scenario like this the government may **accept** that inflation will result from a policy designed to reduce unemployment quickly because it's more important to get people back to work.

Changes in **Aggregate Demand** are likely to cause **Conflict** between objectives

1) **Short run economic growth** is caused by the AD curve shifting to the **right**. This could be due to an **increase** in any of the **components** of **aggregate demand** (C + I + G + (X – M)).

2) For example, if the AD curve shifts to the right from AD to AD_1 then there will be an **increase** in **output** (i.e. economic growth) from Y to Y_1 and, as a result, there will be a **decrease** in **unemployment** (because of the derived demand for labour).

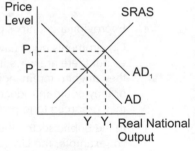

3) However, a shift to the right of the AD curve will also result in an **increase** in the **price level** from P to P_1. Higher prices may also lead to a **lack** of **competitiveness** internationally, meaning a **decrease** in exports, a **rise** in imports and therefore a **worsening** in the current account of the **balance of payments**.

4) So, in this case, an increase in aggregate demand will only help the government to achieve **two** of its macroeconomic objectives.

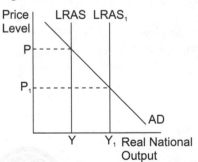

5) However, a shift in the LRAS (or AS) curve will enable a government to achieve **all four** of the main macroeconomic objectives at the **same time**.

6) For example, if the LRAS curve shifts to the right to $LRAS_1$ then this will lead to an **increase** in **output** (from Y to Y_1) and **reduce unemployment**. The **price level** will also **fall** (from P to P_1) and this will **improve** the country's **competitiveness** — **improving** the **balance of payments**.

7) This suggests that if the government **only** used **demand-side policies** (see p.168) to achieve its macroeconomic objectives then this would lead to **conflict** between the objectives. However, **supply-side policies** (see p.176) are more likely to help a government achieve their four main macroeconomic objectives in the **long run**.

Learn the **Main Causes** of **Conflict** between the **Macroeconomic Objectives**

Make sure you understand the **cause** of these **key conflicts** between **government objectives**. Remember, these objectives are likely to conflict in the **short run**, but in the **long run** these conflicts may **not** occur if **aggregate supply increases**.

Inflation and Unemployment

There's a lot more detail on p.162-164.

- When unemployment is **reduced** and the economy begins to **approach** full capacity, there are **fewer** spare workers, so **demand** for workers increases — especially for **skilled** workers. This will lead to an **increase** in wages and the **extra cost** of this may be passed on by producers to consumers in the form of **higher prices** — causing **cost-push** inflation.
- Low unemployment may cause consumers to **spend** more because they feel more **confident** in their **long-term** job prospects. This may cause **prices** to **rise** due to **demand-pull** inflation.
- So reducing unemployment makes it more **difficult** to keep inflation at the **preferred low rate**.

Conflicts Between Economic Objectives

Economic Growth and Environmental Protection

Economic growth can put a **strain** on the **environment**. For example:
- New factories and increases in production can raise levels of air and water **pollution**, as well as increase the amount of **waste** that needs **disposing** of.
- Economic growth will tend to increase the use of **natural resources** — this can be a major problem if these resources are **non-renewable**.
- Ecosystems might be **damaged** or even **destroyed** by the **construction** of new factories, housing, etc. — in the most **extreme** cases, this can lead to the **extinction** of certain animals or plants.

Economic Growth and Inflation

1) A rapidly **growing** economy can cause large **increases** in **prices**, due to an increase in **demand**. This will cause a **higher** than desirable level of **inflation**.

2) Similarly, attempts to keep **inflation low** can **restrict** growth. For example, if **interest rates** are kept **high** to reduce inflation by **discouraging** spending (and encouraging saving), this can **restrict economic growth**.

> This can also cause conflict between growth and equilibrium in the balance of payments, as high inflation is likely to worsen the BOP (see p.153).

Inflation and Equilibrium in the Balance of Payments

1) **Sometimes** the government's objectives for low inflation and equilibrium in the balance of payments will be **compatible**, but at other times they'll **conflict**.

2) For example, if **inflation** is **low**, this implies that prices are **rising slowly**. If prices rise **more slowly** than those in other countries, then **exports** to other countries will **increase** and **imports** will **decrease**. This would **increase a surplus** on the balance of payments, but **reduce** a balance of payments **deficit**.

3) However, low inflation is often **maintained** by **high interest rates**. High interest rates **encourage** foreign investment, which **increases demand** for the domestic currency — **increasing** its **value**. This will make exports **more expensive** and imports **cheaper**, so **exports** will **decrease** and **imports** will **increase**. This would **reduce a surplus** on the balance of payments, but make a **deficit worse**.

Economic Growth and a Reduction in Wealth Inequality

1) Economic growth can increase inequality, as not everyone benefits equally from a growing economy.

2) For example, as an economy grows, highly skilled workers (e.g. those that work in hi-tech industries) may become more in demand, while the demand for low-skilled workers (e.g. those that carry out routine manual tasks which can be done instead by machines) may fall.

3) Governments can choose to use increased tax revenue from economic growth to decrease this inequality by:
   - Increasing welfare payments.
   - Using progressive taxes (i.e. taxes where the rich pay a higher rate than the poor).
   - Increasing the minimum wage in line with increases in the average wage.

4) However, increasing taxes or welfare payments may damage future economic growth. For example:
   - High taxes may be a disincentive for individuals and businesses to earn and grow.
   - Extra welfare payments may not encourage people to work.

> However, some welfare benefits can help the economy to grow (e.g. help with childcare costs might allow parents to return to work).

5) Supply-side policies that help people back to work and reduce geographical and occupational labour immobility would encourage growth, while reducing the welfare budget and unemployment.

Warm-Up Questions

Q1 Explain why a government aiming for low unemployment and low inflation might encounter policy conflicts.

Q2 Briefly explain how a government's objectives for economic growth and inflation might conflict.

PRACTICE QUESTIONS

Exam Question

Q1 Explain, using a diagram, how a government could improve all four of its main macroeconomic objectives at the same time.

[12 marks]

My macaroni-economic policy involves eating lots of pasta and cheese...

Eeeh... running an economy sounds tricky. You need to know about all the bear-traps awaiting unsuspecting governments as they go about trying to achieve useful things. The stuff on these pages is hated by governments, but loved by Economics examiners.

Tackling Unemployment and Inflation

Economists argue about the link between unemployment and inflation. But governments can't wait for economists to agree before they have to start making policies. These pages describe some of the economists' arguments, and how governments often try to tackle unemployment and inflation in practice. **These pages are for all boards.**

The **Natural Rate of Unemployment** occurs at **Labour Market Equilibrium**

1) The **natural rate of unemployment** (NRU) is the rate of unemployment when the **labour market** is in **equilibrium** — this is when the **labour demand** is **equal** to **labour supply**.

2) When there's equilibrium in the labour market that means there's **enough jobs** for **every worker** in the **labour force**, but that **doesn't** mean that every worker will be **in a job** (because of **frictional** and **structural unemployment**). There can be unemployment when the labour market is in equilibrium, and the rate of that unemployment is the **NRU**.

3) The **NRU** can be seen as corresponding to **full employment**, as it's **not possible** for **every** person in the workforce to have a job. No matter how much aggregate demand is increased, frictional and structural unemployment will **always exist**.

The **Short Run Phillips Curve** shows an **Inflation/Unemployment Trade-off**

1) The **short run Phillips curve** shows an apparent **trade-off** between inflation and unemployment. By plotting **historical** inflation and unemployment data, the economist A.W. Phillips found that as **inflation falls**, **unemployment** seems to **rise**, and vice versa.

2) So it looks like if the government wants to **reduce unemployment**, then it can **increase aggregate demand** to achieve this... as long as it's prepared to **accept higher inflation**.

3) However, **not** everyone **agrees** that it's quite this simple. One problem is that once inflation has gone **up**, people seem to **expect** it to **remain high**, and they change their behaviour accordingly.

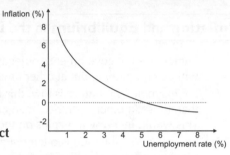

This is the idea of 'adaptive expectations' — i.e. people using the past to predict what's going to happen in the future. So if inflation is high today, then people will expect it to be high tomorrow as well. This can lead to high inflation becoming 'embedded' in an economy, even if the government is trying to reduce it (see p.163).

Keynesian economists say the **Phillips Curve** relationship is basically **True**

The Phillips curve above shows the **same** idea as appears in the curved section of a **Keynesian LRAS curve**.

- **Below A** (i.e. where **output** is **low** and **unemployment** is **high**), workers will take jobs even if the wages are low — output increases with **little effect** on inflation.

- **Between A and B**, as output increases (and unemployment falls), there is an **increase** in **prices** (i.e. **inflation**). This is the **same relationship** as the one shown in the Phillips curve.

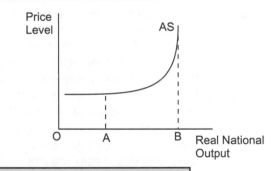

The non-accelerating inflation rate of unemployment (NAIRU)

- The non-accelerating inflation rate of unemployment (**NAIRU**) is the lowest rate of **unemployment** that can exist in the long run **without** leading to **changes** in the rate of **inflation**.

- For example, if NAIRU is 5%, then unemployment **below** this level **will** lead to **increases** in inflation, but unemployment **above** this level will **not**.

- In practice, NAIRU and NRU are very **similar**.

The **Phillips Curve** relationship has sometimes **Broken Down**

1) In the 1950s and 1960s, governments used the Phillips curve to try and **manage** the **trade-off** between **inflation** and **unemployment**.

2) However, in the 1970s, the relationship between unemployment and inflation seemed to **break down**. There was a period of '**stagflation**' — a **stagnant** economy (with low growth and high unemployment) along with high **inflation**.

3) It was **monetarist** economists who put forward an explanation for this. They said that the short run Phillips curve only takes into account the **current rate of inflation** — it doesn't take into account the influence of the **expected** rate of inflation. That's where the **long run Phillips curve** comes in.

Tackling Unemployment and Inflation

Expectations about Inflation can cause Inflation Rises to become Embedded

1) **Assume** that an economy that's at **point A** on the diagram has **unemployment** at its **natural rate** (U_N) — that's the **NRU**.

2) At point A **inflation** is **0%**, so the **economic agents** (workers, firms, etc.) in the economy will **expect** that inflation will **stay at 0%** and this will influence things like **workers' wage negotiations**.

3) However, if **aggregate demand increases** and this **forces** unemployment **below** the **NRU** (to U_1), then this will cause **wage demands** to **go up** and **inflation** will **increase** (to **3%**).

4) At **point B** economic agents will now **expect inflation** to **stay** at **3%**. As a result, future **wage negotiations** will be **based on** inflation being at 3%.

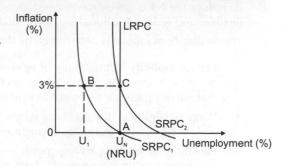

5) **Higher wage demands** will mean firms are **less willing** to take on workers, so **unemployment** will **rise back** to the NRU (to U_N). So the **short run Phillips curve** ($SRPC_1$) will **shift right** to $SRPC_2$.

6) When the $SRPC_1$ curve **shifts right** to $SRPC_2$ (and the economy is at **point C**), you can see that, **despite** unemployment returning to the **NRU**, an **inflation rate** of **3%** has become '**embedded**' in the economy. Further **increases** in **aggregate demand** will mean that **higher inflation rates** can become embedded in the economy.

7) This shows how important it is for governments to use policies that **stop** inflation **rising continuously**. In the UK, the Bank of England is tasked with keeping inflation **close** to the target rate of **2%** so that the **expectations** of economic agents are based on 2% inflation. On top of this, governments will use policies to **lower unemployment** and even **lower** the **NRU**.

Monetarist economists say there is No Trade-off between Inflation and Unemployment

1) In the example above, the increase in AD caused **inflation** to **rise**. However, there was **no long-term effect** on **unemployment** — this eventually returned to the **NRU**.

2) This idea led the monetarist economists who first suggested the idea of adaptive expectations to conclude that there was **no long-term link** between **inflation** and **unemployment**.
   - No matter how the SRPC shifts, **unemployment** will always **return** to the **NRU**.
   - So the **long run Phillips curve**, **LRPC**, will always be a **vertical line** coming up from U_N.
   - This means that in the **long run** there is **no trade-off** between **unemployment** and **inflation**.

3) In fact, many economists say the short run Phillips curve relationship (i.e. that you can trade off inflation against unemployment in the short run) **doesn't exist** either.

4) The significance of the Phillips curve isn't clear. **Supply-side** policies may mean that low unemployment and low inflation **can exist** at the same time (see p.177). However, at times it does seem that the unemployment-inflation trade-off **does** exist. In practice, the Phillips curve is now only used in **short run** economic policy-making.

Demand-side Policies can reduce Cyclical Unemployment

Economists argue over the **theory** of how an economy works. Governments have to get on with the **practical** business of **making policies**. Here's some of the **issues** they face, and the **solutions** they can try to use.

1) To **reduce unemployment**, governments need to understand what **type** of unemployment they're trying to tackle.

2) During a **recession** an economy is likely to have **cyclical unemployment**, so a government would need to introduce policies that **boost aggregate demand**. For example, the government could use **reflationary fiscal policies**, such as decreasing taxes or increasing welfare payments, or **expansionary monetary policies**, such as a lowering of interest rates.

There's more about this in Section 11.

3) However, there are **problems** with these kinds of demand-side policies.
   - A **lack of information** about the **size** of an economy's **output gap** may mean that the government **overspends** when it tries to **boost aggregate demand** and causes the economy to '**overshoot**' (i.e. grow too quickly) — leading to **inflation**. Alternatively, the government might **under-spend** and **prolong** a **recession**.
   - A **lack of information** about the size of the **multiplier** can cause problems too. For example, if the multiplier in a country is **bigger** than the government **expects**, then an increase in government spending could cause **inflation**.

4) It's **hard** for a government to use demand-side policies to **fine-tune** the economy — they can be quite **clumsy** and **cause more problems**. **Time lags** can also mean that improvements are **slow** to develop — governments may think that their policies aren't working, so they **increase spending further** and create inflation.

Tackling Unemployment and Inflation

Supply-side Policies reduce the Natural Rate of Unemployment

1) To **reduce** the NRU governments need to use **supply-side policies** that make the labour market more **flexible**, and **reduce frictional** and **structural unemployment**.

2) The **flexibility of labour** is determined by **three important factors**:

- **Labour mobility** — the ability of workers to **switch jobs easily**. The more **transferable skills** workers have, the more easily they can switch jobs — so labour mobility will depend on **how skilled workers are**. On top of that, labour mobility will also depend on the **willingness** of workers to **move** to where there are jobs.
- **Wage flexibility** — the ability of **wages** to **change** with changes to the labour market (i.e. respond to supply and demand). For example, during a **recession**, employers can **lower wages** to avoid having to **lay workers** off.
- **Flexibility of working arrangements** — the ability of **employers** to **hire workers** in a way that **suits them**. Things such as **part-time work**, **short-term contracts** (or **zero-hour contracts**) and **shift employment** make it **easier** and **cheaper** for firms to **hire** or **fire** workers and **respond to changes** in the **market**.

3) So, policies that **improve labour market flexibility** will focus on **improving** these **three factors**. For example:
- Labour mobility can be tackled by the **same policies** that are used to **reduce structural unemployment** (see below).
- Governments can improve wage flexibility by **scrapping** the **NMW** and **limiting trade union power**.
- The flexibility of working arrangements could be improved if the government **passed laws** that made it **easier** for firms to **hire workers** on **short-term** or **zero-hour contracts**.

4) **Frictional unemployment** will be reduced by policies which **encourage** people to find a job and **speed up** this process:
- **Reducing benefits** will give unemployed workers a greater **incentive** to find a job and it will help the government **avoid** the **unemployment trap** (where unemployed workers are better off than those working on low wages).
- **Income tax cuts** will **increase** the **incentive** for workers to find a job, or encourage them to **work longer hours**.
- **Increased information** about jobs will help workers find the **right job** for themselves **more quickly**.

5) **Structural unemployment** will be reduced by policies which tackle **geographical** and **occupational immobility**:
- Governments can improve **occupational mobility** by **investing** in **training schemes** that help workers to **improve** their **skills**, or by **encouraging firms** to **set up** their **own training schemes**.
- **Geographical immobility** can be tackled by giving workers **subsidies** to move to different areas or by building **affordable houses** in areas that need workers. However, workers will still often be **reluctant** to leave their homes and families.
- Governments can **bring jobs** to areas with **high unemployment** by providing benefits to firms that locate in certain areas. This might be **combined** with **training schemes** to give local workers the skills required for the jobs provided.

Monetary Policy is usually used to tackle Demand-pull Inflation

1) Governments also need to use policies that deal with **demand-pull** and **cost-push inflation**.

2) **Monetary policy** is usually used to **tackle demand-pull inflation** — you'll find out how monetary policy works on p.173.

3) The **supply-side policies** described **above** to **tackle frictional** and **structural unemployment** are the kinds of policies often used to **tackle cost-push inflation**. For more supply-side policies see p.176.

Warm-Up Questions

Q1 Briefly explain how rises in inflation can become embedded in an economy.

Exam Question

Q1 Explain how a government could reduce the natural rate of unemployment in a country. [8 marks]

I'm going to be embedded under a duvet if I hear any more about inflation...

That Phillips curve 'argument' is complicated — here's a bit more info about where economists disagree... The short run Phillips curve trade-off relies on the idea of 'money illusion' — i.e. the confusion of nominal wages (how much money you have) with real wages (how much stuff your money can buy). If people suffer from money illusion, then the Phillips curve can work. But monetarists don't believe people suffer from money illusion, so they don't believe in the Phillips curve trade-off.

Inequality and Poverty

Some inequality is probably inevitable in any country, but there's a problem if inequality leads to poverty.
To start, you need to know a bit more information about inequality... so that's up first. **These pages are for all boards.**

Income and **Wealth** are **Not** distributed **Equally** in a market economy

1) An individual's **income** is the amount of money they receive over a **set** period of time, e.g. per week or per year. Income comes from **many sources**, e.g. **wages**, **interest** on bank accounts, **dividends** from shares and **rent** from properties.

2) Wealth is the **value** in money of **assets** held — **assets** can **include** property, land, money and shares.

3) In the **UK**, and most other economies, income and wealth **aren't** equally distributed. There are a number of factors affecting the **distribution** of **income**:

   - People earn **different wages** — certain skills are **more** in demand than others, so workers with those skills are likely to receive **higher** wages (see p.106).
   - **Unwaged** people (e.g. unemployed or pensioners) often rely on **state benefits**, so their **incomes** tend to be **lower**.
   - **Tax** and **state benefits** — in the UK there's a **progressive** tax system (to some extent, see p.169). Those with **higher** incomes are taxed a **higher percentage** of their earnings over certain levels. Some of this tax is then **redistributed** as benefits, e.g. to the unemployed, or to people with disabilities.
   - Compared to the **private sector**, workers in the **public sector** (on average) earn more per week.
   - Average full-time earnings also differ considerably between **different regions**. In 2019, the **highest** paid regions were London and the South East. The North East and Northern Ireland were the two **lowest** paid regions.

4) Wealth is **more unevenly** distributed than income:

   - Wealth often **earns** income — e.g. shares may **increase** in value and **generate** more income. Those who **earn income** from their **wealth** could **invest** that income again (e.g. by buying more shares), which in turn will generate **more income**, and so on. This means the **wealthy** become even wealthier, whereas those with **low** wealth don't have much (if anything) to invest, so their wealth will only grow by a **small** amount (if at all).
   - **Assets** tend to **increase** in **value** more quickly than **income rises**.
   - In the UK, income is **taxed**, but wealth isn't — so it's much **easier** to redistribute income than wealth.

Lorenz Curves show the **Extent** of **Inequality**

1) The **Lorenz curve** can be used to represent the **distribution** of income graphically.

2) Along the **horizontal** axis is the cumulative percentage of the **population**, and up the **vertical** axis is the cumulative percentage of income.

3) The **diagonal** line represents **complete equality** — e.g. 10% of the population have 10% of the income, 20% have 20% of the income, and so on.

4) The **further** the Lorenz curve is away from the diagonal, the greater the inequality in the country.
   - In this graph, the **lowest-earning 50%** of the population **earn only 8%** of the country's total income.
   - So the **highest-earning 50%** earn **92%** of the total income.
   - This represents a **large** amount of **income inequality**.

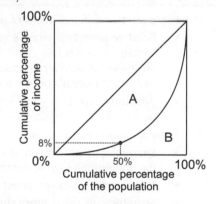

Gini Coefficients also describe the **Extent** of **Inequality**

1) The **Gini coefficient**, a **measure** of **inequality**, can be found from the Lorenz curve.

2) The Gini coefficient is calculated using the formula below:

$$\text{Gini coefficient} = \frac{\text{area A}}{\text{area A} + \text{area B}}$$

The Lorenz curve and Gini coefficient can also be used to represent the distribution of wealth.

3) A coefficient of **0** represents **complete equality** — i.e. **everybody** earns the **same**. A coefficient of **1** represents **complete inequality** — i.e. **one person** earns **all** the income in the country.

4) Wealth and income **inequality** have become **greater** in many countries (including the UK) since the early 1980s, with the **highest** incomes growing **particularly quickly**.

The UK income Gini coefficient has risen from around 0.27 in 1979 to 0.33 in 2019.

Inequality and Poverty

Equity and Equality are Different things

1) **Equality** means that everyone is treated **completely equally** — they all get **exactly** the **same** things.

2) **Equity** is more about **fairness** — people have different **circumstances**, so it's more about people getting what they **need**.

3) Equality is **positive** (it's **objective** and deals with **facts**), whereas equity is **normative** (it's **subjective** and based on **opinion**).

4) There are **two** types of equity:
   - **Horizontal equity** — people with the **same circumstances** are treated **fairly** (i.e. they're treated the **same**).
   - **Vertical equity** — people with **different circumstances** are treated **fairly** but **differently**.

EXAMPLE	
1)	People with the **same level of income** are taxed the **same amount** — this is **horizontal** equity.
2)	People with **higher incomes** are taxed **more** — this is **vertical** equity.

The Distribution of income and wealth has big Impacts on the Economy

There are both **positives** and **negatives** to an **unequal** distribution of income and wealth:

POSITIVES

1) Inequality provides **incentives** for people to work harder and earn more — so **rewarding** hard work **increases productivity**.

2) It encourages **enterprise** by those who have the funds available to start businesses.

3) It also **encourages** people to **work** instead of claiming benefits.

4) It may create a **trickle-down effect** — some economists argue that if there's **inequality** and **greater economic growth**, the **rich** will become even **richer** and **spend more** on goods and services, providing **more income** for the **poor**. This is known as the **trickle-down effect**. As a result, **relative poverty** may **increase**, but **absolute poverty** will **decrease**.

NEGATIVES

1) **Absolute** and **relative** poverty can remain **high** (see below).

2) It **restricts** economic growth and wastes people's talent, because the **poorest** people won't have the **funds** to start businesses.

3) As incomes rise **even higher**, people generally **spend more** on **imports**, so this money would **leave** the circular flow.

4) **Crime** is likely to **increase** because people don't have what they **need**.

A perfectly equal distribution of wealth and income could also be seen as inequitable — e.g. it wouldn't reward people who chose to work hard or took risks to start a new business.

Big Differences in Income and Wealth often mean there's Poverty

1) There are **two** different types of poverty:
   - **Relative poverty** is when someone has a low income **relative to other incomes** in their country (e.g. people whose income is less than 50% of the average income might be classed as living in relative poverty). So someone from a **rich county** might be classed as living in **relative poverty**, even though someone in a much **poorer** country with the **same income** might be considered **wealthy**.
   - **Absolute poverty** is when someone can't afford the very **basics** — e.g. food and shelter. The minimum income needed for these basics is called the **poverty line** (e.g. the World Bank uses a poverty line income of $1.90 per day).

2) There are many **causes** of poverty:
   - **Unemployment** — even in a country where the state gives **unemployment benefits**, the unemployed are likely to be at the **bottom** level of income in that country.
   - **Low wages** — workers **most likely** to receive low wages are those with **few** skills or qualifications.
   - State benefits rising **more slowly** than wages — this means the **relative incomes** of people relying on state benefits **fall** over time.

The Poverty Trap

- The poverty trap can affect people who are in poverty — these may be people relying on **state benefits**, or those on **low wages** and **means-tested benefits** (these are just benefits based on a person's income).
- When these people earn **higher wages**, they may only **actually receive** a **small** percentage of their wage increase. This is because they'll need to pay income tax and National Insurance contributions (in the UK), and have their benefits **reduced** (because they're earning more money).
- In some cases, this could even cause a **drop** in their disposable income, and this means their **marginal tax rate** will be **high**.
- So the combination of income tax, National Insurance and the benefit system can result in a **disincentive** for these people to **find work**, or to **increase** the number of hours they work. Governments may attempt to **remove** these disincentives (see p.176).

Marginal tax rate is just the percentage (tax) that'll be taken from the next pound you earn.

Government Policies to Tackle Poverty

A government can do various things to reduce poverty in its own country. **This page is for AQA and Edexcel.**

Governments often Intervene to try to Alleviate Poverty

Governments can use the first three policies below to **redistribute** income and wealth **after** it's been earned. The final two policies try to **change** the **amount** of income people receive instead.

Benefits

1) **Benefits** are used to **redistribute** income — tax revenue (mostly from those with **higher** incomes) is used to **pay** for the benefits of those who **need** them.

2) However, as **means-tested state benefits** contribute to the **poverty trap** (see p.166), governments might:
   - **Remove** means-tested benefits completely. This would **increase** the **incentive** to work. However, at least in the short term, it would cause **larger** differences in income, and **relative** and **absolute** poverty would **increase**.
   - **Change** means-tested benefits to universal benefits. But the **cost** of these extra benefits might mean that those on low incomes are **taxed more**.
   - **Reduce** means-tested benefits more gradually as income increases.

State provision

1) **State-provided** services, such as **health care** and **education**, help to **reduce** inequalities caused by **differences** in income — e.g. someone on a **low income** can receive the **same** health care as someone on a **high income**.

2) State-provided services also **redistribute income** because most of the money to **pay** for them comes from taxing people with **higher incomes**. But **free** access **reduces** the incentive to work and is expensive to provide.

Progressive taxation

1) **Progressive taxation** means a **bigger** percentage of tax is taken from workers with **high incomes** than those with **low incomes**. It helps to **reduce** the difference between people's **disposable incomes**, reducing **relative poverty**.

2) But progressive taxation can contribute to the **poverty trap**. Also, if high income earners are taxed **too much**, some may **move** to a country where they're **taxed less**. This will mean a **loss** of labour and money from the economy.

Economic growth

1) Perhaps the most **effective** way of reducing poverty is through **economic growth**. This will mean **jobs** are created and **unemployment** will be **reduced**. It also tends to lead to **higher wages**, meaning the government will gain **more tax revenue**, which it can use to provide services.

2) However, economic growth can be **difficult** to achieve. It can also result in **larger** inequalities in income — for example, economic growth might **mainly** benefit the rich so that they become even richer. It can also cause problems such as the using up of **finite resources**, which might mean **more** poverty and inequality in the future.

National minimum wage (NMW)

1) A **national minimum wage**, if it's set at a sensible level, will **reduce poverty** among the lowest paid workers. It will provide an **incentive** to work, and will help those on **low incomes** to afford a reasonable **standard of living**. A NMW can also **counteract** monopsony power (see p.63) — e.g. if an employer with monopsony power is paying low wages, resulting in workers being in **relative** or **absolute** poverty.

2) However, the NMW might mean some employers employ **fewer** people. This would mean a **rise** in **unemployment**, and therefore a rise in **poverty**. A NMW also **doesn't** take into account that the cost of living **varies** depending on where someone lives, so the **standard of living** for people who are earning the NMW will **vary** depending on where they live (while anyone who's **unemployed** won't benefit from a NMW at all).

Warm-Up Questions

Q1 Explain the difference between equity and equality.

Q2 Define: a) horizontal and vertical equity   b) absolute and relative poverty.

PRACTICE QUESTIONS

Exam Question

Q1 Comment on the likely effectiveness of using a national minimum wage and means-tested state benefits to alleviate poverty in a country where absolute and relative poverty are both quite high.   [10 marks]

I caught nothing with my poverty trap — it was really poor...

There's an unequal distribution of income and wealth in most economies. In fact, in capitalist economies (where the free market dominates), inequality is likely. Governments use the idea of equity to help achieve an acceptable level of inequality.

Fiscal Policy

The next few pages are about the macroeconomic policy tools that governments can use to achieve their macroeconomic objectives. Before you tackle this section, make sure you're clear on aggregate demand and aggregate supply (pages 132-143), and on policy objectives (pages 144-167). **This page is for all boards.**

You've got to learn the Key Features of Fiscal Policy

1) **Fiscal policy** (or budgetary policy) involves **government spending** (public expenditure) and **taxation**. It can be used to **influence** the **economy as a whole** (macroeconomic effects) or **individual firms** and **people** (microeconomic effects).

2) Fiscal policy can be used to **stimulate aggregate demand**:

- **Reflationary fiscal policy** (sometimes called 'expansionary' or 'loose' fiscal policy) involves **boosting** aggregate demand (causing the AD curve to shift to the right) by **increasing** government spending or **lowering** taxes. It's likely to involve a government having a **budget deficit** (government spending > revenue).

- **Deflationary fiscal policy** (sometimes called 'contractionary' or 'tight' fiscal policy) involves **reducing** aggregate demand (causing the AD curve to shift to the left) by **reducing** government spending or **increasing** taxes. It's likely to involve a government having a **budget surplus** (government spending < revenue).

3) A reflationary fiscal policy is likely to be used during a **recession** or when there's a **negative output gap**. It'll **increase economic growth** and **reduce unemployment**, but it'll also **increase inflation** and **worsen** the **current account** of the **balance of payments** because as incomes increase, more is spent on imports.

Reflationary and deflationary fiscal policy is known as demand-side fiscal policy — it affects aggregate demand.

4) A deflationary fiscal policy is likely to be used during a **boom** or when there's a **positive output gap**. It'll **reduce economic growth** and **increase unemployment**, but it'll also **reduce price levels** and **improve** the **current account** of the **balance of payments** because as incomes fall, less is spent on imports.

5) A government's **fiscal stance** or **budget position** describes whether their policy is reflationary (known as an **expansionary** stance), deflationary (a **contractionary** stance), or neither (a **neutral** stance). If a government has a neutral fiscal stance then government spending and taxation has **no net effect** on AD.

Deflationary policy reduces demand — it doesn't necessarily cause deflation.

6) There are **two important features** of fiscal policy that you need to be aware of:

- **Automatic stabilisers** — Some of a government's fiscal policy may **automatically** react to changes in the economic cycle. During a **recession**, **government spending** will **increase** because the government will pay out more benefits. The government will also receive **less tax revenue**, e.g. due to unemployment. These automatic stabilisers **reduce** the problems a recession causes, but at the expense of creating a **budget deficit**. During a **boom**, the automatic stabilisers create a budget surplus as **tax revenue increases** and **government spending** on benefits **falls**.

- **Discretionary policy** — This is where governments **deliberately** change their level of spending and tax. At **any given point** a government might choose to spend on improving the country's infrastructure or services, and increase taxes to pay for it. On other occasions the government might take action because of the **economic situation**, e.g. during a recession the government might spend more and cut taxes to stimulate aggregate demand.

Cyclical and Structural Budget Positions are Different

1) A **structural budget position** is a government's **long-term** fiscal stance. This means their budget position over a whole period of the **economic cycle** (see page 145), including booms and/or recessions.

2) A **cyclical budget position** is a government's fiscal stance in the **short term**. This is affected by where the economy is in the economic cycle — automatic stabilisers are likely to create a **surplus** (i.e. a contractionary budget position) during a **boom** and a **deficit** (i.e. an expansionary budget position) during a **recession**.

3) A **budget deficit** caused by an expansionary **cyclical budget position** is known as a **cyclical budget deficit**. This will be **balanced out** by a **budget surplus** during boom times (when the cyclical budget position is contractionary).

4) A **budget deficit** caused by an expansionary **structural budget position** (where spending is more than revenue in the long term) will add to **national debt**. This is called a **structural budget deficit** (there's more about deficits on page 170).

5) Government spending can be split into **current expenditure** — repeated spending on things which are **used up** quickly (e.g. wages), and **capital expenditure** — spending on **assets** (e.g. infrastructure) which will last a long time.

The government also makes transfer payments — this is where money is transferred according to need (e.g. welfare benefits). Unlike with current and capital expenditure the government gets no goods or services in return.

EDEXCEL ONLY

A government may have a budget position on **current expenditure** which is different from their overall position. For example they may want current expenditure to be funded from **revenue**, but be willing to borrow for **capital expenditure**. So their budget position on current expenditure would be **neutral** or **contractionary**, but their **overall position** may be **expansionary** because of their capital expenditure.

This is the 'golden rule' that the UK government aimed to follow before 2008 — see page 171.

Fiscal Policy

Most of the money that governments spend comes from taxation. Taxes aren't just about paying the bills though. For example, they can also have a social impact by redistributing income. Who knew tax could be so exciting? ***This page is for all boards.***

There are **Different Types** of **Tax System**

1) Taxes should be **cheap to collect**, **easy to pay** and **hard to avoid**, and they **shouldn't** create any **undesirable disincentives**, e.g. discouraging people from working or from saving.

2) On top of this, governments may want taxes to achieve **horizontal** and **vertical equity** (for more on equity see p.166).

    • **Horizontal equity** will mean that people who have **similar incomes** and **ability** to **pay taxes** should pay the **same amount** of tax.

    • **Vertical equity** will mean that people who have **higher** incomes and **greater ability** to **pay taxes** should pay **more** than those on **lower incomes** with **less ability** to **pay** taxes.

3) Governments may also want taxes that **promote equality** in an economy. This might involve using taxes to **reduce major differences** in people's **disposable income**, or to **raise revenue** to pay for **benefits** and the **state provision** of **services**.

4) Governments **raise tax revenue** through **direct taxation** (e.g. income tax) and **indirect taxation** (e.g. VAT or excise duty). They also use **different tax systems** to achieve different economic objectives — the ones you need to know are **progressive taxation**, **regressive taxation** and **proportional taxation**.

    See page 86 for direct/indirect tax.

5) **Progressive taxation** is where an **individual's taxes rise** (as a percentage of their income) as their **income rises**, and it's often used to **redistribute income** and **reduce poverty**. A government can use the tax revenue from those on high incomes and **redistribute** it to those on low incomes in the form of benefits or state-provided merit goods (e.g. health care or education) — **increasing equality**. Progressive taxation follows the **'ability to pay' principle** (the tax achieves **vertical equity**).

6) **Regressive taxation** is where an **individual's taxes fall** (as a percentage of their income) as their **income rises**, and they're used by governments to **encourage supply-side growth**. By **reducing** the taxes of the **rich** the government will hope that the economy will **benefit** from the **trickle-down effect** (see p.166). A regressive tax system gives people more of an **incentive to work harder** and **earn more income**, but it may **increase inequality**.

• **Supply-side economists** argue that increasing direct taxes creates a **disincentive** to work and will **reduce a** government's **tax revenue**. This is shown on the **Laffer curve**.

• The Laffer curve shows that **as taxes increase**, eventually this will lead to a **decline in tax revenue** because people will have **less incentive to work**.

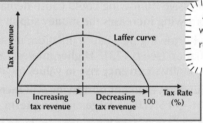

A 100% tax rate will result in no tax revenue because no one would work.

---

7) **Proportional taxation** (a 'flat tax') is where everyone pays the **same** proportion of tax **regardless** of their **income** level. This tax system can achieve **horizontal equity**, but setting a fair tax rate to apply to all members of society is **difficult**. For example, a 25% tax on income might be too high for those on lower incomes to afford, and it might not raise enough revenue from those on higher incomes for the government to be able to pay for all of the public goods and services it provides.

• Supporters of a flat tax argue that it can **simplify** the tax system, **reduce** the incentive to **evade and avoid** paying taxes (flat taxes often charge high earners less than variable rates), and **increase** the incentive to **earn more**.

• However, flat rate tax systems may bring in **less tax overall** than variable rate tax systems.

• Flat rate tax systems also don't have **vertical equity**, but they can be made more **progressive** by having a **tax free allowance** (where you don't pay any tax until you earn a certain amount).

The **UK Government** uses **Various Different Taxes**

1) In the UK there's a **sales tax** on most products, known as **VAT** (value-added tax). VAT is a **proportional tax** — it's a **fixed percentage** regardless of the selling price of a product. However, it can also be seen as a **regressive tax**. This is because the **percentage** of **total income** that the **rich** spend is **less** than that of the **poor** (e.g. because the rich can afford to save more of their income), so that means the percentage of total income that the rich spend on VAT will be **less** than it is for the **poor**.

2) A more **progressive system** of **VAT** might be to tax **luxury goods** at a **higher tax rate**.

3) It's argued that the UK has a **progressive income tax system**. There's a **tax-free allowance** (£12 500 for 2019/20), and then individuals on **low-to-middle income** have their extra income over the allowance taxed at **20%**. Those on a **high income** are taxed at **40%** on their extra income over a certain threshold, and those on a **very high income** are taxed at **45%** on their income over a further threshold.

4) But it's also argued that the UK tax system is **regressive** because if you consider **direct** and **indirect** taxes **together**, the **lowest earners** in the UK economy have to pay a **higher proportion** of their income as tax than the **highest earners** do.

Fiscal Policy

The 'budget balance' is the difference between a government's spending and the revenue it brings in (e.g. from tax). It's important, because both a deficit (spending > revenue) and a surplus (spending < revenue) have their downsides. Read on... **All boards.**

The **Size** of **Government Spending** can be affected by several things

1) The **size** and **structure** of a **country's population** will affect levels of government spending. For example, a country with a **large population** may require greater levels of government spending than a country with a **small population**, and a country with an **ageing population** will have **greater demand** for **state-funded health care**.

2) Government policies on **inequality**, **poverty** and the **redistribution of income** will alter the amount of government spending — this might vary from government to government depending on their **political views**. For example, a government that wants to redistribute income may **spend more** on **benefits**.  *There's more on this on the next page.*

3) The **fiscal policies** governments use to tackle **certain problems** in a country will also have an effect. During a **recession** a government may increase public spending to **encourage growth** and **reduce unemployment**, but if these policies lead to a **large national debt** then the government may introduce **'austerity measures'** and **severely reduce** their spending.

Large Budget Deficits can cause Big Problems

A budget deficit (PSNB) is what a government borrows in a single year. The national debt (PSND) is the total debt (run up over time).

1) A **budget deficit** (also known as **public sector net borrowing — PSNB**) must be **paid for** by **public sector borrowing**, so that the government can spend **more money** than it **receives** in **revenue**.

2) In the UK, the government can borrow the money it needs from **UK banks**, which will create **deposits** that the government can spend. It can also **borrow money** from the private sector by selling **Treasury bills**, which the government will **pay off over a period of time** (e.g. 3 months), or it can borrow money from foreign **financial markets**.

3) This kind of borrowing is **fine** in the **short run**, especially if the borrowed money is used to **stimulate demand** in a country. But there will be **problems** if there's **excessive borrowing**:

   • Excessive borrowing could cause **demand-pull inflation** (see p.152), partly due to the fact that government borrowing **increases** the **money supply**, so there's **more money** in the economy than can be **matched** by **output**.

   • As borrowing may cause inflation, it can also lead to a **rise** in **interest rates** to curb that inflation (see p.173). **Higher** interest rates will **discourage investment** by firms and make a country's **currency rise in value**, meaning that its **exports** are **less price competitive**.

4) **Continued government borrowing** will **increase** a country's **national debt** (also known as **public sector net debt — PSND**). A **large** and **long-term** national debt can cause **several problems** too:

   • If a country's debt becomes very large then it may cause **firms** and **foreign countries** to **stop lending** money to that country's government. This will **constrain** the country's ability to **grow** in future.

   • **Future taxpayers** will be left with **large interest payments** on **debt** to pay off. Debt repayments have an **opportunity cost** as future governments may have to **cut spending** to pay off a debt, which may **harm economic growth**.

   • A **large national debt** suggests that there's been **excessive borrowing**, which **causes inflation** and **interest rates** to **rise** (see above). It also suggests that public sector spending is very large, which may **'crowd out'** private sector spending. Although, if government spending **boosts** the economy there may be **'crowding in'** instead (public sector spending may increase private sector spending) — firms will **invest** more if the economy is **growing quickly** (see p.141).

   • A country with large debt is **less attractive** to **foreign direct investment** (**FDI** — see p.194), as foreign countries will be **uncertain** how the debtor nation's economy will do in future and whether it will be a good bet for investment.

5) Methods to **correct** a **budget deficit** will depend on what kind of budget deficit it is.

   • A **cyclical budget deficit** is caused by **recessions** and comes about due to a government's **automatic stabilisers** (when government spending on benefits increases and tax revenue falls). This kind of deficit will be **corrected** when the economy **recovers** again — the deficit will be replaced by a surplus.

   • However, a **structural budget deficit**, caused by **excessive borrowing**, is much harder to solve. To cure this problem, governments will have to **raise taxes** and **reduce public spending** so that they can pay off their debt (these are known as **'austerity measures'**). However, these actions could **harm economic growth** and cause other problems.

Budget Surpluses are Not Ideal either

   • A budget surplus is **generally more desirable** than a budget deficit — however, it's **not** always a good thing either.

   • A budget surplus might suggest that **taxes are too high** or that governments **aren't spending** enough on the economy. Both of these things could **harm** or **constrain economic growth**.

   • **Lowering taxes** or **increasing government spending** would **correct** a budget surplus.

Fiscal Policy

Governments follow **Fiscal Rules** to **Avoid Overspending**

1) The **UK government** first brought in **fiscal rules** in 1997. One of these was the **golden rule** — over the economic cycle (see page 145) the government can borrow to **invest** in things like infrastructure (which should generate future growth), but cannot borrow to fund **current expenditure** (e.g. wages).

2) Following fiscal rules like these should help to **prevent** a government from **continuously borrowing** and **overspending** to promote growth, which increases national debt and inflation. It'll also help governments to achieve **economic stability** as they'll **avoid** uncertainty and fluctuating inflation.

3) Fiscal rules can also influence the behaviour of **businesses** and **consumers**, by increasing **confidence** in future economic stability. For example, consumers may be more willing to spend and firms may increase investment if they're confident in the country's economic stability.

4) However, this will only work if there is a belief that governments will **keep to** the rules they've set.

> For example, there was disagreement over whether the golden rule was actually being followed between 1997 and the 2008 financial crisis, as it's not clear how an economic cycle is defined. (The rule was abandoned after 2008.)

5) In 2010 the UK government created the **Office for Budget Responsibility** (**OBR**) — an independent body that:

   • Publishes reports **analysing** UK **public spending**, **taxation**, and government **predictions** of future spending.

   • Assesses the **performance** of the government against the **fiscal targets** it's set for itself.

   • Uses **long-term projections** to analyse how **sustainable** government spending and revenue is.

6) By doing this, the OBR **helps** the government to keep its fiscal policy **under control**.

Governments use fiscal policy to **Tackle Poverty**

> For more information on poverty and ways to tackle it, turn to pages 165-167.

• Fiscal policy can be used to **reduce poverty** in a country. **Three** key ways a government can do this is through **benefits**, **provision** of **certain goods** and **services**, and **progressive taxation**.

• Government spending on **benefits**, e.g. Universal Credit, pensions and disability benefits, is a way of **helping** those who are **unemployed** or **unable** to work, and reducing **absolute poverty**.

• A government can also spend its tax revenue to **provide** goods and services, such as free health care or education, to enable those who are suffering from poverty to have **access** to these things.

• Furthermore, by **providing** some **goods** and **services** to poorer members of society, a government will be **investing** in the **improvement** of its country's **human capital** — i.e. this spending may make **labour** (one of the factors of production) **much more productive**.

• **Progressive taxation** may **reduce relative poverty** by **narrowing** the **gaps** between people's **disposable income**, and the revenue raised can pay for benefits and the state provision of goods and services. On top of this, governments could **provide tax cuts** and **discounts** for the **poor**.

• Finally, if fiscal policy creates **growth**, then this may reduce both **relative** and **absolute poverty**. Greater economic growth will mean **more jobs**, **higher incomes** and a **better standard of living**.

The government's physical policy was a big hit with Claude and Sue.

For more information on poverty and ways to tackle it, turn to pages 165-167.

Warm-Up Questions

Q1 Briefly explain the difference between automatic stabilisers and discretionary fiscal policy.

Q2 What does the Laffer curve show?

Q3 Give three examples of problems caused by large, long-term national debt.

Q4 Explain the role of the Office for Budget Responsibility.

Exam Questions

Q1 Distinguish between a cyclical budget position and a structural budget position. [4 marks]

Q2 Loose fiscal policy is most likely to be used when:
   A the economy is in a boom phase.   B a country has a large national debt.
   C there is a negative output gap.   D the government's budget position is neutral.   [1 mark]

Q3 Evaluate whether fiscal rules are effective in creating economic stability. [12 marks]

Q4 Discuss how taxation can be used to help a government reduce inequality in a country. [10 marks]

People laugh, but I love the automatic stabilisers on my bike...

Governments sometimes aim for a balanced budget. This is one of those terms that's used in different ways by different people (hurray). It can mean government spending is <u>equal</u> to revenue, or that spending is <u>no more than</u> revenue (i.e. spending ≤ revenue).

Average and Marginal Tax Rates

If you're doing OCR then you need to know a bit more about taxation, and what tax revenue is spent on. **OCR only.**

You can calculate **Average** and **Marginal** tax rates

1) An **average tax rate** is the **percentage** of some total amount (e.g. total income or total profits) paid as tax. With income tax this is the **total amount of income tax** you pay as a percentage of your **total income**.

$$\text{average income tax rate} = \frac{\text{total income tax paid}}{\text{total income}} \times 100$$

2) A **marginal tax rate** is the rate of tax you pay on any **extra money**. For income tax this 'extra' is the **last £1** you earn — the marginal income tax rate is the rate paid on the last £1 of income.

$$\text{marginal income tax rate} = \text{rate paid on last £1 of income}$$

3) In the UK the marginal income tax rate increases as you earn over certain **thresholds**. It's only the **extra income** (over the threshold) that's taxed at the higher rate, **not** your whole income.

4) Here's an example using the **marginal rates of income tax** in the UK for 2019/20:

Income (x)	Marginal tax rate
£0 ≤ x ≤ £12 500	0%
£12 500 < x ≤ £50 000	20%
£50 000 < x ≤ £150 000	40%
Over £150 000	45%

EXAMPLE: average and marginal tax rates on an income of £62 000

- You don't pay tax on income **up to £12 500**.
- On income between **£12 500 and £50 000** you pay **20% tax**. Work out how much **income** is in this bracket:

  Income between £12 500 and £50 000 = £50 000 – £12 500 = **£37 500**

  Then work out how much **tax is paid** on this income:

  20% of **£37 500** = 0.2 × 37 500 = **£7500**

  *If your income is **more** than the threshold then subtract from the **threshold**. If your income is **less** than the threshold then subtract from your **income**.*

- On income between **£50 000 and £150 000** you pay **40% tax**. Work out how much **income** is in this bracket:

  Income between £50 000 and £150 000 = £62 000 – £50 000 = **£12 000**

  Then work out how much **tax is paid** on this income: 40% of £12 000 = 0.4 × 12 000 = **£4800**

- So the **total tax paid** on an income of £62 000 is: £7500 + £4800 = **£12 300**

- Then the **average tax rate** = $\dfrac{\text{total tax paid}}{\text{total income}} \times 100 = \dfrac{12\,300}{62\,000} \times 100 = \underline{\textbf{19.84\%}}$

  It's actually a bit more complicated for people earning £100 000 or more, but this is the basic idea.

- The **marginal tax rate** is just the rate paid on the last £1 of income. £62 000 is between **£50 000 and £150 000**, so this is **40%**.

The Government **Spends Tax Revenue** on **Benefits** and **Services**

You need to know where the government gets most of its **tax revenue** from, and how this revenue is **spent**.

Main sources of tax revenue:

- **Income tax** (roughly 30% of central government tax revenue)
- **VAT** (about 20%)
- **National Insurance** payments (about 20%)
- **Excise duties** on goods like **alcohol** and **fuel** (about 10%)
- **Corporation tax** (about 8%)
- **Council tax** and **Business rates** (paid to local government)

Main areas of Government expenditure:

- **Social support** including pensions (about 40%)
- **National Health Service** (about 20%)
- **Education** (about 15%)
- **Debt interest** (about 6%)
- **Police, law courts** and **prisons** (about 5%)
- **Defence** (about 5%)

Warm-Up Questions

Q1 What is a marginal tax rate?

Exam Question

Q1 Use the UK marginal tax rates table above to calculate the average income tax rate on an income of £26 000. [2 marks]

I've found this page pretty taxing to be honest...

These average and marginal tax calculations can look a bit nasty at first, but they're not too tricky once you've had a bit of practice. The example on this page should help if you're struggling — once you've made sense of it try the practice exam question above.

Monetary Policy

Monetary policy is largely about setting interest rates. But there's a lot of things to take into account as you do it. **These pages are for all boards.**

Monetary Policy is about Controlling Money

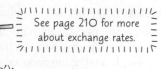

The money supply is measured in different ways — here, it means the amount of notes and coins in circulation, plus the amount of money held in bank accounts.

1) **Monetary policy** involves making decisions about **interest rates**, the **money supply** and **exchange rates**.

2) Monetary policy has a huge effect on **aggregate demand** — it's a **demand-side** policy.

3) The most important tool of monetary policy is the ability to set **interest rates**. Changes to interest rates affect **borrowing, saving, spending** and **investment**.

4) Interest rates also affect the other components of monetary policy — the **money supply** and **exchange rates**. For example, a **high** interest rate can **restrict** the money supply as there'll be **less demand** for loans.

See page 210 for more about exchange rates.

5) Monetary policy can either be **contractionary** ('tight') or **expansionary** ('loose'):

- **Contractionary monetary policy** — this involves **reducing** aggregate demand (AD) using high interest rates, restrictions on the money supply, and a strong exchange rate.

- **Expansionary monetary policy** — this involves **increasing** aggregate demand using low interest rates, fewer restrictions on the money supply, and a weak exchange rate.

6) As with **demand-side fiscal policy** (see p.168), monetary policy **can't** help achieve **all** of a government's macroeconomic objectives simultaneously — there's a **trade-off**. For example, using monetary policy to **increase economic growth** and **reduce unemployment** may mean **increasing inflation** and **worsening the current account** of the balance of payments.

7) In the UK, the main aim of monetary policy is to ensure **price stability** — i.e. **low inflation**. But it also has the aims of **promoting economic growth** and **reducing unemployment**.

Interest Rates are set by the Monetary Policy Committee (MPC)

1) The **Monetary Policy Committee** (**MPC**) of the **Bank of England** sets interest rates in order to meet the inflation target that's set by the government — this target is currently **2% inflation**, as measured by the **Consumer Price Index** (CPI). This is known as **inflation rate targeting**.

2) The MPC has a **symmetric target** — if the inflation rate misses the 2% target by more than 1% **in either direction** (i.e. if it's less than 1% or more than 3%), then the governor of the Bank of England has to write to the Chancellor (see below).

3) So if the MPC believed that inflation was likely to go **above 3%** with current interest rates, it would **increase** the official rate of interest (sometimes called the **Bank Rate** or **Base Rate**) to **reduce** aggregate demand and keep inflation close to 2%.

Some central banks have an **asymmetric inflation target**. For example, the **European Central Bank** (ECB) aims to keep inflation **close to but below 2%**.

4) A low rate of inflation that's **stable** and **credible** (i.e. trustworthy and accurate) stops higher rates of inflation becoming **embedded** in the economy (see p.163). It also helps a government achieve **macroeconomic stability** — a high or rapidly changing rate of inflation creates **uncertainty**, prevents **investment**, and makes it difficult to **plan** for the future.

5) To achieve this **stability** and **credibility**, the Bank of England is **independent** and **accountable**:

- The Bank of England's **independence** means that interest rates **can't** be set by the government at a level that will win votes, but which might not be right for the economic circumstances at the time.

- The Bank of England is **accountable** — if the inflation rate is **more than 1%** away from the **target rate** (either above or below), then the Bank's governor must write an open letter to the Chancellor explaining why, what action the MPC is going to take to deal with this, and when they expect inflation to be back to within 1% of the target.

6) Although price stability is the **main objective** of monetary policy, the Bank of England must pursue this in a way that **doesn't harm** the government's other macroeconomic policy objectives (e.g. economic growth or low unemployment).

7) When the MPC is making a decision on interest rates it will look at important **economic data**, such as:
- house prices,
- the size of any output gaps,
- the pound's exchange rate,
- the rate of any increases or decreases in average earnings.

There's more about this on page 181.

8) The MPC has to consider interest-rate changes very carefully, since these changes can have a **huge** effect (see next page).

Monetary Policy

A **Rise** in **Interest Rates** causes a **Ripple Effect**... usually

1) Even very small changes in interest rates can create a '**ripple effect**' through the whole economy.

2) Here are some likely effects of an **increase** in interest rates:

> - less **borrowing**,
> - less **consumer spending** (i.e. less **consumption**),
> - less **investment** by firms,
> - less **confidence** among consumers and firms,
> - more **saving**,
> - a decrease in **exports**,
> - an increase in **imports**.

All these 'ripple effects' are explained by the transmission mechanism — see next page.

3) A **decrease** in interest rates will have the **opposite effects**.

4) However, when people are particularly **pessimistic** about the future state of the economy, they may prefer to keep hold of the money they already have (rather than spend or invest it), and they're unlikely to want to borrow any more. In this case, lowering interest rates **won't** create the above 'ripple effect', and monetary policy will become **ineffective**. This situation is known as a **liquidity trap**.

Quantitative easing (see page 181) won't work either, as the extra money will just be held on to.

Markets affect **Interest Rates** too

1) The **Bank Rate** is the lowest rate at which the Bank of England will lend to financial institutions (e.g. banks). But it **isn't** the rate of interest that you'd pay if you applied to a high-street bank for a **mortgage** or took out a **bank loan**.

2) However, these various types of interest rates are **linked** — if the Bank Rate goes **up**, then that will usually lead to interest rates charged on mortgages and bank loans also **increasing**. The same happens in reverse if the Bank Rate **falls** — i.e. other interest rates in the economy will also **fall**.

3) But the Bank Rate is **not** the **only** thing that affects these 'market' interest rates.

4) For example, banks often need to **borrow** the money that they then **lend out** to firms and consumers from other lenders. If lots of banks are trying to borrow money at the same time, then they'll have to pay a **higher rate** of interest themselves, which will affect the cost of mortgages and loans they offer to **consumers**.

Interest rates are affected by other things as well as the Bank Rate and the supply and demand for credit. But these are the things you need to be particularly aware of.

Interest Rates affect **Exchange Rates**

1) When interest rates are **high** in the UK, big financial institutions (such as large banks or insurance companies) want to **buy the pound**. They do this so that they can put their money into UK banks and take advantage of the **high rewards** for savers brought about by the high interest rates. This is likely to be a short-term movement of money and it's called '**hot money**'.

2) An **increased demand** for the pound means its **price goes up** — i.e. the pound's exchange rate **rises**.

3) Unfortunately, a **high exchange rate** makes UK exports **more expensive**.

> - Suppose the **exchange rate** of the pound against the dollar is **£1 = $2**. And suppose a British firm makes pens that cost, say, £1.
> - To buy one of these British pens, someone in the USA would first have to buy the pound. This would mean that the price of one of these pens in the USA is effectively **$2**, since it costs them **$2** to buy **£1**, and then they can spend this £1 on buying a pen.
> - Now suppose the exchange rate **changed** to **£1 = $4** (i.e. the pound's exchange rate goes up, or the pound becomes **stronger**).
> - Someone in the USA would now have to spend **$4** to pay for the same £1 pen. Remember, the pen's price in the UK **hasn't changed** at all — this **extra cost** to the person in the USA is **all** to do with the **cost** of **buying pounds**.

4) When this happens **exports go down**, **worsening** the current account on the **balance of payments**.

5) For the same reason (but in reverse), **high** UK interest rates mean **imports** from abroad become **cheaper**. Again, this **worsens** the current account.

6) And remember... imports are a **leakage** in the circular flow of income, and so more spending on imports means a **reduction** in AD.

7) When UK interest rates **fall**, the opposite happens:

Remember though, this depends on the price elasticity of demand of exports and imports.

> - The **exchange rate** of the pound **falls**.
> - UK **exports increase** (as UK goods become cheaper) and **imports decrease** (as foreign goods become more expensive).
> - The **balance of payments improves**.

Jimmy always got excited when the decisions of the Monetary Policy Committee were about to be announced.

Monetary Policy

The diagram on this page looks fairly intimidating, but it's only describing things you've already read about. So don't panic.

The **Transmission Mechanism** shows the effect of **Interest-Rate Changes**

The **knock-on effects** that a change to the official Bank Rate can have are best shown by the **transmission mechanism** — this is shown in the diagram below. The **end result** of any **change** in the **official Bank Rate** will be a **change** to the level of **inflation**.

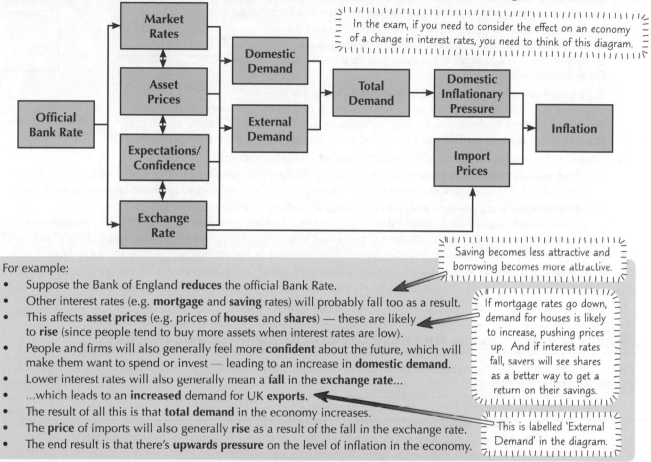

In the exam, if you need to consider the effect on an economy of a change in interest rates, you need to think of this diagram.

For example:

- Suppose the Bank of England **reduces** the official Bank Rate.
- Other interest rates (e.g. **mortgage** and **saving** rates) will probably fall too as a result.
- This affects **asset prices** (e.g. prices of **houses** and **shares**) — these are likely to **rise** (since people tend to buy more assets when interest rates are low).
- People and firms will also generally feel more **confident** about the future, which will make them want to spend or invest — leading to an increase in **domestic demand**.
- Lower interest rates will also generally mean a **fall** in the **exchange rate**...
- ...which leads to an **increased** demand for UK **exports**.
- The result of all this is that **total demand** in the economy increases.
- The **price** of imports will also generally **rise** as a result of the fall in the exchange rate.
- The end result is that there's **upwards pressure** on the level of inflation in the economy.

Saving becomes less attractive and borrowing becomes more attractive.

If mortgage rates go down, demand for houses is likely to increase, pushing prices up. And if interest rates fall, savers will see shares as a better way to get a return on their savings.

This is labelled 'External Demand' in the diagram.

Monetary policy needs to look about **Two Years** into the **Future**

1) The effect of changing interest rates is **not** felt straight away — it takes time for the effects to feed through the transmission mechanism shown in the diagram above.
2) For example, reducing interest rates **won't** usually cause a **sudden surge** in investment or house buying.
   - Firms **plan** investment projects **very carefully** — it can take months or years before they increase their spending.
   - **House buying** can also take a long time — people need to **find** a suitable home, and the purchase can take a long time too. **Fixed-rate mortgage** holders won't notice the effect of an interest rate change until their fixed-rate period ends.
3) In fact, the **time lags** between changes in the Bank Rate and its effect on the economy can be very long indeed.
   - The maximum effect on **firms** is usually felt after about **one year**.
   - The maximum effect on **consumers** is usually felt after about **two years**.

These are 'typical' lags — actual lags may be different.

4) So the Bank of England has to look up to **two years** into the future when it's making a decision about interest rates.

Warm-Up Questions

Q1 Use the transmission mechanism to show why an increase in the official Bank Rate can put downward pressure on inflation.

Exam Question

Q1 Outline the objectives of the Monetary Policy Committee when setting the UK's official interest rate. [4 marks]

Use the transmission mechanism from this book to your brain...

Yeah, that diagram's not at all scary. Piece of cake. Okay... you saw through me, it looks awful I agree. But don't get down about it... just write down the steps involved for an increase and a decrease in interest rates a few times, and you'll get a feel for it. I mean it...

Supply-side Policies

Supply-side policies are very popular at the moment among economists. That goes for Economics examiners too. **All boards.**

Supply-side Policies aim to Increase the economy's Trend Growth Rate

1) The aim of supply-side policies is to **expand** the **productive potential** (i.e. long run aggregate supply) of an economy, or to increase the **trend rate** of growth, as shown in these diagrams.

2) Supply-side policies are about the government creating the **right conditions** to allow **market forces** to create **growth**, as opposed to the government creating growth **directly** by, for example, increasing its spending.

3) Supply-side policies involve making **structural changes** to the economy to allow its 'individual parts' to work **more efficiently** and **more productively**. For example, they might do this by helping **markets** function more efficiently, or creating **incentives** for **firms** or **individuals** to become more **productive** (or more **entrepreneurial**).

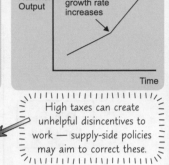

High taxes can create unhelpful disincentives to work — supply-side policies may aim to correct these.

4) Supply-side policies can be divided into **free market** and **interventionist** policies:

   • **Free market supply-side policies** aim to increase efficiency by **removing** things which **interfere** with the free market. They include tax cuts, privatisation, deregulation, and policies to increase labour market flexibility.

   • **Interventionist supply-side policies** are usually aimed at **correcting market failure**. They include government spending on education (see below), subsidies for research and development, funding for improvements to infrastructure (e.g. ports that help firms to export their goods), and industrial policy (this is policy aimed at developing a particular industry or sector of the economy, e.g. through subsidies).

5) The effects of supply-side policies are generally **microeconomic** — i.e. their direct effects are usually on **individual** workers, firms or markets. However, these changes can have a powerful **macroeconomic** effect.

6) Supply-side policies can make an economy more **robust** and **flexible**.

Supply-side policies can Increase the Efficiency of various Markets

Here are some examples of supply-side policies that might be used in different kinds of markets:

There are more examples of supply-side policies on page 118.

The Product Market

• Create incentives for firms to invest, for example:
  – Offer firms tax breaks (i.e. reductions in the amount of tax they need to pay) if they invest profits back into the business instead of paying dividends to shareholders.

• Trade liberalisation — this means removing or reducing trade barriers, and allowing goods and capital to flow more freely between countries.

• Encourage competition, for example:
  – Deregulation (see p.93) can lead to improved efficiency in a market.
  – Privatisation (see p.92) may be effective if nationalised industries are inefficient.
  – Contract services out — this means the government asks private firms to bid to carry out services on its behalf (though the government retains responsibility for the service).
  – Provide extra support for new and small firms, or make it easier to set up a new company.

The Capital Market

Deregulation of financial markets — e.g. The 'Big Bang' of 1986 removed a lot of the traditional 'restrictive practices' that were felt to have made British financial markets (e.g. banks and stockbrokers) inefficient.

The Labour Market

• Reduce unemployment benefits — to create incentives for people to take a job (even a low-paid one) rather than live on benefits. Making it easier for people to find out about what jobs are available can also help.

• Reduce (or reform) income tax — introducing progressive taxation with the aim of creating more incentives for people to work (e.g. by ensuring that people don't become worse off if they take a job or earn a pay rise).

• Improve education and training:
  – E.g. apprenticeships allow people to learn practical skills while gaining relevant qualifications.
  – Improvements in education will not only allow employees to become more productive, but can also lead to greater occupational mobility (see p.113).

Progressive taxation is on p.169.

• Improve labour market flexibility — e.g. through trade union reforms, or by making it easier for firms to make workers redundant when times are tough.

See p.118 for more about labour market supply-side policies.

• Reduce regulations on firms — this would reduce firms' non-wage costs and may encourage them to employ more workers.

Supply-side Policies

Suitable **Demand-side** policies are needed alongside supply-side policies

1) Supply-side policies aim to make an economy more able to **supply** products. But for maximum benefit there needs to be a **demand** for those products — this means appropriate **demand-side policies** are also necessary.

2) Nowadays, supply-side and demand-side policies are often used together, but to achieve different aims:
   - **Supply-side** policies create **long-term growth**,
   - **Demand-side** policies **stabilise** the economy in the **short term**.

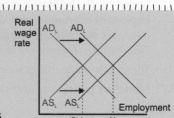

> The Keynesian AS curve on page 143 shows how increasing supply doesn't help when demand is very low. It also means that during a global recession, supply-side policies might not have their full impact until other countries' economies start to recover as well.

Example — Tackling unemployment

- Using an expansionary fiscal policy to boost **aggregate demand** might reduce unemployment. However, a supply-side economist would say that reducing unemployment in this way **doesn't change** the natural rate of unemployment (NRU — see p.162). So when the effects of your expansionary fiscal policy end, unemployment is likely to **return** to its 'pre-boost equilibrium'.

- A supply-side approach to this problem might be to try to **reduce the NRU** itself, i.e. create a **new equilibrium position** in the labour market. The hope is that this effect is likely to be more **long-lasting**. In the diagram, for example:
  - **Tax breaks** encouraging firms to **invest** have created **greater demand** for labour (i.e. the AD_L curve shifts right).
  - **Increased incentives** to work have created a **greater supply** of labour (i.e. the AS_L curve shifts right too).
  - The overall effect is that the equilibrium position in the labour market has moved to the **right** (meaning employment has risen, and that the NRU should **fall**).

- However, demand-side policies can still be useful in tackling **short-term** surges in unemployment.

There are huge potential **Benefits** of supply-side policies

Increasing the economy's **trend growth rate** makes it easier for a government to achieve its **macroeconomic objectives**, with fewer **conflicts** between **objectives** (such as those described on p.160-161) — which isn't the case with demand-side policies.
- For example, **unemployment** should fall as the **economy grows** and output expands.
- And **cost-push inflation** should be reduced, as greater efficiencies (and lower costs) are achieved.
- The **current account** of the **balance of payments** should also improve because of increased international **competitiveness**.

Supply-side policies are **Not Perfect** in every way

1) It can take a **long time** to see the results of supply-side policies, so they **can't** be used to fix the economy **quickly**. For example, it'll take **many years** to see the effects on an economy's labour supply that occur from **improvements** in **education**.

2) There can be **unintended consequences** — e.g. the deregulation of financial markets (starting with the 'Big Bang' in 1986) led to excessive **risk-taking** in financial markets, which contributed towards the recent recession.

3) Supply-side policies can be **unpopular**, and there are also concerns about whether some are **inequitable** (i.e. **unfair**).
   - For example, **benefit cuts** can lead to the poorest people in society worrying about their ability to cope financially.
   - **Greater flexibility** in the labour market and **trade-union reforms** could lead to some people having **less job security**.

> Inequality has increased in the UK since the early 1980s (see page 165).

4) So while a government may hope that improved economic performance will lead to **greater prosperity** overall in the **long term**, it can be very difficult in the short term to introduce some of these policies.

Warm-Up Questions

Q1 Why are suitable demand-side policies important if supply-side policies are to be effective?

Q2 Explain some of the possible criticisms of supply-side economic policies.

PRACTICE QUESTIONS

Exam Question

Q1 To what extent should government macroeconomic policy focus on supply-side policies rather than demand-side policies? [25 marks]

Supply-side policies aren't perfect — they're useless for making a lasagne...

In practice it's actually quite difficult to create increases in trend growth rate using supply-side policies. But at the moment, supply-side policies are economists' and governments' favourite tool for trying. So they're probably just going to have to try quite hard and for quite a long time, given that there are few alternatives around that are clearly better. Okay... see what you remember.

Different Approaches to Macroeconomic Policy

Government macroeconomic policy changes over time. One reason for this is that people's understanding of economics develops by seeing how successful (or unsuccessful) different policies have been in the past. **These pages are for all boards.**

Government Intervention became Popular as a result of the Great Depression

1) The **Great Depression** was a period of **falling output**, **deflation** and **high unemployment** around the world — the depression spread from the US, where it began in **1929**, and lasted until the late 1930s.

2) As the Great Depression hit the UK, **government revenue** fell, and the cost of providing **unemployment benefits** rose. The government was expected to face an increasing **budget deficit**.

3) In the 1920s the classical economic idea that **balancing the budget** is the government's **most important economic goal** was the mainstream view. This meant that the UK government followed **deflationary** fiscal policy of cutting government spending during the Great Depression. There were major cuts to **public sector pay** and **unemployment benefits**.

4) These cuts made things **worse** — unemployment kept rising, and the economy stayed in **recession**.

5) **Monetary policy** was also **contractionary**, because of Britain's membership of the **Gold Standard**:

   - The **Gold Standard** is a system where currency can be swapped for a fixed amount of gold from the **central bank**, so the amount of currency in the system is fixed, depending on how much gold the central bank holds.

   - This meant that countries in the Gold Standard couldn't use expansionary monetary policy (see page 173) such as expanding the **money supply** or lowering **interest rates**. It also meant that **exchange rates** were effectively fixed (with the pound overvalued, so British exports weren't competitive).

6) The economy only began to recover when Britain left the Gold Standard in 1931, and could then lower interest rates and devalue the pound. This had an **expansionary** effect — **consumption** and **investment** increased. For example, more houses were built, which provided **jobs** and contributed to **growth**. Increasing **defence spending** (in response to the rise of Nazi Germany) also had an expansionary effect.

   The US experienced similar problems with the Gold Standard, and similar positive effects when they left in 1933.

7) Economic policies in the US during the Great Depression (under President Hoover) were **laissez-faire** — this means leaving the economy to market forces, with minimal interference by the government.

8) Taxes were generally kept low to encourage businesses to **invest more** and consumers to **spend more**. However, as **government revenue** fell during the Great Depression, taxes were increased (as in the UK) to avoid a **budget deficit**.

9) As the depression **worsened** the government was criticised for not intervening to help the **unemployed** and **poor**.

10) In 1933, **Franklin D. Roosevelt** became the new President of the USA. Roosevelt ended laissez-faire policies, and introduced the '**New Deal**' — this included **expansionary policies** which increased government spending, e.g. government-funded **jobs** for the unemployed and large **infrastructure projects**.

"You sort out the economy, I'll vacuum the White House."

11) These projects reduced **unemployment** and **poverty**. However, unemployment began to **rise** again in the late 1930s. It eventually fell when **defence spending** during WW2 contributed to economic recovery (as it had in the UK).

Keynesian Fiscal Policy was Widely Used in the Mid 20th Century

1) The experience of the Great Depression contributed to rising interest in the work of **Keynes**, which argued that **government spending** could boost an economy during recession and get it back on track.

2) **Keynesian** demand management policies of adjusting **government spending** to control **economic growth** were popular in the middle of the 20th century — in the UK the government focused on **full employment**, and adjusted **taxation** and **spending** to influence demand and try and smooth out the **economic cycle**.

   This relies on the multiplier effect (page 131) to create an increase in national income that's bigger than the government spending.

3) There was **steady growth** and near **full employment** in the UK in the 1950s and 1960s, as well as fairly **low and stable inflation**. There were boom and bust cycles, but the downturns were fairly weak.

Different Approaches to Macroeconomic Policy

Keynesians think the Economy Adjusts Slowly

- **Keynesians** believe that the government often needs to **intervene** to get the economy closer to reaching **full employment**, and operating at **full capacity** (i.e. on the vertical part of the Keynesian LRAS curve — see page 141).

- They think when there's a shock like a recession that causes **aggregate demand** (AD) to drop, it takes a very long time for demand to recover, because **prices** and **wages adjust slowly**.   So the economy is likely to be operating **below** capacity (and below full employment) for a **long time**, unless the government steps in to **boost demand**.

- **Classical economists** think that the economy generally operates at full capacity (and full employment) on its own (i.e. it's usually on the classical LRAS curve — see page 140).

- They believe that when demand falls the economy **recovers quickly**, because **wages** and **prices** easily adjust.

- **Monetarists** take the **classical view**, i.e. the economy is quick to adjust back to full capacity.

EDEXCEL ONLY

Keynesian Policies were Questioned in the 1970s

1) **Inflation** began to rise in the late 1960s, and the UK economy became more **volatile** in the 1970s:
   - **Rising oil prices** and **wage demands** kept inflation high (between 1973 and 1974 oil prices trebled).
   - The economy was in **recession** during 1973 and 1974.
   - By 1975 **inflation** had reached 25%, and **unemployment** began to rise steeply.

   This was caused by a supply-side shock.

2) Many saw this as a **breakdown** of the Phillips curve relationship of inflation as the **trade-off** for full employment (there's more on this on page 162).

3) Keynesian **demand management policies**, which were based on this relationship, began to be **questioned**. It was argued that these policies were actually making things **worse**.

4) One of the main reasons for questioning these policies is that the government spending **multiplier effect** is **small** — partly because government spending is **paid for** by **taxes**, so **increases** in **government spending** may be **matched** by **increases** in **taxes** (a withdrawal from the circular flow).

5) There are a **few other reasons** why demand-side fiscal policy has become **less popular**:
   - Government spending 'crowds out' spending by the **private sector**, **discouraging enterprise**.
   - **Continuous** government spending, paid for by **borrowing**, will lead to **inflation**, a **budget deficit** and an **increase** in **national debt** (see p.170).
   - It's **difficult** to **control** the effects of fiscal policy. To be successful it requires **very accurate information**, and getting it wrong can lead to '**stop-go cycles**'.
   - Policies that **only** affect aggregate demand will lead to **conflicts** between the **four main macroeconomic objectives** (see p.160-161).

   A reflationary fiscal policy may cause an economy to 'overshoot' (i.e. grow too quickly), causing high inflation. A government may then 'apply the brakes' with a deflationary fiscal policy, which might cause a recession.

The government's approach to fiscal policy has Changed

Governments now generally use fiscal policy **differently** to the Keynesian approach:

Supply-side fiscal policy is used to increase **aggregate supply**, which will help a government to achieve all four of its main economic objectives (unlike demand-side fiscal policy). For example, **tax cuts** could be offered to entrepreneurs to encourage them to start up new businesses that will increase the **productive potential** of the economy.

Fiscal policy is used on a **microeconomic** level to influence the behaviour of **consumers** and **firms**. For example, **demerit goods** are **taxed** to decrease consumption, and **merit goods** can be provided by the state or **subsidised** to increase their consumption. Fiscal policy can also be used to help governments achieve their **environmental policy objectives**. For example, the government could introduce '**green taxes**' that discourage the use of coal or oil, or provide **subsidies** to firms that use renewable energy (e.g. solar or wind power).

Government spending can be directed at **specific regions** that need extra help. For example, if a region loses a big employer and is suffering from **structural unemployment**, then the government could **invest** in that region to **create jobs**, or encourage **firms** to move there with **subsidies** and **tax breaks**.

Progressive taxation allows the government to **redistribute** wealth from those who are **better off** to those who are **less well off** (for more see p.169).

But Keynesian fiscal policy was used during the 2008-2010 recession (see next page).

Different Approaches to Macroeconomic Policy

Guess what — another juicy double page of macroeconomic policy approaches. I'm far too good to you. Not all of this is for all boards, so you could skip some of it, but you might find it useful for understanding the stuff you do need to know. **All boards.**

EDEXCEL ONLY

Inflationary Policy was used in the UK and the US after the 2008 Financial Crisis

1) Fiscal policy has generally moved away from the **Keynesian** demand-side approach since the 1970s (see pages 178-179). But during the recession which followed the **2008 financial crisis** the UK government brought in policies aimed at stimulating the economy which used a more Keynesian approach.

2) Inflationary **fiscal policies** were used, such as:

   • A temporary **cut to VAT** from 17.5% to 15%, aimed at increasing consumer spending.
   • Bringing forward planned **capital expenditure** (see page 168), to raise national income during the downturn.
   • As well as this **discretionary policy**, spending increased through **automatic stabilisers** (see page 168).

3) Expansionary **monetary policy** was also used — the **base rate** was lowered to 0.5%. As this wasn't considered enough to boost demand, other monetary policies such as **quantitative easing** were also followed (see the next page for more).

4) This approach was influenced in part by the lesson of the **Great Depression**, where deflationary fiscal policy aimed at balancing the budget and an inability to use expansionary monetary policy had made the problem **worse** (see page 178).

5) Another contrast between the Great Depression and the 2008 financial crisis was the reaction to **bank failures**. During the Great Depression banks were allowed to **collapse**, which reduced the **money supply**, **damaged the economy** further, and caused **widespread panic** as people feared losing their savings. During the 2008 financial crisis the UK government used **public money** to take over several major banks and prevent them from failing. The US government followed a similar policy.

6) The post 2008 recession ended up being much **less severe** than the Great Depression, possibly because of these policies. However, the combined effect of the **crisis** and the **expansionary policies** resulted in the government running a large **budget deficit**, and **national debt** levels increased sharply.

7) After the worst of the crisis had passed, the government brought in **tax increases** to begin to deal with this, and after the change of government in 2010 policy became particularly focused on reducing the **budget deficit**. Deflationary fiscal policy was brought in, mostly in the form of **spending cuts**. There was also a **VAT increase** from 17.5% to 20%.

8) GDP growth per capita **fell** in the UK from 2010 to 2012. The Office for Budget Responsibility has stated that deflationary fiscal policy **reduced growth** in this period, but that other factors such as rising **oil prices** also contributed to falling GDP.

9) In the US, the initial response to the financial crisis was very similar — **interest rates** were lowered and **quantitative easing** was used. There was also a programme of **government funding** of banks and **investment** in the motor industry.

10) However, these inflationary measures have been phased out more **slowly** in the US than they were in the UK. Some economists think that this is one reason why the **recovery** from the financial crisis was **faster** in the US than in the UK. But there may have been **other factors** which contributed to this — the UK was more heavily affected by economic problems in the **EU** than the US. Also, **oil prices** increased much more in the UK than the US, which affected household income.

AQA ONLY

Funding for Lending and Forward Guidance aim to Stimulate Lending

After the 2008 financial crisis, bank **lending** to households and businesses was **falling**, which contributed to **slow growth**. **Funding for Lending** and **forward guidance** are policies to **encourage lending**, with the aim of stimulating the economy.

Funding for Lending was launched in July 2012. It involves the Bank of England lending money to commercial banks below market rates, with the intention that these cheap loans would be passed on to households and businesses.

The scheme was closed for household lending when the government decided the housing market had recovered, and was also adjusted to favour lending to small and medium sized businesses over large corporations.

The success of Funding for Lending has been questioned. More mortgages were approved and mortgage interest rates fell, but there may not have been much benefit for the wider economy. However, without the scheme things might have been worse.

Forward guidance involves the central bank publicly announcing its intentions to keep the base rate at a certain level for a set period of time, or while certain economic conditions remain (e.g. while unemployment is above a certain rate).

The aim is to allow businesses and individuals to plan their borrowing and spending, without having to worry about sudden changes in interest rates.

The Bank of England has used forward guidance since 2013.

Different Approaches to Macroeconomic Policy

Quantitative Easing injects New Money into the Economy

1) **Quantitative easing** (QE) is used when it's necessary to adopt a 'loose' monetary policy to **stimulate aggregate demand** (or create upwards pressure on **inflation**) at a time when interest rates are already very **low** (or **negative**).

2) QE **increases** the **money supply**, which will enable individuals and firms to spend more.

3) It involves the Bank of England (or another central bank) 'creating new money' and using it to **buy assets** owned by **financial institutions** and other firms. The hope is that these will then either **spend** the money or **lend** it to other people to spend.

Aggregate demand was low because the 2007 'credit crunch' (when banks suddenly cut back the amount they were willing to lend) had reduced aggregate demand.

4) QE was introduced in the UK in 2009. **Aggregate demand** needed to be stimulated after the **2008 recession**, but **interest rates** were already at a very **low** rate (0.5%).

Treasury bills are a form of government debt.

- The Bank of England **bought assets** (e.g. government Treasury bills) from firms such as insurance companies and commercial banks.

- However, QE was **slow to work** at first because the banks were still reluctant to lend money after the credit crunch. Instead they used it just to increase their reserves of money.

- Eventually these banks did begin to **lend** money to other firms and individuals — who used the money to, for example, invest in new machinery, start new businesses or buy houses.

- All of this spending boosted **aggregate demand** and led to an increase in the rate of **inflation** (see below).

5) Using QE to bring up the rate of inflation (rather than decreasing interest rates) has the added benefit that it will keep a **currency weak** (i.e. its exchange rate will remain low). This can increase the **competitiveness** of an economy and **boost exports**.

6) QE also provides a boost to overall **confidence** in an economy (especially during a recession), as consumers and firms see the central bank taking action.

7) One **danger** of using QE is that financial institutions may initially use this 'new money' to increase their reserves, and only **lend** it out when the **economy improves**. This **extra lending** at a time when **inflation** may already be **increasing** can lead to demand-pull inflation becoming harder to control.

Although the Bank of England could use QE 'in reverse' — i.e. sell assets to institutions to decrease the amount of money in circulation.

The Bank of England also has to consider the Wider Economy

1) The **main aim** of monetary policy in the UK is to ensure **price stability** — i.e. keep **inflation** close to its **target rate**. Under normal circumstances, this would mean that during a period of **high inflation**, interest rates would **increase**.

2) But between January 2010 and March 2012, inflation was **3%** or **higher** (and so was outside the 1% limit above the 2% target), but the Bank of England **kept** interest rates at 0.5% during this entire period and **continued** its use of QE.

3) The reason is that the UK economy had suffered some **'economic shocks'**, and there were concerns about the possibility of entering the second dip of a **'double dip'** recession.

4) The Bank of England reasoned that raising interest rates was **unnecessary** — it said inflation would fall **naturally** even without an interest rate rise, and that if it did increase interest rates, then a double dip recession was **more likely**.

5) Remember... as long as inflation is under control, the Bank has a duty to support the government's economic objectives. The Bank therefore continued with its very **loose monetary policy** in order not to further harm the economy.

Warm-Up Questions

Q1 Why has demand-side fiscal policy become less popular?
Q2 What is forward guidance?
Q3 Explain quantitative easing.

Exam Question

Q1 Briefly discuss differences in the UK policy responses to the Great Depression and the 2008 Financial Crisis. [6 marks]

I use quantitative easing to squeeze into my favourite jeans...

Lots to take in here, so go through it all carefully. Demand-side fiscal policy had gone out of fashion before the financial crisis, but it's had a bit of a comeback. It's got its problems though — amongst other things it can lead to overspending for little reward.

The Financial Sector and Financial Markets

The financial sector (i.e. everything to do with banks, shares, bonds, and so on) is vital to the smooth running of any major economy. But it's tricky to understand until you get a few basic ideas under your belt. **These pages are for all boards.**

The **Financial Sector** is a **Major Part** of the economy

1) The most basic purpose of banks and other financial institutions is to **make money available** to those who want to **spend** more than their income (e.g. a business wanting to expand) using the **savings** of those who **don't** currently want to spend (e.g. someone with savings in a bank account or a pension fund).

2) To do this, they:
   * Help people and firms **save** — through **bank accounts**, **pension funds**, **bonds** and other financial products.
   * Provide **loans** to **businesses** and **individuals**.
   * Allow **equities** and **bonds** to be issued and traded on **capital markets** (see p.183).

Everyday Forms of Borrowing for Individuals

* **Personal loans** are loans to **individuals** to be paid back over a **small number** of years. These can be **secured** (where a bank can force the sale of an asset, like a house, to recover the loan's cost if it isn't repaid) or **unsecured**. Unsecured loans have a **higher rate** of **interest** than secured loans because they're **riskier** (see p.185).
* **Mortgages** are loans to buy **property**. The bank **owns** the **property** until the loan is repaid.
* **Credit cards** allow their holders to **borrow** money from a bank when **purchasing goods** or **services**.
* **Pay-day loans** are **short-term**, **small**, **unsecured loans**, usually with **high rates** of **interest**.
* **Overdrafts** are loans to firms and individuals that occur when the **funds** in their account **fall below zero**. A **fee** might need to be paid for using an overdraft, and **interest** may need to be paid on the money borrowed.

Firms Use Equity and Debt Finance to Fund Their Activities

* **Equity finance** is raised by selling **shares** in a company. Raising funds in this way means that the person providing the finance (by buying shares) becomes a **shareholder** in the firm and can claim some **ownership** of it. This entitles the shareholder to a share of the firm's **profits** in the form of **dividends**.
* **Debt finance** is borrowing money that has to be **paid back** (usually with **interest**). This can involve **borrowing** from **financial institutions** (e.g. banks), or issuing **corporate bonds** (see p.183).

3) **Financial institutions** and **financial markets** also perform various other functions in an economy.
   * They make trade **easier** by allowing buyers to **make payments** quickly and easily.
   * They provide **insurance cover** to firms and individuals.

The financial sector **Helps Economic Growth**

1) **Effective** and **efficient** financial institutions and financial markets enable **economic growth** to **occur**, while **unstable** institutions and markets can cause **major problems**.

2) Economic growth is driven by the **spending** of **individuals** and **firms**, much of which relies on **credit**.

3) **Businesses** (small firms especially) are **unlikely to grow** without credit. If firms don't grow, this means **fewer new jobs** and lower **exports**.

4) Firms in **developing countries**, where the financial sector tends to be quite **weak** or **underdeveloped**, **struggle** to get **credit** and this **restricts** their growth.

The financial sector is the engine of an economy — necessary to make progress but a bit of a nightmare when it goes wrong.

The **Banking Industry** is **Regulated**

1) Banks are **private-sector** organisations that aim to make **profits** for their shareholders. But in some ways banks are treated quite **differently** from most other private firms.

2) This is partly because problems in a **bank** or in the **banking industry** can have an impact beyond those with bank savings — they could potentially **destabilise** a country's **whole economy** (see p.188).

3) **Greater profitability** in banking is also often associated with taking **bigger risks** (see p.185), so there are **incentives** for banks to take financial risks in the hope of making a large profit.

4) The **huge economic importance** of banks combined with the **incentive to take risks** means that banking is a **regulated industry** — i.e. there are **rules** to control the **behaviour** of banks, and **penalties** for any banks that **break** the rules.

5) **Financial institutions** are **regulated** to:
   * **Reduce** the **impacts** of **financial market failure**.
   * **Protect consumers** by **policing individuals** and **firms** to ensure that they act **fairly** and **legally**.
   * **Ensure** the **integrity** and **stability** of financial institutions and the **services** they provide.
   * **Maintain confidence** in the financial sector and **avoid sudden panics**.

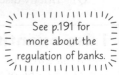

See p.191 for more about the regulation of banks.

The Financial Sector and Financial Markets

You need to know about **Three** types of **Financial Market**

Money Markets provide **Short-term Finance**

Money markets provide **short-term finance** to **banks** (and other financial institutions), **companies**, **governments** and **individuals**. This **short-term debt** will have a **maturity** (i.e. a repayment period) of **up to about a year** (and it could be as little as **24 hours**).

> Inter-bank lending (see p.186) is arranged via a money market.

Capital Markets provide **Medium** and **Long-term Finance**

1) Capital markets provide **governments** and **firms** with **medium-** and **long-term finance**. Governments and firms can raise finance by **issuing bonds** (see below). Firms can also raise finance by **issuing shares** (see p.182) or by **borrowing** from **banks**.

2) A capital market has a **primary market** and a **secondary market**:
   - The **primary market** is for **new share** and **bond issues**.
   - The **secondary market** is where **existing securities** are traded (e.g. a stock exchange). This **increases** their **liquidity** (i.e. being able to sell them means it's easier to 'convert them to spendable cash', see p.185).

> A security is basically a certificate with some kind of financial value which can be bought and sold (e.g. shares and bonds).

Different Currencies are bought and sold on the **Foreign Exchange Markets**

1) **Foreign exchange markets** are where **different currencies** are **bought** and **sold**. This is usually done to allow **international trade** and **investment**, or as **speculation** (to make money on fluctuations in currency prices).

2) A foreign exchange market is split into what's known as the **spot market** and the **forward market**:
   - The **spot market** is for **transactions** that happen **now**.
   - The **forward market** is for transactions that will happen at an agreed time in the **future**.

Forward Markets: Prices are agreed on the day of the deal, but delivery happens later

- On a forward market, contracts (called **futures**) are made at a **price agreed today** but for **delivery later**.
- Futures are useful for firms who **export** and **import** goods, as they '**lock in**' an agreed exchange rate between the buyer's and seller's currencies. This **certainty** allows both firms to be more confident about their **future plans**.
- Either firm **could** lose out if the exchange rate changes, but this '**risk sharing**' encourages more trade.
- Forward markets also exist for **commodities** — e.g. a price for a future trade in coffee can be agreed **in advance**.

AQA ONLY

Bonds are a form of **Borrowing**

1) Governments and large firms can issue bonds to **raise money** (e.g. a government might need to finance a **budget deficit**, while a firm might want to **invest** in new machinery).

> UK government bonds are called 'gilts'.

2) Investors buy new bonds at their 'face value' (called the **nominal value**) and become **bondholders**.

3) **Interest** is paid to the bondholder — the **amount** of interest paid (e.g. £5 per year) is called the **coupon**.

4) After they've been issued, bonds can be traded in **secondary capital markets**. Investors can buy or sell bonds at **any price** — this '**market price**' may be **bigger** or **smaller** than the bond's **nominal value**. Coupons are paid to the **current bondholder**.

5) The bond's **yield** is the annual **return** an investor will get from the bond. The **less** someone pays for a bond, the **higher** its **yield**.

$$\text{Yield} = \frac{\text{Coupon}}{\text{Market price}} \times 100$$

> Calculate the yield on a bond with a **coupon** of **£6** and a current **market price** of **£75**.
>
> $$\text{Yield} = \frac{\text{Coupon}}{\text{Market price}} \times 100 \implies \text{Yield} = \frac{£6}{£75} \times 100 = 8\%$$

> The coupon might be described as a percentage of the nominal value. E.g. a coupon of 6% per year on a bond with a nominal value of £100 would pay £6 per year.

6) When the bond **matures**, the **current bondholder** is paid the **nominal value** of the bond by the issuer. This means the issuer's original **debt** has been **repaid**.

Warm-Up Questions

Q1 What is the difference between a money market and a capital market?

> PRACTICE QUESTIONS

Exam Question

Q1 Explain the importance of regulation in the banking industry. [4 marks]

Ahhh, corporate and government bonds — I've been expecting you...

There's quite a bit of economics-y jargon being thrown around on these pages. Stick with it — things will get better.

Banks and Money

Banks and Money — now <u>this</u> is what I expect to see in an Economics book.
These pages cover different types of bank, as well as other types of financial institution. **These pages are for all boards.**

Learn the **Difference** between **Commercial** and **Investment Banks**

Commercial Banks

1) Commercial banks (e.g. TSB and NatWest) have these **main roles**:
   - To **accept savings**.
   - To **lend** to individuals and firms.
   - To be **financial intermediaries** (i.e. move funds from lenders to borrowers).
   - To allow **payments** from one person or firm to another.

2) Commercial banks also provide **other financial services** to customers, such as **insurance** and **financial advice**.

3) Commercial banking is split into **two areas**:
   - **Retail banking** — providing services for **individuals** and **smaller firms** (e.g. savings accounts and mortgages). Retail banks are often called 'High Street banks'.
   - **Wholesale banking** — dealing with **larger firms'** banking needs. ← *The term 'commercial banking' is sometimes used to mean just wholesale banking.*

4) Commercial banks help **firms grow** by providing **loans** and **financial advice**, and by facilitating **overseas trade**.

Investment Banks

1) Investment banks **don't** take deposits from customers. Instead, their role is to:
   - Arrange **share** and **bond issues**.
   - Offer advice on **raising finance**, and on **mergers and acquisitions**.
   - **Buy and sell securities** (e.g. shares and bonds) on behalf of their clients.
   - Act as **market makers** to make trading in securities easier. ← *A market maker for a security allows companies and individuals to buy and sell that security without the need to use a stock exchange.*

2) Investment banks also engage in **higher risk** (but potentially very **profitable**) activities. For example, **proprietary trading** involves a bank buying and selling shares using its **own money**.

Commercial Banks can also Operate as Investment Banks

- Many large banks operate as **both** commercial **and** investment banks (e.g. Barclays and HSBC).
- Allowing banks to operate as **both commercial banks** and **investment banks** creates a **systemic risk** (i.e. a risk that a **whole market** or even the **whole financial system** might collapse), because banks may wish to **use deposits** from the **commercial banking side** of their business to **fund investment banking activity**. If they **lose money** in **bad investments** then **their depositors' money** could be at risk.

Banks **Aren't** the only **Financial Institutions**

There are **other financial institutions** operating in global financial markets — it's not just banks. For example:

- **Pension funds** — these **collect** people's **pension savings** and **invest** them in **securities**. When a client **retires**, the pension fund **pays out** their savings and the **returns** they've generated. Pension funds also provide **long-term**, **large-scale investment** in **companies**.

- **Insurance firms** — insurance firms **charge** customers fees to provide **insurance cover** against all kinds of risk. This is important for the economy — e.g. businesses can insure against the risk of customers **not paying** (which **encourages trade**).

- **Hedge funds** — firms that invest **pooled funds** from different contributors in the hope of receiving **high returns**. They usually invest in a number of **different markets**, but the desire for **high returns** (and the fact that they're only **lightly regulated**) can lead to **risks** for the contributors, and for the wider economy (see below).

- **Private equity firms** — these **invest** in **businesses** (e.g. by buying equity) and then try to make the **maximum return**. This could mean helping a business become **successful** so that it can be **sold** for a **profit**. However, they're often **criticised** for **asset-stripping** (selling a firm's assets) and **cutting jobs**.

The Shadow Banking System

- The shadow banking system includes **unregulated financial intermediaries** and the **unregulated activities** of **otherwise regulated** financial institutions. The shadow banking system has become **much larger** in **recent years** (but since it isn't regulated, it's hard to tell exactly how large).
- **Hedge funds** and **private equity firms** are often considered part of the shadow banking system.
- The shadow banking system supplies an **increasing** amount of **credit**.
- But the lack of **regulation**, the absence of the sort of **emergency support** available to normal banks (see p.190), and its **large** (but **unknown**) **size** add to the risk of the shadow banking system helping to cause a **financial crisis**.

Banks and Money

Saying what's meant by 'the money supply' isn't easy — money doesn't have to mean just banknotes and coins.

Money has Different Levels of Liquidity

1) Any **financial instrument** (e.g. coins, notes, shares, bonds) that **satisfies** the four main **functions** of money (see p.37), and that's also **portable**, **widely accepted**, **difficult to forge** and **durable** can be classified as **money** and counted as part of the **money supply**.

2) Different types of money (and other assets) have different levels of **liquidity**. Liquidity refers to **how easily** something can be **spent** — for example, notes and coins are **very liquid** because they can be **spent easily**, but **shares** (and **houses**) are **less liquid** (they're **illiquid**) because they need to be **converted** into **cash** before they can be used to buy things.

3) Economists have '**narrow**' and '**broad**' **definitions** of money, based on the **liquidity** of the different forms.

> • **Narrow money** refers to the **notes** and **coins** in **circulation**, plus **balances** held at a **central bank**. In other words, narrow money consists of financial instruments that are **very liquid**.
>
> • **Broad money** includes assets that are **less liquid**, as well as all of the things that make up narrow money.

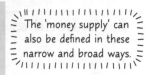
The 'money supply' can also be defined in these narrow and broad ways.

Banks have to Balance Profitability and Liquidity

1) Banks are businesses, and one of their aims is to **maximise profits** for the benefit of their shareholders.

2) The **rate of return** on **illiquid assets** (e.g. corporate bonds) is generally **higher** than that on more **liquid assets** (e.g. deposits at the Bank of England). So banks **don't** want to have too many liquid assets.

3) However, banks need to have a certain amount of liquid assets available. This is because banks tend to **lend** money over a **long term** — i.e. they're paid back over a long period of time. But **depositors** who give their money to banks expect to be able to withdraw their savings **immediately**.

4) So banks need **enough** liquidity to be able to **repay depositors** when asked, but **not too much** liquidity, or they might become **unprofitable**. This means they have to calculate very carefully the amount of **liquid reserves** they hold.

5) Banks actually rely on depositors **not all** wanting to withdraw their savings at the **same time**. If **too many** depositors want to withdraw their money at short notice, a bank may not have the **liquidity** to be able to repay them (and it **can't** immediately demand money **back** that it's **lent** out **long-term**).

6) This usually **won't** be a problem, as it's **very unlikely** everyone would suddenly decide to withdraw their savings at the same time.

7) However, if people thought their savings were **at risk** for any reason, then lots of people probably **would** withdraw their savings very quickly (this is called a '**run on the bank**'), and the bank could quite quickly **run out** of liquid assets.

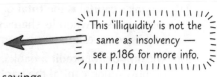
This 'illiquidity' is not the same as insolvency — see p.186 for more info.

8) This is why it's really important that people **trust** the banking system with their savings. It's also why a **central bank** is needed to act as an emergency **lender of last resort** (see p.190).

Risk is Profitable but... Risky

1) **Risk** is a key idea in finance. All other things being equal, risky investments will **usually** generate a **higher return** (i.e. be more profitable) than less risky ones. Investors will want **high rewards** for **risking** their money. This is why different **interest rates** are charged in different **money markets** — the **more secure** an investment is, the **lower** the rate of interest that will be earned.

2) All investors (including banks) must **balance** the **security** of an investment against its **profitability**.

3) This is especially important if an investor is using **someone else's money**, or if the firm they're working for is particularly important to the **stability** of the financial system.

See next page for more about how banks balance profitability, liquidity and security.

Warm-Up Questions

Q1 What is an investment bank?

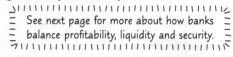

Exam Question

Q1 Explain why a bank's need for liquidity is not compatible with its desire to maximise profits. [4 marks]

These pages are a bit dry — they need some liquidity...

Remember, banks are businesses, so they need to make profit in order to be successful. However, the need to make profit sometimes conflicts with the job that banks must perform for their customers. That's when problems can occur.

Banking and Interest Rates

Banks do a bit more these days than lock up loads of money in big vaults. **This page is for AQA and OCR only.**

AQA & EDEXCEL

Commercial banks **Create Credit** and **Money**

1) Most of the money in the economy is **created** by commercial banks when they **make loans**.

2) When a **loan** is **granted**, the bank creates a **deposit** in the **customer's account** — this is new money, so it **increases** the **money supply**.

3) The customer becomes a **debtor** of the bank — they need to repay the loan, plus interest.
   - The loan is an **asset** for the bank (anything that's **owned by** or **owed to** the bank is an asset).
   - The customer's deposit is a **liability** for the bank (anything that the bank **owes** is a liability).

The deposit counts as a liability because if the customer wanted to withdraw it, the bank would have to pay.

Banks **Lend** to **Each Other**

1) **Inter-bank lending** is lending **between banks** and occurs on the **inter-bank lending market** (a **money market**). The loans given between the banks are **very short-term** — usually **less** than **one week**, and often only **overnight**.

2) On any day, some banks will have **excess liquidity** and others will have a **shortage** (e.g. because they've received more or less than they expected in payments). Inter-bank lending means that banks with a **temporary shortage** of liquidity can **borrow** to **meet** their **customers' needs**. Banks with excess liquidity **earn interest** on what they lend.

3) The **rate** charged is called the **inter-bank lending rate**, or the **overnight rate**.

Banks have **Balance Sheets**

1) Like all businesses, banks have **balance sheets**. A bank's balance sheet is a **snapshot** of its **assets** and **liabilities** on a particular date.

2) On a balance sheet, total assets should always **equal** total liabilities.

Levels of **Capital** are **Vital**

1) A bank's **capital** is the **total** of its **share capital** (the money raised when its shares were **first issued**) and its **reserves** (made up from **retained profits**).

2) The amount of **credit** a bank can create depends on how much **capital** the bank holds. This is because banks will usually want to keep the **ratio** of **loans to capital** within a certain **limit** (and central banks sometimes **insist** on it — see p.191).

3) If the value of one of the bank's assets **falls**, the bank's **capital** is **reduced** by the **same amount** (so that **total assets** still equal **total liabilities**).

For example, if a borrower defaults on a loan, the value of that loan as an asset would fall, and the bank's level of capital would also fall.

4) If the total value of a bank's assets falls by a **large amount**, the bank could **'run out'** of capital (i.e. if the bank's capital is less than the amount lost). The value of the bank's **assets** would be **less than** the value of its **liabilities** and the bank would be **insolvent**. An insolvent bank would normally have to **close down** — central banks **don't** usually lend to **insolvent** banks.

XYZ Commercial Bank — Balance Sheet: Jan 1st

Assets		Most liquid
	Cash (notes & coins)	
	Balances at the Bank of England Most UK banks will have an account with the Bank of England.	
	Money at call and short notice Funds the bank has lent out, but which it can insist are repaid very quickly — e.g. inter-bank lending.	
	Commercial and Treasury Bills These are securities issued by companies or governments — they're similar to bonds, but the interest is paid in a slightly different way.	
	Investments (e.g. bonds)	
	Advances (money the bank has lent out e.g. loans and mortgages)	
	Fixed assets (e.g. land and buildings)	Least liquid
Liabilities	**Deposits from savers**	
	Short-term borrowing (e.g. from money markets)	
	Long-term borrowing (e.g. bonds the bank has issued)	
	Reserves (retained profits)	
	Share capital	

A bank's capital is a liability, because if the bank ceased trading, this money would be returned to shareholders (once all the bank's outstanding debts had been paid).

Banks need to achieve a balance of **Liquidity, Security** and **Profitability**

A bank will aim to hold a **variety** of different types of asset to achieve a suitable balance of **liquidity, security** and **profitability**. For example, **unsecured** loans are more **profitable** (but **riskier**) than **secured** loans (e.g. mortgages).

- If someone defaults on a **secured** loan (e.g. a mortgage), the bank can **repossess** the house (or other asset) that's been used as **security** (and the value of the bank's assets doesn't fall too much).
- If someone defaults on an **unsecured** loan, that asset is **removed** from the bank's balance sheet.

Banking and Interest Rates

Right... a page about interest rates. This is harder than it looks, so concentrate. **This page is for OCR and AQA only.**

OCR ONLY

Interest Rates are determined by Supply and Demand

You need to be able to explain, using a **diagram**, how **interest rates are determined**. Here are a couple of **examples** that show how it can be done.

The Loanable Funds Theory says interest rates are set by Savers and Borrowers

1) **Loanable funds** are the total amount of money available for **borrowing**. The loanable funds theory says the **interest rate** is **determined** by the **supply of**, and **demand for**, **loanable funds**.

2) At **higher** interest rates, the **supply** of loanable funds will **be higher** (since people **save more**) and **demand** will **be lower** (since people **borrow less**).

3) The market for loanable funds is at **equilibrium** where the supply and demand curves cross — the interest rate (IR_e) is the **equilibrium price**.

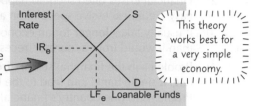

This theory works best for a very simple economy.

The Liquidity Preference Theory says people balance Risk and Reward

1) In the **liquidity preference theory**, **demand** for liquid money depends on how people want to hold their wealth.

2) The theory assumes that people can hold their wealth **either** as **liquid money** **or** in the form of **illiquid bonds**:
   - Holding your wealth as bonds means you **earn interest** (i.e. your wealth will **steadily increase**). But the **price** of bonds **changes** — this means your **wealth** could go **down** if the price of bonds falls.
   - The **value** of liquid money is **stable** — this means your wealth **won't fall**, but it **won't earn interest**.

   For the purposes of this theory, '**bonds**' means '**any illiquid interest-earning asset whose price can change**', while '**liquid money**' is best thought of as '**cash in your pocket**' (i.e. it's **not** in a bank account **earning interest**).

3) If interest rates are **high**, bonds are **more attractive** — the **reward** of the interest **outweighs** the **risk** of a price fall. If interest rates are **low**, bonds are **less attractive** — the **risk** of a price fall **outweighs** the **reward** of the interest.

4) **Demand** for **liquid money** also depends on people's **expectations** of **future** interest rates.
   - When interest rates are **high**, people might expect them to **fall** soon, which will lead to a **bond-price increase** (see below). **Speculators** expecting this will want to hold their wealth as **bonds** and will demand less **liquid money**.
   - Similarly, **demand** for liquid money might **increase** if interest rates are **low** (as speculators will be expecting them to **rise** soon, leading to a **bond-price fall**).

5) The result is that **high** interest rates mean **demand** for money is **low**, and **low** interest rates mean **demand** for money is **high**. In other words, the **liquidity preference schedule** (**LP**, the **demand curve** for money) slopes **downwards**.

6) The interest rate (IR_e) is at the **equilibrium** between **supply** (MS) and **demand** (LP).

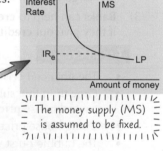

The money supply (MS) is assumed to be fixed.

OCR ONLY

Interest Rates can be expressed in Nominal Terms and Real Terms

1) A **nominal** rate of interest is one that **hasn't** been **adjusted** to allow for **inflation**.

2) **Real** rates of interest have been **adjusted** to show changes in the **purchasing power** of money that's been saved. They're defined as: **Real rate of interest = Nominal rate of interest – Rate of inflation** E.g. if a bank offered a **nominal** interest rate of **5%** but **inflation** was **3%**, the **real** rate of interest would be **2%**.

AQA ONLY

Market Interest Rates and Bond Prices have an Inverse Relationship

The **yield** of a bond will approximately match the **rate of interest** on other investments with **similar risk levels**. This means that as interest rates **rise**, bond prices **fall**, and vice versa.

E.g. A bond with a nominal value of £100 was issued with a coupon of £5 per annum (i.e. 5% of the nominal value). If **interest rates** are currently **8%**, find the **approximate market price** of the bond.

$$\text{Yield} = \frac{\text{Coupon}}{\text{Market price}} \times 100 \implies \text{Market price} = \frac{\text{Coupon}}{\text{Yield}} \times 100 = \frac{£5}{8} \times 100 = £62.50$$

Interest rates have risen from 5% to 8%, leading to a fall in the bond's price.

Exam Question

Q1 Explain, using the loanable funds theory, how interest rates are determined. [9 marks]

I have nominal interest in these theories — sorry, I mean, *real* interest...
I know what you're thinking... but I'm afraid it's too late to switch from Economics to something easier (e.g. rocket science).

Financial Market Failure

Market failure in the financial sector can have huge consequences for a whole economy.
So it's a good idea to understand the kind of things that can lead to market failure. **These pages are for all boards.**

A **Financial Crisis** can create a **Systemic Risk**

1) There are various kinds of **financial crisis** — e.g. a sudden sharp fall in the **price of assets** (e.g. shares or houses), or a **government defaulting** on its loans.

2) Financial crises often seem to happen after a **long period** of **prosperity** (e.g. because of low interest rates, easy credit, excessive speculation and overconfidence), and often lead to a **recession**.

3) It usually takes **longer** for an economy to recover after a recession accompanied by a **financial crisis** than it would from a 'normal' recession.

4) Problems in the financial sector also involve **systemic risk** — the risk that a problem in one part (e.g. a single bank) can lead to the breakdown of a **whole market** or perhaps even the **whole financial system**. Problems in one country's financial sector can also **quickly spread** around the world. What looks like a fairly minor local problem can quickly become a much more **serious** international situation.

Banks have helped to create **Market Bubbles**

1) **Speculation** means aiming to make a profit by **buying** assets **relatively cheaply** and **selling** them at a **higher price**. Speculation always carries some **risk** (because if asset prices **fall**, a speculator will **lose money**).

2) Excessively **high estimates** of future **asset price rises** can lead to **market bubbles** (or 'asset price bubbles'). For example:

   See also p.148.

   - Investors **expecting** the **price** of an **asset** to **continue to rise** can **overpay**, creating a **market bubble** (where **prices** in a market are much greater than the assets' true worth).

   - When investors eventually **lose confidence**, the **bubble** will **'burst'** and investors will **rush** to **sell** their assets to avoid large losses. This leads to **prices plummeting**, leaving investors with **large debts** (if they **borrowed** the money they invested) and **worthless assets**.

3) **Banks** can help to **create market bubbles** if they give out **credit** too easily.

   Speculators often borrow the money to fund their purchases.

Credit Crunch

- The **financial crisis of 2008** was partially caused by a speculative bubble in the US housing market.
- Growth in the **'sub-prime'** mortgage market (the mortgage market for borrowers with a poor credit rating) caused **house prices** to rise, as demand increased.
- Rising house prices led to more and more people investing in property, **pushing prices up** further.
- The bubble burst when people who'd taken on mortgages they couldn't afford began to **default**, and **house prices** began to **fall**.
- This meant that banks' levels of **capital** fell (see p.186), so banks **reduced** their **lending**, creating a **'credit crunch'**.
- This triggered a **loss of confidence** in the wider economy, a **fall** in **aggregate demand**, and a deep **recession**.

Externalities exist in Financial Markets

1) There are **negative externalities** in financial markets. Some of these come about because of the **importance** of banks and the financial sector to the **wider economy**.

2) In the financial sector, **mismanagement** of **risk** is one cause of externalities.

3) For example, the risks financial institutions took that eventually led to the **2008 financial crisis** were 'paid for' by **taxpayers** — government money was used to prevent the collapse of major banks.

The bank's risk adviser admitted that, to a non-expert, the health and safety info might seem excessive, but he was taking no chances after last week's fiasco.

4) Other negative externalities of the 2008 financial crisis included **large drops** in **GDP**, **falling salary levels** for many workers, and a **significant rise** in **unemployment**.

Too Big to Fail

- The need for a bailout of the banks was partly because some were considered to be **'too big to fail'** — they had become **so big** that a **systemic risk** was created.
- If **one or two** of these large banks collapsed, it could have led to **panic** and a run on other banks, causing them (and possibly the **whole financial sector**) to collapse.
- The UK government felt it **had to rescue** these banks, even though it cost **billions** of pounds.

Financial Market Failure

Asymmetric Information leads to Adverse Selection and Moral Hazard

1) **Asymmetric information** (see p.82) occurs when **one party** to a contract (e.g. a seller) has **less information** than the **other party** (e.g. a buyer).

2) For example, borrowers often **know better** than lenders **how likely** it is that they'll be able to **repay** a loan.

3) Asymmetric information can lead to **adverse selection** and **moral hazard**:

- **Adverse selection** occurs when the **most likely buyers** of a product are those that the **seller** would probably prefer **not** to sell to (and the seller may not be able to tell the difference between a 'good buyer' and a 'bad one' at the time of the sale).
- Adverse selection leads to a firm unknowingly taking **greater risks** than it intended.
- Adverse selection can be a problem in some **insurance** markets.
  - For example, suppose a company sells **medical insurance**. It will calculate the insurance **premiums** (the **cost** of buying a policy) based on who it believes is likely to buy it.
  - However, the premiums might be **too high** for people to be willing to pay if they're in **good health** (these people would be very **profitable** for the insurance company, as they'll need less medical treatment).
  - But it might be **good value** for those in **poor health** (who will require **more** medical treatment and who could therefore **cost** the company large amounts of money).
  - This results in the insurance company selling only to the **most unprofitable** customers — i.e. the company **risks** making a huge **financial loss** that could lead to it **collapsing**.
  - And if the insurance company **increases** its premiums to try and solve the problem, the result is that the problem will just get **worse** (since the only people willing to pay these even **higher** insurance premiums would be those in the **worst** health).

- **Moral hazard** occurs when someone is more willing to **take risks** because they know that **someone else** will have to pay the **consequences** if anything goes **wrong**.
- For example, a bank might **provide risky loans** (to chase higher profits) if it **knows** that it'll be **bailed out** by taxpayers if things go wrong.

See p.82 for more about moral hazard.

EDEXCEL ONLY

Market Rigging is Illegal and leads to Market Failure

1) **Market rigging** occurs when traders on financial markets, or others working in the financial sector, **collude** to **deliberately manipulate markets** to make **huge profits** for themselves and the firms they work for.

2) For example, they may make the **demand** for securities appear **higher** than it really is to artificially 'inflate' their price. This **prevents** the market from **working** as it should.

3) There are **laws** and **regulations** designed to **stop market rigging** and **punish** those that engage in it, but if the **penalties aren't tough enough**, or the laws **aren't strictly enforced**, then they **won't** be a **deterrent**.

4) In recent years many banks have been **fined billions of pounds** by regulators for market rigging. Some of the biggest fines have been as a result of rigging **foreign exchange markets** as banks colluded on the buying and selling of currencies.

Warm-Up Questions

Q1 Give three examples of market failure in the financial sector.

Q2 Briefly explain why some banks might be considered 'too big to fail'.

Exam Question

Q1 Which of the following is **not** an example of market failure in the financial markets?
A) Banks increasing interest rates charged to higher-risk customers.
B) Bankers giving loans to lots of customers, including those with a high risk of defaulting.
C) Traders using insider information to make large profits.
D) Banks reducing their liquidity, knowing a central bank will not allow them to collapse.

[1 mark]

Money laundering can lead to market bubbles...

What made the financial crisis so bad was that a lot of these forms of market failure occurred at once, creating a big mess. That's why governments are keen to avoid the same mistakes and have introduced more regulations (see pages 191-192).

The Role of the Central Bank

This page builds on the information about central banks and their activities back in Section Eleven, so you should read this page with those things in mind (e.g. the role of the central bank in controlling inflation). **This page is for all boards.**

Central Banks act as a Lender of Last Resort to banks

1) Central banks play an important role in a country's **economy**. Two key roles are to:
   - Act as a **banker** to the **government** (see below).
   - Help to **support banks** by acting as a **lender of last resort.** ← *A central bank is a kind of 'banker to the banks'.*

2) A **lender of last resort** is crucial for a country's **financial stability**.
   - Because banks **borrow short-term** but **lend long-term**, they can sometimes face a **shortage of liquidity** (p.185).
   - If an individual bank that's **solvent** (i.e. it has enough assets to meet all its liabilities, see p.186) faces a temporary shortage of liquidity, the central bank can 'provide liquidity' by **lending** the bank **money**.
   - The **Bank of England** has different schemes to **provide liquidity** to banks — a **predictable** and 'routine' need for liquidity is dealt with under one scheme, while 'emergency' liquidity problems are dealt with under another.
   - The central bank charges a **higher** rate of interest for emergency funds to create an **incentive** for the bank to behave **more carefully** in the future.

3) Central banks can also take action at times of **systemic crisis** (i.e. when it's not just a single bank that's in trouble). This **more widespread** type of emergency intervention happened during the 2008 financial crisis — central banks in various countries provided 'emergency liquidity assistance' to ensure banking stability.

4) Having central banks acting as a **lender of last resort** has **advantages**:
   - It helps to **prevent panic** and a **run on the banks**.
   - It helps to reduce the **impact** of **financial instability**.

5) However, it also has **disadvantages**:
   - It can lead to **moral hazard** (see p.189) and encourage banks to take **excessive risks**.
   - It can lead to banks not holding **sufficient liquidity**.
   - It can seem **unfair** that the central bank will try to **save** financial institutions, but **not** non-financial firms.

Central banks have various Other Functions

They act as 'banker to the government'

- A central bank can help the government **manage** its **national debt** — e.g. by trying to reduce the interest paid. This might involve issuing government **bonds**.
- It can also offer **advice** to the government on economic matters, and help them in their **negotiations** with other **international financial organisations**.

They can help regulate the financial sector

A central bank can **impose rules** to prevent financial **market failure** and **instability** (see p.191 for more on regulating the financial sector).

Macroeconomic stability in an economy is unlikely without financial stability.

They can implement monetary policy

- A central bank can manage the money supply by affecting the availability of credit or its cost. This is mainly done through controlling interest rates, but it can also be done through other methods, such as quantitative easing.
- It can also affect the amount of loans banks make by setting capital requirements (see p.191) — i.e. the reserves of capital a bank must keep.
- It can influence the exchange rate through buying and selling currencies and changing interest rates.
- It's also usually responsible for controlling the issuing of banknotes and ensuring that confidence in the currency is maintained (e.g. by working to prevent the counterfeiting of banknotes). *See Section 11 for more.*

1) While a central bank **can** do all of these things, what they actually do **varies** from country to country — some governments will give certain tasks to particular **government departments** or to **other organisations** instead.

2) For example, in the UK, it's the **Debt Management Office** (**not** the Bank of England) that **issues** 'gilts' (government bonds).

Exam Question

Q1   Evaluate the argument that central banks should act as a lender of last resort to banks.   [8 marks]

The Debt Management Office — or my parents, as I sometimes call them...

Central banks play a really important role in the financial sector — essentially they're there to keep things ticking over and manage any crises. Despite having their disadvantages, they provide an added layer of protection in case things go wrong.

Regulation of Financial Markets

The 2008 financial crisis has been described as a 'perfect storm' of market failure, which was partly caused by poor regulation of the financial markets. Now, governments are trying to put this right. **These pages are for all boards.**

In the past, **Financial Markets** were **Less Regulated**

1) From the **mid-1980s** until the **2008 financial crisis**, **regulation** in many financial markets across the world **wasn't very strict**. This was partly due to a process of **deregulating financial markets** in the **1980s** known as the Big Bang.

2) Less regulation in the financial markets helped them to be **more profitable**.

3) But a lack of regulation in the financial sector also led to **market failure** and other problems which contributed to **instability**:

In the UK, deregulation has been a key factor in helping London to become a major financial centre.

- **Excessive risk-taking** by financial institutions — e.g. many financial institutions, especially investment banks, made **very risky investments** in the hope of making **large profits**.

- **Commercial banks** acting as investment banks — the **deregulation of investment banking** in the **1980s** led to many commercial banks getting involved in investment banking activities. When some of those banks made **massive losses** in their **investment banking activities** during the 2008 financial crisis, it also affected their **commercial banking**.

- **Fraud** and other **illegal activity** — e.g. several major banks have been involved in **market rigging** (see p.189).

- The **growth of market bubbles** — speculative bubbles, e.g. in the housing market, were **allowed** to **develop**, and were **made worse** by the **over-provision of credit** (see p.188).

Regulation of financial markets targets the **Causes** of **Market Failure**

1) Since the financial crisis, governments have tried to **improve** the **regulation** of financial markets.

2) **Regulation** usually **focuses on**:

- **Competition** — making financial markets **competitive** to **benefit consumers**.

- The **structure** of **firms** and **risk management** — ensuring firms are **stable**. This might be achieved by requiring banks to meet **capital and liquidity ratios**, or by **preventing them** from taking **excessive risks** (and making senior individuals within the bank **personally accountable** if they do).

A bank's capital is the funds it holds from profits and issuing shares (see p.186).

Capital and Liquidity Ratios

- A 'capital ratio' measures the ratio of a bank's **capital to loans**. It gives a measure of the **risks** associated with the bank's lending, and of the bank's **stability**.

- A 'liquidity ratio' measures the ratio of **highly liquid assets** to the **expected short-term need for cash**. It also gives an idea of the bank's **stability**, as well as its ability to meet its **short-term liabilities**.

- Using these two ratios **together** gives a better understanding of the bank's **overall stability**.

- Strengthening **rules** and **principles** that financial institutions **must abide by**, or face **tough punishments** if they don't.

- **Systemic risks** — **identifying** systemic risks in the financial markets and finding ways to **manage** or **remove them**.

E.g. plans are now made to allow banks to 'fail safely' if necessary — i.e. allow a bank to go bust without disrupting the whole financial system. The hope is that this will encourage safer banking practices, because banks will know they won't be bailed out.

3) There are **two types** of financial regulation:

- **Microprudential regulation** — to ensure that **individual firms** act fairly towards their customers and **don't** take excessive risks or break the law.

- **Macroprudential regulation** — to tackle **systemic risks** (see p.188) in financial markets and **avoid large-scale financial crises** that can hurt a country's economy.

4) As well as regulation introduced by individual governments, there have been **international agreements** to regulate financial markets. For example, the **Basel Committee** (a committee of global banking authorities), have made recommendations on **minimum liquidity and capital levels** for banks. These should help to **increase** the **financial stability** of banks by making sure they have a **buffer** in case of a **fall** in **asset values** or a **bank run**.

5) Several countries have brought in (or are soon to bring in) a policy of '**ring fencing**' commercial banking activity. This means keeping the commercial banking side of a bank **separate** from the investment banking side. For example, since 2019, UK banks with a large commercial side **aren't** allowed to use the **deposits** of **retail customers** and **small firms** for their investment banking activities.

> Remember, **regulation** is likely to have some **drawbacks** (see p.93) and **regulators** can be vulnerable to **regulatory capture** (see p.99). If the regulation of the financial markets is **too strict** it can lead to **restrictions** on **credit** which **harm economic growth**. It may also lead to the **growth** of the **shadow banking system**, which **isn't regulated**.

Regulation of Financial Markets

In the UK, the **Bank of England** and the **Financial Conduct Authority** (FCA) are responsible for **regulating financial markets**.

The Bank of England

The **Bank of England** regulates the financial markets through the work of **two** bodies under its control — the **Financial Policy Committee** (FPC) and the **Prudential Regulation Authority** (PRA). The FPC is a **macroprudential regulator** and the PRA is a **microprudential regulator**, but they **work together** to ensure the **stability** of financial markets.

Financial Policy Committee (FPC)

The work of the FPC involves:

- **Identifying, monitoring** and **protecting against systemic risks** in the financial system.
- **Issuing instructions** to the **PRA** and **FCA** (see below) to tackle problems that threaten the financial system.
- **Advising the government** on managing the financial markets.

Prudential Regulation Authority (PRA)

The work of the PRA involves maintaining the stability of banks and promoting effective competition by:

- **Supervising** firms and financial institutions to ensure that they **successfully manage risk**.
- Setting **industry standards** for **conduct** and **management** and making sure they're followed.
- **Specifying capital and liquidity ratios** (see p.191) for financial institutions.

Financial Conduct Authority (FCA)

The **FCA** is a **microprudential regulator** which aims to **protect consumers** and **increase confidence** in **financial institutions** and **products**. It does this by:

- **Supervising** the **conduct** of **firms** and **markets** to ensure that things are done **legally** and **fairly**.
- **Promoting competition** in financial markets so that **better deals** are provided for **consumers**.
- **Banning financial products** that **don't** benefit consumers.
- **Banning**, or forcing firms to **change**, **misleading adverts** for financial products and services.

The **IMF** and **World Bank** regulate the **Global Financial System**

1) The **World Bank** and the **International Monetary Fund** (IMF) aim to ensure that the global financial system is **well regulated** and **resilient** to **crises**. Through the **Financial Sector Assessment Program** (FSAP), the IMF and World Bank evaluate the **strengths and weaknesses** of a country's **financial markets** and **recommend policies** to help **reduce the chance** of a **future financial crisis**.

See p.224 for more info about the IMF and the World Bank.

2) The IMF and World Bank have both stepped in to **help countries** in the **aftermath** of the **financial crisis**. For example:
   - The **IMF** provided funds in 2008 to help Iceland **support** its **banks** and **stabilise** its **currency**.
   - Between 2008 and 2011, the **World Bank** provided **developing countries** with **$189 billion** in financial support to help them with their health, nutrition, education and infrastructure needs after the financial crisis.

3) However, the IMF and World Bank have been **criticised** for the way they acted during the financial crisis. Much of their support for affected countries had **conditions** attached requiring those countries to impose '**austerity measures**' that **reduce public spending**. Austerity measures generally affect the **poorest people** in a country the most.

4) Decision-making at the IMF and World Bank is also **dominated** by the **richest countries**. Many people believe that this results in both organisations putting the interests of **developed countries** ahead of those of **developing countries**.

Warm-Up Questions

Q1 What are macroprudential regulation and microprudential regulation?

Q2 What is the Financial Conduct Authority?

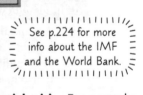

Exam Question

Q1 Explain two ways in which financial-sector regulation might help prevent a future financial crisis. [8 marks]

I closely monitor my finances — right now I've got 37p and an old bus ticket...

So here's an interesting thing the world has learnt recently — when people can act without consequences and without anyone checking if they're doing anything naughty, bad things happen. Who knew? Well, we know now, so it's regulation all the way...

Globalisation

There are many aspects to globalisation — it's all about the world's economies increasingly becoming more like one economy, through things such as increased trade and the movement of labour and capital. **These pages are for all boards.**

You'll need to understand what developed, developing and emerging countries (or economies) are for this section:
- Developed countries are **richer**, **industrialised** countries such as the UK, Japan and Australia. They have **high** GDP per capita figures.
- Developing countries, such as Colombia and Angola, largely rely on **manufacturing**, **agriculture** and other **labour-intensive** industries. They'll have **low** GDP per capita figures and lower **standards of living** than developed countries.
- Some developing countries are called emerging countries because they're **not** yet developed, but are **further** along the development process than other developing countries — e.g. countries such as China, which are **growing quickly** but aren't yet developed.

Globalisation is about the world becoming more like a **Single Economy**

1) **Globalisation** is the **increasing integration** of economies **internationally**. The **main characteristics** of **globalisation** are:

- The **free movement** of **capital** and **labour** across international boundaries.
- **Free trade** in **goods** and **services** between different countries.
- The availability of **technology** and **intellectual capital** (e.g. the knowledge of employees) to be used (and patented) on an **international scale**.

2) In the last 50 years, the **scale** and **pace** of globalisation has dramatically **increased** (see the next page for the reasons).

3) **Globalisation** also involves **political** and **cultural** factors:
- For example, **international bodies**, such as the United Nations (UN), tend to lead to a **convergence** of **political decisions** — i.e. there are more joint decisions made between countries, and more international cooperation.
- Examples of **cultural globalisation** include the spread of things such as **McDonald's** and **yoga** across the world.

4) Some of the other **characteristics** of globalisation include:
- **International** trade becoming a greater **proportion** of **all** trade.
- An increase in **financial capital flows** between countries.
- Increased **integration** of **production** — e.g. different parts of a product being produced in different countries.
- A **greater number** of countries becoming **involved** in **international trade**.
- An **increase** in **foreign ownership** of firms.
- **De-industrialisation** of developed countries, and the **industrialisation** of developing/emerging countries.
- More international **division** and **movement** of labour — i.e. the labour used to produce products is **divided** between **more countries** or **moves** from developed to less developed countries. For example:

- Developing countries, particularly emerging countries, are increasingly obtaining the levels of **skills** and **technology** needed to produce goods for **more developed** countries. Furthermore, labour is also **relatively cheap** in developing/emerging countries compared to developed countries.
- These factors have led to foreign companies starting to **produce goods** in developing/emerging countries, especially if there are other appealing factors for foreign companies, such as a **good transport network** in the developing country.
- For example, **India** provides **software development** for many **European** companies.

Many firms **Operate** in **More Than One Country**

1) A **key** feature of globalisation is the growth of **multinational corporations (MNCs)**.

2) MNCs are firms which function in **at least** one other country aside from their country of origin — e.g. Nissan and KFC®.

3) Factors which **attract** MNCs to **invest** in a country are:
- The **availability** of **cheap labour** and **raw materials**.
- Good **transport** links.
- **Access** to different markets.
- **Pro-foreign investment** government policies.

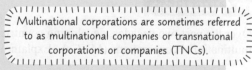
Multinational corporations are sometimes referred to as multinational companies or transnational corporations or companies (TNCs).

4) MNCs may choose to **divide** their operations and **locate** each part in the country with the **lowest costs**.

5) For example, this can be done by **offshoring** (setting up a company abroad) and by **outsourcing** (subcontracting work to another organisation).

Globalisation

There are many **Causes** contributing to **Globalisation**

Trade liberalisation — this is the **reduction** or **removal** of tariffs and other **restrictions** on international trade (i.e. reducing protectionism). Countries might **negotiate** these trade agreements using the **World Trade Organisation (WTO)**.

See p.202-205 for more on the WTO and protectionism.

The **WTO** has brought about an increase in **global product standards**, e.g. through agreements on product standards, which allow consumers to have **more confidence** in imported goods.

A reduction in the **real cost** and **time needed** for the transportation of goods means that it's **cheaper** to export and import. For example, due to the development of **larger cargo ships**.

Improvements in **communications** technology — for example, the internet is making the communication needed for international trade **easier** and **cheaper**.

Globalisation had allowed Bo to fulfil her life-long dream of performing on the West End.

Firms, especially MNCs, wishing to **increase profits** — for example, this means they might **invest** in setting up a factory in a developing country where labour is **cheaper**. So there's an **increase in foreign direct investment (FDI)** by MNCs. Foreign direct investment just means a firm **based** in **one country** making an investment in a **different country**. For example, there have been large amounts of **capital invested** in China from **overseas**.

Firms expanding overseas to exploit **economies of scale** (see p.42).

An increased **number** of MNCs and the growth of their **significance** and **influence** — for example, as MNCs have a greater influence, there's likely to be more **international trade** of goods and services, and more **international investment**.

Governments wishing to obtain the **benefits** of increased trade (see p.198) — so, for example, a government might provide **incentives** for foreign firms to **encourage** them to invest in their country.

The **opening** of new (or more) markets to **trade** and **investment** — for example, following the **collapse** of the Soviet Union after the Cold War, many communist Eastern European countries (including Russia) previously had **closed economies**. Also, China **opening** its economy to trade and then **joining** the WTO in 2001 has had a **big** impact on globalisation.

Growth in **international trading blocs** (see p.204), e.g. there's more trade now between EU countries.

Increasing investment by sovereign states — e.g. Norway **invests** some of its **oil revenues** in **foreign companies**.

More international **specialisation** (see p.198) — if countries specialise in making the products they're best at making, this will **encourage international trade**.

Warm-Up Questions

Q1 Briefly define what is meant by globalisation.
Q2 Give three characteristics of globalisation.
Q3 Give three causes of globalisation.

PRACTICE QUESTIONS

Exam Question

Q1 Over the past two decades, developing countries, such as India, have seen increased investment from multinational corporations (MNCs). Explain why an MNC might invest in a country like India.　　　[6 marks]

Globalisation has many more characteristics — it's optimistic, adventurous...

So globalisation is about all the world's economies integrating to become more like one, single, big economy. This can't happen unless economies are open to trade and investment, so a key part of globalisation is the reduction or removal of any barriers. Don't forget that as well as trade between economies, globalisation involves other factors, such as the existence of MNCs.

Costs and Benefits of Globalisation

Many people see globalisation as a positive thing for economies, but there are still some important drawbacks.
These downsides affect both the economies and the environment. ***These pages are for all boards.***

Globalisation has brought many **Benefits** to economies

1) Trade encourages countries to **specialise** in the goods and services they're best at producing/providing, which **increases output**.

2) So globalisation can allow countries to produce the things where they have a **comparative advantage** (see p.199), leading to an improvement in **efficiency** and the **allocation of resources**.

3) **Producers** can benefit from **economies of scale** and **lower** production costs because markets become **bigger** when countries trade. Global sourcing (i.e. countries buying things, such as raw materials, from anywhere in the world) has also led to **lower** raw material **costs**.

4) **Lower production costs** are also sometimes passed on to **consumers** in the form of **lower prices**.

5) Globalisation provides consumers with a greater **choice** of goods and services to purchase.

6) **World GDP** has risen as a result of globalisation due to many factors — for example, increased **efficiency** means firms can **increase output**. Countries which **aren't** open to trade have seen a **reduction** in their growth rates.

7) Globalisation has also helped to **improve** living standards and **reduce** the levels of **absolute poverty** in the world. A key reason for this is because levels of world **employment** have **increased**, as increased output has meant the creation of **more jobs**.

8) Increased **growth** and **employment** help governments to achieve two of their **macroeconomic objectives**.

9) Increases in **competition** brought about by globalisation can lead to lower prices for consumers.

10) There has been an **increased awareness** of, and quicker response to, **foreign disasters** (e.g. earthquakes) and **global issues** (e.g. **deforestation**) and their consequences.

Globalisation also has **Drawbacks** for economies

1) Globalisation is causing the **price of some** goods and services to **rise** — **increasing world incomes** lead to **increasing demand** for goods and services, so when **supply** is **unable** to meet this demand, **prices rise**.

2) Globalisation can lead to **economic dependency** (i.e. countries' economies being dependent on each other), so this can lead to **instability** in economies — for example, if the US economy goes into a **recession** and **reduces** its imports, this may cause **European** economies to go into a recession too.

3) Increasing **world trade** has led to global **imbalances** in balance of payment accounts. Some countries, e.g. the USA, have large **deficits** and others, e.g. China, have large **surpluses**. These balances are **unsustainable** (see p.156), leading to calls for increased protectionism.

4) **Specialisation** can lead to **overreliance** on a few industries by an economy, which is risky (see p.198).

5) Individual firms may be **outcompeted** by foreign firms and go out of business.

Karen had just been told that the price of baked beans was now £15 per tin.

Costs and Benefits of Globalisation

MNCs have both Positive and Negative Effects

Positive Effects

- Foreign direct investment (FDI) by MNCs creates **new jobs**, and brings **new skills** and **wealth** to an economy. MNCs also **buy** local goods and services, leading to **inflows** of foreign currency.
- MNCs can benefit from **economies of scale**, helping them to be **more efficient**, i.e. they can produce products more cheaply.
- Some people believe MNCs **raise living standards** by providing **employment**.

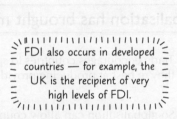
FDI also occurs in developed countries — for example, the UK is the recipient of very high levels of FDI.

Negative Effects

- Some people argue MNCs **exploit** workers in developing countries by paying them **lower wages** than in **developed** countries.
- MNCs can force local firms **out of business** — for example, because local firms might be **unable** to obtain similar **economies of scale**, they'll be **less competitive**.
- MNCs can relocate rapidly and cause **mass unemployment**.
- They can **withdraw profits** from one country and place them in another with **low tax rates** — so the former country **won't** be able to gain **tax revenue** from those profits.
- They can use their economic power to **reduce choice** and **increase prices**.
- MNCs can **influence** government policies in other countries to their advantage, which can be **unfair** to local people or **unhelpful** to the domestic economy.
- Governments may be forced to **reduce corporate tax levels** to attract or keep MNCs in their country.

Globalisation has a Big Impact on the Environment

1) Environmental **degradation** has resulted from globalisation. For example, international trade leads to an increase in the **international transportation** of goods — this means **more** fossil fuels are used, contributing to **climate change** and causing **resource depletion** (see p.81).

2) Carbon emissions are also increased by, for example, **rising production levels** of manufactured goods to meet rising **global demand**.

3) Other threats to the environment that are **linked** to globalisation include:
   - **Deforestation** — from logging for wood and the clearing of forests for factories or farmland.
   - Increasing depletion of other **non-renewable** resources, e.g. metal ores.

4) Some people argue that international trade is **not sustainable** at current levels if its **environmental impact** is considered.

Due to climate change, Irina now has to go shopping for some ice...

Warm-Up Questions

Q1 What effect can the increase in competition have for consumers?

Q2 What are two positives to come from MNCs operating in an economy?

Q3 Give two environmental costs of globalisation.

PRACTICE QUESTIONS

Exam Question

Q1 Which of these is an argument against globalisation?
A) It can help provide an organised worldwide response to a global influenza outbreak.
B) It allows a country to specialise in the mining and exporting of copper, leading to improved extraction techniques.
C) The increase in world trade that it causes will result in an asymmetry in the balances of payments.
D) The resulting growth of MNCs may lead to increased employment. [1 mark]

FDI — Federal Desk of Investigation...

Although globalisation has a big impact on the environment, it's an important part of the global economy that provides many benefits. So implementing any kind of change requires careful planning in order to avoid serious damage to the economy.

Globalisation and Development

As well as all the general consequences of globalisation from the last couple of pages, some consequences are more likely to affect developing countries than they are developed ones — and vice versa. ***This pages is for all boards.***

Globalisation **Consequences** differ for **Developing** and **Developed** countries

1) Globalisation may have contributed to **increasing** levels of **inequality** within many countries (both developed and developing).

2) In some **emerging countries**, such as China and India, the gaps between their **wealthiest** and **poorest** citizens have increased **significantly** in recent years.

3) MNCs can bring **extra tax revenue** to both developed and developing countries, but **regulation** is often needed (e.g. of **transfer pricing**) to make sure governments don't lose out on this revenue. Imposing this regulation can be **costly**.

> *Transfer pricing is setting prices for goods/services that are transferred between divisions of the same company. MNCs could try to manipulate these prices in order to save money on tax.*

Consequences of globalisation for developing/emerging countries

- **Health and safety laws** are generally **less strict** in **developing/emerging** countries — MNCs may take advantage of this.
- MNCs may **exploit** workers by offering very **low wages**.
- **Skilled workers** often **leave** developing/emerging countries to work in more developed countries. This **reduces** the developing country's **potential** for **economic growth**.
- However, globalisation **creates** jobs, **reducing** unemployment.
- MNCs often bring **more efficient** production methods and **technology** to developing countries.
- There's an **increase** of investment in developing/emerging economies — e.g. through **FDI**.

Jeff was starting to regret not reading the health and safety information...

> *There are varying opinions on whether globalisation is a good thing for developing countries — you need to weigh up the costs against the benefits.*

Consequences of globalisation for developed countries

- **Cheap** overseas production of goods has led to a severe **reduction** in some industries in **developed** countries, causing **structural unemployment** (see p.150). For example, cheap clothes from countries such as Bangladesh have **contributed** to the **collapse** of the **textile industry** in the UK.
- Such collapses lead to **de-industrialisation**, which has **further impacts** on economies — such as a **fall** in exports.
- The success of **emerging economies**, e.g. China and India, impacts on developed countries — for example, emerging economies' share of global GDP has increased at the expense of **more developed** nations.
- **Increased** levels of **imports** result from increased trade and have a **negative effect** on a country's balance of payments.
- Globalisation gives countries **greater access** to cheap raw materials and semi-manufactured goods from other countries, which can be used in the **production** of domestic goods. These goods can then be exported or sold domestically.
- MNCs gain access to **cheap labour**, which leads to **lower production costs** and **lower prices** for consumers.

Warm-Up Questions

Q1 Give a positive consequence of globalisation for developed countries.

Q2 Explain how globalisation can cause structural employment in developed countries.

(PRACTICE QUESTIONS)

Exam Question

Q1 Evaluate the likely advantages and disadvantages of globalisation for a developing or emerging country. [15 marks]

I took a photo of Columbia, but it's still developing...

For some globalisation questions, you'll have to consider the different effects on the various parties involved — make sure you remember that globalisation can have both positive and negative effects in developing/emerging and developed countries.

Trade

When countries trade internationally, they tend to start to specialise in the products they're best at producing.
The law of comparative advantage can be used to help judge the amount of output that countries should produce.
However, there are limits to how much countries should specialise. **These pages are for all boards.**

There are many **Advantages** to **International Trade**

- Countries **can't** produce all the things they **want** or **need** because resources are **unevenly distributed**.
- **International trade**, which is the **exchange** of goods and services **between** countries (i.e. imports and exports), can give countries **access** to resources and products they otherwise **wouldn't** be able to use — countries can **export** goods in order to **import** the things they can't **produce** themselves. For example, the UK exports goods so that it can import things such as tea, rice and diamonds.
- By trading internationally, not only do a country's consumers enjoy a **larger variety** of goods and services, but increased **competition** resulting from international trade can lead to **lower** prices and **more** product innovation — so people's **standards of living** are raised by having more **choice**, and **better quality** and **cheaper** products.
- **Additional markets** (i.e. markets abroad) allow firms to exploit more **economies of scale** — if the additional markets mean there's an **increase** in **demand** for their products.
- International trade can also expose firms to **new ideas and skills** — for example, an MNC might bring **new manufacturing skills** to a **developing** country.

International Trade allows countries to **Specialise**

1) International trade allows countries to **specialise** in the goods and services they're **best** at **producing**.
2) Countries specialise because:
   - They have the **resources** to produce the good or service **efficiently**.
   - They're **better** than other countries at producing the good or service.
3) Specialisation has its **advantages**:
   - **Costs** are **reduced**, which can be passed on to **consumers** in the form of **lower prices**.
   - The world's resources are used **more efficiently**.
   - Global output is **increased** and living standards are **raised**.

International Trade and **Specialisation** also have their **Disadvantages**

International Trade

1) Trading internationally usually involves **higher transport costs**.
2) **Currency exchanges** when trading abroad can carry costs, potentially resulting in **financial losses**.
3) There are other **costs** to firms that trade internationally, such as **complying** with other countries' legal and technical requirements, **translating** legal documents and advertising material, and **performing market research** for overseas markets.
4) International trade increases **globalisation**, which has its own **disadvantages** — see p.195.

Toby specialised
in cuteness.

Specialisation

1) Domestic industries may be forced to shut down because foreign firms are better at producing the goods or services provided by that industry.
2) Specialisation can lead to overreliance on one industry — if something happened to negatively affect that industry, it would have a severe impact on the whole economy.
3) Countries are vulnerable to cuts in the supply of goods that they don't produce themselves.
4) Specialisation can have negative impacts on a country's economy. For example, if a country begins to specialise in a particular industry, other industries may decline, and workers from those industries may struggle to get work (as they might not have the relevant skills).

Trade

It's useful to consider Absolute Advantage when looking at Trade

1) A country will have an **absolute advantage** when its output of a product is **greater per unit of resource used** than any other country.

2) To explain absolute advantage economists make a number of **simplifying assumptions**.

> **Example 1 — absolute advantage**
>
> Assume:
> - There are only **two countries** in the world, **A** and **B**, who each have the **same amount** of resources.
> - They both produce **only crisps** and **chocolate**.
> - If each country splits its resources **equally** to produce the **two goods**, then output would be:
>
> | | Units of crisps output per year | Units of chocolate output per year |
> |---|---|---|
> | **Country A** | 1000 | 5000 |
> | **Country B** | 2000 | 3000 |
>
> *Before specialisation, world production of crisps is 1000 + 2000 = 3000 units, and of chocolate is 5000 + 3000 = 8000 units.*
>
> - Country A has the **absolute advantage** in producing chocolate and country B has the **absolute advantage** in producing crisps.
> - So if the countries **specialised** in the products they have an absolute advantage in, then **world production** of crisps would rise to 4000 units (all produced by country B) and of chocolate to 10 000 units (all produced by country A). (Remember — each country **splits** its resources **equally** between the two products, so if country A **only** made chocolate, then the **half** of its resources that **were** used to make **crisps** would be used for **chocolate** instead, and chocolate production would **double**.)
> - Through specialisation, **more output** is produced using the **same amount** of resources — so the **cost per unit** is **reduced**.

Comparative Advantage uses Opportunity Costs

1) **Comparative advantage** uses the concept of **opportunity cost** — the opportunity cost is the **benefit** that's **given up** in order to do something else. In this case, it's the number of units of one good not made in order to produce one unit of the other good.

2) A country has a comparative advantage if the opportunity cost of it producing a good is **lower** than the opportunity cost for other countries.

> **Example 2 — comparative advantage**
>
> Make the same **assumptions** as above, but this time country A and country B produce **only wheat** and **coffee**. If they each split their resources **equally**, they can produce the following quantities:
>
> | | Units of wheat output per year | Units of coffee output per year | Opportunity cost of wheat | Opportunity cost of coffee |
> |---|---|---|---|---|
> | **Country A** | 3000 | 3000 | 1 unit of coffee | 1 unit of wheat |
> | **Country B** | 2000 | 1000 | ½ unit of coffee | 2 units of wheat |
> | **Total output before specialisation** | 5000 | 4000 | – | – |
>
> - Country A has the **absolute advantage** in producing both wheat and coffee.
> - Country A has the **lower opportunity cost** in producing **coffee**, and therefore the comparative advantage — i.e. if country A makes **one extra unit of coffee**, it must give up **one unit of wheat**, but if country B makes **one extra unit of coffee**, it must give up **two units of wheat**.
> - Country B has the **lower opportunity cost** in producing **wheat**, and therefore the comparative advantage — i.e. if country B makes **one extra unit of wheat**, it must give up **half of a unit of coffee**, but if country A makes **one extra unit of wheat**, it must give up **one unit of coffee**.

Flip to the next page to see what happens when the countries specialise.

3) The law of comparative advantage is based on several **assumptions**, which make it hard to apply to the **real world**. For example, it assumes that there are **no economies** or **diseconomies** of scale, there are **no transport costs** or **barriers** to trade, there's **perfect** knowledge, and that factors of production are **mobile**. Also, externalities are **ignored**.

Trade

Specialising Fully often Won't maximise output

> **Example 3**
>
> - Using example 2 from the previous page, if the countries specialise fully in the goods they have a comparative advantage in, allocating all of their resources to one product, total output of coffee will increase from 4000 to 6000 units, but total output of wheat will decrease from 5000 to 4000 units (see the table below).
>
> - However, it's possible to increase the output of both goods by only reallocating some resources. Countries can split production and then trade. For example, in the bottom row of the table below, ¼ of country A's resources are allocated to wheat and ¾ to coffee, while country B just specialises in wheat. By using partial specialisation, wheat and coffee output are both greater than they were before specialisation.
>
> | | Units of wheat output per year | Units of coffee output per year | Opportunity cost of 1 unit of wheat (1W) | Opportunity cost of 1 unit of coffee (1C) |
> |---|---|---|---|---|
> | **Country A** | 3000 | 3000 | 1 unit of coffee (1C) | 1 unit of wheat (1W) |
> | **Country B** | 2000 | 1000 | ½ unit of coffee (½C) | 2 units of wheat (2W) |
> | **Total output before specialisation** | 5000 | 4000 | | |
> | **Total output after specialisation** | 4000 | 6000 | | |
> | **E.g. of total output with partial specialisation** | 1500 (country A) 4000 (country B) | 4500 (country A) | | |
>
> *If country B specialises in wheat and stops making coffee, it can only double its wheat output to 4000 units with the resources it has.*
>
> - Countries are unlikely to specialise 100% — instead they produce at a level where their combined production of both goods is greater than without specialisation.
>
> - For trade to benefit both countries, the terms of trade must be set at the right level (see below).
>
> - If the opportunity cost of production is the same in both nations, there would be no benefit from trade.

Usually, for trade to occur between two countries, **both** countries must **benefit** from trading, or at least not be any **worse off** than if they **hadn't** traded. So, **neither** country will **pay more** for a good than it would **cost** for them to **produce** it themselves, and **neither** will **accept less** for a good than it **costs** for them to **produce** it.

If a country's Terms of Trade Rises then it's Better Off — if it Falls then it's Worse Off

1) A country's **terms of trade** is the **relative** price of its **exports** compared to its **imports**.

2) In the real world, a country's **terms of trade** is often described using an index number. It's **calculated** using the formula:

$$\text{terms of trade index} = \frac{\text{index of average price of exports}}{\text{index of average price of imports}} \times 100$$

3) If the price of a country's **exports rises**, but the price of its **imports stays the same**, its **terms of trade index** will **increase** — e.g. if a country exports lots of tea and the price of tea **rises**, its terms of trade index is likely to **rise** (e.g. from 102 to 120). This increase will mean it'll effectively become '**better off**', as it'll be able to afford more imports.

> *Think of a country's terms of trade as the 'rate of exchange' used between it and the rest of the world — i.e. the amount of imports it can buy per unit of exports.*

4) And if a country's terms of trade index **falls** (e.g. from 110 to 105), it'll effectively be **worse off**.

5) For example, during the recession in 2008-2010, the UK's terms of trade index fell — this was because the price of its imports rose more quickly than the price of its exports.

Trade

Comparative Advantage can be seen using Production Possibility Frontiers

1) Remember, a production possibility frontier (PPF) shows the **maximum amounts** of two goods/services that an economy can produce with a **fixed** level of resources.

2) The diagram shows the **PPF curves** for the two countries in example 3 on the previous page — e.g. if country A produces **only wheat**, it can produce **6000** units.

3) The **gradient** indicates which country has the **comparative advantage** in each good. The **steeper** gradient of **country B's PPF** shows it has the comparative advantage in **wheat**, whereas the **gentler** gradient of **country A's PPF** shows it has the comparative advantage in **coffee**.

4) By using **specialisation** and **trade**, countries can consume **outside** of their PPF.

5) For example, using example 3 from the previous page, country A splits production, so it produces 1500 wheat and 4500 coffee, and country B produces 4000 wheat and no coffee. If country B **exports 2000 wheat** to country A, and country A **exports 1500 coffee** to country B, then country A will consume at **point P** and country B will consume at **point Q** — which are both **beyond** their respective PPFs.

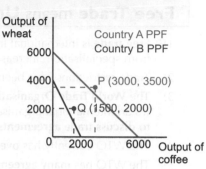

The country with the gentler PPF gradient has the comparative advantage in the good on the x-axis, and the country with the steeper PPF gradient has the comparative advantage in the good on the y-axis.

Trade is Important for Developing and Developed countries

1) You also need to think about how the benefits of trade **vary** for **developed**, **developing** and **emerging** economies, e.g.:

For developed countries

- Imports are **crucial to maintaining high standards of living** in developed countries.
- Products will often be **cheaper** when bought from abroad — e.g. due to **increased competition** and **cheaper labour** in developing countries.

For developing countries

- Developing countries can **import** goods they don't have the technology to produce themselves, which results in a **higher** standard of living.
- Trade also gives these countries access to **new materials**, meaning **new industries** will be **created** because they can produce **new products**. This will help to **improve** the economies of developing countries.

Due to Shelly's fear of heights, she wasn't keen on a high standard of living.

2) **Emerging** economies will experience **some** of the benefits of both developed and developing countries. For example, emerging economies will be able to purchase **cheaper** products from **developing** countries, and they'll also benefit from **importing** products and services they don't have the **technology** to produce themselves.

3) For more on the **benefits** of **globalisation** see p.195, and for more on the benefits of **trade** see p.198.

Warm-Up Questions

Q1 What is international trade?

Q2 What is the difference between absolute and comparative advantage?

Q3 List three assumptions of comparative advantage which make it hard to measure in the real world.

Exam Question

Q1 Explain two possible benefits of international trade for developing countries. [6 marks]

The opportunity cost of not learning these pages is X marks in your exam...

Although there are disadvantages to international trade and specialisation, most countries choose to trade because the benefits seem to outweigh the costs. However, for trade to be beneficial, things such as comparative advantage need to be considered.

Free Trade, Protectionism and the WTO

The World Trade Organisation (WTO) wants to promote free trade, but countries often impose protectionist policies for various reasons — for example, to protect their domestic industries. **These pages are for all boards.**

Free Trade means Unrestricted international trade

1) **Free trade** is international trade **without restrictions** such as tariffs or quotas (see below). Free trade provides **benefits** from specialisation, increased competition and the ability to transfer resources (see p.198 for more trade benefits).

2) Trade restrictions have been **reduced** in recent years — mainly amongst members of **trading blocs** (see p.204).

3) The **World Trade Organisation (WTO)** aims to help trade to be as **free** as possible. It's an international organisation which provides a forum for its **member governments** to **discuss trade agreements** and **settle disputes**, using a set of **trade rules**.

4) The WTO currently has **over 150 members**, including the countries with the biggest economies.

5) The WTO has **many agreements** its members must follow — some examples of the principles behind them are:

   - Countries must treat **all** their **trading partners**, and **foreign** and **domestic** goods, **equally**.

   - The WTO wants to **encourage** competitiveness and **discourage** trade barriers, such as subsidies.

6) The WTO has played a big part in the **movement towards free trade** in recent years.

Governments might want to use Protectionist Policies

1) Governments might want to impose certain **trade barriers** to tackle the **disadvantages** of **free trade**:

   - **To protect jobs** — there might be a risk of too many **job losses** if domestic firms are **outcompeted** by foreign firms.

   - **To protect infant industries** — industries that are just starting out, particularly in developing countries, struggle to compete with **international** companies. Governments might choose to impose trade barriers until the companies **are** big enough to compete. However, there's a **risk** that the industry may never become **truly** competitive, and in the meantime, **domestic consumers** are stuck with **higher** prices or **lower quality** goods.

   - **To ban certain goods** — the government may simply want to **ban** certain goods altogether because they consider them to be **bad** for **society**, e.g. firearms or drugs.

   - **To avoid overdependence** — specialisation could lead to **overdependence** on **one** industry (see p.198).

   - **To protect against dumping** — when companies sell goods abroad at a price that's **below** the production cost to try to **force** other countries' domestic producers **out of business**.

   - **To correct imbalances in the balance of payments** — see p.156.

2) There are various tariff and non-tariff **policies** governments can use to **protect** domestic industries:

   - **Tariffs** can be imposed in the form of a tax on selected imports. This makes imports more expensive, which helps **domestic** manufacturers to compete and raises **tax revenue** for the government.

   Non-tariff policies are just any barriers which don't involve actual tariffs.

   - **Quotas** can be fixed, which limit the **quantity** of a certain good that can be imported — any demand for the good **above** the quota will be **diverted** to **domestic products**.

   - **Embargoes** (bans) can be imposed on certain products — these are usually restricted to **extreme** cases, e.g. drugs or elephant ivory, but may also be for **political** reasons, e.g. if two countries are having a **disagreement**, they might impose embargoes on imports from **each other**. Embargoes tend to be **less** about protecting **domestic industries** and **more** about politics or enforcing laws.

   - The value of the currency can be **reduced** — this **raises** the price of **foreign** imports and **lowers** the price of **domestic** exports.

   - Tight **product standard regulations** can be imposed — foreign products which don't comply with the requirements **cannot** be imported. Product standard regulations could include things such as **high safety** standards, or **low emissions** requirements. These might be used for **environmental** or **consumer protection**, or to help to protect **domestic** industries that **can comply** with the **regulations**.

   - **Subsidies** can be given to domestic producers — this **reduces** the cost of production of domestic products, making them cheaper to buy, but subsidies can be **costly** to a government.

3) Some of these policies, particularly **tariffs** and **subsidies**, can be used to make a country's products **seem more competitive** — e.g. by making domestically produced products **relatively cheaper** (see p.215 for more).

4) **Trade disputes** occur when one country or trading bloc (see p.204) is seen to be acting **unfairly** when trading internationally. Trade disputes might be caused by the use of **protectionist policies** — for example, one country may see the subsidies paid by **another country's government** to one of its **domestic industries** as **unfair**.

Free Trade, Protectionism and the WTO

Tariffs (or Customs Duties) are a Tax imposed on certain Imports

1) Tariffs are a common form of **protectionism**. They're a tax that can be a **fixed amount** per unit or *ad valorem* (i.e. a percentage of the value of a good).

2) In this example, a **fixed** tariff per unit is imposed on imports — this **increases** the price for **domestic consumers** from P_e to P_1. The tariff is P_1 minus P_e:

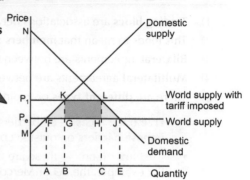

- Domestic demand **reduces** from E to C.
- The **consumer surplus** reduces from P_eNJ to P_1NL.
- Domestic supply **increases** from A to B.
- The level of **imports falls** from AE to BC.
- The domestic **producer surplus** increases from MP_eF to MP_1K.
- The level of **tax revenue** raised by the government is **KLHG**.
- There's a **net welfare loss** of **FGK** and **HJL**.

Quotas can be set to Limit the amount of Imports of certain goods

1) Quotas can be used to **divert demand** for certain goods to **domestic** products by limiting the amount that can be imported.

2) In this diagram, **before** a quota is imposed on imports:

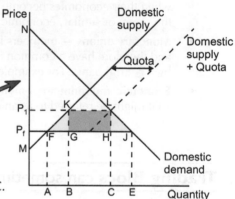

- A foreign country, country X, is willing to supply at P_f — so the quantity of the product demanded domestically is **E**.
- A is supplied by **domestic** suppliers, and the rest (**AE**) is **imported** from country X.

3) A quota is imposed, shown on the diagram, which **restricts** the supply of goods from abroad. **Total supply** is now limited to domestic supply **plus** the quota of imports. This means there's a **new equilibrium** at price P_1 and quantity C:

- Price **increases** from P_f to P_1 and domestic demand **reduces** from E to C.
- The **consumer surplus** reduces from P_fNJ to P_1NL.
- Domestic supply **increases** from A to B (they supply everything they're willing to **up to** price P_1).
- The rest is imported — but **imports fall** from AE to BC (which is the amount set by the quota).
- The **producer surplus** (for domestic producers) increases from MP_fF to MP_1K.
- **KLHG** is an increase in the **producer surplus** for foreign exporters (i.e. the firms domestic consumers are importing from).
- There's a **welfare loss** of **FGK** and **HJL** — HJL is **lost completely** and FGK is **inefficient** production by domestic producers.

Some people don't think Protectionism is a good thing

1) Restricting imports **reduces** specialisation, **diverting** resources away from their **most efficient** use — this reduces **allocative** and **productive efficiency**.

2) Protectionism will mean **prices** tend to be **higher** (for both consumers and producers), as there's a **lack** of **specialisation** and **competition** (and **imports** may be more expensive, e.g. through tariffs).

3) If the prices of **everyday goods** (e.g. food) rise, this will have a **bigger** impact on the **poor** than on the **rich**. As a result, there might be an increase in **inequality**, and it's likely that **living standards** will **fall**.

4) Protectionism also **reduces choice** for consumers.

5) Once trade barriers are in place, it can be **difficult** to **remove** them — industries may **depend** on them to **survive**, so removing them could **destroy** domestic industries.

6) If **demand** for imports is **high**, this could be due to **poor domestic efficiency** — a **lack** of competition **doesn't** encourage firms to **improve** their efficiency, so there'll continue to be a **misallocation of resources**. Firms are likely to make **more** money, especially in the long run, if they improve **efficiency** instead of relying on protectionist policies.

7) Trade barriers imposed by one country may lead to **retaliation** by other countries — this is often referred to as a **'trade war'**. It **reduces** world trade, worsening other problems — e.g. there'll be a further **misallocation** of resources caused by **inefficiency** and a **lack** of **specialisation**.

Free Trade, Protectionism and the WTO

Sometimes countries form trading blocs, which have both positive and negative effects on free trade.

Trading Blocs are Agreements between governments about Trade

1) **Trading blocs** are associations between different governments that **promote** and **manage** trade.

2) This tends to mean that **members** make agreements to **remove** or **reduce** protectionist barriers between them.

3) **Bilateral** agreements are between **two** countries or trading blocs, e.g. between the EU and one other country.

4) **Multilateral** agreements are between **more than two** countries or trading blocs.

5) There are **different types** of trading blocs:

- **Free trade areas** — all barriers to trade are **removed** between members, but **individual** members can still **impose barriers** on outside countries. For example, the United States-Mexico-Canada Agreement (USMCA).

- **Customs unions** — these are **free trade areas** where there are also **standard tariffs** imposed on **non-members**. For example, the EU or Mercosur (made up of some South American countries).

- **Common markets** (sometimes referred to as **single markets**) — these are **customs unions** with the addition of the **free movement** of factors of production between members. For example, the Single European Market (SEM) (see p.208).

- **Economic unions** — trading blocs might be referred to as economic unions when their economies become **more integrated**, e.g. member states adopt the **same**, or **similar**, economic policies, regulations and rules.

- **Monetary unions** — members implement a **single**, **common currency**, and therefore have a common **monetary policy**, usually controlled by a **central bank**. For example, the Eurozone.

> *You might see slightly different definitions of each type of union, especially for economic unions and monetary unions — but just make sure you're aware of the key features of each.*

- **Economic and monetary union** — a monetary union will usually **also** be an economic union, so it might be referred to as an economic and monetary union.

Trading Blocs can sometimes Help with WTO Objectives

1) Trading blocs can lead to **trade creation** — this is when patterns of trade change after barriers are removed, as a result of products being bought from the cheapest source. Removing barriers also allows countries within the trading bloc to **specialise** in the products where they have a **comparative advantage**. This **helps** with **WTO** objectives, as it **opens** up trade, **encouraging** competitiveness and therefore **improving** efficiency.

2) For example, assume country B is the **most efficient** producer of tea:

- Country A is a member of a customs union which imposes a **tariff** on importing tea. The price of tea in country A is P_1, which is the price country B **exports** tea at (P_2) **plus** a tariff (the tariff = $P_1 - P_2$).

- With the tariff, Q_3 of tea is consumed in country A. Q_2 of this is supplied **domestically** and Q_2Q_3 is **imported** from country B.

- If country B **joins** the customs union then the tariff will be **removed**. The new price for tea in country A is P_2 (the price country B is willing to export at).

- Consumption of tea in country A increases to Q_4. Domestic supply is cut to Q_1 and imports from country B increase to Q_1Q_4.

- So **trade** has been **created** — country A is importing more tea from the **most efficient** producer.

- The government of country A loses tariff revenue of **BCDE** and producer surplus reduces from GP_1B to GP_2A — however, consumer surplus **increases** from P_1HE to P_2HF.

- This means the loss of tariff revenue and reduction in producer surplus **aren't** a loss to the country — they just become **consumer surplus** instead of producer surplus and government revenue.

- So the overall gain for country A is **ABC + DEF**.

> *This diagram and the one on the next page are for OCR only.*

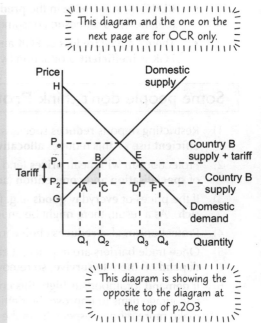

> *This diagram is showing the opposite to the diagram at the top of p.203.*

Free Trade, Protectionism and the WTO

Trading Blocs can sometimes Conflict with the WTO

1) Trading blocs can also lead to **trade diversion** — if **trade barriers** are imposed on non-members, trade will be **diverted** away from any **cheaper non-members**. So countries outside the trading bloc **aren't** able to fully use their **comparative advantage** by specialising, as trade is **restricted**. This **conflicts** with WTO objectives, as it **interferes** with competition, **preventing** the lowest-cost, most efficient products from being traded.

2) For example, assume country D is the **most efficient** producer of pens:

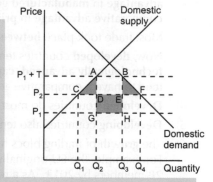

- **Country C isn't** a member of any trade agreements and imposes a **tariff** (**T**) on **importing** pens. Country D is willing to supply pens at price P_1, so with the tariff the price of pens in country C is $P_1 + T$.
- Q_3 of pens is consumed in country C. Q_2 of this is supplied **domestically** and Q_2Q_3 is **imported** from country D.
- Country C joins a **customs union** so the tariff on importing pens from other **member countries** is **removed**. **Country E**, another country in the customs union, is willing to supply pens at P_2 to other customs union members, which is **cheaper** than pens from country D (these still cost $P_1 + T$ as country D is **not** a member of the customs union).
- Country C **switches** to importing pens from country E and the price of pens in country C **reduces** to P_2.
- Consumption in country C increases to Q_4. Domestic supply is cut to Q_1 and imports from country E are Q_1Q_4.
- Trade has been **diverted** away from country D, the **most efficient** producer of pens.
- There's a gain of **CAD + EBF** (these were part of the net welfare loss when there was a tariff imposed — see p.203). However, there's a loss of **GDEH**, which previously formed part of the government revenue from tariffs.

The WTO and Trading Blocs impact on Developing countries

1) Trading blocs can **limit** the development of developing countries who **aren't** members and **cannot** trade on equal terms.

2) Trading blocs can help to **reduce protectionism** on a **global** scale by **reducing** the number of parties that have to **negotiate** a trade agreement. However, they can **limit** progress towards **free trade** if there's **excessive** trade diversion.

EXAMPLE
- The EU's **Common Agricultural Policy (CAP)** has caused **disputes** between the EU and other countries.
- The CAP uses measures such as **subsidies** and **buffer stocks**, along with **import restrictions** on goods from outside the EU, to guarantee a **minimum price** for many agricultural products (see p.100). For example, **tariffs** are placed on **imported goods** to allow the guaranteed minimum price level to be maintained.
- When stocks build up, governments **sell** these excess stocks at a **low price** outside of the EU — this **harms** farmers outside the EU, including in developing countries, who **cannot compete** with such **low prices**.
- After disputes with other countries, in recent years the EU has reformed the CAP. As a result, prices have **moved closer** to the **market price** — but there are still problems with the policy.

3) The WTO played a part in the **reduction** of the level of subsidies on the EU's agricultural goods — this reduction has led to developing nations' agricultural products becoming **more competitive**.

4) Developing countries might be **prevented** from **protecting** infant industries by WTO policies — stopping them from **diversifying** away from agriculture. Not only will this harm **individual** economies, but it might **hold back** worldwide improvements in efficiency, e.g. through **specialisation**.

5) However, **free trade** has been a **major** factor in the rapid economic development of nations such as **China** and **India**.

Warm-Up Questions

Q1 What is the WTO?
Q2 Give two arguments for protectionism and two arguments against protectionism.
Q3 How might a trading bloc conflict with the WTO?

Exam Questions

Q1 How might a government use protectionist policies to protect infant industries?   [10 marks]
Q2 What is meant by a 'customs union'?   [2 marks]

I think these pages are just tariff-ic...

The WTO aims to promote free trade, but countries often don't trade freely, as they want to protect their own industries. Many countries are members of trading blocs, who'll trade freely between themselves, but impose restrictions on non-members.

Patterns of Trade

Trade is an important factor affecting the development of countries. The pattern of trade has changed dramatically over the last century — emerging countries such as China are now playing a major role in international trade. **For all boards.**

World Patterns of trade are Changing

1) A hundred years ago, **developed** countries, such as the **UK**, had a **comparative advantage** in **manufactured** goods, whereas **developing** countries had a **comparative advantage** in **primary** goods, such as commodities.

2) Most trade took place **between developed** and **developing** countries.

3) Now, **developed** countries tend to have a comparative advantage in **high** value, **technologically advanced**, **capital-intensive** products, and **developing** countries tend to have a comparative advantage in **low** value, **labour-intensive** products.

4) **Developed** countries do most of their trade with **other developed** countries.

5) **Developing** countries also tend to do **most** of their trade with **developed** countries.

6) The **growth** of trading blocs has contributed to changes in world trade patterns. For example, the EU originally had six member states in the 1950s, and had grown to 28 members by 2013. As a result, there has been **increased trade** between members.

7) Emerging economies, such as **China** and **India**, have had a big impact on the recent pattern of world trade. China and India are both now important **global** traders.

8) China is the **largest exporter** and the **second largest importer** of goods in the world. Its **main** exports are **electronic equipment** and **machinery**.

9) China's **high-tech industry** has seen **rapid growth** in recent years — it's now the **largest** exporter of **high-tech** goods.

10) India's **main** goods exports are **fuels** and **materials**, e.g. **glass**. It's also a big exporter of **services**, such as **IT services**.

Megan had the pattern part sorted — it was just the trade that wasn't going so well.

UK trade has seen a Rise in Imports and a Fall in Exports

1) The UK has **high levels** of imports and exports. It's the **second** largest **exporter** of **services** in the world.

2) The UK's main **exported goods** are things such as **cars**, **fuels** and **pharmaceuticals**.

3) The country with the **biggest** market for **UK exports** is the **USA** — but just under **half** of the UK's exports go to countries in the **European Union (EU)**.

4) Like many other countries, the UK often **imports** and **exports** the **same types** of goods — the UK's main **imported goods** are **cars**, **fuels** and **pharmaceuticals**.

5) Most UK **imports** come from the **EU**, **China** and the **USA**.

6) The UK has a **trade deficit** in **goods** and a **trade surplus** in **services**.

Recent pattern of UK trade

- The **general** pattern in UK trade since 2000 has seen exports **fall** and imports **rise**.

- The **decline** in UK exports is similar to that seen in most other **major industrialised** countries, and is due to **competition** from **emerging** and **newly industrialised** economies, such as China.

- UK imports have tended to **rise** for similar reasons — goods are often **cheaper** to buy from **less developed** countries. However, the country the UK imports the **most** from is **Germany**.

- UK exports to countries such as **China**, whose economies are **growing** extremely quickly, are **rising**.

- However, the level of the **exports** going to **China** and **India** are both **less than 5%** of the UK's total exports.

Warm-Up Questions

Q1 List four changes in the pattern of world trade that have taken place over the last 100 years.

Q2 List three changes in the pattern of trade in the UK since 2000.

(PRACTICE QUESTIONS)

Exam Question

Q1 Discuss how the growth of China and India's economies may affect the UK.   [8 marks]

CGP imports 83% of its jokes from Vanuatu...

Emerging economies such as China are having a big impact on patterns of international trade — China's now the biggest exporter of goods in the world. But most trade still occurs between developed countries — e.g. the UK imports the most from Germany.

Economic Integration

*Different trading blocs (see p.204) are at different stages of economic integration. Some are happy with little integration — others work towards fuller integration. **This page is for all boards.***

There are Several Stages of Economic Integration

1) **Economic integration** is the process by which the economies of different countries become **more closely linked**, e.g. through free trade agreements or common currencies.

2) The types of **trading bloc** listed on p.204 show the **stages** of **economic integration** — free trade areas, customs unions, common (single) markets, economic unions and monetary unions. The list goes from **least** integrated to **most** integrated.

3) For example, the United States-Mexico-Canada Agreement (USMCA) is a free trade area — it's made up of the **USA**, **Canada** and **Mexico**. The Association of South-East Asian Nations (ASEAN) is also a free trade area with **ten** members. These are at the **first** stage of economic integration.

4) The **EU** is a **customs union**, whilst the **Eurozone** (or **euro area**) is a **monetary union** (or **economic and monetary union**).

Economic Integration can have Positive and Negative impacts

1) There's the possibility of **trade creation** within a trading bloc — e.g. when **tariffs** are **removed**, consumers may switch from **high-cost** domestic producers to **lower-cost** trading partners.

2) So if there's **more trade** within the bloc, this can lead to **greater efficiency** — e.g. as a result of increased **competition**, **specialisation** and **economies of scale**.

3) **Non-members** may **gain** from things such as **improvements** in **efficiency** and **infrastructure** within the bloc, as these things will lead the price of exports from the bloc to **fall**.

4) The **removal** of **tariffs** will **increase** consumer surplus, but producer surplus and government revenue from tariffs will both be **reduced**.

> Trade creation and diversion are short run impacts of economic integration. Changes in efficiency are long run impacts.

5) **Trade diversion** can occur when **trade barriers** (imposed on non-members) divert trade **away** from **cheaper**, **more efficient** non-members.

6) Not only might this mean there's **no overall increase** in trade, but there may be a **reduction** in **efficiency** as trade is diverted to **less efficient** producers, and non-members **aren't** able to fully exploit their **comparative advantage**.

Monetary Unions have Costs and Benefits for Domestic economies

- By adopting a **single currency**, countries **don't** need to consider **costs** related to buying **another currency** when they buy goods and services from countries within the monetary union, and it makes **price comparisons** very simple.

- There are also no **exchange rate risks** when trading within the monetary union.

- The **policies** countries need to adopt in a monetary union, e.g. fiscal and monetary policies, **might** be **beneficial** to their economies, especially in the **long run**. For example, there might be **fiscal rules** (see p.171) to stop countries from having **long-term budget deficits**.

- However, the policies which must be adopted to **suit** the **whole** union may **not** be helpful for **individual** countries' economies. For example, a member state might be in a **recession**, but if the central bank, e.g. the European Central Bank (ECB), **raises interest rates** to restrain inflation in other member states, then the recession may **worsen**.

- Countries lose a certain amount of **sovereignty** (i.e. their ability to make decisions on and control their own economies) in a monetary union as they **lose control** of their **monetary policy** — they can **no longer** change interest rates and exchange rates to help with their **macroeconomic objectives**. **Only the central bank can change interest rates and exchange rates.**

Warm-Up Questions

Q1 Briefly explain the stages of economic integration.

Exam Question

Q1 Discuss the possible costs and benefits to a country of joining a monetary union.

[12 marks]

Trade diversion — redirecting all the chocolate-carrying lorries to my house...

It's really important that you understand the different stages of economic integration, and the positive and negative effects it can have on economies. A lot of the downsides relate to the amount of control a government has over its own economy.

The European Union

You've seen bits about the European Union — but here's a whole double page dedicated to everything European.
These pages are for AQA only, but may be useful for Edexcel and OCR too.

The **European Union** is a **Customs Union**

1) The number of countries in the EU **isn't fixed**. There are several countries waiting as **candidates** to join, and in 2020 the UK **left** the European Union.

2) The EU is made up of **various** bodies and institutions. Two of the **main** ones are:

   - The **European Commission** — has **one Commissioner** from **each** member country. Amongst other things, it **allocates** EU funding, **manages** budgets, and **proposes** laws and helps to **enforce** them.
   - The **European Central Bank (ECB)** — **manages** the euro and tries to keep prices **stable**. It sets **interest rates** to help control inflation, **issues** euro banknotes and manages **foreign currency reserves** to maintain the euro's exchange rate.

3) In the EU, there's **free trade** between members and **common external tariffs** are imposed — so the EU is a **customs union**.

4) The **Single European Market (SEM)** was created in 1993. It meant that the EU became much more like a **common** (single) **market**. As well as free trade of **goods** and **services**, the SEM allows:

While Tony was distracted by his book, Edna liked to check out the singles market.

   - Free mobility of **labour** — **people** are allowed to **move freely** between countries to **live and work**.
   - Free mobility of **capital** and **currency** between countries.

There are **Several** countries **Waiting** as candidates to **Join** the **EU**

1) **Enlargement** of the EU by the **addition** of **new members** will have impacts on both **new** and **existing** members.

2) For example, the impacts of **previous** enlargements and the **potential** impacts of **future** enlargements include:

	Advantages	Disadvantages
Existing members	• **Increased** economies of scale and price competition, which should lead to **higher efficiency** and **lower prices**. • **Migration** from **new** member states to **old** member states will increase **aggregate supply** for the old member states, helping with their **economic growth**. • Migrants tend to be employed at **lower** hourly rates than domestic workers — this can **reduce** production costs and **increase** productive capacity. • Migration might also bring **skilled workers** to existing members.	• The **migration** from **new** member states to **old** member states might lead to **overcrowding** in cities, and it's likely there'll be an **increase** in demand for **services, housing** and **benefits**. • Migrants might contribute to **domestic unemployment**. • If **new** member states are **poorer** than **existing** member states, there might be **increased inequality** as people **migrate** from the **new** to **existing** member states. • **Increased competition** from new members may drive **domestic** firms out of business.
New members	• New members will also benefit from **increased** economies of scale and price competition (and **higher efficiency** and **lower prices**). • People in the new member states will gain the **freedom** to **live** and **work** wherever they choose in other member states. • Joining the EU has meant some countries, which previously had trade barriers to contend with, can now **trade freely** with EU countries.	• New members will have to **comply with EU laws** — which might **conflict** with what the government thinks is **best** for their country. • There may be **increased costs** for firms and the government — for example, in order to comply with regulations on product safety. • **Migration** from **new** to **existing** member states might lead to a domestic **shortage** of labour. • There's a risk of **unemployment**, particularly structural unemployment, if firms **can't compete** with those in existing member states.

The European Union

There are many arguments For and Against the UK's EU Membership

Although the UK **left** the EU in 2020, you still need to **know** about the UK's EU membership, and understand the **pros and cons**:

1) Along with the advantages for existing EU members given on the previous page,
   the arguments **for** the UK's membership of the EU include:

   - **Avoiding job losses** — some people argue that firms would **relocate** to one of the EU's remaining members if the UK was no longer a member of the EU. There could also be a **reduction** in **FDI** in the UK from countries outside of the EU.

   - The UK does much of its trading with other EU countries, such as Germany. Leaving the EU would risk **losing** some of this trade — as a result there'd be **less** money injected into the UK economy and jobs would be **lost**.

2) Arguments **against** the UK's membership of the EU (along with the disadvantages given on the previous page) include:

   - **Control** over migration — if the UK wasn't an EU member, it could **restrict** migration from other EU countries.

   - Some people argued that the UK could remain in a **free trade area** with the EU (but **not** be a member of the customs union), so the UK would still benefit from trade, but be **free from** restrictions imposed by the EU in other areas (e.g. free from EU fishing quotas, and the UK could make its own trade agreements with countries outside of the EU).

The EMU is a further step in European Economic Integration

1) The European **Economic and Monetary Union (EMU)** involves:

   - A **common monetary** policy — this is dealt with by the ECB.

   - Member states **coordinating fiscal** and **economic** policies.

   - Member states using a **common currency** — the **euro**.

2) **Not all** members of the EU are part of the EMU. The UK was a **member** of the **EU**, but **wasn't** a member of the **single currency area** (the Eurozone). If members want to **join** the EMU, they need to meet **convergence criteria** — this means keeping budget deficit, inflation, exchange rate and interest rate levels all close to **specified** levels.

3) Monetary unions have many **costs** and **benefits** — see p.207. These were some of the further arguments on **either side** of the debate on whether the UK should have joined the Eurozone:

Reasons for

- **FDI** into Eurozone countries may have **increased** as, if the UK joined the Eurozone, there would have been a **bigger** market with **reduced transaction costs**. **Not** joining the euro may have meant that the UK **loses** some inward FDI.

- There was the potential that with **reduced transaction costs**, there may have been **increased trade**, which could have lead to **higher** growth and employment.

  It also could have improved living standards and the balance of payments.

- There would have still been **fiscal policy** tools available for the UK government to use to manage the UK economy, though these would have been in line with **EU policies** on, for example, budget deficits.

Reasons against

- **Price stability** is a major aim of the ECB — **Eurozone inflation targets** are **less flexible** than UK ones. **Slower** growth may result from having to meet these targets.

- Various problems have been encountered within the Eurozone recently as a result of the **global financial crisis**. For example, **falls** in real GDP, **weak** consumer spending and capital investment, and **high** unemployment.

- There's a large amount of **structural unemployment** within the Eurozone. This, along with the **widening divergence** in trade balances within the Eurozone, indicates problems with **competitiveness** within it — for example, **Germany** has a large current account **surplus**, and **Cyprus** has a current account **deficit**.

Warm-Up Questions

Q1 What are the main characteristics of the Single European Market (SEM)?

Q2 Give one advantage and one disadvantage to current members of adding new members to the EU.

Exam Question

Q1 Evaluate the costs and benefits of EU membership for the UK.   [15 marks]

EMU — that's bound to ruffle some feathers...

You don't need to know loads of details about EU bodies — just make sure you know the main functions of the two on the previous page. When the UK left the EU in 2020, the truth is that nobody really knew exactly what would happen. This is why it was such a hotly debated topic, with lots of arguments for and against. We'll have to see what the future holds.

Exchange Rates

Exchange rates have an impact on many aspects of the economy, such as economic growth, inflation and the balance of payments. Some countries set a fixed exchange rate, whilst others mainly leave a floating exchange rate to market forces. **For all boards.**

There are **Two** main types of **Exchange Rate Systems**

1) A fixed exchange rate is where the government or its central bank (see p.190) sets the exchange rate. This often involves maintaining the exchange rate at a target rate (see below).

2) A floating exchange rate is free to move with changing supply of, and demand for, a currency.

3) A **hybrid** exchange rate system is a mixture of fixed and floating. There are a number of different hybrid systems, e.g.:

- **Managed floating** — the exchange rate is mainly left to **market forces** (i.e. to float freely), but the government will occasionally **intervene** to influence the exchange rate. For example, to **reduce** the impact of an economic shock on the value of its currency.

- **Semi-fixed** — the exchange rate is only allowed to **fluctuate** within a **set band** of exchange rates.

- **Pegged** — the **value** of the currency is 'pegged' to **another** currency or **group** of currencies. This peg can be **moved** periodically, or as the government sees fit.

Fixed exchange rates have to stay at a **Target Rate**

1) **Fixed** exchange rate systems, and certain **hybrid** exchange rate systems, have a **target** rate.

2) A **government** or **central bank** will maintain the exchange rate at the target rate by **controlling** interest rates and by **buying** and **selling** the currency (using foreign currency reserves) to keep supply of, and demand for, the currency **stable**.

There are **Various** ways of **Measuring** exchange rates

1) **Nominal** exchange rate — an **unadjusted** or 'direct' comparison of the value of currencies.

2) **Real** exchange rate — this is a nominal rate which is **adjusted** to take **price levels** into account (see p.213 for more).

- Nominal exchange rates **don't** always reflect the **true worth** of currencies (i.e. how much they can actually buy).

- Real exchange rates **overcome** this problem by taking **prices** in the different countries into account (using a **price index**, e.g. the CPI, for each country).

> Purchasing power parity (PPP) is an example of using the concept of real exchange rates — see p.123 for more on PPP.

3) **Bilateral** exchange rate — the comparison of just **two** currencies, e.g. a nominal bilateral exchange rate could directly compare the US dollar and the pound, so it might show that £1: $1.50 (£1 is worth $1.50).

4) **Effective** exchange rate — a country's currency is compared to a **basket** of currencies (usually of its **trading** partners). It's a **weighted average** — e.g. the **proportion** of the country's trade with each partner determines the **size** of the weighting. The aim is to give a kind of '**summary**' of the **overall value** of a currency compared to several others.

Market Forces or **Government Intervention** cause exchange rates to **Fluctuate**

1) The **devaluation** of a **fixed** exchange rate occurs when the exchange rate is **lowered** formally by the government. They can achieve this by **selling** the currency.

2) The **opposite** of exchange rate **devaluation** is exchange rate **revaluation** (achieved by **buying** the currency).

3) The **depreciation** of a **floating** exchange rate is when the exchange rate **falls**. This might occur naturally due to **market forces**, although government action (e.g. **lowering** interest rates) might **affect** it indirectly.

4) The **opposite** of exchange rate **depreciation** is exchange rate **appreciation**.

5) **Competitive devaluation** can occur in fixed or hybrid exchange rate systems. This is when governments **deliberately** devalue their own currencies to **improve** international competitiveness (see p.215).

6) **Competitive depreciation** can occur in floating or hybrid exchange rate systems — government intervention might indirectly **reduce** the value of the currency, **improving** the country's international competitiveness.

This crowd **really** appreciated the exchange rate.

Exchange Rates

Floating and Fixed exchange rates have Advantages and Disadvantages

	Advantages	Disadvantages
Floating	Under **fixed** exchange rate systems, central banks require **foreign currency reserves** so that they can intervene to maintain their exchange rate target — a **floating** exchange rate will **reduce** the need for currency reserves.	Floating exchange rates can **fluctuate** widely, which makes business planning **difficult**.
Floating	A floating exchange rate can help to **reduce** a BOP current account **deficit** — a BOP deficit will lead to a **fall** in the value of the currency, so if demand for exports and imports is moderately **price elastic**, exports will **increase** and imports will **decrease**, reducing the BOP deficit.	Speculation can **artificially strengthen** an exchange rate — this would cause a country to **lose competitiveness**, as domestic goods will become **over-priced**.
Floating	A floating exchange rate means that a government **doesn't** need to use monetary policy, e.g. interest rates, to help to maintain the exchange rate — it can use it for **other objectives**.	**Falls** in exchange rates can lead to inflationary pressures — for example, if demand for imports tends to be **price inelastic**.
Fixed	**Speculation** may be **reduced** — unless dealers feel that the exchange rate is no longer **sustainable**.	If speculators feel a fixed exchange rate **isn't sustainable**, they might take advantage of this by **selling** the currency.
Fixed	**Competitive pressures** are placed on firms — they need to keep costs **down**, **invest** and **increase productivity** to remain competitive.	The country effectively **loses control** of interest rates, as they need to be used to keep the **exchange rate** at the desired level.
Fixed	Fixed exchange rates create **certainty**, which is likely to **encourage** investment (including FDI).	Fixed exchange rates are **difficult** to maintain.

The various hybrid systems have a **mixture** of advantages and disadvantages of both floating and fixed systems. For example, a **pegged** system creates **more certainty** than a freely floating system, so this might lead to **more investment**. However, the country will also lose **some** control of interest rates, as they'll need to be used to **influence** the exchange rate.

Supply and Demand determine Floating exchange rates

1) Floating exchange rates are determined by **changes** in **supply** and **demand** for a currency. For example, an **increase** in the **supply** of pounds to S_1 will cause a **decrease** in the **value** of the pound to P_1. This increase in supply may be due to things such as an **increase** in **imports** to the UK and **increased selling** of the pound.

2) A **decrease** in the **demand** for pounds to D_1 will cause a **decrease** in the **value** of the pound to P_1. This decrease in demand may be due to, for example, a **decrease** in **exports** from the UK and **decreased buying** of the pound.

3) Supply and demand **fluctuations** are caused by many other factors, for example:

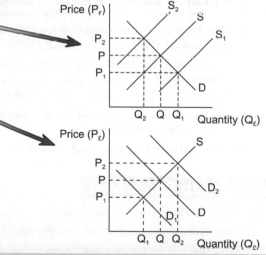

- **Speculation** — where people **buy** and **sell** currency because of changes they **expect** are going to happen in the future.
- The **official** buying and selling of the currency by the **government** or **central bank**.
- **Relative inflation rates** — if a country's inflation rate is **higher** than its **competitors'**, then the **value** of its currency is likely to **fall**. Prices in the country will become **less competitive**, leading to **reduced exports** and **increased imports**, so **demand** for the currency **decreases** and **supply increases**.
- **Relative interest rates** — **high** interest rates **increase demand** for a currency because there's an **inflow** of 'hot money' (see p.157 and 174).
- **Confidence** in the state of the economy — there'll be **greater demand** for a currency if people feel confident in, for example, a country's **growth** and **stability** (this will include a country's **economic** and **political** stability — investors are **unlikely** to have confidence in **unstable** governments).
- The balance on the **current account** of the balance of payments has a **small** effect on the exchange rate — for example, a current account **deficit** will mean there's a **high supply** of the currency due to the **purchase** of **imports**.

Exchange Rates

Fluctuations in the Exchange Rate have Impacts on the economy

1) If the value of a currency **falls**:
   - **Exports** will become **cheaper**, so domestic goods will become **more competitive**.
   - This means that **demand** for **exports** will **increase**.
   - **Imports** will become **more expensive**, so **demand** for **imports** will **fall**.
   - A current account **deficit** should therefore be **reduced**, but a surplus should **increase**.

2) The current account deficit will only reduce if the **Marshall-Lerner** condition holds — see below.

3) The **J-curve** shows how the current account may actually **worsen** in the **short run**, but **improve** in the **long run** — see below.

4) A **fall** in the value of a currency can also mean:
   - If exports increase and imports decrease, there'll be **economic growth** caused by an **increase** in aggregate demand.
   - **Unemployment** may also be **reduced** through the **creation** of more jobs from economic growth.
   - **Inflation** may **rise** if demand for imports is **price inelastic**.
   - **Increased** import prices can also cause **cost-push** inflation.

5) A **rise** in the value of a currency will tend to have the **opposite** effects on an economy.

6) For example, **exports** will become **more expensive** and **imports** will become **cheaper**. This will potentially mean:
   - An **increase** in the size of a current account **deficit**, or a **reduction** in a current account **surplus**.
   - A **fall** in aggregate demand, which is likely to lead to a **fall** in output.
   - **Unemployment** may **rise**.
   - The impact on inflation will depend on the **price elasticity of demand** for imports and for domestic goods.

A Fall in the Value of a currency Might Not improve a current account Deficit

1) A fall in the value of a currency will only reduce a current account **deficit** if the **Marshall-Lerner condition** holds.

2) The Marshall-Lerner condition says that for a **fall** in the value of a currency to lead to an **improvement** in the balance of payments, the price elasticity of demand for **imports plus** the price elasticity of demand for **exports** must be **greater than one**, i.e. $PED_M + PED_X > 1$.

The J-curve shows the effect of Inelastic demand for imports and exports in the Short Run

1) The Marshall-Lerner condition might hold in the **long run**, so there'll be an **improvement** in a current account deficit if the value of a currency **falls**.

2) However, in the **short run** a current account deficit is likely to **worsen**, as demand for imports and exports will be **inelastic** — e.g. because it takes time for people to switch to a cheaper substitute.

3) In the short run, the **overall** value of **exports falls** and the **overall** value of **imports rises**, so the current account deficit worsens.

4) This is shown on the **J-curve**.

Current account of the balance of payments (£bn)

+ve

0

−ve

Time

Warm-Up Questions

Q1 What is an effective exchange rate?

Q2 Give one advantage and one disadvantage of floating exchange rates.

Q3 Give one advantage and one disadvantage of fixed exchange rates.

Q4 What impact might a fall in the value of a country's currency have on a current account deficit?

PRACTICE QUESTIONS

Exam Question

Q1 Explain the likely impact of hosting a major sporting event on a country's currency.   [4 marks]

I lost £7 learning that floating exchange rates are nothing to do with water...

Exchange rates play an important part in all economies — they directly affect exports and imports, which have knock-on effects on other aspects of the economy, such as economic growth, unemployment, inflation and the balance of payments. As well as understanding the exchange rate's impact on the economy, make sure you know the factors which can affect the exchange rate.

International Competitiveness

International competitiveness is all about making sure that, as a country, you're making things that people want to buy and selling them at prices that they're happy to pay. **These pages are for Edexcel and OCR only.**

Competitiveness involves a lot of **Price Factors**

1) International **competitiveness** is a complex thing to try to **measure** — it involves trying to measure a country's **ability** to provide better-value goods and services than its rivals.

2) This will, to a large extent, depend on the **price** at which a country can produce and sell those goods and services. Various measures give an indication of this:

The 'relative' part of these terms means 'in comparison with competing countries'.

- **Relative unit labour costs** — unit labour costs measure the cost of the **labour** needed to generate output. If one country has **lower** unit labour costs than another country, then (all other things being equal) that country will be **more competitive** — i.e. better able to sell its products. To **compare** unit labour costs in different countries, you need to convert each country's unit labour costs to the **same currency**. In fact, comparisons are usually carried out by converting the costs to an **index number** that tries to allow for differences between countries, to make comparisons more valid.

- **Relative productivity** — increasing productivity (e.g. the output per worker per hour) will have a similar effect on competitiveness to reducing unit labour costs — i.e. all other things being equal, **higher** productivity means **greater competitiveness**. There's more on this below.

- **Relative export prices** — exchange rates (see below and p.210) are a key determinant of relative export prices. For example, if the value of a country's currency **falls**, its exports will become **relatively** cheaper and its competitiveness will **increase**. The cost of **labour** will also have a significant effect on relative export prices, especially in **labour-intensive** industries, such as many manufacturing industries. (In **capital-intensive** industries, it's **less useful** as a guide to overall competitiveness.)

3) These are all **price factors**, but often **non-price factors** are used to judge competitiveness too. For example:

- **Design** — are a country's products what people want to buy?
- **Quality** — are products well made, and do they work properly?
- **Reliability** — do a country's products keep working?
- **Availability** — is it easy to buy a country's products?

Strong management and investment in technology can play a big part in improving some of these factors.

Competitiveness is **Influenced** by many factors

There are many factors which influence competitiveness and that can therefore be taken into consideration when trying to decide **how competitive** a country is. For example:

Real Exchange Rates and Relative Inflation Rates

- **Real exchange rates** affect the **relative export prices** of different countries, impacting on a country's competitiveness — e.g. if the **pound** was **strong** compared to the **dollar**, then other countries would be more likely to buy **US exports**.

- The **real exchange rate** is the **nominal exchange rate** (the exchange rate determined by the foreign exchange rate markets — see p.210), but it's **adjusted** to take into account the **price levels** within the countries being compared.

- It's worked out using the following **formula**:

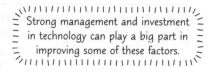

$$\text{real exchange rate} = \text{nominal exchange rate} \times \frac{\text{price level in a country}}{\text{price level abroad}}$$

- So, the real exchange rate will be **affected** by changes to the **nominal exchange rate** and the **rate of inflation** in a country or abroad. This means, for example, the real exchange rate will **fall** if the nominal exchange rate **falls** or if the price levels abroad **rise** relative to domestic prices.

Productivity

- Productivity will be affected by the level of **human capital** in workers...
- ...which is affected by the levels of **education** and **training** of the population.
- The amount and sophistication of **capital equipment** used by workers will also be a factor here.

See p.103 for unit labour costs and productivity — these influence more than one of these competitiveness factors.

International Competitiveness

More factors **Influencing** competitiveness

Wage Costs and Non-Wage Costs

- As well as **wage costs** (what a firm spends on wages), **non-wage costs** will affect the competitiveness of a country's firms.
- Non-wage costs will include things like:
  - employers' **national insurance** contributions and **pension** contributions,
  - costs incurred as a result of **environmental protection** or **anti-discrimination** laws, or **health-and-safety** regulations.

Labour Market Flexibility

- A flexible labour market is one where the **supply** of labour is able to **adapt** quickly to the **changing** needs of businesses (for example, workers can **transfer between activities** quickly — see p.118 for more).
- So factors affecting flexibility include the strength of **trade unions**, levels of **skills** and **qualifications** amongst workers, the ability for firms to hire/fire workers **easily**, and the willingness of workers to work **part-time** or on **flexible** contracts.

Research and Development

A country that's able to **innovate** and create **new products** (and perhaps even whole **new markets** as a result) or new, more efficient **methods of production** is likely to have an advantage when it comes to competing internationally.

Regulation

Regulations often **increase costs** for firms, forcing them to **raise** prices and become **less competitive** internationally.

Governments can try to improve the **Economy's** competitiveness

1) To improve **firms' competitiveness**, and the competitiveness of the economy **as a whole**, governments can introduce a range of **supply-side** policies. For example:

> See p.176-177 for more on supply-side policies.

- Improve **education and training** (which will also improve labour market flexibility)
  - E.g. apprenticeships allow people to learn **practical skills** while gaining relevant **qualifications**.
  - Improvements in education will not only allow employees to become more **productive** (and therefore **reduce** unit labour costs), but can also lead to greater **occupational mobility** (see p.113).
- Improve **labour market flexibility** in other ways
  - E.g. in the past, policies have been introduced that weakened some of the powers of **trade unions** — firms are now able to make workers **redundant** more easily when times are tough.
- **Create incentives** for firms to **invest**
  - E.g. offer firms **tax breaks** (i.e. reductions in the amount of tax they need to pay) if they **invest** profits **instead** of paying **dividends** to shareholders. There can be many outcomes of investment — for example, investment in **research** can lead to improvements in **product quality** and **productivity**.
- **Improve infrastructure**
  - E.g. build faster transport links or improve communication links.
- **"Cut red tape"**
  - This means **removing** any **regulations** that no longer seem necessary and which may be increasing firms' costs unnecessarily — e.g. outdated **environmental** or **health-and-safety** regulations.
  - Making it easier to set up a company can lead to more **entrepreneurship** and **innovation**.
- **Encourage competition**
  - E.g. **deregulation** (see p.93) can lead to improved **efficiency** in a market.
  - **Privatisation** (see p.92) may be effective if **nationalised** industries are **inefficient**.
- **Encourage immigration**
  - Foreign workers may have the **skills** that businesses need.
  - This can be a very quick way to obtain the **human capital** needed in an economy.
- **Maintain economic stability**
  - E.g. by keeping **inflation** low, **exchange rates** steady, and the **balance of payments** under control.

2) It may **not** be **simple** to introduce these policies though, and it may take a **long time** to feel their full effect.
- For example, it takes a long time to plan and build extra schools and colleges to improve **education** and **training**.
- Some policies may be **controversial** — e.g. trade union reforms can be unpopular with some people.
- There may also be difficulties in **affording** these policies — e.g. the government may not be able to spend money on **improving infrastructure**, or firms may not be able to **invest** at the most appropriate time.

International Competitiveness

Governments can Influence prices more directly

1) Some governments may **devalue** their currency —
   i.e. **reduce** its **value** against other currencies (see p.210).

2) Devaluing a country's currency can lead to **increased demand** from abroad for that country's **exports**. But it also means **imports** become more expensive, so people in that country are more likely to buy **domestically** produced goods.

Decreasing interest rates would usually lead to a fall in the exchange rate — so you might think a government could devalue the currency that way. But in the UK, interest rates are set by the Bank of England rather than the government.

3) Overall, the country should become **more competitive**, and there should be improvements in the **balance of payments**.

4) But devaluation can lead to **cost-push inflation** (see p.152) if imports are used in the production of other goods. It may also mean that firms aren't under as much pressure to **reduce their costs**, something that will be necessary in the long run if they're hoping to compete with foreign firms.

5) **Tariffs** can also be used to **increase competitiveness** (at least domestically), and similarly a government could use **subsidies** to allow domestic producers to supply their goods more cheaply than similar ones produced abroad (see p.202).

6) Both tariffs and subsidies have the **disadvantage** that, like devaluation, producers may not seek the **efficiency improvements** that are necessary for them to **genuinely** compete internationally.

Competitiveness is Usually a good thing

1) In general, being internationally competitive is a **good** thing:
   - If a country's **exports** are **relatively cheap**, there'll be **higher** demand for them. This will mean **increased** aggregate demand, economic growth and levels of employment.
   - Many countries have current account **deficits** — increasing exports (and reducing imports) helps to **correct** this imbalance.

2) Falling competitiveness can have **serious consequences**:
   - A country that's less able to sell its products is likely to experience a worsening in its **balance of payments**, because **exports** will **fall** while **imports increase**.
   - In addition, as economic activity generally decreases, **unemployment** will probably **increase**.
   - Remaining competitive is particularly important for countries whose industries rely on **international trade** to achieve **economies of scale**.

As the 'Enhancing Productivity' company bonding day neared its climax, Sandy was sure it wasn't falling competitiveness that was uppermost in her mind.

There can be Downsides to being Internationally Competitive

1) It's **not** always good to be internationally competitive:
   - If a country has a current account **surplus**, relatively cheap exports will **worsen** this imbalance.
   - If a country is so competitive that it's **over-reliant** on exports, this leaves it **vulnerable** to **shocks** (e.g. if a major trading partner suffers from a recession).

2) Focusing on competitiveness can lead to other problems. For example:
   - A **flexible labour market** is useful for competitiveness — but this can lead to **difficulties** for workers because of the **uncertainty** it creates, e.g. a lack of job security.
   - Countries might **neglect** the environment, e.g. by **not** keeping **pollution** levels down.

Warm-Up Questions

Q1 How can real exchange rates influence a country's competitiveness?

Q2 How might a devaluation of a currency help a country regain its competitiveness?

PRACTICE QUESTIONS

Exam Question

Q1 Discuss some of the approaches that may be used by a government to help improve its country's overall competitiveness.

[20 marks]

Changing devalue of the currency isn't always an option...

International competitiveness is important to countries — if they're not competitive, they're likely to face all sorts of problems, such as struggling to grow their economies. There are loads of things that can affect competitiveness, so time to get learning.

Measures of Economic Development

This section is all about economic development — this is related to economic growth, but is not the same thing. First up, measuring development. There's more on this in Section 8, but this page will give you a recap. **These pages are for all boards.**

Economic Development is **Not** just about economic growth

1) **Economic growth** is relatively easy to define — it's an **increase** in the size of a country's **GDP**.

2) **Economic development** is more complicated to define and measure, because it's a **normative** concept. It involves making **value judgements** about what would make up a '**more developed**' country.

3) But the aim is to somehow measure how **living standards** and people's **general welfare** in a country **change** over time.

4) The size of a country's **economy** is important when measuring its development, but so are things such as the **size** and **health** of the **population**, and the **quality of life** they have.

5) To some extent, measuring **development** means assessing not just the amount of **economic growth** that has occurred, but also its '**quality**' — e.g. the effect it has on **people's lives** or the **uses** extra income resulting from that growth is put to.

> **Examples**
> - Economic growth that causes vast amounts of **pollution** would be considered **less beneficial** than the same amount of economic growth but with much **less** pollution.
> - Economic growth that directly **improves** the lives of a **large part** of the population (e.g. by improving access to clean drinking water) would be considered **more positive** than growth that brings financial benefits to just a **small** number of **already wealthy** people.

National Income Figures like **GNI Per Capita** don't tell the whole story

1) One important measure of economic development is **national income data**, such as **real GDP per capita** or **real GNI (gross national income) per capita**.

   Real GDP and GNI have the effect of inflation removed — GDP and GNI are covered on page 122.

2) Using GDP or GNI **per capita** (i.e. **per person**) will give a better indication of people's **standards of living**. This will be very important if the size of a country's population is **changing**. Using 'per capita' figures also means you can **compare** figures **between countries** whose populations are different sizes.

3) Comparisons between different countries based on national income data make use of the principle of **purchasing power parity**, **PPP** (see p.123). This is important as $1 will buy **more** in a **less developed** country than in a **developed** one.

4) Generally speaking, countries with a **higher** GDP or GNI per capita have **higher standards of living**, but national income data **doesn't** tell you about lots of '**quality of life**' factors, such as the amount of **leisure time** people have or their **health**.

5) National income data also **ignores** economic welfare brought about by the **hidden economy** — i.e. economic activity that's **not recorded** by government statistics (which is a **large** chunk of some developing countries' economies).

   There's more about the limitations of comparing countries using GDP on page 123.

6) The **Genuine Progress Indicator** (**GPI**) is an economic indicator that tries to give a fuller picture of the effects of growth than GDP. It uses GDP, but also takes into account the negative effects of growth (e.g. pollution), as well as things that affect **quality of life** but aren't included in GDP (e.g. volunteer work).

7) The GPI is useful because it means policies can be aimed at increasing **overall welfare**, rather than just GDP. However, it's quite **difficult** to put a value or cost on things like volunteering or pollution, so these figures will be quite **subjective**.

The **Human Development Index** considers a **Wider Range** of indicators

1) The United Nations **Human Development Index** (**HDI**) is an attempt to describe people's welfare and a country's economic development in a way that goes beyond just looking at national income figures.

2) It takes into account people's **health** (measured by life expectancy), **education** (measured by years of schooling), and **standard of living** (measured by real GNI per capita, adjusted for purchasing power parity). (There's more information about HDI on page 128.)

3) It **doesn't** capture all the information that's relevant to people's welfare or economic development, but it does place a **greater emphasis** on the **quality of life** of a country's people instead of just considering **economic growth**.

The Human Development conference was interesting, but not really what Susan had expected.

4) Countries' HDI figures can be used to **rank** those countries from **most developed** to **least developed**. Or a country's HDI figure (a number between 0 and 1) can be used to assess its **general** level of development — e.g. a figure **above 0.8** signifies a **high** level of human development, while a figure **below 0.5** shows a **low** level of human development.

5) Two countries can achieve a similar HDI in very **different** ways, e.g. one country might have **high** life expectancy but a **poorly developed** education system, while another has **low** life expectancy but a **successful** education system.

Measures of Economic Development

Extreme Inequality is usually seen as a Problem

1) Development can help to reduce **inequality** between countries, but even when a country's national income grows, inequality **within** that country can still cause problems.

2) In **developing** countries, those with very low wealth and incomes can suffer **hardship** if circumstances change (e.g. if harvests fail or demand for their goods decreases).

3) In **developed** countries, those with the lowest wealth and incomes may not be in **absolute poverty**, but they may still be in **relative poverty** (see p.166), or at risk of **social exclusion** (i.e. they may not have access to all the opportunities or resources needed to **fully participate** in society, such as employment opportunities and decent health care).

4) Some people say that inequality is an **inevitable consequence** of economic development (i.e. some people will always do better than others). Others say that some inequality is actually **necessary** for capitalism to function effectively, since inequality gives people an **incentive** to work hard and succeed.

If the benefits of development go to those who are already wealthy, extreme poverty can exist alongside genuine affluence.

5) However, it can also be argued that inequality can **slow down** economic development, for various reasons:

- The **poorest** within a country may find it difficult to **start businesses**. They may not have the resources to **invest**, will find it difficult to **save**, and their lack of **assets** (for use as **collateral**) may make it difficult for them to get **loans**. Access to **credit** is often particularly limited in developing countries — banking can be too expensive for people to use, and getting to a bank may be difficult.

Collateral means goods that you promise to give to a lender if you aren't able to repay a loan.

- People on higher incomes may well spend a lot on **imports**, or invest their money **abroad** (see p.218) — so this money will **leave** the economy.

6) Inequality and social exclusion may also be linked to **social problems** in a country, such as higher levels of **crime** or **health problems**.

There's more on the positives and negatives of inequality on page 166.

Inequality can be measured using the Lorenz Curve or Gini Coefficient

1) Causes of inequality will **vary** between countries, but the following are important factors:

- wage and tax levels
- unemployment levels
- education levels
- property ownership and inheritance laws
- level of government benefits

There's more on the causes of inequality on page 165.

2) The amount of **inequality** in a country can be shown using a **Lorenz curve** or a **Gini coefficient**.

The Lorenz curve
- The Lorenz curve for a country is shown in **red** in this diagram.
- Remember... **perfect equality** would be shown by a **straight line**.
- A 'saggier' curve means a **greater share** of the country's overall income goes to a relatively **small number** of people.

The Gini coefficient
- Remember... the Gini coefficient (G) is always a value **between 0** (everyone earns the same) **and 1** (one person gets all the country's income).
- $G = \dfrac{A}{A + B}$ *See p.165 for more about the Lorenz curve and Gini coefficient.*

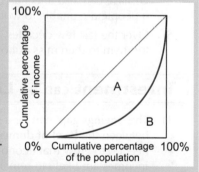

Warm-Up Questions

Q1 Describe why national income figures don't give a true indication of economic welfare in a country.

Q2 What is the HDI? What three factors are assessed in order to work out a country's HDI?

PRACTICE QUESTIONS

Exam Question

Q1 Explain why inequality may slow down economic development. [4 marks]

The Genie coefficient — how many wishes you get after rubbing a magic lantern...

Economic development is tricky — it sounds like a similar kind of thing to economic growth, but it's actually quite different. Economic development is a lot more general, and involves people's overall quality of life rather than just their income. Inequality is important here too — some degree of inequality is probably inevitable, but extreme inequality can lead to all sorts of problems.

Limits to Growth and Development

All countries are different, but there are some common obstacles that developing nations frequently face. **All boards.**

Poor Infrastructure makes it difficult for an economy to grow

1) The **infrastructure** of a country means the **basic facilities** and **services** needed for the country and its economy to function. For example:
   - roads
   - schools
   - water supplies
   - sewerage
   - railways
   - hospitals
   - electricity supplies
   - telephone / internet services

2) Poor infrastructure makes it **difficult** for a country's economy to grow or be internationally competitive. For example:
   - If **energy supplies** are unreliable, then firms and factories won't be able to operate efficiently.
   - If **transport links** are poor, it can be difficult to **move** goods **around** or **out of** the country.
   - If **telephone** and **internet services** are scarce, then businesses will find it difficult to coordinate their operations and communicate with customers.

3) Poor infrastructure also makes it very difficult to attract **foreign direct investment** (FDI).

4) **Foreign aid** (see p.220) is often used to **improve** or **maintain** infrastructure, but developing nations can sometimes persuade foreign investors to help **improve** their infrastructure — perhaps because these nations have important **raw materials** or because they would become attractive **new markets** for foreign firms.

> For example, Chile has large reserves of **minerals** and has attracted large amounts of **FDI** in various parts of its economy, such as in its **energy** and **communications** industries.

The natural resources available in a country can also affect how it develops.

Disease and lack of Education can cause Human Capital Inadequacies

1) If a country's **population** grows **faster** than its **economy**, then this will lead to a fall in **GNI per capita** (and probably also a fall in people's **standards of living**). Developing nations, such as those in certain parts of Africa, have some of the fastest growing populations in the world.

2) A fast growing population means there'll be lots of **children**, which can put pressure on a country's **education system**.

See p.216 for more about development and a country's population.

3) However, household poverty is a major factor in keeping children **out** of school, and if children **don't** go to school, this can lead to further problems. **Low educational standards** are likely to mean a workforce that's **less productive**, as they have less **human capital**. A less productive workforce will make it difficult to attract **FDI**. It can also be difficult for people to access **professional training** (e.g. medical school) in developing countries, which causes similar problems.

4) **Disease** can also affect a country's economy — e.g. it can result in **lower productivity** if people are unable to work, and put a strain on the country's **health care system**.

5) Over the last few decades, **HIV/AIDS** has also led to a huge number of children being **orphaned** — it's common for them to then miss out on going to **school**, with long-term consequences both for them and the economy.

Investment can be Limited in Developing Countries

1) The 'savings gap' can be a problem when incomes are low — it's the **gap** between the **level of domestic savings** in an economy and the **investment** needed to grow that economy. This lack of investment in **capital** means incomes are likely to remain **low**, as shown in the diagram.

See p.220 for the importance of savings in the Harrod-Domar model.

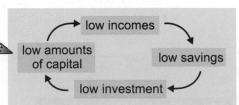

2) **Capital flight** is when people start holding their savings **abroad** (often as a result of high tax rates or political instability). This lack of domestic investment makes economic growth more difficult to achieve. It also means that **less tax** is collected (since the government won't receive taxes due on those savings).

3) Many developing countries borrowed heavily in the past. Just **servicing** (i.e. paying the **interest** on) these debts can be vastly expensive, leaving **less** money available for **health** and **education**, for example, or investment in **capital**.

4) A **foreign exchange gap** (or **foreign currency gap**) means capital outflows from a country are greater than capital inflows. This is more likely when a country:
   a) is dependent on **exports** of **primary products**, or **imports** of **manufactured goods** (see next page),
   b) has to spend a lot of money **servicing debt**.

5) An **absence of property rights** can also cause problems — if people aren't sure they will be able to keep the land they have, then they may not **invest** in improvements to their **homes**, or in setting up **businesses**. This can harm development.

This may be because the rule of law is weak (i.e. there's no functioning system to get people to keep to the law)

Section Fourteen — Economic Development

Limits to Growth and Development

Primary Product Dependency has many potential Disadvantages

1) Many countries depend on **primary products** (commodities) — i.e. products taken directly from the earth. These might include **minerals** like copper and iron ores, or **plants** like rice, wheat or fruits, where the 'value added' is low.

> 'Value added' describes how much a firm increases what a product is worth. Many primary products are 'low value added' — this means they won't generate huge profits (see p.221).

2) **Demand** for primary products is usually **price inelastic** — this means that a change in **demand** will have a **large** effect on the **price**.

3) **Supply** of some primary products (e.g. agricultural products) will be **price inelastic** in the short term, since supplies can't quickly increase or decrease (e.g. because it takes time for plants to grow). **Agricultural** products are also easily damaged by **natural disasters** and **extreme weather events**.

4) This **volatility** of commodity prices means that producers' **incomes** and earnings from **exports** can **change quickly**. If supply and demand are both price inelastic then **slight changes** in either will cause **big fluctuations** in price. The **uncertainty** this creates makes it very difficult to **plan**, and attract **investment**.

5) **Developed** countries may use **protectionist policies** to protect their own primary industries — e.g. EU policies such as the Common Agricultural Policy (CAP) make it difficult for farmers in **developing** nations to compete on equal terms.

6) The **Prebisch-Singer hypothesis** describes how countries that rely on **exporting** primary products and **importing** manufactured goods may become steadily **worse off** over time, as there'll be a decline in the **terms of trade** (see p.200).

The Prebisch-Singer hypothesis says that:

- Demand for **primary products** is income inelastic — as incomes rise, demand changes very little.

- However, demand for **manufactured products** is more income elastic — as incomes rise, demand for these goods rises quickly. This will usually then lead to **large** increases in **price**.

- As the price of manufactured goods increases, countries **exporting** mainly **primary products** will find they're able to **import fewer** manufactured goods for a **given level** of exports.

7) The Prebisch-Singer hypothesis suggests that overreliance on, say, **cash crops** (i.e. crops grown for profit) is **not** an effective long-term development strategy. However, there are criticisms of this hypothesis:
- As the world's **population** grows, greater demand for agricultural products to eat may push prices **up**.
- Demand for some primary products (e.g. gold or oil) is **income elastic** — as incomes rise, demand rises **even quicker**.
- If a country has a **comparative advantage** in producing primary products, then it makes sense to use that country's resources for this purpose.

Corruption and Civil Wars stop an economy functioning efficiently

1) **Corruption** occurs when power is abused for **personal gain** (e.g. by government officials accepting **bribes**). The result is often that the country's resources are **diverted away** from their most productive use, so governments and private firms become **less efficient**.

> E.g. some African firms export goods using much longer routes than necessary to avoid having to pay bribes.

2) The effects of corruption can be even worse. For example, if the police expect to be paid the same **bribe** by people whether or not they've broken the law, there's little incentive for people to act honestly. The effect is that the **legal system**, and eventually even the **government**, stop working properly.

3) Even if there's little corruption, an **unreliable bureaucracy** in a country (e.g. a tax office that's unable to collect the taxes that are due) can also make development difficult to achieve.

4) **Civil wars** are also a disaster for a country's economy, and are **more likely** in less developed nations. Large numbers of people are **killed** or become **refugees**, **absolute poverty** generally increases and **infrastructure** is damaged. Even after the war ends, **capital flight** and **military spending** usually remain high.

5) All these effects make it very difficult to **compete internationally** and attract **foreign direct investment** (FDI).

Warm-Up Questions

Q1 List three factors that can limit a country's economic development.

Exam Question

Q1 Explain how primary product dependency can limit a country's economic development. [8 marks]

Capital flight — in economics, this doesn't mean a trip to Paris or Rome...

The factors on these pages are bad enough and can hugely hamper a country's development. But they aren't the only problems to face developing countries. For example, landlocked countries (i.e. those with no coastline) tend to be less economically successful than those on the coast. Although you can't shift a country and give it a coastline, development policies can help.

Ways of Promoting Growth and Development

There are lots of policies to help improve economic development, but each has its pros and cons. **These pages are for all boards.**

Different Strategies are used in international development

1) The **policies** on the next few pages are mostly based on one of the following **strategies** for helping countries develop:
   - **Aid** and **debt relief** (see below).
   - **Structural change** — e.g. development of the **agricultural**, **industrial** or **tourism** sectors (see next page).
   - Policies favouring <u>either</u> an **interventionist** approach <u>or</u> a **market-orientated** approach — see pages 222-223.

2) Since all developing countries are **different**, each will need a particular **mix** of **strategies** and **policies**, probably involving both **markets** and the **state**. But there's **no guarantee** that what's worked in one country will be successful in another.

Aid means Transferring Resources from one country to another

1) In economics, **aid** means the **transfer of resources** from one country to another. There are various types:
   - **Bilateral aid** — when a donor country (i.e. the country sending the aid) sends aid **directly** to the recipient country.
   - **Multilateral aid** — when donor countries pass the aid to an **intermediate agency** (e.g. the World Bank — see p.224), which then distributes the aid to recipient countries.
   - **Tied aid** — aid sent **on condition** that the money is spent in a particular way (e.g. on imports from the donor country).

2) Aid can be used as **emergency relief** (for example during a drought or a war), but it's also used to **promote development** — this is known as **development aid**.

3) There are arguments for and against using aid to assist in **development:** ⟵ *But offering emergency aid after natural or man-made disasters is uncontroversial.*

Arguments in favour of development aid:
- It reduces **absolute poverty**.
- If it leads to improvements in **health** and **education**, this will improve a country's **human capital**.
- It helps to fill the **savings gap** (see the Harrod-Domar model below) and the **foreign exchange gap**.
- There can be 'multiplier effects'. For example, if aid is used to improve a country's **infrastructure**, there will be a **direct** increase in aggregate demand. An increase in aggregate demand will mean more people will have **jobs** (and **money** to spend), and this will lead to further increases in aggregate demand.

Harrod-Domar model	The **Harrod-Domar model** says that the growth rate of an economy is directly linked to: • the level of **saving** in the economy, • the efficiency with which the **capital** in the economy can be used. If either of these factors can be **increased**, then economic growth should be **faster**.

Arguments against development aid:
- Some people claim that aid leads to a **dependency culture**, meaning that countries start to count on receiving aid **indefinitely**, instead of **developing** their own economies.
- Aid can be **misused** by **corrupt** governments, meaning the money doesn't help the people it was meant to help.
- Some say aid is aimed more at securing 'favours' for the **donor country** than helping the **recipient countries**.

Debt Relief means Not expecting Existing debts to be repaid

1) A country with **large debts** has to spend a large amount of its income on **servicing** those debts (i.e. paying the **interest**).

2) For **low-income** countries, debt servicing can use up a **large proportion** of their total income. This leaves **less** money available for other services, such as **health care** or **education**.

3) **Debt relief** means **cancelling** some of the debts owed by developing countries. Again, there are **pros** and **cons**:

Arguments in favour of debt relief:
- It frees up money for **public services**, such as **health care** and **education**.
- The money saved by the developing country can be invested in **capital goods** to help grow its economy.

Arguments against debt relief:
- Some people claim that cancelling debt creates a risk of **moral hazard** (see p.82) and a **dependency culture**. For example, countries may feel that **future** debts will also be cancelled, so they may just **borrow** more.
- Cancelling the debt of countries run by **corrupt** governments may mean more money is **misused** — e.g. for **personal gain** or to buy **weapons** for internal repression (i.e. using force to control the country's people).
- Debt cancellation can be used by a donor country as a way to secure **influence** in the recipient country.

Ways of Promoting Growth and Development

Development often means changing the structure of the economy (the balance between the primary, secondary and tertiary sectors) — this is covered in more detail on page 129. The policies on this page can be thought of as part of a structural change strategy.

Developing the **Agricultural Sector** can help

1) The agricultural sector is often seen as a **low-productivity** sector (i.e. the **output** is low compared to the **inputs** required) where it's difficult to **add value**.

2) Although there are potential problems for a country if it depends too much on **primary products** (see p.219), it can be worth a country developing its agricultural sector if that's where it has a **comparative advantage**.

3) Developments in the agricultural sector can be seen as a **stepping stone** to developing other sectors. For example, if improvements in the agricultural sector lead to increases in national income, **other** sectors can then be **invested** in.

The **Lewis Model** describes the development of the **Industrial Sector**

1) The **Lewis model** has been used to argue that increasing an economy's **industrial sector** is the key to development. It says growth in industry and manufacturing can be achieved **without** reducing agricultural output or increasing inflation.

> **Lewis model**
> - The Lewis model assumes that there's **excess labour** in the **agricultural** sector (i.e. the same amount of agricultural output could be produced by fewer people). This means that there's **no opportunity cost** if agricultural workers transfer to **industry** to take advantage of the **higher wages** available.
> - So industry develops **without** reducing agricultural output. And while there's excess labour (i.e. 'spare workers') in agriculture, wages in industry **don't rise** — i.e. a country can industrialise **without** causing **inflation**.
> - **Profits** from industry can be reinvested in **capital goods**, leading to greater **productivity gains**.
> - The reduction in excess labour in agriculture will also mean **agricultural productivity** increases.
> - Eventually, an equilibrium will be reached where everyone is **better off** than they were, and **profits** (and savings) are increased, leading to even more **investment** and **growth**.

2) Like all models, the Lewis model involves a lot of **simplifications**. In practice, things often work out **differently**.

3) It may not be easy to **transfer labour** to industry — workers (often young males) **migrating** from the countryside will leave fewer people to do physically demanding agricultural labour, while at **harvest times** there may be **no** 'spare workers' at all. **Investment** in **education** and **training** is also needed to develop the **human capital** needed to expand industrial output.

4) Also, profits **aren't** always reinvested locally — they may be invested **abroad** or used for **consumption**.

5) And if industrial production is **capital intensive** and involves little **human labour**, economic growth may not provide many additional **jobs**.

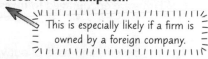
This is especially likely if a firm is owned by a foreign company.

Developing the **Tourism Industry** involves some **Risks**

1) Developing a country's **tourism industry** can improve a country's economy, though it's not without problems.

2) Increasing tourism will mean that a country earns **foreign currency** from tourists. It also means it's likely to attract **foreign investment** (e.g. from multinational hotel chains).

3) **Employment** should also increase. However, employment in the tourism industry may be **seasonal**, and multinational companies may want to bring in their own **management**, meaning that the **local** jobs created will be **low-skilled**.

4) An increase in tourism is likely to mean that more goods are **imported** (either **capital** goods to build facilities or goods demanded by **tourists** on holiday). This will be **bad** for the country's **balance of payments**.

5) Extra tourism may lead to **environmental damage** or **inconvenience** for the locals, as **tourists'** needs are prioritised.

6) Also, demand in the tourism industry is likely to be **income elastic** — it will increase quickly as people's incomes increase. The disadvantage is that during **economic downturns**, demand is likely to **fall quickly** too. And tourist destinations **aren't** guaranteed to remain popular forever — tourists' **tastes** can **change** quickly.

Warm-Up Questions

Q1 Explain some of the advantages and disadvantages of using aid to help a country develop its economy.

Q2 What is meant by the phrase 'debt relief'? Explain some of the arguments for and against it.

Exam Question

Q1 Discuss how expanding the industrial and tourism sectors may affect the development of a country's economy. [12 marks]

The Lewis model — to speed up your economy, shift it up a gear...

Development is difficult, and each country will be difficult in its own particular way. Just because a way has been found to promote development in one country, that doesn't mean the same method will work in a different country.

Ways of Promoting Growth and Development

The first section on these pages describes policies that make use of either an interventionist approach or a market-orientated one.

Protectionism is **Inward-Looking** — Free Trade is **Outward-Looking**

1) Inward-looking strategies seek to 'protect' domestic industries until they're ready to compete internationally.

- The main policy adopted is one of import substitution. Goods that were previously imported are replaced by domestically made goods. This is achieved by imposing tariffs and quotas on imported goods (see p.202-3).

- Subsidies might be provided either to domestic producers to allow them to sell their goods at competitive prices, or on certain necessary products that everyone will need (even if they're imported from abroad), allowing them to spend more of their own income on domestically produced goods.

- A currency might be maintained at an artificially high exchange rate, allowing the country to import selected goods from abroad cheaply — e.g. raw materials in order to reduce production costs for domestic firms.

2) The aim in the short term is to create jobs, reduce poverty and improve the country's balance of payments.

3) In the long term, the idea is that domestic industries will grow, benefit from economies of scale, and gain the necessary knowledge to compete on equal terms with firms from other countries.

4) However, being protected from international competition can result in inefficiency. And it can lead to a country's resources being misallocated — a country's comparative advantage may not be exploited as fully as it could be.

5) **Outward-looking** strategies, on the other hand, emphasise **free trade**, **deregulation** and the promotion of **foreign investment**.

Countries like India and China have used outward-looking policies to great effect in recent decades.

6) Firms are encouraged to **invest** and seek new **export markets**.

7) The benefits and costs of outward-looking strategies are what you might expect from greater **free trade** — **increased efficiency** and **competitiveness**, but more **economic dependency** between countries. See Section 13 for more information.

Interventionist strategies used to be popular...

- Interventionist strategies are similar to inward-looking strategies — e.g. they often involve import substitution, subsidies and high exchange rates. They may also involve industries being nationalised (i.e. taken into government ownership), and policies forcing producers to sell their goods to government-run distributors to keep prices low.

- They were popular in the past and were based on 'dependency theory', a theory that claims developing countries are still held back economically because of the way they were previously exploited by richer ones — e.g. by being forced to specialise in primary products. In practice these interventionist strategies were associated with low rates of economic growth, balance of payments problems, government deficits, corruption and general inefficiency.

Some interventionist strategies may be more successful, and are still popular. For example, investing in developing human capital through the education system (see page 176), or encouraging joint ventures between global companies and local companies or government.

Ways of Promoting Growth and Development

...but now Free-Market strategies are more common

- From about the 1980s, **free-market strategies** (also called market-orientated strategies) have been more popular. Free-market strategies recommend **less government intervention**, and place a much greater emphasis on **free trade**. There's a lot more information on pages 202-205. These are very similar to the **outward-looking** strategies described above — they aim to **increase efficiency** by **freeing the market**, for example by removing subsidies.

- **Floating exchange rate systems** (see page 210) are an example of a market-orientated strategy. Allowing exchange rates to be set by the market means exporting firms aren't protected against **currency fluctuations** (see page 212), but it may improve **efficiency** and **productivity** because it helps the market to react easily to international demand.

Tanja was not happy when she found out she still had to pay for her fruit in a free market.

Microfinance involves making Small Loans to Businesses and Individuals

1) **Microfinance** means providing loans to **small businesses** and low-income **individuals** who may not be able to get loans from traditional banks. The aim is for people in developing countries to use the loans to become more **financially independent** — either by developing **businesses** or investing in **education**.

2) Although microfinance works for **some people**, it's not clear that microfinance can reduce poverty on a **large scale**.

Fair Trade schemes guarantee producers a Minimum Price

1) **Fair trade** schemes aim to offer **individual farmers** (or **groups** of small producers) in developing countries a **guaranteed minimum** ('fair') price for their goods. In return, the producers usually have to accept certain **conditions** (e.g. they must agree to **inspections**, use **approved** farming techniques, and treat employees **fairly**).

2) The guaranteed price makes **long-term planning** easier for producers — they're not subject to the large fluctuations in price that are often associated with primary products (see p.219).

3) However, the **distortion** of the **market price** can lead to **overproduction** — farmers may not realise that a **low price** is a sign that they should grow a **different** crop. So when prices are low, farmers may flood the market and drive the price down **further** — affecting producers who **aren't** in the fair trade scheme.

These schemes rely on buyers being willing to pay above the market price, which may not be the case.

Warm-Up Questions

Q1 Describe the differences between inward-looking and outward-looking development strategies.

Q2 What is the main difference between interventionist strategies and free-market strategies?

Q3 What is microfinance?

Exam Questions

Q1 Discuss the effectiveness of fair trade schemes for promoting growth and development in developing countries. [12 marks]

Stop staring out the window — that outward-looking strategy won't help...

There's no 'magic development wand' that can be waved to make everything better. Economies are (very) complex things, and trying to steer an economy towards a particular outcome is tricky. So be ready to recognise the pros and cons of any approach.

Ways of Promoting Growth and Development

Not quite done yet, sorry. You need to know how institutions and NGOs can support development. **OCR and Edexcel only.**

International Institutions and Non-government Organisations also offer help

International Monetary Fund (IMF)

- The IMF was set up in 1945 to "ensure the stability of the international monetary system".
- Most countries in the world are members of the IMF. Each member has a 'quota', based on the size of its economy. A country's quota determines the amount of financial resources it has to make available to the IMF.
- The IMF uses these resources to offer loans (as well as technical advice) to developing countries in order to fight poverty and to help countries facing economic difficulties (e.g. problems with their balance of payments).
- If necessary, the IMF can borrow further funds from member countries under the New Arrangements to Borrow (NAB) scheme. Up until 2019, there was also a General Arrangement to Borrow (GAB) scheme.
- Nowadays, the IMF offers policy advice to countries so they can maintain economic stability and raise living standards. It also carries out economic research, making the data available to member countries.

The International Bank for Reconstruction and Development (IBRD) — part of The World Bank

- The IBRD aims to reduce poverty in middle- and low-income countries, and promote sustainable development (see next page) that helps to improve employment prospects. It offers loans, grants and advice to its member countries.
- It raises most of its funds from commercial financial institutions, where it can borrow at favourable rates as a result of it being backed by most of the world's governments.

These loans (called 'credits') are either interest-free, or interest is charged at very low rates.

The International Development Association (IDA) — another part of The World Bank

- The IDA aims to reduce poverty in the world's poorest countries by offering loans, grants, debt relief and advice.
- It concentrates on funding schemes that relate to:
  - **health care** (especially in reducing the impact of HIV/AIDS, malaria and TB),   – **education**,
  - **infrastructure** improvements — e.g. after civil war or natural disaster,   – **clean-water** provision,
  - **institutional reforms** — reform of state institutions (e.g. government departments or the police) to reduce corruption or improve opportunities for businesses.

Non-government organisations (NGOs) — these include **private organisations** and **charities**

They may be large institutions, but the work they do is often on a **small scale**. For example, they may offer **microfinance**, **training** in business skills, **technical** or **medical** assistance, or **advice** on environmental sustainability.

The involvement of International Institutions can be Controversial

1) There's **disagreement** over how **effective** international institutions are at promoting economic growth and development.
2) IMF and World Bank loans are often **conditional** on countries following certain **economic policies**, such as deregulation, privatisation and spending cuts. Supporters of these loan conditions argue that the policies **reform economies** so that the problems that led them to seek financial help aren't **repeated**, and that this **promotes growth** (now and in the future).
3) But it can be argued that these conditions **limit development**, as opening up an economy to the free market may increase **inequality**, and the poorest may lose access to services like **health care** and **education**. So reforms can be **controversial**.
4) The policies adopted to help any particular country will depend on what it's thought has **caused** that country's problems. Various **economic theories** are used to justify different approaches (e.g. 'dependency theory' on p.222).
5) But all developing countries are **different**, so each country will require its own particular **mix** of **policies**. What worked well in one country may not have the same effect in another — it's important to find out what works **in practice**.

Warm-Up Questions

Q1 How can NGOs support economic growth and development?

PRACTICE QUESTIONS

Exam Question

Q1 Outline the role of international institutions such as the IMF in promoting international growth and development. [2 marks]

If IDA pound for every acronym I'd learnt in Economics...

International institutions can support development by offering funding, advice and information. This can help relieve poverty and raise living standards. It's not all roses though — some developing countries struggle with the debt they've ended up with.

Sustainable Development

Sustainability is a fairly easy thing to understand, but it's often quite difficult to achieve in practice. ***This page is for OCR only.***

Sustainability is about being **Fair** to **Future Generations**

1) **Sustainability** is quite a simple idea: **Sustainability** is about meeting the needs of people **now**, without making it more difficult for people **in the future** to meet their own needs.
2) For example, a country may be able to **boost** its economic development, but if it uses up its **natural resources** in the process, this may lead to problems **maintaining** this economic progress in the future.
3) The world's population is **increasing** and the economies in many developing countries are **growing**, leading to an ever-increasing **demand** for resources. It's feared that the world's production and consumption are **unsustainable** in the long run — i.e. we won't be able to carry on producing and consuming **forever** in the way we currently are.

There's **No Agreed** way to measure **Sustainability**

1) There **isn't** an **internationally agreed** way to measure **how sustainable** a country's economic growth is. However, this is what the **Index of Sustainable Economic Welfare** (**ISEW**) tries to do.
2) **ISEW** is an **adjusted** version of GDP — it measures improvements in **standards of living**, while taking into account the **environmental damage** and **resource depletion** caused as a result. Other adjustments allow for factors that affect people's **economic welfare** (either for the better or for the worse), but which **aren't included** in the 'normal' GDP figure.
3) For example, if an activity leads to a lot of **pollution**, **resource depletion** or increased **inequality**, then the GDP figures are adjusted **downwards**. As well as this, ISEW excludes **'defensive' spending** — i.e. spending needed to **repair** the **damage** caused by other spending. For example, the cost of treating smoking-related illnesses isn't included in the ISEW figures.
4) Although ISEW is an attempt to produce a **more comprehensive** measure of welfare, it's criticised for having certain **value judgements** built into the way it's calculated. For example, the cost of increased inequality is difficult to measure **objectively**.

   But any measure includes some value judgements — GDP assumes that the value or cost of these things is zero.
5) This is one of the major problems with measurements of this kind — it's hard to work out what to **include**, what can be **ignored**, and what **monetary value** should be attached to each benefit or cost.
6) But measures that help governments understand the **'true cost'** of economic activities are useful. For example, if economic activities have large **negative externalities**, then a government can introduce policies to internalise them.

Introducing **Policies** to achieve **Sustainable** growth **Isn't Easy**

1) Governments will usually want to create **economic growth** and bring people out of **poverty**, but this can often involve a **trade-off** with **environmental sustainability** (see p.161). For example, growth may depend on cheap **energy** (e.g. for factories to run efficiently). But if, as in China, much of this comes from coal-fired power stations, then **pollution** can be high.
2) This isn't an easy problem to solve. Deciding whether to remove people from poverty **now** or develop environmentally friendly technologies to maintain the environment for **future generations** is not an easy choice for a government to make.
3) It's especially difficult for governments in **politically unstable** countries to take measures whose benefits will only be felt in the **long term**. They may prefer instead to introduce popular policies with much greater benefits in the **short term**.
4) **International agreements** are often vital for ensuring sustainability. For example, if one government introduces measures to reduce **pollution** from vehicles (e.g. a new tax on carbon dioxide emissions), then that might put its transport industry at a disadvantage compared to **other countries**. This means it's important for countries to **work together**.
5) Governments also need to be careful that growth is reasonably evenly spread throughout a country. **Regional policies** (i.e. policies aimed at helping particular areas) can offer **incentives** to create growth in **disadvantaged** regions, and can help make the best use of local **resources**, and ensure **uneven development** doesn't lead to **social problems**.

Warm-Up Questions

PRACTICE QUESTIONS

Q1 How can economic indicators like ISEW be used to support sustainable development?

Q2 Describe some difficulties often encountered when trying to achieve sustainable economic development.

Exam Question

Q1 Define sustainable development. [2 marks]

Rules for sustainability: 1) Don't take the last biscuit in the packet...

If I've said it once, I've said it a thousand times... sustainable development is not an easy nut to crack. But it's not all doom and gloom. Some people argue that with economic growth and greater prosperity, cleaner technologies can be afforded. We shall see.

Get Marks in Your Exam

These pages explain how you'll get marks in the exams. To do well you need to satisfy four different Assessment Objectives (AO1, AO2, AO3 and AO4), each of which requires different skills. Prove you've got the skills and you'll get the marks.

Make Sure You Read the Question Properly

It's easy to **misread** a question and spend 10 minutes writing about the **wrong thing**. A few simple tips can help you avoid this:

1) <u>Underline</u> the **command words** in the question (the ones that tell you **what to do**). Here are some common ones:

   - **Calculate** — you'll need to do some **maths** to find the **value** you're asked for (pretty obvious really).
   - **Explain** — you should write about **why** it's like that (i.e. give reasons). You might also need to do some **analysis** (see below).
   - **Assess, evaluate, discuss, examine** — these words basically mean the same thing. You'll need to write about the **advantages** and **disadvantages** OR the **arguments for** and **against**. You'll then need to give your **opinion** on which side is **stronger**, and **back this up** with reasons why.

2) <u>Underline</u> the **key words** (the ones that tell you **what it's about**), e.g. productivity, sustainability, market failure.

3) **Re-read** the question and your answer **when you've finished** to check that your answer addresses **all parts** of the question. A **common mistake** is to **miss a bit out** — like when questions say 'refer to the data from...' or 'illustrate your answer with...'.

There are Four Assessment Objectives the questions will cover

These are the **assessment objectives** you'll be marked on in your exams:

AO1 marks are for **content** and **knowledge**.
- This means things like knowing the **proper definitions** for **economics terms**.
- **Most** questions will include **at least one** AO1 mark, but you'll **rarely** get a question that **only** has AO1 marks. It's always good to give a **definition** of the key term(s) from the question, or to give the **formula(s)** if you're doing a calculation, to make sure you get your AO1 marks.

AO2 marks are for **application**.
- This means **applying** your knowledge to a situation. Again, **most** questions will include AO2 marks.
- Use your knowledge to **explain** your answer and give **reasons**. You'll need to **apply** your **own ideas** and your **economic knowledge** to show **why** you think something has happened or will happen.

AO3 marks are for **analysis**.
- This means thinking about benefits, costs, causes, effects and constraints.
- If there's **disagreement** about something (e.g. whether a particular policy is good or bad for economic growth), then consider **both sides** of the argument — you'll only get **limited** analysis marks by looking at **one side**.
- If there's data, say what the figures **mean**, talk about what might have **caused** them and say what **effect** you think they will have on the economy in the **future**.

AO4 marks are for **evaluation**.
- This means using your **judgement**. Questions with AO4 marks will **always** have AO3 marks too — you'll have to **weigh up** both sides of the argument **before** using your judgement.
- You need to give a **balanced** answer, so talk about the **different viewpoints** on the subject (i.e. consider the **advantages** and **disadvantages**).
- It's good to say which **side** of the argument you think is **strongest**, but you **don't need** to give a **definite** answer. You can point out that it **depends** on various factors — as long as you say **what those factors** are, and say **why** the issue depends on them. Use your judgement to say what the **most important factors** are. The main thing is to **justify** why you're saying what you're saying.

1) The **command words** can give you a bit of a clue about **which** assessment objectives the question includes:
   - 'Explain' questions **won't** require you to evaluate (AO4), but **could** involve all the other objectives (see below).
   - 'Evaluate', 'discuss', 'assess' and 'examine' questions will have marks for **each** of the four assessment objectives.

2) You should **always** look at the **number of marks** a question is worth — this gives you a **good indication** of how much you need to write. For example:
   - If you're asked to **explain** something and the question is worth **4 marks**, you **won't** need to write very much to earn all the marks — there'll probably only be **AO1** and **AO2** marks.
   - If you're asked to **explain** something and the question is worth **15 marks**, you'll need to write **more** — there'll almost certainly be some **AO3** marks too, so you'll have to include some **analysis** in your answer.

Get Marks in Your Exam

It's **Important** that you make your answers **Clear**

Some of the following might sound **pretty obvious** — but you'd be surprised how **easy** it is to panic in an exam and focus **too much** on getting all the facts down, and **not enough** on making your answer clear and understandable:

- It's really **important** that your answers are **clear** and **well-written**, particularly in **extended** answer questions (i.e. questions worth 8 or more marks).
- Try to write **formally** and **arrange relevant information clearly** — write a **well-structured 'essay'**, not a list of bullet points.
- You should use **specialist vocabulary** when it's appropriate — it's well worth **learning** some of the **technical terms** used in this book.
- Try to write **neatly** enough for the examiner to be able to read your answer.
- **Spelling, grammar** and **punctuation** are important too — using them correctly will help you to make your answers **crystal clear**.
- If your handwriting, grammar, spelling and punctuation are **so** far up the spout that the examiner **can't understand** what you've written, **expect problems**.

If you're taking the **OCR** exams, there are **specific** questions that assess the **quality** of your extended responses — these are marked with an **asterisk** (*). For these questions, you **must** write your answers clearly as described above — you **won't** be able to get full marks for them if you don't.

Impressive... but it won't get you any marks.

Jotting down a quick 'essay' plan will help you to structure your essay-style answers.

Data-response questions will ask you to refer to extracts given in the exam. These could be tables of data, or pieces of text.

Use the **Data** for **Data-response Questions**

Again, that sounds pretty obvious, but there are some things you need to bear in mind:

1) If a question asks you to **refer** to a table of data, a graph, or some text, make sure you **use** it in your answer.
2) **Don't** just copy out loads of data — any data you use in your answer must be **relevant** to the specific point you're making.
3) If a data-response question asks you to 'explain', you'll need to use the data as well as your **economic knowledge** to **back up** the points you make.
4) You'll need to show that you **understand** the information, and you might need to **analyse** and **evaluate** it.
5) If you need to draw a diagram, do it in **pencil** so you can rub it out if you make a mistake. However, label your diagrams in **pen** so they're nice and clear.
6) Sometimes you might need to do a **calculation**. You can use a calculator to find the answer, but **write down** your **working out**. If you get the answer **wrong** you can still **pick up marks** for using the correct method.
7) **'Quantitative skills'** questions (i.e. questions involving some **maths**) will make up around **20%** of the marks in your exams. Don't worry though — a lot of these marks are just for **reading** tables or graphs and **using** the data in your answers.

Don't forget to include **All** the **Skills** in **Extended Answer Questions**

1) Longer essay-style questions need a bit of **planning**. Jot down a **rough outline** of what you want to say — remember, you need to make your answer **balanced**, so make a list of the **advantages** and **disadvantages**, or the arguments **for** and **against**.
2) **Diagrams** are a quick and easy way of explaining quite difficult concepts in your answers, but make sure you **explain** what your diagrams show and **always** refer to them in your answers. **Label** your diagrams properly so they're clear.
3) In an essay answer you need to show **all** the skills — **don't jump** straight to the **evaluation** part. So, if you're asked to evaluate the extent to which lowering the price of exports can bring about the recovery of the UK economy, you need to:

- **Define** what is meant by exports and recovery (this will get you your **AO1** marks).
- Explain how an increase in exports is **relevant** to the recovery of the UK economy (for **AO2** marks).
- Give the **advantages** and **disadvantages** of lowering the price of exports (for **AO3** marks).
- Finally, for the **AO4** marks, **weigh up** both sides of the argument and **decide** how successful, in your opinion, lowering the price of exports would be in helping the UK economy to recover.

Learn this stuff for some inflation of marks...

Of course, to do well in the exam, you've got to know all that economics stuff inside out — but these pages will give you an idea of how you can put that knowledge to best use in the exam. Keep in mind that you don't just need to learn the facts — you've got to prove to the examiner that you understand them and can apply them to various scenarios. So all very simple, really...

What to Expect in the Exams

It'll be handy if you're familiar with how the exams are structured for your exam board, and the types of question you might face. All exam boards use multiple-choice questions, so make sure you have a look at the last section on this page.

A-Level Economics is divided into Three Exams

1) Whichever exam board you're doing, you'll sit **three exams** for A-Level Economics — you'll have **2 hours** for each exam.

2) Paper 1 will be on **microeconomics**, paper 2 will be on **macroeconomics** and paper 3 will be a **combination** of the two.

3) For **AQA** and **OCR**, each paper is worth **80 marks**, so you should aim to pick up a mark roughly every **one and a half minutes**. For **Edexcel**, each paper is worth **100 marks**, so you should aim to pick up a mark every **minute or so**. There's a slightly different format for each paper, depending on your exam board:

AQA	**Papers 1 & 2**	• **Section A** is worth **40 marks** and contains **extracts** of information about two different contexts — you have to **choose one** of these contexts to answer a range of **data-response** questions about. • **Section B** is also worth **40 marks**. It contains three **essay-style** questions — you have to **choose one** to answer. Each question is split into a **15 mark** part and a **25 mark** part.
	Paper 3	• **Section A** contains **30 multiple-choice questions** (see below) worth **1 mark** each. • **Section B** involves a **case study** made up of **extracts** — there's a mix of questions worth a total of **50 marks**.

EDEXCEL	**Papers 1 & 2**	• **Section A** is made up of **multiple-choice** and other **short answer** questions. It's worth **25 marks**. • **Section B** involves **data-response** questions based on **extracts** of information. It's worth **50 marks**. • **Section C** has a **choice** of two **25 mark**, **essay-style** questions.
	Paper 3	• **Sections A and B** are worth **50 marks** each. They both involve using **extracts** to answer **data-response** questions. This includes a **choice** of two **25 mark**, **essay-style** questions — you have to **choose one** of these in each section.

OCR	**Papers 1 & 2**	• **Section A** is worth **30 marks** — it contains **stimulus material** followed by some short answer and some extended answer **data-response** questions. • **Sections B and C** are each worth **25 marks**. You have to **choose one** of two **essay-style** questions to answer for each section.
	Paper 3	• **Section A** contains **30 multiple-choice questions** which are worth **1 mark** each. • **Section B** contains **stimulus material**, followed by a mix of short answer and extended answer **data-response** questions worth a total of **50 marks**.

Here's an example Multiple-Choice Question and Answer

For **multiple-choice** questions, you'll have to indicate the **correct answer**:

> **1** The diagram shows a firm operating under conditions of perfect competition. Which one of the following is true?
>
> **A** The market has high barriers to entry.
>
> **B** The area PXQO represents the firm's total costs.
>
> **C** In the short run the firm experiences supernormal profits.
>
> **D** The lack of profit available acts as a disincentive to firms entering the market.
>
> Answer [C] ← *You'll get the 1 mark for giving the correct answer.*
>
> 1 mark

To answer multiple-choice questions, go through each option **one by one**. You should be able to spot the **correct** answer, but it can help to **rule out** answers you **know** aren't right too — e.g. for the question above, you might think:

Option A is incorrect as there are no barriers to entry in a perfectly competitive market. A firm's total costs will be cYQO, so option B is also incorrect. When perfect competition exists a firm can experience supernormal profits in the short run, so C is the correct answer. These profits act as an incentive for firms to enter the market, so D is incorrect.

Sample Questions and Worked Answers

You've seen an example multiple-choice question already — but there are loads of types of questions you could get in the exams.

The **Next Three Pages** give some **Example Questions** and **Answers**

1) These three pages **don't** cover **all** the question types that might come up in your exams — just a small selection.

2) There are **four** sample questions with worked answers. Each example includes **notes** on the answer, pointing out **good** features and areas for **improvement**, and an **explanation** of the number of marks that answer would earn.

3) **Don't** just read what's here — where the example answer **wouldn't** earn full marks, it's a good idea to try to write your own **improved answers**.

Here's an example **Data-Response Question** and **Answer**

Extract A: Index of average house price in the US 2000-2011.

Year	2000	2001	2002	2003	2004	2005
Index of average house price	234.53	252.06	268.02	284.70	311.28	346.52
Year	2006	2007	2008	2009	2010	2011
Index of average house price	371.38	375.63	356.94	337.29	323.63	311.52

Source: Adapted from US Federal Housing Finance Agency

Extract B: The 2007/8 Global Financial Crisis.

Leading up to the global financial crisis of 2007/8, in the US, mortgages were given to borrowers who were likely to struggle to pay back the loans. The banks did this because house prices were rising and they believed that they would continue to rise. So if they had to sell the house of someone who couldn't pay their mortgage, then the rising house prices would cover their costs. Because banks were willing to give credit to most people, this increased demand for housing, causing house prices to rise even further, and created a bubble in the housing market.

1

5

2   **Extract B** (lines 5-7) states that the banks' willingness to lend to most people created a bubble in the housing market.

Using the data from the extracts and your economic knowledge, explain the causes of the bubble in the US housing market and what effect this had on house prices over time.   **8 marks**

Market bubbles are created when estimates of the future worth of assets are excessively high.

> Defining the main term(s) given in the question will often earn you a mark or two.

In the US leading up to the global financial crisis of 2007/8, banks believed that house prices would continue to rise. This led them to give mortgages to people who were unlikely to be able to pay back the loans, because the banks believed increasing house prices would cover their costs if people were unable to pay back what they owed. This allowed more people to get mortgages, and therefore demand for housing increased. This in turn caused house prices to increase further, and a housing market bubble was created.

From Extract A, you can see that the index of the average house price in the US rose by 50.17 from 2000 to 2003. From 2003 to 2006 it rose by 86.68. This indicates that house prices were rising more quickly from 2003 to 2006 — this sharper increase was likely caused by increased demand for housing. The growth slowed significantly between 2006 and 2007, and then house prices actually began to fall — this is likely to be the point where investors lost confidence in the housing market and rushed to sell their assets.

> This is a good use of the data in Extract A, but the explanation could be made a bit more thorough, e.g. by including figures for the growth from 2006 to 2007 and beyond.

This answer could receive 6 marks. It shows a good understanding of what led to the housing market bubble and the effect this had on house prices. It could be improved with some references to Extract B where appropriate, and perhaps by linking the Extract A data into the second paragraph.

Sample Questions and Worked Answers

An example question using a **Diagram**

3 (a) Using a diagram, explain the negative externalities linked to increasing levels of travel via road transport.

15 marks

Travelling by road (e.g. by car or lorry) generates negative externalities, so increasing use of road transport means that the impact of these negative externalities will be increasing. The negative externalities of production can be seen on the diagram.

In this diagram the socially optimal output level of this service (where MSC = MSB) is Q_1 and the optimal price is P_1. However, in the free market only private costs are considered, so output would be Q_e and the price would be P_e. This would cause overproduction and underpricing of this service — more is produced and sold at a lower price than is desirable for society. This means that for each unit of road transport produced between Q_1 and Q_e the marginal social cost is greater than the marginal social benefit.

Increased road transport will result in increased levels of pollution, which will be damaging to the environment. Road transport can also have negative impacts for local residents. For example, their health may be affected by emissions from vehicles, which could result in increased costs for the NHS. Also, people who live next to roads may lose out financially — if they live next to an increasingly busy road, the value of their house could fall. More road transport could also increase pressure on the NHS and emergency services, as it may mean there is an increase in road accidents.

There are many negative externalities linked to increased road transport that can increase costs to society. Increasing the cost of travelling by road may help reduce the overuse of road transport.

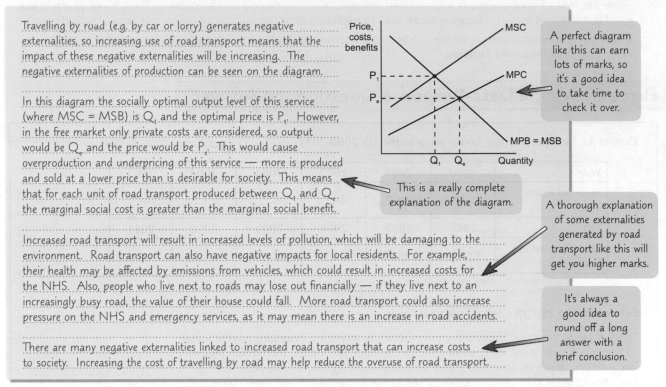

A perfect diagram like this can earn lots of marks, so it's a good idea to take time to check it over.

This is a really complete explanation of the diagram.

A thorough explanation of some externalities generated by road transport like this will get you higher marks.

It's always a good idea to round off a long answer with a brief conclusion.

This answer could get 11 marks. It's a good answer but it's missing a definition of negative externalities (e.g. that MSC are greater than MPC). You can get quite a few marks here for a perfectly labelled diagram (as shown in this answer). You need to give a couple of examples of negative externalities that can be generated (e.g. pollution due to increased emissions) and then explain their effects (e.g. could cause increased NHS costs).

Here's an example **Calculation Question** and **Answer**

This question is like the data-response ones (including a calculation) that you might get in your exams.

Extract A: Average hourly wage for full-time employees in the UK in 1986 and 2011 and the % change in this period (1986-2011).

Full-time employees		Hourly wage (£)*		Percentage change (%)
		1986	2011	
Lowest earners	Bottom 1% earn less than	3.48	5.93	+ 70
	Bottom 10% earn less than	4.80	7.01	+ 46
	Average	7.78	12.62	**?**
Highest earners	Top 10% earn more than	14.78	26.75	+ 81
	Top 1% earn more than	28.18	61.10	+ 117

*1986 wages converted to 2011 prices

4 Using **Extract A**, calculate to the nearest whole number the percentage change in the average wage of a full-time employee between 1986 and 2011.

2 marks

Answer:

Percentage change = $\dfrac{12.62 - 7.78}{7.78} \times 100 = \dfrac{4.84}{7.78} \times 100 = 62\%$

This answer would get both marks. You'd get both marks just for the correct answer, but it's important to show your working — if your final answer was wrong but your working was correct, you could still earn 1 mark.

Do Well in Your Exam

Sample Questions and Worked Answers

An example **Essay-Style Question** and **Answer** to give you some tips

Extract B: Wage rates and the introduction of the National Minimum Wage.

The National Minimum Wage (NMW) sets a legal minimum hourly wage rate for employees of [1]
different ages. It was introduced by the Labour government in 1999 to help prevent workers from
being exploited by being paid such a low wage that they would not be able to afford a decent standard
of living. A key aim of the NMW was to increase the earnings of the poorest workers in society and
create a more equitable distribution of income. For example, if a worker was in a low-paid job the [5]
introduction of the NMW may have increased their hourly wage and therefore increased their earnings.

From looking at data collected about full-time UK workers between 1986 and 2011, the introduction
of the NMW seems to have had the desired effect of increasing earnings of workers on the
lowest wages. Between 1986 and 1998 (before the NMW was introduced) the bottom 1% of
earners experienced a 15% increase in real wages. However, after the introduction of the NMW [10]
(1998-2011) the bottom 1% of earners experienced a larger increase in real earnings of 51%.

When the NMW was being introduced it had some strong opponents who suggested
that it would have negative impacts for the UK labour market and economy as a
whole. However, on reflection the introduction of the National Minimum Wage has
been considered one of the most successful government policies of recent times. [15]

5   **Extract B** (lines 12-15) suggests that the National Minimum Wage in the UK was not universally
popular before its introduction but that it's now considered to have had an overall positive impact.

Using the data and your economic knowledge, evaluate the impacts on the UK
labour market associated with the introduction of the National Minimum Wage.   25 marks

---

The National Minimum Wage is a pay floor. This means that employers can't pay a wage less than the NMW.

Introducing a NMW can have several positive impacts on the labour market. One impact that it can have
is to increase the wages of the poorest workers in society and help reduce poverty. For example, if you are on
a low wage and the NMW means that your hourly wage rate increases, then this can make a real difference
to the amount you earn. The NMW having an impact on the wages of low earners is demonstrated in
the data in Extract B because it shows that after the NMW was introduced, the bottom 1% of earners
experienced a higher increase in real wages than during a similar period before its introduction. This boost
in earnings might also act as a morale boost, resulting in happier workers who might be more productive.

> There is some good evaluation here. It's important to use the data as this is asked for in the question.

Also, the NMW helps to encourage people to seek work. For example, having a minimum wage might
act as an incentive to unemployed people to take jobs that would previously have paid less than the
NMW. In addition, increasing the number of people in work is good for the economy. An increased
number of people willing to work means that the supply of workers in the labour market increases.

> You could use diagrams to support this answer — e.g. a diagram showing the excess supply of labour when wages rise. This is a good way of picking up marks.

Having a NMW can have some negative impacts though. It might lead to a decreased level of employment
in a labour market. This is because an increased wage rate could result in reduced demand for labour due to
increased wage costs for firms, although the impact on firms might vary depending on the staff they employ.
If a firm has lots of staff below the NMW then the introduction could considerably increase their wage costs,
but if they only employ a small number of staff below the NMW then it might not have much of an impact.

A NMW may not actually decrease poverty. This is because many of the poorest
people in society, such as the elderly and disabled, are not in work, so aren't able
to benefit from the increased earnings that a NMW could bring.

> The last sentence isn't specifically about the labour market, so wouldn't get any marks.

A NMW might also decrease the competitiveness of UK firms compared to firms in
other countries that have lower wage costs. UK firms may pass on their increased costs
to consumers by increasing their prices, and this could contribute to inflation.

> There's no conclusion to this essay — it's always best to put one in.

*This essay is a good effort. There's quite a lot of analysis and there's definite discussion of the pros and cons of
introducing a NMW. However, there's a bit of discussion that isn't directly relevant to the question and there's
no conclusion. A diagram or two would really help your discussion too. This answer would get about 19 marks.*

Answers

Section One — The Economic Problem

Page 7 — The Economic Problem

1   Maximum of 6 marks available.   <u>HINTS</u>:
- Pick three factors of production that would be necessary for someone opening a new restaurant, and explain why each is important.
- E.g. 'Labour will be important, since a new restaurant will need people to carry out all the various tasks involved, such as cooking food, serving customers, managing the accounts, and so on.'

Page 9 — Production Possibility Frontiers

1   Maximum of 1 mark available.   <u>HINTS</u>:
- The answer is B.
- W, Y and Z all show combinations that can be made using existing resources, since they all lie inside or on the PPF.
- But X lies outside the PPF, so this combination cannot be made using existing resources.
2   Maximum of 5 marks available.   <u>HINTS</u>:
- Start by defining the term opportunity cost, e.g. 'the next best alternative that you give up in making a particular decision'.
- Then explain that only combinations of cars and butter shown by points inside or on the production possibility frontier (PPF) can be made using the existing resources.
- Now you need to show an opportunity cost on this diagram. E.g. 'Suppose the combination of goods shown by point Y is currently being produced (20 000 cars and 9000 tonnes of butter), but it was then decided that more butter was needed. This could only be achieved by producing fewer cars. For example, if production were shifted to point Z, then this would mean 11 300 tonnes of butter would be produced, but with current resources only 10 000 cars could be produced. So the opportunity cost of producing an extra 2300 tonnes of butter is the lost production of 10 000 cars.'

Page 11 — Markets and Economies

1   Maximum of 5 marks available.   <u>HINTS</u>:
- Start by explaining what a command economy is, e.g. 'A command economy is where the government decides how resources should be allocated, rather than leaving it to the market.'
- Then you need to give reasons why a command economy could lead to a lack of efficiency, e.g. 'Because government-owned firms don't need to make a profit, they have no incentive to try to reduce inefficiency by, for example, improving their production methods to make them more efficient. This means that command economies as a whole lack efficiency because they're made up of inefficient firms.'
- You could also mention that there might be a lack of efficiency because all economic decisions need to be made by the government and this can be slow.
- You don't need to write too much — there are only 5 marks for this question.

Page 13 — Economic Objectives

1   Maximum of 1 mark available.   <u>HINTS</u>:
- The answer is B.
- To find the marginal revenue of the fourth chair you need to work out the additional revenue gained from selling the fourth chair.
- So, the marginal revenue of the fourth chair is £195 – £158 = £37.

Page 15 — Behavioural Economics

1   Maximum of 8 marks available.   <u>HINTS</u>:
- Start by explaining what is meant by behavioural economics, e.g. 'Behavioural economics looks at the impact of social, psychological and emotional factors on the decision making of individuals in an economy to try to gain a more accurate idea of how economic agents act.'
- You then need to give examples of how a government can use behavioural economics and choice architecture to create its policies, e.g. 'When individuals are presented with a choice where there is a default option, they are more likely to choose (or stick with) the default option. This means that a government could introduce a scheme where employees are automatically enrolled onto a pension scheme so that the default option will lead to individuals saving more.'
- Give some other examples of choice architecture that a government could use to create its policies — for example, a government could encourage the creation of tax-free saving accounts which will act as a 'nudge' to encourage people to save more.

Section Two — Competitive Markets

Page 17 — Demand

1   Maximum of 8 marks available.   <u>HINTS</u>:
- Start by stating that the demand for tiles is a derived demand.
- Then explain what is likely to happen to the demand for tiles — 'The demand for tiles is likely to decrease in line with the falling demand for houses.'
- To maximise your marks you need to provide more detail. So here you could say that if the housing market is in decline there would be less demand for tiles because fewer new houses would be built — so fewer tiles are needed. You could also say that there will always be some demand for tiles even when the housing market is slow (due to people redecorating and refurbishing etc.), but the fact that tile retailers are cutting back expansion plans suggests they have seen a drop-off in demand for tiles.

2   Maximum of 4 marks available.   <u>HINTS</u>:
- Define what's meant by complementary goods, e.g. 'Complementary goods are goods that are often used together, so they are in joint demand. When demand rises for one good, then demand will also rise for the other good.'
- State what is likely to happen to the demand for crackers — 'The demand for crackers is likely to decline if the demand for cheese falls due to a price increase.'
- For full marks you could mention any complicating factors — e.g. you could say that people also buy crackers without cheese, so an increase in cheese prices may not have a dramatic impact on cracker sales.

Page 19 — Price, Income and Cross Elasticities of Demand

1   Maximum of 1 mark available.   <u>HINTS</u>:
- The correct answer is B.
- This question is a case of calculating PED using the numbers you've been given. As it's a calculation there's only one correct answer.
- percentage change in demand = $\frac{200}{200} \times 100 = 100\%$
- percentage change in price = $\frac{-1.5}{3} \times 100 = -50\%$
- PED = $\frac{100}{-50} = -2.0$

Page 21 — Uses of Elasticities of Demand

1   Maximum of 6 marks available.   <u>HINTS</u>:
- Start by explaining what price elasticity of demand (PED) is, and what different values for PED mean for a business — e.g. 'Price elasticity of demand shows how the quantity demanded of a product responds to a change in its price. A value greater than 1 (ignoring minus signs) signifies elastic demand — i.e. that a change in price will cause a proportionally larger change in the quantity demanded, while a value between 0 and 1 signifies inelastic demand — i.e. that a change in price will cause a proportionally smaller change in the quantity demanded.'
- Then you should explain how the firm can use this knowledge to maximise revenue — e.g. 'The firm should set the price at the level where PED = 1. If it were to set the price at a level where PED < 1, then a reduction in price would lead to a proportionally larger increase in sales, which would lead to an increase in revenue. If it were to set the price at a level where PED > 1, then an increase in price would lead to a proportionally smaller decrease in sales, which would also lead to an increase in revenue.'

Page 23 — Supply

1   Maximum of 1 mark available.   <u>HINTS</u>:
- The correct answer is A.
- A cut in the price causes a movement down the curve. The other options are incorrect because they would all cause the supply curve to shift (as they cause an increase or decrease in the amount of the product supplied at every price).
2   Maximum of 1 mark available.   <u>HINTS</u>:
- The correct answer is C.
- You need to work out which option would cause the supply curve to shift to the right. This is C because increased production speed results in increased output, which increases supply (and causes the supply curve to shift to the right). Options A, B and D all result in a decrease in supply and shift the supply curve to the left.

Page 25 — Price Elasticity of Supply

1   Maximum of 4 marks available.   <u>HINTS</u>:
- There are several possible answers for this question.
- In general supply is more inelastic in the short run as at least one factor of production will be fixed (e.g. it takes time to expand banana plantations to allow for an increase in supply).
- More specific reasons include that bananas are perishable, so can't be stored for long, and take time to grow — both of which mean that suppliers can't respond that quickly to a change in price.
- Make sure you give two clear reasons for this question to get the marks.
2   Maximum of 4 marks available.   <u>HINTS</u>:
- Your answer to this question is likely to focus on the fact that the firm employs 'highly skilled' workers to create hand-made furniture.
- For example, the firm may find it difficult to expand its workforce as it needs to find highly skilled workers and/or take time to train new unskilled staff.
- You could also mention that the furniture produced by the firm is likely to take a long time to make, which limits the ability of the firm to increase supply in the short run.

Page 27 — Market Equilibrium

1   Maximum of 1 mark available.   <u>HINTS</u>:
- The correct answer is D.
- The equilibrium point moves when the demand curve shifts.
  A is incorrect as the equilibrium is where the demand and supply curves meet.
  B is incorrect as a fall in supply causes the supply curve to shift and the equilibrium point to move. C is incorrect because it is supply and demand which determine the equilibrium point, not the other way round.

Answers

Page 28 — Price and the Allocation of Resources

1 Maximum of 4 marks available. <u>HINTS</u>:
- Start by explaining what the price mechanism is — 'when a change in the supply or demand for a good/service leads to a change in its price, which in turn leads to a change in the quantity bought/sold, until supply is equal to demand'.
- Then talk about how price can act as an incentive — e.g. 'higher prices are attractive to firms because they can mean higher profits for the firm — this encourages firms to increase production/supply'.

Page 31 — Subsidies and Indirect Taxes

1 Maximum of 1 mark available. <u>HINTS</u>:
- The correct answer is D.
- EFJK shows the area above the market price of the good if there was no subsidy. A, B and C are incorrect — A is the total cost of the subsidy, B is not part of the subsidy and C is the consumer gain from the subsidy.

2 Maximum of 6 marks available. <u>HINTS</u>:
- For this question it's a good idea to draw a diagram to show what happens when a tax is put on a product.
- Draw a diagram that shows how a tax shifts the supply curve to the left.
- Explain what the diagram shows — i.e. the price of the product increasing above the free market equilibrium price and the quantity demanded/supplied of the product falling.

Page 33 — Demand and Supply — Oil

1 Maximum of 12 marks available. <u>HINTS</u>:
- Explain the influence of a subsidy on price and demand for biofuels — e.g. it lowers the price of biofuel and increases demand for it.
- Draw a diagram showing how a subsidy on biofuels would shift the supply curve to the right.
- Explain what the diagram shows — i.e. the price of the product decreasing below the free market equilibrium price and the quantity demanded/supplied increasing.
- Biofuels are a substitute for oil-based fuels, so explain how a reduction in the price of biofuel could affect the demand for oil (i.e. decrease it).
- Discuss other factors that could affect demand for biofuels and crude oil — e.g. if it is cheap and easy to switch to biofuels demand for them could increase hugely, but expensive switching, difficulties in use or limited uses could limit an increase in demand.

Page 35 — Demand and Supply — Transport

1 Maximum of 10 marks available. <u>HINTS</u>:
- For this question you can discuss a variety of different factors that can have an impact on housing prices in different areas.
- The supply of houses in an area impacts prices — large supply leads to lower prices. Supply depends on factors such as costs and availability of land, materials and construction workers.
- Government regulations — incentive schemes to build in a certain area may lead to a large supply of houses to buy and cause house prices to be lower than other areas without such schemes.
- Levels of employment play a role — in areas with high levels of unemployment house prices will be lower due to lower levels of demand.
- Desirability of an area — in a fashionable part of the country with nearby amenities and good transport links, house prices may be higher.
- Availability of cheap rental properties — this may reduce demand for houses to buy and therefore reduce average house prices.

2 Maximum of 4 marks available. <u>HINTS</u>:
- Start by explaining broadly what the effect of higher fuel prices will be — e.g. 'higher fuel prices would lead to a fall in demand for car usage'.
- You then need to include details about how the price elasticity of demand for car travel would determine the size of the fall in demand — e.g. 'The price elasticity of demand for travelling by car is low, so changes in the cost of driving are unlikely to have a large effect on demand.'

Section Three — Business Economics

Page 39 — The Costs of a Firm

1 Maximum of 1 mark available. <u>HINTS</u>:
- The correct answer is B.
- The marginal cost is the additional cost of producing one more unit of output, so it only depends on variable costs. Because Firm X and Firm Y have the same variable costs, they must also have the same marginal cost.
- The firms have the same variable costs but different fixed costs, so they must also have different total costs and average costs. This lets you rule out options A, C and D.

2 Maximum of 2 marks available. <u>HINTS</u>:
- To get both marks, make sure you give a clear explanation, e.g. 'Average fixed cost = total fixed costs ÷ quantity produced. This means that when output is increased, the average fixed cost falls because the total cost is being divided between a greater quantity of output.'

Page 41 — The Law of Diminishing Returns

1 a) Maximum of 3 marks available. <u>HINTS</u>:
- Start by describing the shape of the marginal cost curve between A and B — i.e. that it decreases as output rises.
- Explain that as the levels of factor inputs that are variable in the short run are increased, the firm is getting more additional output from each unit of input, so the cost per unit of that additional output is decreasing.

b) Maximum of 3 marks available. <u>HINTS</u>:
- Start by describing the shape of the marginal cost curve between B and C — i.e. that it increases from its minimum value as output rises.
- Explain that this is the result of the law of diminishing returns — as the levels of factor inputs that are variable in the short run are increased, the firm is getting less additional output from each unit of input, so the cost per unit of that output will be greater.

Page 43 — Economies and Diseconomies of Scale

1 Maximum of 5 marks available. <u>HINTS</u>:
- State that what's being described in the question is a firm encountering 'diseconomies of scale' — this is where the average cost per unit increases as the firm's output rises.
- Give examples of how diseconomies of scale can arise, e.g. 'Larger firms whose output has grown can suffer from increases in wastage and loss, as materials may seem in plentiful supply', or 'As a firm grows and its output increases, communication between workers may become less efficient.'

Page 44 — Long Run Average Cost

1 Maximum of 6 marks available. <u>HINTS</u>:
- Start by explaining what a long run average cost (LRAC) curve shows — i.e. the minimum possible average cost at each level of output.
- Explain what happens in the short run — e.g. 'In the short run a firm will have at least one fixed factor of production, which means the firm will be operating on a particular short run average cost (SRAC) curve. As the firm varies its output, it can move along this SRAC curve. However, this SRAC curve will only meet the LRAC curve in a single place, and this may not be the required level of output.'
- State that to produce the required level of output at the cost shown on the LRAC curve, it may be necessary to move to a different SRAC curve, and this will involve varying the levels of all factors of production — this is something that can only be done in the long run.

Page 45 — Returns to Scale

1 Maximum of 6 marks available. <u>HINTS</u>:
- Start by defining returns to scale — e.g. 'Returns to scale describe the effect on output of increasing all factor inputs by the same proportion. For example, increasing returns to scale describe the situation when doubling the levels of all factor inputs, say, leads to output more than doubling. Similarly, decreasing returns to scale describe a situation when doubling the levels of all factor inputs leads to output less than doubling. And constant returns to scale describe a situation when doubling the levels of all factor inputs leads to output also doubling.'
- Explain when a firm might experience increasing, constant and decreasing returns to scale and how each of these affects average costs — e.g. 'As a business grows over the long run, it will often find it can initially achieve increasing returns to scale — i.e. more output is being produced per unit of input, so the average cost of output falls.'

Page 47 — The Revenue of a Firm

1 Maximum of 2 marks available. <u>HINTS</u>:
- For each output level, MR = $TR_n - TR_{n-1}$

Quantity sold	Price (£)	Total Revenue (£)	Marginal Revenue (£)
0	12	0	—
1	10	10	10 – 0 = 10
2	8	16	16 – 10 = 6
3	6	18	18 – 16 = 2
4	4.50	18	18 – 18 = 0
5	3	15	15 – 18 = -3

2 Maximum of 15 marks available. <u>HINTS</u>:
- Start by defining a price-making firm — i.e. it's a firm that has enough market power to set the price they sell their goods at.
- Then explain that for a price-making firm, the higher it sets the price, the lower demand will be — its demand curve will slope downwards.
- But the firm's demand curve will also be its average revenue (AR) curve (since a demand curve and an average revenue curve both show what quantity of a product the firm will be able to sell at a particular price). This means the firm's average revenue curve will also slope downwards.
- The firm's marginal revenue (MR) curve must also slope downwards, because to increase sales, the firm has to reduce the price. In fact, the firm's MR curve will be twice as steep as its AR curve.
- Then define a price-taking firm — i.e. it's a firm that has no market power and so has to sell its goods at the price determined by the market. If it increases prices, it won't sell anything, and there's no need to decrease prices.

Answers

- Explain that for a price-taking firm, average revenue will be the same, no matter what quantity of goods it sells — i.e. its average revenue curve will be horizontal.
- Finish by explaining why the MR curve is horizontal, e.g. 'Marginal revenue = average revenue, because each extra unit sold brings in the same revenue as all the others — so the MR curve is also horizontal.'

Page 49 — Profit

1 Maximum of 4 marks available. <u>HINTS</u>:
- Explain that there are two options available for a company whose average costs exceed its average revenue in the long run, and that which option a firm chooses will depend on whether its average revenue is greater than or less than its average variable costs — e.g. 'If the firm's average revenue is greater than its average variable costs, the firm will continue to trade in the short run, but if the firm's average revenue is less than its average variable costs, the firm will shut down immediately.'
- In the long run, the firm will have to close down, since it will be making less than normal profit.

2 Maximum of 1 mark available. <u>HINTS</u>:
- The correct answer is D.
- If marginal revenue (MR) is greater than marginal cost (MC) at a particular level of output, the firm would increase its profit by increasing output, because the revenue gained by doing so will be bigger than the cost. This rules out options A, B and C.
- If MR is less than MC, the firm would increase its profit by reducing output, because it cost the firm more to produce the last unit of output than it received for it in revenue. This rules out option E.
- Therefore, since it's a profit-maximising firm, it'll output at a level where MC = MR.

Page 51 — The Objectives of Firms

1 Maximum of 25 marks available. <u>HINTS</u>:
- Start by explaining that the traditional theory of the firm assumes that firms aim to maximise profit, but state that there are also other objectives that many firms try to achieve.
- You'll need to then describe some other objectives that are commonly pursued by firms and give possible reasons why — e.g. 'Firms may choose to maximise sales or revenue rather than profit, perhaps to increase their market share or to make it easier to obtain finance. However, pursuing any of these objectives will reduce profit, at least in the short term.'
- Explain that even if a firm is prioritising an objective other than profit maximisation in the short term, this may in fact be a way to maximise profit in the long term — e.g. 'A new firm may be aiming to increase output as quickly as possible in the short run in the hope of achieving its minimum efficient scale of production (MES). Although this means sacrificing profit in the short run, this may allow the firm to maximise profits in the longer term.'
- You should also discuss who decides what objectives a firm should pursue — e.g. 'The divorce of ownership from control means that it may not be a firm's owners who set the objectives but the directors and managers, and these may have priorities other than profit maximisation, such as enjoying the prestige of running a large firm.'
- For this question, you'll need to evaluate all your points and come to some kind of balanced conclusion — e.g. 'While long run profit maximisation is an objective pursued by many firms, there are good reasons to believe that other firms will have different objectives, even if only in the short term. It may even be that some of these firms' owners would like to pursue profit maximisation, but that those in day-to-day control are actually prioritising something else without their knowledge.'

Page 53 — Why Firms Grow

1 Maximum of 10 marks available. <u>HINTS</u>:
- Start by defining horizontal integration — e.g. 'Horizontal integration is when firms at the same stage of the production process for similar products are combined to form a single company.'
- Then explain some of the benefits this might bring — e.g. 'The new, larger firm may be able to achieve economies of scale that weren't available to the smaller firms. These could be of various types, including marketing economies of scale, financial economies of scale, and technical economies of scale.'
- Explain that the integration would result in less competition in the market, so the new firm would possibly be able to further increase its market share.
- 'Discuss' means your answer needs to include some kind of 'weighing up', and so you should also mention that there are risks when firms merge to create a new, larger firm — e.g. 'Large firms can become complacent and less efficient, or they might not be able to react as fast as a smaller firm to changing circumstances. There are also other diseconomies of scale that the new firm might face — for example, communication might become more difficult, and it might be harder to coordinate all the actions of the larger firm.'

Page 55 — Business Growth and Demergers

1 Maximum of 1 mark available. <u>HINTS</u>:
- The correct answer is A.
- If a firm splits into two separate companies, it's unlikely to increase purchasing economies of scale because one big firm has split into two smaller firms.
- B, C and D are all likely impacts of a demerger.

2 Maximum of 5 marks available. <u>HINTS</u>:
- Start your answer by giving an advantage to this firm of staying small, e.g. 'A small, successful firm might want to stay small because of the risks involved in expanding — the firm's owner(s) may be happy trying to maintain the current level of success.'
- Give at least two other reasons why the firm may want to stay small, such as keeping stronger, more personal relationships with customers and a strong emphasis on high-quality craftsmanship, while avoiding the diseconomies of scale it might experience if it expands.

Section Four — Market Structures

Page 57 — Perfect Competition

1 Maximum of 15 marks available. <u>HINTS</u>:
- Draw some diagrams to show how the long run equilibrium position will be reached. You should include diagrams similar to those shown below.

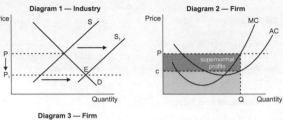

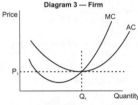

- Explain that diagram 1 shows initial supply (S) and demand (D). A firm will produce quantity Q at price P (shown on diagram 2).
- Describe how diagram 2 shows the supernormal profit a firm will make (the dark grey area), and explain how this will attract new firms to the market.
- State that this will shift the industry supply curve from S to S_1 (see diagram 1), and firms will undercut each other until they all make normal profit — so the long-term industry equilibrium is at E.
- Finish by explaining that — as the price falls from P to P_1 — the firm will reduce its output from Q to Q_1. So, in the long term, the equilibrium for this firm is at price P_1 and quantity Q_1 (shown on diagram 3).

Page 59 — Perfect Competition

1 Maximum of 5 marks available. <u>HINTS</u>:
- Briefly define dynamic efficiency — e.g. the ability to improve efficiency or products over time.
- Explain that the strategies to achieve dynamic efficiency involve investment and risk, and therefore if they are to take place, they need adequate reward.
- Explain that this means dynamic efficiency won't be achieved in a perfectly competitive market, e.g. 'Firms in a perfectly competitive market make normal profit, so there's no incentive to take risks as there's no reward — so dynamic efficiency won't be achieved in a perfectly competitive market.'
- State that, however, even in the most competitive real-life markets, some dynamic efficiency can usually be achieved.

Page 61 — Barriers to Entry

1 Maximum of 5 marks available. <u>HINTS</u>:
- Define barriers to entry, e.g. 'A barrier to entry is any potential difficulty or expense a firm might face if it wants to enter a market.'
- Explain why branding can be a barrier to entry — it creates familiarity, so it often makes a product the first choice for consumers.
- Finish by giving the possible ways in which an incumbent firm can create this barrier to entry — for example, the incumbent firm might create a strong brand by producing a product which is genuinely better than the competition, or it might create a strong brand using effective advertising.

2 Maximum of 15 marks available. <u>HINTS</u>:
- Define barriers to entry.
- Give examples of various barriers to entry — those which come from anticompetitive behaviour, e.g. 'Incumbent firms might lower prices to a level that new entrants can't match, therefore driving new entrants out of business', and those which don't, e.g. 'Economies of scale exist in some industries, so there will naturally be a cost advantage for large incumbent firms.'
- You'll need to weigh up the various barriers to entry and use this reasoning to give a conclusion on the extent to which they result from anticompetitive behaviour.

Answers

Page 63 — Monopolies

1 Maximum of 10 marks available. <u>HINTS</u>:
- Define supernormal profit — e.g. 'Supernormal profit occurs when a firm's total revenue exceeds its total costs.'
- You need to include a diagram similar to the one on the right.
- Explain that a firm will aim to maximise profits, so it'll output where MC = MR.
- Go on to explain how this means that the firm will make a supernormal profit shown by the dark grey area.

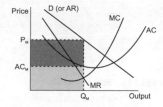

- Finish by using barriers to entry to explain why the firm will continue to make this supernormal profit in the long run. E.g. 'Barriers to entry in a monopoly market are total — so no new firms can enter the market, and the supernormal profit won't be competed away. This means that, in the long run, nothing will change, so the firm will continue to make the same supernormal profit.'

Page 65 — Price Discrimination

1 Maximum of 10 marks available. <u>HINTS</u>:
- Define price discrimination, e.g. 'Price discrimination occurs when a seller charges different prices to different customers for exactly the same product.'
- Explain how price discrimination will lead to the transfer of some, or all, of the consumer surplus to the producer — so producers' revenues increase, which is a good thing for producers, but not consumers. Use diagrams to demonstrate this.
- Go on to give the possible benefits to consumers of price discrimination — explain that the extra revenue might be used, for example, to improve products, or that those who can afford higher prices might effectively be subsidising the lower prices paid by other consumers.
- Conclude your answer, e.g. 'So price discrimination is good for producers, but it can have both positive and negative effects for consumers.'

Page 67 — Oligopolies

1 Maximum of 10 marks available. <u>HINTS</u>:
- Briefly define an oligopoly, e.g. 'An oligopoly is a market which is dominated by just a few firms. There may be high barriers to entry, differentiated products, interdependency and the use of competitive or collusive strategies.'
- Mention the anticompetitive behaviour that might exist in an oligopoly — for example, collusion on prices might result in higher prices for consumers. This means firms would be making supernormal profits at the expense of consumers.
- Explain that there are possible benefits to consumers too — e.g. 'Firms might try to differentiate their products from those made by firms they're colluding with, which can lead to improved products.'
- The word 'extent' in the question is key — make sure you emphasise the importance of each argument you make to the interests of consumers. For example, explain that even with price collusion, prices are unlikely to be very high as this would probably attract new firms to the market — even if there are high barriers to entry. This may limit the negative effects on consumers.

Page 69 — Interdependence in Oligopolistic Markets

1 Maximum of 15 marks available. <u>HINTS</u>:
- Include a diagram of the kinked demand curve to back up your answer.
- Give the two assumptions of this model — e.g. 'This model assumes that if one firm raises its prices, then other firms will not raise their prices, but if one firm lowers its prices, then other firms will also lower theirs.'
- Explain what these assumptions will lead to — i.e. that when price is increased, demand is price elastic, and when price is decreased, demand is price inelastic.
- Give the consequences of firms raising or lowering prices — i.e. that any firm that either raises or lowers its prices will lose out as a result.
- Conclude by explaining, for example, 'Firms have no incentive to change prices, because they'll lose out either way — therefore there is price stability.'

Page 71 — Monopolistic Competition

1 Maximum of 12 marks available. <u>HINTS</u>:
- Start by explaining that in the short run, monopolistic competition resembles a monopoly market because of barriers to entry (even though they'll usually be quite low) and/or product differentiation — use a diagram.
- Explain that the long run position of monopolistic competition is more like perfect competition, and explain why — e.g. 'Barriers to entry either don't exist or are very low in markets with monopolistic competition, so new entrants will join the market, and therefore in the long run it'll behave more like there's perfect competition than like a monopoly market.'
- Explain that this is because a firm's demand curve shifts to the left as new firms join the market (because demand is split between more firms). State that this continues until only normal profit can be earned — include a diagram like the one at the bottom of p.70.
- Mention that firms aren't productively or allocatively efficient — and explain why. But state that if there's monopolistic competition, it's likely to be more efficient than a monopoly market, and that prices will generally be lower.

Page 73 — Contestability

1 Maximum of 10 marks available. <u>HINTS</u>:
- Start by giving a definition of high contestability — e.g. 'A market is highly contestable if barriers to entry and exit are low, and supernormal profits can potentially be made by new firms.'
- Explain that if incumbent firms were to achieve large supernormal profits, this would attract new firms to the market, so incumbent firms are likely to set relatively low prices to avoid attracting new entrants — because they don't want increased competition.
- Give some further effects of high contestability on incumbent firms, e.g. 'High contestability is more likely to encourage firms to create high barriers to entry.'
- Explain the long run effect — that firms in highly contestable markets will move towards productive and allocative efficiency.

2 Maximum of 6 marks available. <u>HINTS</u>:
- Give an explanation of what is meant by technological change, e.g. 'Technological change occurs through invention and innovation — for example, the invention of a new product or a new service.'
- Explain the effect of technological change on barriers to entry and give examples, e.g. 'Technological change can reduce barriers to entry — for example, a new production method may reduce the cost of production for a particular product, and therefore reduce the barriers to entry for its market.'
- Make sure you include examples of how technological change can also increase barriers to entry.

Section Five — Market Failure

Page 75 — Externalities

1 Maximum of 6 marks available. <u>HINTS</u>:
- The question asks for a diagram so you must include one.
- Explain why the MPC curve can be seen as the supply curve and the MPB curve can be seen as the demand curve. Then you can say that this means equilibrium occurs where MPC = MPB and refer to the diagram, saying this is at price P_e and output Q_e.
- Say that this isn't the socially optimum level, e.g. 'This is not the socially optimal level of output — this occurs when the external costs and benefits to society have been included, which is where MSC = MSB.'
- Again, refer to the diagram by saying that this means the socially optimal price is P_1 and the socially optimal level of output is Q_1.

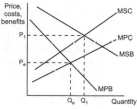

Page 77 — Externalities

1 Maximum of 12 marks available. <u>HINTS</u>:
- Draw a diagram showing positive consumption externalities like the one on the right.
- To get all of the marks for this question you need to explain what your diagram shows. Make sure you correctly label the curves and axes.
- Explain how the consumption of education has a higher MSB than MPB and how, if it's left to the market, education will be consumed at a level below the socially optimal point (where MSC = MSB).
- Talk about how the free market level of production causes the loss of a potential welfare gain (you need to make it clear where this is on your diagram).

Page 79 — Merit and Demerit Goods

1 Maximum of 6 marks available. <u>HINTS</u>:
- Give a definition of a merit good, e.g. 'Merit goods are goods which have greater social benefits than private benefits.'
- Draw a diagram to show how merit goods are underprovided by the free market — this should look like the merit good diagram on p.78. Your diagram should show that the MSB curve is above the MPB curve and that the free market equilibrium is below the socially optimal level (where MSC = MSB) of consumption/production of the merit good.

Page 81 — Public Goods

1 Maximum of 1 mark available. <u>HINTS</u>:
- The correct answer is D.
- A flood defence system is a public good so it will be affected by the free rider problem. This means that the free market won't provide a flood defence system because consumers will be unwilling to pay for a service that they could get for free if other consumers paid for it.
- Option A is incorrect because sufficient knowledge to build adequate flood defences exists or could be acquired.
- Option B is incorrect because flooding only helps some forms of farming and isn't a reason to prevent the construction of a flood defence system.
- Option C is incorrect because a flood defence system is a public good and in a free market it wouldn't be possible to set a price for individuals to be charged that truly reflected the system's value to them.

Answers

Page 82 — Imperfect Information

1   Maximum of 4 marks available. <u>HINTS</u>:
- Define what imperfect information is, e.g. 'Imperfect information is when buyers and/or sellers have incomplete knowledge of the price, costs, benefits and availability of products.'
- Give a couple of examples where this imperfect information causes market failure and the overprovision of demerit goods. For example, provision of alcohol, cigarettes and unhealthy foods.

Page 83 — Inequity

1   Maximum of 4 marks available. <u>HINTS</u>:
- Describe what is meant by market failure, e.g. 'Market failure occurs when the price mechanism fails to allocate scarce resources in a suitable way.'
- Then you need to explain how income and wealth inequality can be seen as market failure. Make sure you mention that this is normative market failure — it's based on opinion. E.g. 'Inequality in the distribution of income and wealth is a normative example of market failure. This is because it's the opinion of some economists that this kind of inequality is unfair (i.e. where the free market distributes income and wealth in a way that means that some people cannot afford to pay for what they need), so is a misallocation of resources. They argue that income and wealth should be redistributed for the benefit of society.'

Page 84 — Immobile Factors of Production

1   Maximum of 4 marks available. <u>HINTS</u>:
- Give a definition of what an immobile factor of production is, e.g. a factor of production which cannot be moved from one location to another or from one part of the economy to another, such as land.
- Explain why immobile factors of production can lead to market failure. E.g. immobile factors of production can lead to inefficient allocation of resources (resources are often unused or underused), which means there's market failure.
- Give an example of where immobile factors of production can cause market failure. For example, a jobseeker may not be able to afford to move to a different area to get a job — this is an example of geographical labour immobility.

Page 85 — Market Failure in Monopolies

1   Maximum of 8 marks available. <u>HINTS</u>:
- It's a good idea to start by explaining what market failure is, e.g. 'Market failure occurs when the price mechanism fails to allocate scarce resources efficiently.'
- Then you'll need to draw a diagram to show how monopoly firms can restrict output and cause an inefficient allocation of resources.
- To get all of the marks for this question you need to explain what your diagram shows, and correctly label the curves and axes.
- Explain that a monopoly is a price maker, which means that it can restrict supply (to Q_m) to get a higher price (P_m), leading to a welfare loss to society.

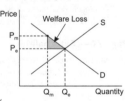

Section Six — Government Intervention

Page 87 — Taxation

1   Maximum of 1 mark available. <u>HINTS</u>:
- The correct answer is D. This is because the tax causes the supply curve to shift left to S_1. The tax revenue is equal to the difference in price (= 25 − 15 = £10) at the new level of demand multiplied by the new equilibrium quantity (80), so the tax revenue is £800.

Page 88 — Subsidies

1   Maximum of 1 mark available. <u>HINTS</u>:
- The correct answer is C. This is because the area ACFJ is equal to the difference between A and C (this takes into account the producer and consumer gain) multiplied by the quantity demanded when the subsidy is in place (equal to A to J). So ACFJ is the total cost of the subsidy to the government.

Page 89 — Price Controls

1   Maximum of 8 marks available. <u>HINTS</u>:
- Draw a diagram that shows the setting of a maximum price like the one on the right.
- Your diagram should have correctly labelled axes and clearly show a maximum price that's below the equilibrium price (e.g. in the diagram above P_m is below P_e).
- Give a complete explanation of what is shown on your diagram. Mention the equilibrium price and quantity and refer to the maximum price that has been set. You need to talk about the excess demand at the maximum price and indicate where this is shown on your diagram (i.e. Q_1 to Q_2 on the diagram above).

Page 90 — Buffer Stocks

1   Maximum of 1 mark available. <u>HINTS</u>:
- The correct answer is B. This is the correct answer because farmers would be paid the minimum price (P_2) when supply is at S_1.
- Option A is incorrect as this is the price that would be received by farmers if there was no buffer stock scheme in place. Option C is incorrect as this is the price farmers would receive for the level of supply shown by S rather than S_1. Option D is incorrect because farmers would not receive this price for the level of supply shown by S_1.

Page 91 — State Provision

1   Maximum of 6 marks available. <u>HINTS</u>:
- Start your answer by explaining that the state provision of health care means that it's likely to be free at the point of use.
- There are several disadvantages that you could go on to explain. These include: state provision can mean there's less of an incentive to operate efficiently due to a lack of the price mechanism; state-provided health care may fail to respond to consumers' demands as there is no profit motive to determine the services offered; self-reliance of patients may be reduced if they know the service is there if they need it; and free health care can lead to excess demand and this can lead to long waiting lists for consumers.

Page 93 — Privatisation, Regulation and Deregulation

1   Maximum of 15 marks available. <u>HINTS</u>:
- Give a brief definition of what a public monopoly is.
- Explain that the lack of competition for a public monopoly tends to mean it'll be inefficient.
- Explain how governments can use privatisation to introduce competition to a market (i.e. a government can sell a publicly owned firm). You'll need to explain why private firms have incentives to be more efficient, e.g. 'Private firms tend to be open to free market competition, so they have an incentive to keep prices down, and therefore keep costs down by being more efficient.'
- Discuss the various advantages and disadvantages of privatisation, e.g. 'Privatisation should improve resource allocation, as privatised firms have to react to market signals of supply and demand.'
- You could argue that, in this case, privatisation alone is likely to result in a private monopoly, so there may be the need for deregulation and/or regulation to increase competition and, therefore, efficiency.
- The question asks you to evaluate, so you'll need to weigh up the advantages and disadvantages and come to a conclusion to get all the marks. Make sure you show why the arguments you've made support your conclusion, e.g. 'Privatisation is likely to be effective at improving efficiency, as long as it results in a competitive market. Therefore the effectiveness of privatisation will depend on the factors which affect the level of competition in the market, such as having an appropriate level of regulation in place.'

Page 95 — Competition Policy

1   Maximum of 10 marks available. <u>HINTS</u>:
- Explain that the Competition and Markets Authority (CMA), and similar bodies, monitor competition to look out for unfair behaviour by firms towards consumers or other firms — you should go on to explain that this is part of the UK government's competition policy, which aims to increase competition, improve fairness to consumers and reduce monopoly power.
- Give some specific examples of what the CMA monitors, such as mergers, agreements between firms (they're looking for anti-competitive agreements) and the opening of markets to competition — e.g. 'The CMA monitors mergers and takeovers so they can prevent those that aren't beneficial to the efficiency of the market or to consumers. They may choose to stop a merger that would give a firm too high a market share (e.g. over 25%) and make it a monopoly, or that would give a firm too much monopoly power.'

Page 97 — Other Methods of Intervention

1   Maximum of 15 marks available. <u>HINTS</u>:
- Briefly explain what tradable pollution permits are and how they work, e.g. 'Tradable pollution permits are a way of controlling pollution by putting a cap on it, and using the market mechanism to internalise the externality of pollution. The government sets an optimal level of pollution and allocates permits that allow firms to emit a certain amount of pollution over a period of time. Firms can trade their permits with other firms and over time the number of permits will be reduced. This will create a market that assigns a cost to firms' pollution and creates incentives for firms to reduce their pollution.'
- You need to consider the advantages of using tradable pollution permits to reduce greenhouse gas emissions, such as the fact that they reward firms who cause low levels of pollution and they raise revenue for the government which could be used for other schemes to reduce greenhouse gas emissions. You also need to write about some disadvantages, such as the fact that it's difficult to set the optimal level of pollution and that the scheme has administrative costs for both firms and governments.
- A strong answer will also consider other possible schemes to reduce greenhouse gas emissions, with some evaluation of their effectiveness compared to using tradable pollution permits. For example, 'A government could impose a tax on petrol to discourage the overuse of cars and lorries and so reduce greenhouse gas emissions. This kind of tax will also internalise the externality of pollution from road transport

Answers

and raise revenue for the government to use for other schemes to reduce greenhouse gas emissions. However, using taxation has problems, for example, it's difficult to put a value on the cost of pollution and set the right level of tax.'
- Finish off with some evaluation of whether you think tradable pollution permits are effective or not, e.g. 'I think tradable pollution permits are an effective way of reducing greenhouse gas emissions as they create strong incentives for firms to reduce pollution. However, their success is dependent on the government setting a level of pollution that is appropriate, otherwise the system won't work.'

2   Maximum of 6 marks available. HINTS:
- You need to explain that governments try to correct market failures that are caused by asymmetric information by providing more information to consumers with the aim of helping them to make rational decisions.
- Describe that in this example governments would try to give more information to consumers about the health problems linked to cigarette consumption in order to reduce the level of demand for cigarettes.
- Give a couple of ways that governments could provide more information about the health implications of cigarettes, e.g. health warnings on cigarette packets and advertising campaigns to increase awareness of smoking-related disease.

Page 99 — Government Failure

1   Maximum of 1 mark available. HINTS:
- The correct answer is C. This is because the high cost involved in implementing the ban is an example of government failure.
- Options B and D are incorrect as they contribute to correcting the market failure associated with the banned substance.
- Option A is incorrect as the boosted opinion of the government hasn't contributed to a government failure.

2   Maximum of 6 marks available. HINTS:
- For this question you need to think about the effects the intervention would have and whether this actually addresses the market failure surrounding cigarette consumption.
- You should talk about how the desired impact of this intervention is to reduce demand for cigarettes and the negative externalities linked to their consumption (e.g. health problems).
- You also need to talk about the likely impact of the neighbouring country having cigarettes at a lower price, e.g. that people may purchase cigarettes from the neighbouring country to avoid the tax, and the consumption of cigarettes may not decrease as the government intended — this would be a government failure.

Page 101 — Examples of Government Failure

1   Maximum of 4 marks available. HINTS:
- There are several different advantages you can talk about for this question. If you think about the problems associated with farm subsidies, there are several of these that would be eased if the size of payments were reduced.
- For example, reducing farm subsidies could: reduce the oversupply of agricultural products and save money for governments if they have to store excess produce; and reduce the cost to the taxpayer.

2   Maximum of 10 marks available. HINTS:
- For this question you need to give arguments for and against road pricing.
- Arguments for a road pricing scheme include: a scheme could reduce the external costs linked to congestion (e.g. increased journey times) and the pollution (e.g. air and noise) it creates; revenue generated by the scheme can be used to contribute to projects that benefit society; and a reduction in health problems linked to traffic emissions inside the area covered by the scheme.
- Arguments against a road pricing scheme include: businesses inside a road pricing area may experience reduced trade because of the scheme; congestion may simply be shifted to areas not covered by the scheme — i.e. the road pricing may not actually reduce the external costs it aims to, just change their location; there may be underutilisation of road space in the road pricing area; schemes have an unfairly large impact on poor motorists; if the road pricing charge is too low then it might not have much impact on congestion levels.
- Include a brief evaluation of what you think about implementing a road pricing scheme to finish off your answer. It doesn't matter whether you're for or against — you just need to back up what you say.

Section Seven — The Labour Market

Page 103 — Labour Demand

1   Maximum of 6 marks available. HINTS:
- There are several factors that can lead to the demand for labour increasing — you need to give two possibilities and explain them fully.
- For example, you could explain how increased demand for the goods/services that labour produces and increased labour productivity can result in increased labour demand, e.g. 'If a firm trains its staff and this increases their productivity, this would decrease the firm's unit labour cost, which would increase its demand for labour.'

Page 105 — Labour Supply

1   Maximum of 15 marks available. HINTS:
- Start off by explaining that the elasticity of the supply of labour is determined by the extent to which the labour supply changes when there's a change in wage rates.

- You then need to explain, using examples, factors which can affect the elasticity of labour supply, e.g. 'The main determinant of the elasticity of labour supply is the level of skills and qualifications needed for a job. For example, a highly-skilled job, such as being a surgeon, will have an inelastic supply of labour (especially in the short run) because it takes time for new surgeons to be trained and gain the qualifications they need.'
- You could also include an example of a low-skilled job and explain why its labour supply will tend to be more elastic.
- Include a discussion of other factors which can influence the elasticity of labour supply, e.g. 'If workers are occupationally mobile, then the supply of labour will tend to be more elastic, as workers will be able to easily move to industries with rising wages.' You could also mention geographical mobility in your answer.

Page 107 — Wages

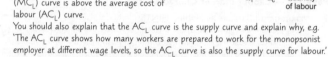

1   Maximum of 8 marks available. HINTS:
- Draw a diagram, such as the one on the right, and use it to explain how wage rates and employment levels are determined in a monopsony labour market.
- Explain why the marginal cost of labour (MC_L) curve is above the average cost of labour (AC_L) curve.
- You should also explain that the AC_L curve is the supply curve and explain why, e.g. 'The AC_L curve shows how many workers are prepared to work for the monopsonist employer at different wage levels, so the AC_L curve is also the supply curve for labour.'
- Now you can describe how wages and employment levels are determined in a monopsony labour market, e.g. 'Firms want to maximise their profits, so they'll employ at point T where $MRP_L = MC_L$. This means they'll employ Q_1 workers and the supply (or AC_L) curve shows that Q_1 workers will accept a wage of W_1. This is below the wage rate (W_C) and quantity of labour supplied (Q_C) in a perfectly competitive market.'

Page 109 — Trade Unions

1   Maximum of 20 marks available. HINTS:
- Start your answer with a definition of market failure — e.g. 'Market failure is the failure of the market mechanism to allocate resources efficiently.'
- Explain how trade unions can cause market failure, e.g. 'Trade unions can cause market failure by negotiating higher wages that are above the market equilibrium wage, which can result in a surplus of labour and therefore unemployment.' You could use a diagram like the one on p.108 to explain how this can occur in a perfectly competitive labour market.
- However, it's important to also give some reasons why these increased wages might not lead to unemployment (and therefore market failure) — e.g. if workers agree to become more productive when receiving a higher wage.
- Explain what happens in a monopsonistic labour market — e.g. 'The presence of a trade union in a monopsonistic labour market can lead to an increase in the wage rate and level of employment.' This could also be explained with the help of a diagram (see p.109).
- Remember, in questions like this you need to give reasons to justify the points you're making (in this case, for and against the idea that trade unions cause market failure).
- Round off your answer with a brief conclusion — you could give your opinion about the extent to which trade unions cause market failure based on the points you've discussed.

Page 111 — Discrimination

1   Maximum of 8 marks available. HINTS:
- Start by explaining what labour market discrimination is, e.g. 'Labour market discrimination is where employers treat a specific group of workers differently to other workers in the same job.'
- Explain some different types of discrimination (e.g. racial and age) and how they can impact the wages that are paid to any workers being discriminated against — in general these workers earn less than those that aren't suffering from discrimination. You can also go on to give other impacts on the wages of these workers, e.g. 'Workers being discriminated against may accept a job paying a low wage that they are overqualified for because they haven't been able to find a more suitable job.'
- You need to also explain how discrimination can impact worker productivity. For example, a worker being discriminated against might not be able to get a job that would make the most of their skills and maximise their productivity.

2   Maximum of 8 marks available. HINTS:
- You could draw a diagram similar to the one on the right (see p.111).
- Using your diagram, explain that firms who discriminate believe that the MRP of their favoured workers (the workers the firm doesn't discriminate against) is higher than it really is, e.g. 'Employers believe the MRP of their favoured workers to be greater than it really is. This means they demand more of these workers, so the MRP curve shifts to the right, increasing the wage rate for these workers from W_e to W_f.'

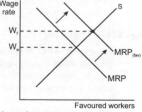

Answers

- Make sure you explain how costs for firms that discriminate can be higher than firms that don't discriminate, e.g. 'This discrimination means that these firms have fewer workers to choose from and have to pay higher wages to the workers they choose to employ — this is shown on the diagram as the MRP curve for favoured workers is shifted to the right, meaning that favoured workers are paid wages above the market equilibrium wage level. By ignoring workers who may have been more suited to a job and more efficient, they increase their costs of production.'

Page 113 — Imperfections

1   Maximum of 4 marks available. <u>HINTS</u>:
- Define occupational immobility, e.g. 'Occupational immobility is when workers lack the skills to be able to move from one occupation to another with ease.'
- Then explain the likely impacts of a high level of occupational immobility on an economy, e.g. 'Occupational immobility can mean that skills shortages persist, i.e. there may be a long term shortage of labour with specific skills. Skills shortages lead to increased wage costs for firms and therefore increased costs of production. This could also mean increased prices for consumers.'
- Make sure you include more than one likely impact — for example, you could explain how occupational immobility can cause unemployment.

Page 115 — Labour Market Characteristics

1   Maximum of 8 marks available. <u>HINTS</u>:
- In your answer you should explain what labour market segmentation means — e.g. 'A segmented labour market is one that consists of many individual labour markets.'
- Explain how the labour market would operate in the absence of barriers to entry and exit, e.g. 'If there were no barriers to entry and exit, workers would move from low wage jobs to high wage jobs until everyone had the same wage. However, in reality there would still be some wage differentials because not everyone has the motivation and talent to do a high-paying job.'
- Explain that the presence of barriers to entry and exit in reality means that segmented labour markets exist. This is because these barriers prevent the free movement of workers between all of the different jobs that are available, so many distinct labour markets exist.
- You could give an example of one of these barriers to entry, e.g. 'A barrier to entry for some jobs is a particular qualification — for example, to get a job as a pharmacist you need a particular university qualification.'

Page 117 — Minimum, Maximum and Living Wages

1   Maximum of 15 marks available. <u>HINTS</u>:
- Start by briefly describing what a national minimum wage (NMW) is.
- Describe and explain some advantages that the introduction of a NMW would bring — for example, reducing poverty for some of the poorest members of society, boosting morale of low-wage workers and increasing their productivity, and increasing tax revenue to allow greater government spending, e.g. 'Introducing a NMW may increase the earnings of people on very low incomes and reduce the number of people living in poverty in a country.'
- Describe and explain some disadvantages surrounding the introduction of a NMW — for example, increasing wage costs for firms leading to them reducing the number of staff they employ, decreasing competitiveness compared to countries with lower wage costs, and increasing prices of goods due to increased wage bills for firms being passed on to consumers, e.g. 'The increased wage costs brought about by the introduction of a NMW might mean that firms pass on these costs to consumers by increasing their prices, which could also contribute to inflation in the economy.'
- Make a conclusion about the impact of introducing a NMW — here you can give your opinion of whether you think introducing a NMW will have a positive or negative impact given the advantages and disadvantages you've discussed. You could mention the fact that this might depend on the level it's set at.

Page 119 — Pensions and a Changing Workforce

1   Maximum of 8 marks available. <u>HINTS</u>:
- You could start your answer by defining what a flexible workforce is, e.g. 'A flexible labour force is one where workers can transfer between activities quickly in response to changes in the economy.'
- You need to mention different methods that governments can use to increase labour force flexibility and discuss the likely effectiveness of each method, e.g. 'The government could provide or subsidise training schemes for workers to increase their flexibility. The skills and knowledge the workers gain from such training will make them more attractive to employers and are likely to allow them to transfer between jobs more easily.'
- Other examples of methods include making it less costly for firms to hire and fire workers, and reducing the power of trade unions.

Page 121 — Migration

1   Maximum of 4 marks available. <u>HINTS</u>:
- You must include a diagram, such as the one on the right, in your answer.
- Explain that the wage rate before immigration is W_1.
- Then describe what happens when migrant workers enter the labour market, e.g. 'Migrant

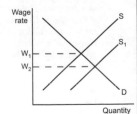

workers expand the labour supply, so there will be a shift of the supply curve from S to S_1. This will cause a fall in the wage rate to W_2.'

Section Eight — Measuring Economic Performance

Page 123 — Measuring Economic Growth

1   Maximum of 8 marks available. <u>HINTS</u>:
- Start by defining the GDP per capita, e.g. 'The GDP (or national output) of a country can be found by calculating the value of all the goods and services that country produces in one year. Dividing this figure by the population size gives the GDP per capita, which is the national output per person.'
- Give a few examples of why this comparison might not be accurate, e.g. 'GDP per capita figures don't take the hidden economy into account — the bigger the difference in the extent of the hidden economy between the two countries that are being compared, the less accurate the GDP per capita will be at making a comparison between their standards of living.'
- You could also mention what the GDP per capita doesn't take into account, e.g. income inequality between the rich and poor in a country, working conditions, number of hours worked per week.

Page 125 — Measuring Inflation

1   Maximum of 6 marks available. <u>HINTS</u>:
- Start your answer by defining inflation, e.g. 'Inflation is the sustained rise in the average price of goods and services over a period of time.'
- Explain what the RPI is, e.g. 'The RPI is a measure of inflation calculated using two surveys — the Living Costs and Food Survey, which looks at what people spend their money on, and a survey of the prices of the most commonly used goods and services.'
- Then give a limitation of the RPI, e.g. 'The information given by people responding to the Living Costs and Food Survey can be inaccurate.'
- The question asks for two more limitations of the RPI as a measure of inflation. You could mention that certain households are excluded from the RPI, and discuss the fact that the basket of goods only changes once a year, so short-term changes are often missed.

Page 127 — Measuring the Balance of Payments

1   Maximum of 4 marks available. <u>HINTS</u>:
- State that one measure is the claimant count.
- Give one advantage and one disadvantage of the claimant count, e.g. 'The claimant count is the number of people who are claiming JSA, so it's easy to obtain the data. However, unemployed people who either choose not to claim JSA, or aren't eligible to claim it, aren't included in the claimant count.'
- State that the other measure is the Labour Force Survey.
- Give one advantage and one disadvantage of the Labour Force Survey, e.g. 'The Labour Force Survey is an internationally agreed measure for unemployment, so it's easy to use it to make comparisons with other countries. However, it's expensive to collect and compile the data.'
2   Maximum of 4 marks available. <u>HINTS</u>:
- Give a definition of the balance of payments, e.g. 'The balance of payments records flows of money in and out of a country.'
- Explain that if the flow of money into a country exceeds the flow of money out of that country, it will have a balance of payments surplus.
- Then say that if the flow of money out of a country exceeds the flow of money into that country, it will have a balance of payments deficit.

Page 129 — Measuring Development

1   Maximum of 12 marks available. <u>HINTS</u>:
- Give a definition of the HDI — mention its three components and how each of them helps to measure the standard of living.
- Give an analysis of each of the three components — explain their limitations. E.g. 'The health component of the HDI is measured by life expectancy. However, a long life expectancy isn't the same as a high quality of life. For example, someone could live for a long time but suffer from poor working conditions or a lack of freedom.'
- Explain why the HDI is more accurate at measuring the standard of living than, for example, the GDP per capita. E.g. 'The HDI gives a more accurate measure of the standard of living in a country than the GDP per capita because it takes more factors into account. The HDI includes real GNI per capita (a similar measure to GDP per capita), but it also looks, for example, at health and education.'
- Mention that other indicators would help to give a fuller picture, e.g. 'Other indicators could help to give a better picture of the standard of living in a country. For example, the number of mobile phones per thousand of the population. If there are lots of mobile phones, this suggests that people are paid enough to be able to afford them. Mobile phones also improve trading, which might lead to a higher level of economic development.'

Section Nine — Aggregate Demand and Aggregate Supply

Page 131 — The Circular Flow of Income

1   Maximum of 6 marks available. <u>HINTS</u>:
- Start by defining the multiplier effect, e.g. 'The multiplier effect is the process by which an injection into the circular flow of income creates a change in the size of national income that's greater than the size of the initial injection.'

Answers

- Then explain that an increase in government spending on the NHS will represent an injection into the circular flow of income, and how this extra money will go around the circular flow of income in the form of increased expenditure and income.
- Finally, explain that the size of the multiplier will depend on the size of leakages from the circular flow of income. So if a lot of money leaks out of the circular flow then the size of the multiplier will be quite small.

Page 133 — The Components of Aggregate Demand

1 Maximum of 6 marks available. <u>HINTS</u>:
- Describe what is meant by consumption, e.g. 'Consumption is the total amount spent by households on goods and services.'
- Then, explain how high taxes affect consumption, e.g. 'High direct taxes (such as income tax) will reduce the amount of disposable income available to consumers, and high indirect taxes will increase the cost of spending. This means that high taxes are likely to lead to a fall in consumption.'
- And then explain how high interest rates affect consumption, e.g. 'High interest rates increase the cost of borrowing, which means that it's more expensive for consumers to borrow money to spend, and they make it more attractive for people to save their money. High interest rates may also reduce the amount consumers have to spend, as loan repayments and mortgages will become more expensive. As a result, high interest rates are likely to lead to a fall in consumption.'

2 Maximum of 6 marks available. <u>HINTS</u>:
- Identify three things that will have an effect on investment, such as risk, business confidence and interest rates, and say what effect they will have.
- The question asks you to describe three factors, so you don't need to provide too much detail.
- Risk — if there is a high risk that an investment will not benefit a firm then it is less likely to invest.
- Business confidence — if business confidence is high and a firm is doing well, then it is more likely to invest.
- Interest rates — if interest rates are high then investment is likely to be reduced because the cost of borrowing to invest is higher.

Page 135 — The Components of Aggregate Demand

1 Maximum of 1 mark available. <u>HINTS</u>:
- The correct answer is C.
- C is correct because both policies will increase aggregate demand. Government spending is a component of aggregate demand, so an increase in government spending will increase aggregate demand. A decrease in taxes will increase people's disposable income, so consumption (another component of aggregate demand) is likely to increase, which means aggregate demand will increase.
- A, B and D are incorrect. Option B will cause aggregate demand to fall, and options A and D may result in a slight rise in aggregate demand, but they're less likely to lead to an increase in aggregate demand than option C.

2 Maximum of 10 marks available. <u>HINTS</u>:
- Start by defining exports, e.g. 'Exports are goods or services that are produced in one country and then sold in another.'
- Then, identify two things that could increase the demand for a country's exports, such as changes to the exchange rate or non-price factors.
- The question asks you to explain two factors, so you'll be expected to give some reasons to support your answers.
- Explain how the exchange rate may affect the demand for a country's exports, and remember to consider the price elasticity of demand — e.g. 'A fall in the value of a country's currency will reduce the price of its exports, so they'll be cheaper for other countries to buy and demand for them will increase. However, the level of an increase in demand will depend on the price elasticity of demand. For example, demand can be price inelastic in the short run, so if the UK's exchange rate fell, there may be a time lag before countries switch to buying exports from the UK instead of from another country. This means that in the short run, demand for a country's exports might not increase, or increase by much.'
- Then go on to talk about the second factor, non-price factors — e.g. 'An improvement in the quality of a country's goods may increase demand for that country's exports, as people are often willing to pay more for good quality products. The level of the increase in demand may depend on who the country exports to — for example, demand for exports might be low if that country's main trading partners are quite poor or suffering from a recession.'

Page 137 — Aggregate Demand Analysis

1 Maximum of 10 marks available. <u>HINTS</u>:
- Give a definition of the multiplier effect.
- Use the multiplier effect to explain how an increase in government spending, e.g. on roads, hospitals and schools, would be likely to lead to a bigger increase in aggregate demand in general.
- Draw a diagram to show how an increase in government spending will cause the aggregate demand curve to shift to the right.
- Point out that the size of the increase in aggregate demand (and, therefore, the size of the shift to the right of the aggregate demand curve) depends on the size of the multiplier effect.
- Explain that the size of the multiplier depends on the size of the leakages from the circular flow of income, e.g. 'If the leakages in the circular flow are small then the multiplier will be big and cause a large shift to the right of the aggregate demand curve.'

Page 139 — Aggregate Demand Analysis

1 Maximum of 4 marks available. <u>HINTS</u>:
- First find MPW using the formula MPW = MPS + MPT + MPM. MPW = 0.3 + 0.4 + 0.1 = 0.8.
- Use the value of MPW to find the multiplier. Multiplier = 1 ÷ MPW = 1 ÷ 0.8 = 1.25
- Now you can use the definition of the multiplier to find the total rise in GDP. Total rise in national income = injection × multiplier = £100m × 1.25 = £125m

Page 141 — Aggregate Supply

1 Maximum of 1 mark available. <u>HINTS</u>:
- The correct answer is B.
- B is correct because the discovery of a new raw material would increase the factors of production that are available to an economy. If there are more factors of production available, in this case a new raw material, then the capacity of the economy will increase and the LRAS curve will shift to the right.
- Options A, C and D are more likely to affect the aggregate demand curve or the short run aggregate supply curve as they will change the costs of production. None of these options will increase the capacity of the economy.

Page 143 — Macroeconomic Equilibrium

1 Maximum of 8 marks available. <u>HINTS</u>:
- Draw a diagram to show a shift to the right of the short run aggregate supply curve.
- Your diagram should look like the one shown on the right.
- Referring to your diagram, explain how a shift to the right of the aggregate supply curve (from SRAS to SRAS₁) means that output will increase (from Y to Y₁) and the price level will fall (from P to P₁). You should also point out that an increase in output will mean that unemployment will fall because labour is a derived demand. If more is being produced then the demand for labour will increase.

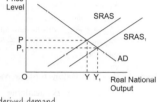

- You should also mention that a fall in the price level will make a country's exports cheaper, so exports will increase and there will be an increase in a balance of payments surplus or a reduction in a balance of payments deficit.

Section Ten — Government Economic Policy Objectives

Page 147 — Economic Growth

1 Maximum of 8 marks available. <u>HINTS</u>:
- You could start by explaining what's meant by an improvement in the standard of living, e.g. 'The standard of living in a country includes many things, such as the level of wealth and access to necessary goods and services. An improvement in the standard of living will occur when there's an improvement in people's economic welfare. This might be the result of increased wages, or improvements in the services that people use.'
- Then you should give at least two reasons why economic growth might improve standards of living, e.g. 'Economic growth means that output is rising, which will lead to an increase in jobs, causing a fall in unemployment, and a rise in wages. If more people are employed and have higher wages, then their standard of living will improve.' You could go on, for example, to mention how economic growth might lead to investment in cleaner, more efficient production processes — this will reduce pollution that harms the environment, and therefore improve living standards, e.g. if the air is cleaner, this may improve people's health.
- Balance your answer by considering how economic growth might not improve the standard of living, e.g. 'Short run economic growth can lead to inflation, and higher prices may mean that some people's standard of living will decrease, even when there's economic growth.'

Page 149 — Economic Instability

1 Maximum of 8 marks available. <u>HINTS</u>:
- Start by explaining what an asset price bubble is, e.g. 'An asset price bubble is when prices of assets such as housing or shares increase until they're much higher than the assets' true value.'
- Now you need to explain why this can be destabilising for an economy, e.g. 'Eventually, these bubbles can burst, meaning asset prices fall further and further after an initial drop in price, as people sell the asset before they lose even more money. This is often accompanied by less confidence and optimism among people, which leads to more saving and less spending in the economy. This can throw the economy into a downward spiral.'

Page 151 — Unemployment

1 Maximum of 8 marks available. <u>HINTS</u>:
- First state what unemployment may mean for an economy, e.g. 'Unemployment means that an economy isn't operating at its full capacity, as there's wasted labour that isn't being used. As a result, there may also be other resources that are not being exploited, such as offices and machines.'

Answers

- Then explain how this will impact upon economic growth, e.g. 'A country's economic growth may be harmed if there's high unemployment because fewer people will have income to spend, which may mean that firms' profits and output will fall. However, a government might respond by increasing its spending on unemployment benefits, so spending might not decrease by a large amount.' You could go on to talk about how it's hard for people who are unemployed for long periods of time to get a job (because their skills become outdated), and how this might affect economic growth.

Page 153 — Inflation

1 Maximum of 12 marks available. <u>HINTS</u>:
- Start by giving a definition of inflation, e.g. 'Inflation is the sustained rise in the average price of goods and services over a period of time.'
- Give examples of the harm high inflation can cause, e.g. 'High inflation can reduce people's standards of living, especially those on fixed incomes. Prices are rising, but their incomes remain the same, so the real value of their money falls.'
- Discuss the potential advantages of keeping the rate of inflation low, e.g. 'If a country's inflation rate is below the inflation rate in its competitor countries, it's likely to become more price competitive.'
- Try to provide a thorough analysis of the positives and negatives, showing that you've considered the likely importance of each.
- You should also mention the difference between cost-push and demand-pull inflation. Demand-pull inflation tends to be less harmful, as it's caused by a rise in demand, whereas cost-push inflation is caused by an increase in the costs of production.
- Explain that deflation is a bad thing, and describe the effects it can have on the economy.
- Make a strong conclusion to your evaluation, explaining that a rate of 2% is considered desirable as some inflation is better than no (or negative) inflation, but that high inflation tends to be harmful.
- There are 12 marks for this question — make sure you provide enough examples and explanations.

Page 155 — The Balance of Payments

1 Maximum of 8 marks available. <u>HINTS</u>:
- Give a definition of the balance of payments, e.g. 'The balance of payments measures international flows of money. It measures flows of money out of a country, e.g. to pay for imports, and flows of money into a country, e.g. from the sale of exports.'
- Define the four sections of the current account, and state whether the UK has a deficit or a surplus in each (as well as their relative sizes — i.e. large or small).
- Discuss the likely reasons for the UK importing more visible goods than it exports, such as high levels of consumer spending, a lack of price competitiveness and, until more recent years, the high value of the pound.

Page 157 — The Balance of Payments

1 Maximum of 15 marks available. <u>HINTS</u>:
- You should start by explaining the possible negative effects of a rise in the value of the Chinese renminbi, e.g. 'A significant rise in the value of the Chinese renminbi is likely to cause a very large increase in the US's current account deficit on its balance of payments, at least in the short term, because it imports a lot of goods from China.' You could go on to mention how a rise in the value of the renminbi may also cause prices to rise in the US because it imports a lot of goods from China.
- You should then explain how the rise in the value of the Chinese renminbi might have a positive effect. For example, if demand was price elastic, then US consumers might stop buying so many Chinese imports and they may switch to buying domestic products. This would improve the US's current account deficit.
- Conclude your answer by stating what you think is most likely to happen — e.g. 'A rise in the value of the Chinese renminbi may not benefit the US balance of payments current account deficit if domestic products aren't suitable substitutes for Chinese imports or if domestic products are still more expensive than imports from China. Both of these factors would mean that the US current account deficit would worsen.'

Page 159 — Other Economic Policy Objectives

1 Maximum of 8 marks available. <u>HINTS</u>:
- Start by explaining how firms might damage the environment, through, for example, carbon emissions or waste disposal.
- Explain that a government will try to measure the cost of the damage caused so they can attempt to internalise the externalities and encourage a change in the behaviour of firms.
- Describe the different methods governments might use to alter firms' behaviour, such as financial penalties, restrictions or bans. Give specific examples, e.g. 'Governments might use tradable pollution permits — these restrict the amount of pollution firms can produce, but firms can buy/sell these permits between themselves.'

Page 161 — Conflicts Between Economic Objectives

1 Maximum of 12 marks available. <u>HINTS</u>:
- Start by explaining what the four main macroeconomic objectives are, i.e. strong economic growth, reducing unemployment, low inflation and equilibrium in the balance of payments.

- Then describe how these four objectives can be achieved by an increase in a country's aggregate supply (or long run aggregate supply) — use a diagram to show this.
- You must explain what the diagram shows, e.g. 'If aggregate supply is increased so that the LRAS curve shifts to the right (from LRAS to LRAS$_1$)then this will achieve an increase in output (from Y to Y$_1$). This increase in output is economic growth, which will lead to a reduction in unemployment. In addition, the price level will fall (from P to P$_1$), so inflation will be controlled. This will also improve the country's competitiveness — so the balance of payments will improve.'

- You should give some examples of how a government could achieve this kind of increase in aggregate supply (i.e. long run economic growth), e.g. 'To shift the LRAS curve to the right a government would need to stimulate an increase in the quantity and quality of the factors of production. For example, it could encourage immigration in order to increase the country's workforce.'

Page 164 — Tackling Unemployment and Inflation

1 Maximum of 8 marks available. <u>HINTS</u>:
- You could start by defining the natural rate of unemployment, e.g. 'The natural rate of unemployment (NRU) is the rate of unemployment when the labour market is in equilibrium.'
- Then give at least two ways that the NRU could be reduced by a government — for example, you could mention some supply-side policies that are used to make the labour market more flexible, or to reduce frictional or structural unemployment, e.g. 'A government could improve occupational mobility by investing in training schemes that help workers to improve their skills.'

Page 167 — Government Policies to Tackle Poverty

1 Maximum of 10 marks available. <u>HINTS</u>:
- Give brief definitions of absolute and relative poverty.
- Discuss the various positive and negative effects on absolute and relative poverty of the introduction of a national minimum wage (NMW), and of means-tested state benefits — you'll need to explain each point. For example, 'A NMW, if it's set at the right level, will reduce poverty amongst the lowest paid workers and increase the incentive to work.' and 'Means-tested benefits can be expensive — they're paid for by tax, so the introduction of means-tested benefits might mean that those on low incomes are taxed more.'
- You can mention how one policy can help in an area that the other can't, e.g. 'A NMW won't help anyone who's in absolute poverty if they're unemployed — especially if they're unable to work. However, means-tested benefits would provide these people with some form of income, reducing their relative poverty and potentially lifting them out of absolute poverty.'
- Make sure you include conflicts between the two policies, such as 'Means-tested benefits and a NMW might be set at a level where the combination worsens the poverty trap — if the NMW isn't high enough, the incomes of the unemployed who are receiving means-tested benefits might actually fall if they start earning the minimum wage, e.g. because of the fall in their means-tested benefits and the increase in their taxes, so there would be no incentive for them to work.'
- Finish by saying how effective you think these policies might be overall.

Section Eleven — Macroeconomic Policy Instruments

Page 171 — Fiscal Policy

1 Maximum of 4 marks available. <u>HINTS</u>:
- First explain what a budget position is, e.g. 'The budget position describes whether a government's fiscal policy is reflationary, deflationary, or neither.'
- Then define a cyclical and a structural budget position, and point out the differences between them. E.g. 'The cyclical budget position of a government is their budget position in the short term. This will be affected by where the economy is in the economic cycle, because automatic stabilisers are likely to create a surplus in boom times, and a deficit during recession. The structural budget position on the other hand is a government's long-term budget position, over a whole period of the economic cycle.'
2 Maximum of 1 mark available. <u>HINTS</u>:
- The answer is C.
- A is unlikely because during a boom phase government is unlikely to stimulate the economy further with loose fiscal policy (i.e. by boosting aggregate demand).
- B is not particularly likely because in the long term a country is less likely to have loose fiscal policy, which involves running a budget deficit (with government spending exceeding revenue), when it has a large national debt.
- D can't be correct because loose fiscal policy means government is boosting aggregate demand, whereas a neutral budget position means government spending and taxation has no net effect on aggregate demand.
- C is the most likely because when there's a negative output gap government is more likely to use loose (expansionary) fiscal policy to boost the economy.
3 Maximum of 12 marks available. <u>HINTS</u>:
- Start by defining fiscal rules, e.g. 'rules a government makes to control its spending and borrowing'.
- Then explain how fiscal rules might create economic stability.

Answers

- You could start by talking about the effect they have on governments, e.g. 'Fiscal rules can help achieve economic stability because they should help to prevent a government from continuously borrowing and overspending to promote growth, which increases national debt and inflation. If these get too high government may need to take action (such as raising interest rates or cutting spending). This can lead to instability as it may result in confidence in the economy falling.'
- Then go on to explain how they might affect firms and consumers, e.g. 'Fiscal rules can also influence the behaviour of businesses and consumers, by increasing confidence in future economic stability. If confidence is high then consumers will be more willing to spend and firms are likely to increase investment.'
- The question says evaluate, so you need to discuss how effective they're actually likely to be. You could talk about whether governments actually follow them, e.g. 'Fiscal rules are only likely to contribute to economic stability if people and firms believe they will be kept to. For example, there isn't agreement on whether the 'golden rule' set by the UK government in 1997 was kept to, before being abandoned in 2008.'
- You could mention the role of the OBR in helping the UK government to keep to any fiscal rules it has set itself.

4 Maximum of 10 marks available. <u>HINTS</u>:
- It's likely that a government would use a progressive tax to reduce inequality, so you could start by explaining how progressive taxation could achieve this, e.g. 'A government might use a progressive taxation system to redistribute income. A progressive tax system is one where an individual's taxes rise as a percentage of their income as their income rises. This means that the rich will pay higher taxes, reducing income inequality. Revenue raised in this way can be used to provide benefits and state-provided services for the poor, which will also help to reduce inequality.'
- You could go on to mention how the government could also reduce inequality by providing tax relief for the poor.
- You should balance your answer by considering why taxation may not be effective at reducing inequality, e.g. 'If a progressive tax is set too high for the rich it might create a disincentive to work and lead to a fall in revenue received by the government. This would mean that the government would have less to spend on benefits and services, which may increase inequality.'

Page 172 — Average and Marginal Tax Rates

1 Maximum of 2 marks available. <u>HINTS</u>:
- First work out the total tax paid — there's no tax on the first £12 500, then 20% is paid on the rest (£26 000 is less than £50 000). So you need to work out 20% of £26 000 − £12 500:
  £26 000 − £12 500 = £13 500
  20% of £13 500 = 0.2 × £13 500 = £2700
- Then work out the average income tax rate.

$$\text{average income tax rate} = \frac{\text{total income tax paid}}{\text{total income}} \times 100 = \frac{2700}{26\,000} \times 100 = 10.4\% \; (1 \text{ d.p.})$$

Page 175 — Monetary Policy

1 Maximum of 4 marks available. <u>HINTS</u>:
- First describe what the MPC's targets are when setting the interest rate. E.g. 'The MPC sets interest in order to meet the inflation target that's set by the government. This target is currently 2% inflation.'
- Then give a bit more detail about how interest rates are set to meet this target. E.g. 'If the MPC believed inflation was likely to go more than 1% above the target it would increase the official rate of interest to reduce aggregate demand.'
- Finally, mention that this isn't their only aim, e.g. 'Controlling inflation is the main aim of the MPC, but when setting interest rates it must also consider the aims of promoting economic growth and reducing unemployment.'

Page 177 — Supply-side Policies

1 Maximum of 25 marks available. <u>HINTS</u>:
- For this question you'll need to look at the advantages and disadvantages of supply-side policies, and also think about what role demand-side policies should play in an economy. You could start by briefly describing the role of demand-side and supply-side policies, e.g. 'Demand-side policies are most useful for managing an economy in the short run, as they can be used to make small adjustments to its performance. Supply-side policies will increase an economy's productive capacity and improve efficiency, which will lead to long run improvements in the economy.'
- You could then talk about the advantages of supply-side policies, e.g. 'Successful supply-side policies are crucial to an economy's long-term growth. For example, policies that improve efficiency in the product market, such as tax breaks for firms that invest their profits back into their businesses, will help a country's firms to produce more and better products. This will improve the country's international competitiveness and its balance of payments.' You could go on to talk about other supply-side policies and their importance to a country's economy, such as those aimed at improving the efficiency of the capital and labour markets.
- It's important to also talk about the drawbacks of supply-side policies. For example, too much deregulation can cause unintended negative effects, such as excessive financial risk-taking.
- You should then discuss when demand-side policies might be more appropriate than supply-side policies, e.g. 'Demand-side policies are more appropriate for short-term management of the economy. For example, sharp rises in inflation can be tackled more effectively by using monetary policies, like raising interest rates, than with long-term supply-side approaches to improve efficiency. Demand-side policies are especially

important during a recession when aggregate demand needs to be stimulated quickly in order to create economic growth and jobs. It might cause too much harm to an economy, in the short run, if a government uses supply-side policies to tackle the effects of a recession.'
- To develop this further you could consider how supply-side policies and demand-side policies could be used together for the benefit of an economy, e.g. 'Supply-side policies will create more supply in an economy, but to bring the maximum benefits to an economy, demand will also need to be stimulated to match that supply. For example, if supply-side policies were introduced to make the labour market more efficient, then this might lead to lower real wages for workers, unless aggregate demand was also increased (e.g. by providing tax breaks for firms that employ more workers).'
- Make sure you conclude your answer with a judgement that sums up your arguments, e.g. 'Supply-side policies are very important for a country's economy and a government should try to increase aggregate supply in order to help it achieve its macroeconomic objectives. However, demand-side policies shouldn't be ignored as they're useful for managing an economy, e.g. controlling inflation, and are an important tool during a recession. In addition, for supply-side policies to be more successful they need to be combined with demand-side policies to create demand for the new supply that's produced.'
- You'll get marks for any relevant diagrams you include — as long as they're correctly drawn and explained.

Page 181 — Different Approaches to Macroeconomic Policy

1 Maximum of 6 marks available. <u>HINTS</u>:
- Mention at least two differences in the policy response to the two recessions. For example: fiscal policy was contractional during the Great Depression, but expansionary in the recession after the 2008 financial crisis; banks were allowed to fail during the Great Depression, but not in 2008; expansionary monetary policy was used after the 2008 financial crisis, but this wasn't an option during the early part of the Great Depression.
- You're asked to 'discuss', so give some explanation of why the response was different in each case, and what the effect of this was. E.g. 'During the Great Depression there was a widely held belief that the most important economic goal of government was to balance the budget (i.e. not to run a budget deficit). This meant that when government revenue fell and spending increased as the recession hit, the government introduced contractionary fiscal policy in order to try and balance the budget. This worsened the situation, and the economy stayed in recession until expansionary monetary policy was brought in. In contrast, after the 2008 financial crisis the government brought in expansionary fiscal policy to try and limit the effect of the shock. This helped to stimulate the economy in the short term by boosting aggregate demand. However, it also contributed to budget deficits during the recession, resulting in rapidly rising national debt.'

Section Twelve — The Financial Sector

Page 183 — The Financial Sector and Financial Markets

1 Maximum of 4 marks available. <u>HINTS</u>:
- Start by explaining what's meant by regulation — e.g. 'Regulation in the banking industry means that there are rules to control the behaviour of banks, and penalties for banks that break those rules.'
- Then explain why regulation is important in banking — e.g. 'Regulation is important because if a bank runs into difficulties, this can destabilise a country's whole economy. Also, in banking, greater profitability is associated with taking bigger risks, so banks have an incentive to behave in a risky way.'
- Finish off your answer by linking the above points together — e.g. 'This combination of banks' huge economic importance and incentives to take risks means that regulation is important in the banking industry.'

Page 185 — Banks and Money

1 Maximum of 4 marks available. <u>HINTS</u>:
- Start by explaining what's meant by liquidity — e.g. 'Liquidity refers to how easily an asset can be converted into spendable cash.'
- Explain why a bank needs liquidity — e.g. 'A bank needs to have a certain amount of liquid assets so that it can repay depositors who want to withdraw their money — banks have to be able to repay this money immediately.'
- Now explain why needing to keep some liquid assets prevents the bank from maximising profits — e.g. 'The rate of return a bank can expect on illiquid assets is generally higher than that for liquid assets, so profits cannot be maximised while the bank holds liquid assets.'

Page 187 — Banking and Interest Rates

1 Maximum of 9 marks available. <u>HINTS</u>:
- Describe what is meant by loanable funds — e.g. 'Loanable funds are the total amount of money that's available for borrowing.'
- Explain the loanable funds theory — e.g. 'The loanable funds theory states that the interest rate is determined by the supply of, and demand for, loanable funds. The supply of loanable funds comes from people's savings, while the demand comes from people wanting to borrow. The interest rate is the price at the equilibrium point in the market, i.e. where the supply and demand curves meet.'
- You could also include a graph to show the supply and demand curves for loanable funds. Mark on it the equilibrium point and the market interest rate.

Answers

Page 189 — Financial Market Failure

1 Maximum of 1 mark available. <u>HINTS</u>:
- The correct answer is A.
- B is incorrect — this is an example of market failure, since giving loans to customers who have a high risk of defaulting could create a market bubble, which will eventually 'burst'.
- C is incorrect — using insider information to make profit is illegal and prevents the market from working as it should.
- D is incorrect — a bank keeping too little liquidity risks not being able to repay depositors, which could destabilise an economy. If a bank takes the risk of holding only a small amount of liquidity while relying on a central bank not to allow it to collapse, then this is an example of moral hazard (a market failure).

Page 190 — The Role of the Central Bank

1 Maximum of 8 marks available. <u>HINTS</u>:
- Explain what's meant by 'lender of last resort' — e.g. 'A lender of last resort can provide liquid funds to a bank facing a shortage of liquidity.'
- Describe the importance of a lender of last resort — e.g. 'Because banks borrow short-term but lend long-term, they can at times expect to face a shortage of liquidity. If a bank is unable to meet its liabilities, then there could be panic and a run on the bank. The lender of last resort will be able to step in to prevent this panic and maintain stability in the financial sector.'
- Describe the risks in having a lender of last resort — e.g. 'Knowing that a central bank can help deal with any liquidity problems might lead a bank to take excessive risks in the hope of making a larger profit, an example of moral hazard. It can also seem unfair that a bank running into difficulties is rescued, while any other business would probably be allowed to fail.'
- Balance the arguments and come to a conclusion — e.g. 'Although there are risks in central banks acting as a lender of last resort, the risks if they don't take on this role are probably greater overall.'

Page 192 — Regulation of Financial Markets

1 Maximum of 8 marks available. <u>HINTS</u>:
- Mention two forms of regulation, and make sure you explain how each one could prevent a future financial crisis.
- Start with the first type of regulation — e.g. 'In the past, there has been excessive risk-taking by financial institutions. Some banks made risky investments in the hope of making large profits. To prevent this continuing, regulation was introduced to ensure firms are stable and meet capital and liquidity ratios. Senior individuals in the bank are now also more personally accountable for the risks their banks take.'
- Now describe a second type — e.g. 'Several major banks have previously been involved in market rigging and other illegal activities, which contributed to instability in the market. The laws and rules that banks and financial institutions must abide by have now been strengthened, with tough punishments for any that break those rules. This should ensure that similar illegal activities cannot lead to a crisis in the future.'

Section Thirteen — The Global Economy

Page 194 — Globalisation

1 Maximum of 6 marks available. <u>HINTS</u>:
- Give a definition of a multinational corporation (MNC) — e.g. 'A multinational corporation (MNC) is a firm which functions in at least one other country aside from its country of origin.'
- Explain what factors might encourage investment from MNCs in developing countries, and why — e.g. 'MNCs look for ways to increase profits and lower costs. The availability of cheaper labour in a developing country, such as India, may encourage an MNC to set up a factory there.' You should go on to discuss at least one other factor that might encourage investment from MNCs, such as the availability of raw materials, or the existence of good transport links in the developing country.

Page 196 — Costs and Benefits of Globalisation

1 Maximum of 1 mark available. <u>HINTS</u>:
- The correct answer is C.
- These are all potential consequences of globalisation. You need to decide which is a drawback. Better response to disaster (A), better efficiency (B) and more employment (D) are all positives.

Page 197 — Globalisation and Development

1 Maximum of 15 marks available. <u>HINTS</u>:
- Start by defining globalisation — e.g. 'Globalisation is the increasing integration of economies internationally.'
- Discuss the advantages of globalisation for developing/emerging economies — make sure you assess the relative importance of each point you make, e.g. 'Globalisation can lead to the creation of jobs in developing and emerging countries — for example, MNCs may build factories in a developing country and employ local workers, which will reduce unemployment. This is important for developing and emerging countries for a number of reasons — for example, if more people are employed, more people will be earning a wage, and demand for domestic products might increase because people have more money to spend. This will create economic growth in that country.'

- Discuss the disadvantages of globalisation for developing/emerging economies — again, you'll need to assess the relative importance of each of your points, e.g. 'Skilled workers often end up leaving developing countries to work in more developed countries. This can massively limit economic growth in those developing countries because they're losing their brightest and most productive workers.'
- Give a conclusion at the end of your answer, summing up whether or not you think that the advantages of globalisation are likely to outweigh the disadvantages.

Page 201 — Trade

1 Maximum of 6 marks available. <u>HINTS</u>:
- You could start by defining international trade, e.g. 'International trade is the exchange of goods and services between countries.'
- The question asks for two benefits — make sure you explain both of them, e.g. 'International trade allows developing countries to import goods they don't have the technology to produce themselves. This raises the standard of living in those developing countries.' You could also mention that trade gives developing countries access to new materials that they can use to produce new products.

Page 205 — Free Trade, Protectionism and the WTO

1 Maximum of 10 marks available. <u>HINTS</u>:
- Give a definition of protectionist policies — e.g. 'Protectionist policies are trade barriers imposed by governments to protect domestic industries from the disadvantages of free trade.'
- Explain why governments might want or need to protect infant industries — for example, when infant industries are just starting out, they might find it hard to compete internationally, so their government may choose to protect them until they are big enough to compete.
- Briefly describe at least two protectionist policies a government might use to protect infant industries, such as tariffs on imports, quotas, reducing the value of its currency, and subsidies. Make sure you explain how each of your examples could be used to protect infant industries, and not just domestic industries in general, e.g. 'To protect an infant industry, a government could impose a tariff on some specific foreign imports. This would make the products produced by the infant industry more competitive domestically, and give it time to become big enough to compete internationally without the help of tariffs.'

2 Maximum of 2 marks available. <u>HINTS</u>:
- E.g. 'A customs union is a group of countries who have removed all barriers to trade between themselves, and impose standard tariffs on non-member countries.'

Page 206 — Patterns of Trade

1 Maximum of 8 marks available. <u>HINTS</u>:
- You should start by explaining that the growth of China and India's economies has led to them producing more and cheaper products — including high-tech goods. You can go on to say that both countries are becoming more important trading partners of the UK.
- Give some examples of how the growth of China and India may affect the UK, e.g. 'UK exports, especially of manufactured goods, have declined and will continue to decline because of competition from newly industrialised economies like China. This will mean that there'll be fewer and fewer manufacturing jobs in the UK.'
- Try to balance the points that you make, e.g. 'The UK may be able to increase exports of services to India and China as their economies grow, which will improve the UK's balance of payments. However, less than 5% of UK exports currently go to each country, so this may mean the UK's balance of payments won't improve greatly — at least in the short run.'

Page 207 — Economic Integration

1 Maximum of 12 marks available. <u>HINTS</u>:
- Start by defining a monetary union, e.g. 'A monetary union is a type of trading bloc where all members use a single, common currency. The countries have a shared monetary policy, which is usually controlled by a central bank.'
- You need to discuss the possible benefits of joining a monetary union, assessing how important each of these benefits is likely to be, e.g. 'When trading within the monetary union, the country won't have to deal with the costs of exchanging currencies. If the country does a lot of trade with the other countries in the monetary union, the country could save significant amounts of money.'
- Discuss the potential costs to a country of joining a monetary union, and their likely importance. For example, the country would lose control over its own monetary policy and it may experience restraints on its economic growth if it has to meet targets set by the central bank of the monetary union.
- Explain why the overall impact of joining a monetary union depends on the specific countries that are involved, e.g. 'The impact of joining a monetary union can vary between trading blocs and between countries — for example, if interest rates are raised by a central bank, this may help one country by restraining its level of inflation, but if another country is experiencing a recession, the rise in interest rates might have negative consequences for its economy.'

Answers

Page 209 — The European Union

1 Maximum of 15 marks available. <u>HINTS</u>:
- You need to discuss the possible benefits to the UK of being a member of the EU, assessing how important each of these benefits is likely to be, e.g. 'FDI into the UK is likely to be higher as a member of the EU. FDI plays an important role in the UK — so this might be a strong argument for the UK to be a member of the EU.' Make sure you mention other benefits to the UK of EU membership, such as greater economies of scale and migration from other member states providing skilled labour, which helps to increase aggregate supply.
- Discuss the potential costs to the UK, and their likely importance, e.g. 'Migration from other member states can lead to overcrowding and put a strain on services such as housing, benefits and health care. The significance of this partly depends on how much migrants are putting into and taking out of the economy overall. For example, it's possible that migrants pay more in taxes than they receive by using services such as the NHS.'
- Conclude your answer by stating whether, given your arguments and their relative importance, EU membership for the UK is more likely to be beneficial or harmful to the UK, e.g. 'Being a member of the EU is likely to be more beneficial than harmful to the UK. The likely benefits of EU membership, such as higher levels of FDI and economies of scale, are likely to outweigh the potential costs, such as possible strains on services.'

Page 212 — Exchange Rates

1 Maximum of 4 marks available. <u>HINTS</u>:
- Describe the likely effect on demand for a currency of a country hosting a major sporting event — e.g. 'A major sporting event, such as the Olympics, can attract tens, or even hundreds, of thousands of visitors to a country. These visitors will require the domestic currency, e.g. to pay for tickets, hotels and transport, so demand for the currency will increase.'
- Explain what effect this will have on the exchange rate — e.g. 'An increase in demand for a currency will cause its value to rise.' You can use a diagram like the one on the right to show how the value of the currency (e.g. the pound) rises as demand increases — make sure you refer to your diagram in your answer.

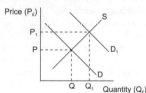

Page 215 — International Competitiveness

1 Maximum of 20 marks available. <u>HINTS</u>:
- Explain that a government can use supply-side policies to improve its country's overall competitiveness. Give at least three examples of supply-side policies a government could use and explain how they can help to improve competitiveness. Make sure you evaluate the points that you make, e.g. 'A government could improve the productivity of workers by improving education in the country or providing apprenticeships to help people to learn practical skills and get qualifications. However, policies like this take a long time to have an effect and aren't appropriate if competitiveness needs to be improved in the short run.'
- Other approaches you could discuss include improving labour market flexibility, improving infrastructure, privatisation, deregulation and maintaining macroeconomic stability.
- You could conclude your answer by saying which approach you think is the most effective and why, e.g. 'Improvements in education are crucial to improve a country's competitiveness. If a country's workforce has greater skills then it's likely that it'll be more productive, and that will lead to significant improvements in competitiveness.'

Section Fourteen — Economic Development

Page 217 — Measures of Economic Development

1 Maximum of 4 marks available. <u>HINTS</u>:
- Give at least two ways that inequality might slow down economic development, for example by preventing the poorest people from starting businesses, and by contributing to social problems such as crime.
- You'll need to explain how these issues limit development to get all the marks, e.g. 'Inequality can lead to social problems, for example crime rates may rise if the poorest people in a country can't meet their basic needs (such as food) in any other way. This will limit development because high crime rates reduce people's quality of life, and could slow economic growth as firms may invest less in buildings and capital equipment if they think this might make them the target of crime.'

Page 219 — Limits to Growth and Development

1 Maximum of 8 marks available. <u>HINTS</u>:
- You could start by giving a definition of primary products, e.g. 'Primary products are products extracted from the earth, like coal or wheat.'
- Give at least two reasons why economic development might be limited in a country dependent on primary products. Examples include: the fact that firms can't add much value to primary products, the Prebisch-Singer effect, and the uncertainty of income from agricultural products because of the possibility of damage from natural disasters or extreme weather.

- For each reason you list, explain exactly how this may limit economic development, e.g. 'Because the value that firms can add to primary products is very low, firms selling these products won't generate large profits. This means there is likely to be little investment in a country which is dependent on primary products, and this will limit economic development.'

Page 221 — Ways of Promoting Growth and Development

1 Maximum of 12 marks available. <u>HINTS</u>:
- Explain how expanding the industrial sector can help an economy develop, e.g. 'The Lewis model argues that there is excess labour in the agricultural sector, so productivity can increase by moving agricultural workers to industry, without wages rising. This means inflation is avoided. The increased profit from the higher output of industry can be invested in equipment which will increase productivity further. Therefore everyone will be better off as savings, investment, and growth all increase.'
- To balance this you also need to evaluate whether this approach is likely to be effective in practice — give some downsides to the approach, e.g. 'However, profits from industry may be invested abroad, especially when firms have foreign owners, so industrialisation may not contribute as much to the economy as the Lewis model suggests.'
- Now do the same for the tourism sector — first explain how it should contribute to economic development, e.g. 'Expanding the tourism industry should bring in foreign currency from tourists, and foreign investment from firms catering to tourists. As well as increasing investment, employment should increase as jobs are created in the industry.'
- To fully evaluate this approach, counter your explanation of the benefits of developing tourism with some reasons why this might not be successful, e.g. 'However, employment in the tourist industry is often seasonal, and jobs may not be secure as demand for holidays is income elastic, so the industry could be badly affected by an economic downturn.'
- Finally, come to a conclusion, commenting on the relative significance of the points you've made, e.g. 'Expansion of these sectors should create economic growth, by increasing output and productivity. However, this growth may not contribute significantly to development if it doesn't provide quality local jobs. If firms bring in foreign workers or develop industries which don't require much labour, then there may not be much of a positive effect on development, because the benefits of growth will not be spread very widely.'

Page 223 — Ways of Promoting Growth and Development

1 Maximum of 12 marks available. <u>HINTS</u>:
- First explain what fair trade schemes are and how they work, e.g. 'Fair trade schemes involve offering farmers in developing countries who are members of the scheme a guaranteed minimum price for their goods. In order to be part of a scheme farmers are required to meet certain conditions, such as agreed farming practices and fair treatment of employees.'
- Then give a few ways in which these schemes might help promote growth and development, for example by raising wages for agricultural workers, by reducing environmental damage by changing farming methods, or by encouraging farmers to invest in capital by giving them more income security.
- Explain exactly how each factor could contribute to growth and development, e.g. 'Farmers in fair trade schemes don't have to deal with large fluctuations in the price they can get for their product, so they're much more able to plan for the long term than they otherwise would be. This means they're more likely to invest in equipment or staff training, which will contribute to development, and may lead to more growth in the future as productivity is likely to increase.'
- Then offer some drawbacks of fair trade schemes to balance your answer, e.g. 'Fair trade schemes distort the market price of the products that farmers produce. This means that farmers in these schemes won't react to the signal that low prices give to limit production. So when prices are low there may be overproduction, which will flood the market with goods, driving the price even lower. This will be detrimental to farmers who aren't part of the fair trade scheme, because they have to accept the market price for their goods.'

Page 224 — Ways of Promoting Growth and Development

1 Maximum of 2 marks available. <u>HINTS</u>:
- Briefly explain how international institutions may promote growth and development, e.g. 'International institutions such as the IMF offer loans and economic advice to member countries. The aim is to maintain economic stability around the world, which should promote growth, and to encourage development by improving living standards in developing countries.'
- You could mention other international institutions too, as the question's not just asking about the IMF, e.g. 'The World Bank supports development by offering funding schemes for basic provision of services such as health care and education to the world's poorest countries.'

Page 225 — Sustainable Development

1 Maximum of 2 marks available. <u>HINTS</u>:
- Give a definition of sustainable development, e.g. 'Sustainable development means improving people's living standards now, through economic growth or other advancements, without making it harder for people in the future to achieve similar living standards.'
- You'll need to explain both words to get both marks — it's not enough to just say it's development that doesn't negatively affect people in the future.

Glossary

abnormal profit See supernormal profit.

absolute advantage A country will have an absolute advantage when its output of a product is greater per unit of resource used than any other country.

absolute poverty This is when someone doesn't have the income or wealth to meet their basic needs, such as food, shelter and water.

accelerator process This is where any change in demand for goods/services beyond current capacity will lead to a greater percentage increase in the demand for the capital goods that firms need to produce those goods/services.

aggregate demand The total demand, or total spending, in an economy at a given price level over a given period of time. It's made up of consumption, investment, government spending and net exports.
Aggregate Demand = C + I + G + (X – M)

aggregate supply The total amount of goods and services which can be supplied in an economy at a given price level over a given period of time.

aid The transfer of resources from one country to another.

allocative efficiency This is when the price of a good is equal to the price that consumers are happy to pay for it. This will happen when all resources are allocated efficiently.

asymmetric information This is when buyers have more information than sellers (or the opposite) in a market.

automatic stabilisers These are parts of fiscal policies that will automatically react to changes in the economic cycle. For example, during a recession, government spending is likely to increase because the government will automatically pay out more unemployment benefits, which may reduce the problems the recession causes.

average cost The cost of production per unit of output — i.e. a firm's total cost for a given period of time, divided by the quantity produced.

average revenue The revenue per unit sold — i.e. a firm's total revenue for a given period of time, divided by the quantity sold.

backward vertical integration See vertical integration.

balance of payments A record of a country's international transactions, i.e. flows of money into and out of a country.

bank rate The official rate of interest set by the Monetary Policy Committee of the Bank of England.

barriers to entry Barriers to entry are any potential difficulties that make it hard for a firm to enter a market.

barriers to exit Barriers to exit are any potential difficulties that make it hard for a firm to leave a market.

black market Economic activity that occurs without taxation and government regulation.

budget deficit When government spending is greater than its revenue.

budget surplus When government spending is less than its revenue.

capital account on the balance of payments A part of the record of a country's international flows of money. This includes transfers of non-monetary and fixed assets, such as through emigration and immigration.

cartel A group of producers that agree to limit production in order to keep the price of goods or services high.

central bank The institution responsible for issuing a country's banknotes, acting as a lender of last resort for other banks, and implementing monetary policy (e.g. setting interest rates).

circular flow of income The flow of national output, income and expenditure between households and firms.
national output = national income = national expenditure

command economy An economy where governments, not markets, determine how to allocate resources.

comparative advantage A country has a comparative advantage if the opportunity cost of it producing a good is lower than the opportunity cost for other countries.

competition policy Government policy aimed at reducing monopoly power in order to increase efficiency and ensure fairness for consumers.

concentration ratio This shows how dominant firms are in a market, e.g. if three firms in a market have 90% market share then the three-firm concentration ratio is 90%.

conglomerate integration Mergers or takeovers between firms which operate in completely different markets.

consumer surplus When a consumer pays less for a good than they were prepared to, this difference is the consumer surplus.

consumption The purchase/use of goods or services.

contestability A market is contestable if it's easy for new firms to enter the market, i.e. if barriers to entry are low.

cost-push inflation Inflation caused by the rising cost of inputs to production.

creative destruction This occurs when the innovation and invention of new products and production methods causes the destruction of existing markets and creates new ones.

cross elasticity of demand (XED) This is a measure of how the quantity demanded of one good/service responds to a change in the price of another good/service.

current account on the balance of payments A part of the record of a country's international flows of money. It consists of: trade in goods, trade in services, international flows of income (salaries, interest, profit and dividends), and transfers.

cyclical unemployment Unemployment caused by a shortage of demand in an economy, e.g. when there's a slump.

demand-pull inflation Inflation caused by excessive growth in aggregate demand compared to aggregate supply.

demand-side policy Government policy that aims to increase aggregate demand in an economy. For example, a policy to increase consumer spending in an economy.

demerger A firm selling off part(s) of its business to create a separate firm, or firms.

demerit good A good or service which has greater social costs when it's consumed than private costs. Demerit goods tend to be overconsumed.

dependency ratio How many people are either too young or too old to work, relative to the number of people of working age.

deregulation Removing rules imposed by a government that can restrict the level of competition in a market.

derived demand The demand for a good or factor of production due to its use in making another good or providing a service.

developed countries Relatively rich, industrialised countries with a high GDP per capita.

developing countries Countries that rely on labour-intensive industries. They have a relatively low GDP per capita.

diminishing returns See law of diminishing returns.

diseconomies of scale A firm is experiencing diseconomies of scale when the average cost of production is rising as output rises.

disposable income Income, including welfare benefits, that is available for households to spend after income tax has been paid.

dividend A share in a firm's profits that is given to the firm's shareholders.

divorce of ownership from control This occurs when a firm's owners are no longer in control of the day-to-day running of the firm (e.g. because it's run by directors). This can lead to the principal-agent problem, where those in control act in their own self-interest, rather than the interest of the owners.

dynamic efficiency This is about firms improving efficiency in the long term by carrying out research and development into new or improved products, or investing in new technology and training to improve the production process.

economic cycle The economic cycle (also known as the business or trade cycle) is the fluctuations in actual growth over a period of time (several years or decades).

economic development An assessment of living standards and people's overall welfare in a country.

economic growth An increase in an economy's productive potential. Usually measured as the rate of change of the gross domestic product (GDP), or the GDP per capita.

economic integration The process by which the economies of different countries become more closely linked, e.g. through free trade agreements.

economic rent The excess a worker is paid above the minimum required to keep them in their current occupation (this minimum payment is their transfer earnings).

economically active population The people in an economy who are capable of and old enough to work.

economies of scale A firm is experiencing economies of scale when the average cost of production is falling as output rises.

emerging countries Countries which are not yet developed, but which are growing quickly and are further along the development process than other developing countries.

equilibrium A market for a product is in equilibrium when the quantity supplied is equal to the quantity demanded.

equity This means fairness.

exchange rate The price at which one currency buys another.

extending property rights When property rights over a resource are given to an individual or firm. This gives them control over the usage of that resource.

external growth A firm growing through mergers/takeovers.

externalities The external costs or benefits to a third party that is not involved in the making, buying/selling and consumption of a specific good/service.

factors of production These are the four inputs needed to make the things that people want. They are: land, labour, capital and enterprise.

financial account on the balance of payments A part of the record of a country's international flows of money. This involves the movement of financial assets (e.g. through foreign direct investment).

Glossary

financial sector Firms that provide financial services (e.g. banks and insurance companies).

fiscal policy Government policy that determines the levels of government spending and taxation. Often used to increase or decrease aggregate demand in an economy.

Fisher's equation of exchange See quantity theory of money.

fixed costs Costs that don't vary with the level of output of a firm in the short run.

foreign direct investment (FDI) This is when a firm based in one country makes an investment in a different country.

forward vertical integration See vertical integration.

free market A market where there is no government intervention. Competition between different suppliers affects supply and demand, and as a result determines prices.

free rider problem This means that once a public good is provided it's impossible to stop someone from benefiting from it, even if they haven't paid towards it.

free trade International trade without any restrictions from things such as trade barriers.

frictional unemployment The unemployment experienced by workers between leaving one job and starting another.

full employment The situation when everyone of working age who wants a job at the current wage rates can get one.

globalisation The increasing integration of economies internationally, which is making the world more like a single economy.

government failure This occurs when government intervention into a market causes a misallocation of resources.

gross domestic product (GDP) The total value of all the goods and services produced in a country in a year.

hit-and-run tactics This is when firms enter a market while supernormal profits can be made and then leave the market once prices have been driven down to normal-profit levels.

horizontal equity This means that people in identical circumstances are treated fairly (i.e. equally).

horizontal integration Mergers or takeovers between firms that are at the same stage of the production process of similar products.

human capital The economic value of a person's skills.

Human Development Index (HDI) A measure of a country's economic development, used by the UN, that combines measures of health (life expectancy), education (average and expected years in school), and the standard of living (real GNI per capita).

imperfect information A situation where buyers and/or sellers don't have full knowledge regarding price, costs, benefits and availability of a good or service.

income Money that a firm or person receives for providing a good or service.

income elasticity of demand (YED) This is a measure of how the demand for a good/service responds to a change in real income.

inequity Another word for unfairness.

inflation The sustained rise in the average price of goods and services over a period of time.

infrastructure The basic facilities and services needed for a country and its economy to function.

inorganic growth See external growth.

interest The money paid to the lender by someone who borrows capital. This will often be a fixed percentage rate — known as an interest rate.

internal growth A firm growing as a result of increasing the levels of the factors of production it uses, rather than through mergers or takeovers.

investment The purchase of capital, such as new machinery, in the hope that this will help generate an increased level of output. Investment can also mean buying shares from the stock market — this is done in the hope of making a future profit or receiving dividend payments.

labour immobility This occurs when labour can't easily move around to find jobs (geographical immobility) or easily switch between different occupations (occupational immobility).

law of diminishing returns The idea that if a firm increases one variable factor of production while other factors stay fixed, then the marginal returns the firm gets from the variable factor will always eventually begin to decrease.

liquidity How easily an asset can be spent (converted to money).

long run A time period in which all the factors of production are variable, so a firm can expand its capacity.

long run aggregate supply (LRAS) In the long run it is assumed that, because factors and costs of production can change, an economy will run at full capacity — so LRAS is the productive potential of an economy.

long run Phillips curve See Phillips curve (long run).

macroeconomics This is the part of economics that looks at the economy as a whole. For example, trends in unemployment and economic growth.

marginal cost The cost to a firm of producing the final unit of output.

marginal product The extra output that's produced when a firm adds one more unit of one of the factors of production they're using.

marginal propensity to consume The proportion of an increase in income that people will spend (and not save).

marginal returns See marginal product.

marginal revenue The extra revenue received as a result of selling one more unit of output.

marginal tax rate The rate of tax you pay on any 'extra' money you receive.

marginal utility The benefit of consuming one extra unit of a good.

market failure This is where the price mechanism fails to allocate resources efficiently.

merger Two firms uniting to form a new company.

merit good A good or service which provides greater social benefits when it's consumed than private benefits. Merit goods tend to be underconsumed.

microeconomics This is the part of economics concerned with individual people, individual firms and individual markets. For example, it covers things like how changes in demand affects the price of a good in a market.

minimum efficient scale of production (MES) The lowest level of output at which a firm can achieve the lowest possible average cost of production.

monetary policy Government policy that involves controlling the total amount of 'money' in an economy (the money supply), and how expensive it is to borrow that money. It involves manipulating interest rates, exchange rates and restrictions on the supply of money.

monopoly A pure monopoly is a market with only one supplier. Some markets will be referred to as a monopoly if there's more than one supplier, but one supplier dominates the market.

monopoly power The ability of a firm to be a 'price maker' and influence the price of a particular good in a market.

monopsony A market with a single buyer.

multinational corporations (MNCs) Firms which function in at least one other country, aside from their country of origin.

multiplier effect The process by which an injection into the circular flow of income creates a change in the size of national income that's greater than the injection's size.

national debt The total debt that a country has run up over time.

National Minimum Wage (NMW) A legal minimum hourly rate of pay, set for different age groups. There's a national minimum wage in the UK.

national output All the goods and services produced in a country in a year.

nationalised industry An industry owned by the government.

natural monopoly An industry where economies of scale are so great that the lowest long run average cost can only be achieved if the market is made up of a single provider.

natural rate of unemployment (NRU) The rate of unemployment when the labour market is in equilibrium (i.e. when labour demand is equal to labour supply).

non-pure public good See quasi-public good.

normal profit A firm is making normal profit when its total revenue is equal to its total costs.

oligopoly A market dominated by a few large firms that offer differentiated products, with high barriers to entry. The firms are interdependent and may use competitive or collusive strategies.

opportunity cost The benefit that's given up in order to do something else — it's the cost of the choice that's made.

organic growth See internal growth.

output gap The gap between the trend rate of economic growth and actual economic growth. Output gaps can be positive or negative.

participation rate The proportion of working age people in an economy that are either in work or actively seeking work.

per capita Another way to say 'per person'.

perfect information This is when buyers and sellers have full knowledge of prices, costs, benefits and availability of products.

Phillips curve (long run) A curve that shows the relationship between inflation and unemployment in the long run — it's always a vertical line positioned at the natural rate of unemployment (NRU).

Phillips curve (short run) A curve that shows the relationship between inflation and unemployment in the short run — as the level of one falls, the level of the other rises.

predatory pricing An aggressive pricing tactic which involves incumbent firms in a market lowering their prices to a level that a new entrant to the market can't match, in order to force them out of the market.

price cap A limit on price rises that makes a market fairer to consumers. A price cap also provides an incentive for firms to increase efficiency. Two common price caps are: RPI – X, and RPI – X + K.

price discrimination This occurs when a seller charges different prices to different customers for exactly the same product.

price elasticity of demand (PED) This is a measure of how the quantity demanded of a good/service responds to a change in its price.

Glossary

price elasticity of supply (PES) This is a measure of how the quantity supplied of a good/service responds to a change in its price.

price maker A firm that has some power to control the price it sells at.

price mechanism This is when changes in the demand or supply of a good/service lead to changes in its price and the quantity bought/sold.

price taker A firm that has no power to control the price it sells at — it has to accept the market price.

price war A situation where one firm in a market lowers their prices, and other firms follow suit, possibly triggering a series of price cuts as firms try to undercut one another.

principal-agent problem See divorce of ownership from control.

privatisation When a firm or a whole industry changes from being run by the public sector to the private sector.

producer surplus When a producer receives more for a good than they were prepared to accept, this difference is the producer surplus.

production possibility frontier (PPF) A curve which shows the maximum possible outputs of two goods or services using a fixed amount of inputs.

productive efficiency This occurs when products are produced at a level of output where the average cost is lowest.

productivity The average output produced per unit of a factor of production — for example, labour productivity would be the average output per worker (or per worker-hour).

profit A firm's total revenue minus its total costs.

progressive taxation A tax system where an individual's tax rises (as a percentage of their income) as their income rises.

proportional taxation A tax system where everyone pays the same proportion of tax regardless of their income level.

protectionism When a government uses policies to control the level of international trade and protect its own economy, industries and firms.

public good A good which people can't be stopped from consuming, even if they've not paid for it, and the consumption of which doesn't prevent others from benefiting from it (e.g. national defence).

public sector The part of the economy that is owned or run by the government.

purchasing power parity (PPP) An adjustment of an exchange rate to reflect the real purchasing power of the two currencies.

quantitative easing (QE) This involves a central bank (e.g. the Bank of England) 'creating new money' and using it to buy assets owned by financial institutions and other firms. It increases the money supply, which will enable individuals and firms to spend more, or lend it to other people to spend.

quantity theory of money This theory is based on the idea that changes in the money supply will cause changes to the price level. It uses the formula: $MV = PT$, which is known as Fisher's equation of exchange.

quasi-public good A good which appears to have the characteristics of a public good, but doesn't exhibit them fully.

quota A limit on the amount of a good that is allowed to be used, produced or imported.

real income A measure of the amount of goods/services that a consumer can afford to purchase with their income, adjusted for inflation.

real wage unemployment Unemployment caused by real wages being pushed above the equilibrium level of employment. It can be caused by trade unions negotiating for higher wages, or the introduction of a national minimum wage.

recession This occurs when there's negative economic growth for at least two consecutive quarters. Typically there's falling demand, low levels of investment and rising unemployment during a recession.

regressive taxation A tax system where an individual's tax falls (as a percentage of their income) as their income rises.

relative poverty This is when someone has a low income relative to other incomes in their country.

returns to scale How much a firm's output changes as they increase input (i.e. increase all factors of production). Returns to scale are increasing if output increases more than proportionally with input, constant if output increases proportionally with input, and decreasing if output increases less than proportionally with input.

revenue The total value of sales within a time period.
It can be calculated using the formula:
price per unit × quantity sold.

satisficing Running a firm in a way that does just enough to satisfy important stakeholders in the firm, rather than trying to maximise something (e.g. profit or revenue).

seasonal unemployment Unemployment due to uneven economic activity during the year.

shadow banking system Firms (or parts of firms) that provide credit, but which are not regulated.

share A share represents a portion of a company's value — giving the share's owner a right to a portion of the company's profits.

shareholders Individuals (or firms) that own shares in a company.

short run A time period in which at least one of a firm's factors of production is fixed.

short run aggregate supply (SRAS) This is aggregate supply when the factors of production are fixed.

short run Phillips curve See Phillips curve (short run).

specialisation Specialisation means people or countries doing only the things they're best or most efficient at.

speculation When things are bought (e.g. shares) in the hope that they will increase in value and can be sold for a profit at a later date.

static efficiency This occurs when allocative and productive efficiency are both achieved at a particular time.

structural unemployment Unemployment (usually) caused by the decline of a major industry, which is made worse by labour immobility (geographical or occupational).

subsidy An amount of money paid by a government to the producer of a good/service to lower the cost of production. This should increase supply, which will lower the price and increase demand for the good/service.

sunk cost This is an unrecoverable cost of entering a market, e.g. advertising. It can act as a barrier to exit.

supernormal profit A firm is making supernormal profit when its total revenue exceeds its total costs.

supply-side policy Government policy that aims to increase aggregate supply in an economy. For example, a policy to increase the productive capacity of the economy.

sustainability This is about meeting the needs of people now, without making it more difficult for people in the future to meet their own needs.

systemic risk This is when a problem in one part of the financial sector can cause the whole financial system to collapse.

takeover One firm buying another firm, which then becomes part of the first firm.

tariff A form of tax placed on certain imports to make them more expensive and discourage their consumption.

tax An amount of money paid to a government. It's paid directly, e.g. income tax, or indirectly, e.g. excise duty.

terms of trade A measure of the relative price of a country's exports compared to its imports.

total cost All the costs for a firm involved in producing a particular amount of output.

total revenue The total amount of money a firm receives from its sales, in a particular time period.

trade creation The removal of trade barriers within a trading bloc, allowing members to buy from the cheapest source.

trade diversion When trade barriers are imposed on non-members of a trading bloc, so trade is diverted away from any cheaper non-members.

trade liberalisation The reduction or removal of tariffs and other restrictions on international trade (i.e. reducing protectionism).

trade union An organisation of workers that acts to represent their interests, e.g. to improve their pay.

trading blocs These are associations between the governments of different countries that promote and manage trade between those countries.

transfer earnings The minimum pay that will stop a worker from switching to their next best paid occupation.

unemployment The level of unemployment is the number of people who are looking for a job but cannot find one. The rate of unemployment is the number of people out of work (but looking for a job) as a percentage of the labour force.

utility The 'benefit' or 'well-being' gained from an action.

variable costs Costs that vary with the level of output of a firm.

vertical equity This means people with different circumstances are treated differently, but fairly.

vertical integration Mergers or takeovers between firms at different stages of the production process of the same product. If a firm takes over another firm that's further forward in the production process it's forward vertical integration, and if a firm takes over another firm that's further back in the production process it's backward vertical integration.

wage differentials The differences that exist in wages between different groups of workers, or between workers in the same occupation.

wage rate The price of labour, i.e. the rate of pay to employ a worker.

wealth The value of somebody's assets.

working population See economically active population.

World Trade Organisation (WTO) The WTO is an international organisation which provides a forum for its member governments to discuss trade agreements and settle disputes, using a set of trade rules. It aims to help trade to be as free as possible.

x-inefficiency Inefficiency caused by unnecessary costs and waste (i.e. organisational slack).

Index

Index

EKHR72